THE THIRD GOSPEL FOR THE THIRD WORLD

The Third Gospel *for the* Third World

VOLUME TWO–A
MINISTRY IN GALILEE
(Luke 3:1–6:49)

Herman Hendrickx, cicm

A Michael Glazier Book
THE LITURGICAL PRESS
Collegeville, Minnesota

THE THIRD GOSPEL FOR THE THIRD WORLD Volume Two-A

Copyright © 1997 by **Claretian Publications**
A division of Claretian Communications, Inc.
U.P. P.O. Box 4, Quezon City 1101, Philippines
TE 921-3984 • Fax (632) 921-7429 • E-mail: claret@cnl.net

Claretian Publications is a pastoral endeavor of the Claretian Missionaries in the Philippines. It aims to promote a renewed spirituality rooted in the process of total liberation and solidarity in response to the needs, challenges and pastoral demands of the Church today.

Library of Congress Cataloging-in-Publication Data

Hendrickx, Herman.
    The Third Gospel for the Third World / Herman Hendrickx.
        p.   cm.
    "A Michael Glazier book."
    Includes bibliographical references.
    Contents: v.   1. Preface and infancy narrative (Luke 1:1-2:52).
    ISBN 0-8146-5870-9
    ISBN 0-8146-5871-7 Volume Two-A
    1. Bible.   N.T.   Luke—Commentaries.   I.   Title.
BS2595.3.H46   1996
226.4' 07—dc20   96-34651
                                                                CIP

Cover design by Maria d.c. Zamora

Biblical texts are taken from the New Revised Standard Version (NRSV) unless otherwise indicated.

TABLE OF CONTENTS

FOREWORD

This book is the first part of the second volume of a commentary on the Gospel of Luke under the general title *The Third Gospel for the Third World*, which will eventually consist of five volumes. The first volume covering the Luke's Preface (Lk 1:1–4) and Infancy Narrative (Lk 1:5–2:52) was published in September 1996. The second volume was supposed to cover The Ministry of Jesus in Galilee (Lk 3:1–9:50). For practical reasons, however, the author decided to divide the said volume into two parts, namely, A (Lk 3:1–6:49) and B (7:1–9:50).

Like the first volume, the present book intends to pay special, though not exclusive attention to whatever may be of particular interest to third world readers. Again we try to deal with questions raised by the sociological approach to the Gospels, as well as anthropological and cultural features, like matters of family, clan and tribe, matters of honor and shame, the conditions of rural and urban life, etc. We also try again to take into account some finding of recent literary criticism. The commentary will especially try to make available to a wider reading public what the author considers to have pastoral implications first and foremost in a third world setting. But it goes almost without saying that many of these features are also of importance to committed first world Christians.

Since this commentary tries to bring together findings of various fields of research, several of which are rather new, it is obvious that we are very much indebted to scholars in these various fields. We trust that the text notes and the bibliography will sufficiently account for the extent of this indebtedness. We tried to make available the insights of present-day Lukan scholarship to people who have no access to the books and periodical articles in which these insights are found and/or cannot afford to buy them.

Like the previous volume, this book is no easy reading, although the author tried to avoid becoming too technical. But the disciplines mentioned above are not exactly easy. So the reader will again have to invest time and effort in order to discover and assimilate the riches of the Third Gospel presented in this commentary. We wish that you may have the courage and stamina to bring this to a fruitful end.

PREPARATION FOR JESUS' MINISTRY
(LK 3:1-4:13)

The emergence of John the Baptist represents the real beginning of Luke's story. The synchronism of Lk 3:1-2 marks the true beginning for Luke's narrative after the "pre-history" of the infancy narrative. John announces and prepares for the coming of Jesus (Lk 3:1-20). Jesus himself makes his beginning with baptism (Lk 3:21-22), and is at this point formally introduced by Luke in terms of his legal human ancestry (Lk 3:23-38). Identified by the divine voice as Son of God and equipped with the Spirit (Lk 3:22), Jesus' filial obedience is put to the test (Lk 4:1-13), prior to his public ministry, in a wilderness encounter with the devil (Lk 4:1-13; Nolland, 1989: 136, 144).

It has been pointed out that the story of John the Baptist is again intertwined with that of Jesus. Passing over Lk 2:1-52, Lk 1:80 continues in Lk 3:3; and passing over Lk 3:1-20, Lk 2:40 continues in Lk 3:21-22. The call, preaching and arrest of John the Baptist can be seen as standing in parallel to Lk 3:21-22; 4:16-27, and 4:28-30. Some scholars, therefore, include Lk 4:16-30 with the preparatory section, since this would make clear the parallel between the use of Isa 40:3-5 to introduce John and Isa 61:1-2 to introduce Jesus (Schweizer, 1984: 68). We prefer to follow, however, the scholars who situate the beginning of Jesus' ministry at Lk 4:14 (Marshall, 1978: 175ff.; Fitzmyer, 1981: 521ff.; Nolland, 1989: 184ff.; C.F. Evans, 1990: 263ff.; Bovon, 1991: 203ff.; Bock, 1994: 386ff.; Ringe, 1995: 49ff.).

1. The Ministry of John the Baptist (Lk 3:1-20)

The fact that the traditions about John the Baptist can be traced to every layer of the gospel tradition points to the early acceptance of a significant role for him in the life of the Church and its understanding of its own mission. The Church could not ignore John, for his preaching nurtured the very roots of its own identity. Its traditions about him are therefore diverse and rich. Even in the New Testament John has been interpreted in different ways. While for the most part these interpretations may not contradict each other, at times they do. For instrance, in Mark and Matthew John is identified with Elijah (Mk 9:11 parallel Mt 17:12; Mt 11:14). One may discuss whether or not Luke is comfortable with that understanding of the Baptist (Miller, 1988: 611-622), but there can be no question that the Fourth Gospel denies it outright (Kazmierski, 1996: 9,25).

The account of John's ministry in Lk 3:1-20 exhibits a clear thematic unity. An inclusion that is formed between verses 1-2 and 19-20 by references to Herod, during whose reign this ministry takes place, his brother Philip, and John himself underlines this unity (O'Fearghail, 1991: 21; van Bruggen, 1993: 104). Lk 3:1-20 contains much *uniquely Lukan material*. Only Luke details the content of John's teaching (Lk 3:10-14). Only Luke cites Isa 40:4-5 (Lk 3:4-6). The lengthened citation (Mark and Matthew cite only Isa 40:3) expresses that Jesus' coming offers salvation for all ("all flesh"). Only Luke mentions the imprisonment of John so early in the account (Lk 3:19-20). But there are also *traditional materials* which have clear parallels elsewhere. The warning about judgment has a practically literal parallel (Lk 3:7-9; Mt 3:7-10). The promise of the mightier one to come has conceptual parallels (Lk 3:15-17; Mk 1:7-8; Mt 3:11-12). The combination of the two types of material describes John's ministry of preparation (Bock, 1994: 278). Luke presents John as a prophet more fully than the other Synoptic writ-

ers. All agree that John was a man whose ministry anticipated Jesus', but Luke explains how John prepared for Jesus.
In addition, Luke's placement of these events on the stage
of world history communicates that they were of international significance (Acts 26:26; Schürmann, 1969: 150; Müller,
1984: 45-46; Danker, 1988: 81; Bock, 1994: 280-281). The
question of the source(s) of Lk 3:1-20 will not be discussed
here (for a critical survey of recent scholarship, see Fuchs,
1995: 23-129).

a. John the Baptist (Lk 3:1-6)

In the first section of the preparation for Jesus' public
ministry there is redundancy: John now appears on the scene,
introduced anew (Lk 3:2), almost as if we had not learned
in the infancy narrative that he is the forerunner of Jesus.
Part of the redundancy is due to Luke's dependence on Mk
1:1-5, a source that lacks an infancy narrative. In the Gospel of Mark, John's appearance on the scene is a simple
preparation for Jesus' public ministry; but Luke's story is more
complicated because of its dependence on Mark and of the
prefixing to his Gospel of an infancy narrative. It is also
complicated by the view of John the Baptist that Luke has
and that is colored in part by the view of saving history
which Luke has worked into his two-volume work, Luke-
Acts (Fitzmyer, 1981: 450). This pericope has a twofold
purpose: to place John's, and therefore Jesus' ministry in
the midst of world history (Lk 3:1-2a; Kremer, 1988: 45)
and to set the ministry of John the Baptist in the midst of
Old Testament hope (Lk 3:4-6). The word of God comes
to John in the wilderness as his ministry renews God's direct activity for people (Lk 3:2b-3; Bock, 1994: 279).

The position of John the Baptist in Luke's Gospel is a
much discussed issue. Some consider John the last of the
prophets, the last of the age of promise. Thus he belongs to
the Old Testament. That is the view of Hans Conzelmann
(1960: 18-27) who notes that the account of John the Bap-

tist is self-contained in Luke. He points out that Luke moves
the account of John's imprisonment up (Lk 3:19-20), so that
Jesus becomes the exclusive focus of the period of fulfillment (so also Schürmann, 1969: 149,183-184; Ernst, 1977:
146; and Fitzmyer, 1981: 450-451, but with some qualifica-
tion). Others consider John a "bridge-figure" in whom the
transition from promise to fulfillment is made (Bovon, 1991:
162; Marshall, 1978: 132; Wink, 1968: 42-86).

Verses 1-2: (1) In the fifteenth year of the reign of Emperor
                  Tiberius,
                  when Pontius Pilate was governor of Judea,
                  and Herod was ruler of Galilee,
                  and his brother Philip ruler of the region of
                  Ituraea and Trachonitis
                  and Lysanias ruler of Abilene,
             (2) during the high priesthood of Annas and
                  Caiaphas,
                  the word of God came to John son of Zechariah
                  in the wilderness.

A sixfold synchronism, that is, a chronological arrangement
of historical events and personages so as to indicate coincidence or coexistence (Webster), marks the beginning of the
Gospel account proper in such a way that Lk 1–2 is rel-
egated to the role of prehistory (contrast the minimal setting in Lk 1:5). Lk 3:1ff, which is parallel to Mk 1:1ff., is
also the real "beginning" for Luke (compare Acts 1:22 :
"beginning from the baptism of John"). This is confirmed
by the fact that none of the insights acquired by the characters in the infancy narrative play any role in the story
line from Lk 3:1ff. onward. Lk 1—2 may orient the reader,
but Lk 3 begins the promised account of "the events that
have been fulfilled among us" (Lk 1:1; see Acts 10:37; 13:24;
Nolland, 1989: 137). The events of Lk 1—2, though full of
promise for the future, had been confined to a small circle
of the pious in Israel. But the events of the Gospel were
"not done in a corner" (Acts 26:26), and the moment when
they begin to pass from the private to the public domain is

strongly underlined by Luke (C.F. Evans, 1990: 228-229). Seven rulers are mentioned, working from the most comprehensive ruler down to the regional spiritual leaders (Bock, 1994: 281-282). In a work that would see God's word open outwards to the ends of the earth (Acts 1:8) and where Jesus and his disciples would come in conflict with both political and religious leaders at all levels, this introduction appears most appropriate (LaVerdiere, 1980: 47).

The synchronism begins at the center of the world (*oikoumenē*), Rome, and with a date, the regnal year of the Roman emperor. Since Tiberius succeeded Augustus in A.D. 14, "the fifteenth year of the reign of Emperor Tiberius" refers most probably to the year A.D. 28-29. However, the existence of various calendars, lack of knowledge about customs concerning the reckoning of the accession (part-) year, and especially a period of co-regency with Augustus make certainty impossible (Nolland, 1989: 139; for the place and role of the emperor in the contemporary scene, especially in connection with the *Pax Romana*, see Hendrickx, 1996: 172-177). A recent study affirms that Luke's reference to the fifteenth year of the reign of Tiberius in Lk 3:1 is in fact calculated from the time of the co-regency with Augustius ca. A.D. 11/12. The accuracy of this interpretation is supported by the proclamation of the "year of the Lord's favor" (Lk 4:19) which refers to a clearly established Jubilee year that in the Jewish chronology of the time may be dated to A.D. 26/27 (Strobel, 1995: 466-469).

Tiberius ruled Palestine from a distance, so that the effect of his reign was experienced only through the governors and others under him. The empire was divided into imperial provinces directly under the emperor's care (e.g., Syria and Galatia) and senatorial provinces under the care of the Senate (e.g., Asia, Macedonia, and Achaia). Rulers in these regions were either legates (military men in charge of the army) or prefects (administrative financial officers in charge of collecting taxes and keeping the peace; from A.D.

53, as the result of a decree of emperor Claudius, called procurators). Prefects were usually of lesser stature than legates. Pontius Pilate was a prefect as shown by an inscription discovered at Caesarea (Marshall, 1978: 133; C.F. Evans, 1990: 232-233; Bock, 1994: 282). The remaining statements in verse 1 are not chronological, but refer to the rulers contemporary with the previous date. They begin with the emperor's representative in Judaea, Pilate, who was prefect from A.D. 26 to 36-37. Judaea was one of the three administrative districts into which Palestine was divided under Roman rule, stretching from the northern border of Samaria to include Idumaea in the south, and from the sea to beyond the Jordan (so Lk 1:65; 2:4; 5:17; 21:21; C.F. Evans, 1990: 232).

Herod is Herod Antipas, son of Herod the Great (Lk 1:5) and Malthace. He was ruler of Galilee and Peraea from 4 B.C. until his deposition by emperor Caligula in A.D. 39. Luke shows a particular interest in him (Lk 3:9; 8:3; 9:7,9; 13:31; 23:7-15; Acts 4:27; 13:1; Marshall, 1978: 133-134). The term "tetrarch, " literally means "ruler over a fourth part," but a tetrarchy, originally one of the four regions into which a kingdom was divided, had become a general term for a division of a Roman protectorate, and hence the term tetrarch was used in the New Testament period for petty rulers. Herod Antipas is the "Herod" of the rest of the Lukan Gospel.

Philip, Herod Antipas' half-brother, the son of Herod the Great and Cleopatra of Jerusalem, ruled peacefully over what Luke calls "the region of Ituraea and Trachonitis," thereby mentioning only two of the small areas over which he ruled. They were located east of the Jordan, to the north bordering on Syria, roughly north of the Decapolis and south of Damascus. Philip ruled from 4 B.C. until A.D. 34 when he died without an heir; his territory became part of the Roman province of Syria (Fitzmyer, 1981: 457).

Lysanias was tetrarch of Abilene, that is, a territory around the city of Abila, northwest of Damascus. It is not clear who was the Lysanias mentioned here, and Luke's mention of Lysanias of Abilene has often been regarded as an historical error. But several persons in power in this period seem to have borne this name (Creed, 1957: 307-309). It is surprising that Luke should mention such a small territory that plays no part in the gospel story. Indeed, if the identity of this petty ruler is problematic, still more so is the reason why Luke has mentioned him at all. Is it because Luke was a Syrian? Did he come from Abilene? We shall never know (Fitzmyer, 1981: 458). It is perhaps for the sake of completeness, since Abilene was part of the territory of Herod Agrippa I (Acts 25:13-26:32; C.F. Evans, 1990: 233).

To the civil leaders Luke now adds mention of religious leaders of Palestinian Judaism. Annas, or Ananus, was appointed high priest by the Roman governor in A.D. 6 and held this position until he was deposed in A.D. 15. He was then succeeded by Ishmael (A.D. 15), Eleazar, his own son (A.D. 16-17), Simon (A.D. 17-18), and eventually by his son-in-law, Joseph, called Caiaphas. The latter held the post from A.D. 18-36. In Acts 4:6 Luke again gives the title "high priest" to Annas, while mentioning Caiaphas simply as a member of "the high-priestly family." It is not clear what Luke intends by "the high-priesthood of Annas and Caiaphas." Literally, he says, "under the high priest Annas and Caiaphas." That is, Luke uses a singular term to refer to two persons. Since there was never more than one high priest at a time, and Caiaphas was undoubtedly the high priest during this time, some scholars have raised questions about either the accuracy of Luke's information or of his interpretation. But it may have been customary to speak of an ex-high priest as "high priest" even if he was already out of office, and Luke may simply be referring to a period when Palestinian Judaism was dominated by two powerful figures during which the call of John took place (Fitzmyer, 1981: 458). Luke may be saying that actual power was really shared and that the religious authority of the region was really a two-man affair, with Annas exercising great power behind the scenes (Ellis, 1974: 88; Schneider, 1977: 82; Marshall, 1978: 134; Bock, 1994: 284). Josephus, *Antiquities* 20. 198, says that people considered Annas very happy in that after he himself had been high priest all his five sons became high priests, which was unprecedented. Hence we may suppose that Annas continued to exercise great influence, and could still be called in a sense high priest. There is a similar combination, or confusion, of names in the Fourth Gospel (compare Jn 18:13,24 with 18:19; C.F. Evans, 1990: 234; Bovon, 1991: 165-166).

"The word of God came to John son of Zechariah." Whereas in Mk 1:4 we are simply told that John the Baptist was preaching in the wilderness, Luke presents his activity as the result of a "call" from God. The wording seems to be borrowed from Jer 1:1LXX, "the word of God, which was (directed) to Jeremiah, son of Hilkiah..." So also Isa 38:4, "Then the word of the Lord came to Isaiah..." and Jer 13:3, "And the word of the Lord came to me a second time..." The phrase "the word of God" (*rhema theou*) is unique in the New Testament but recalls "the word of God" in the Septuagint of which Luke is very conscious here (Leaney, 1966: 106). Some hold that *rhema* suggests a particular message of God rather than the entire scope of his message as *logos* would do (Plummer, 1901: 85). Moreover, the term *logos* is particularly Lukan (nineteen out of twenty-six Synoptic uses; Luke-Acts: thirty-three out of sixty-eight New Testament uses). Others relate *rhema* to the specific call to begin one's ministry, as the verbal parallelism to Jer 1:1-4 suggests. This latter sense gives a specificity to *rhema* that is quite plausible here (Bock, 1994: 285). The allusion thus relates the call of John to that of the prophets Jeremiah and Isaiah, specifying the prophetic character of his role (recall Lk 1:76; see 7:26; Fitzmyer, 1981: 458; Webb, 1991b: 169). So, while in the other Gospels John the Baptist simply makes his appearance in fulfillment

of scripture, Luke traces his appearance back to a divine call
(C.F. Evans, 1990: 234). But the Baptist's call to prophetic
ministry is more than the call of any Old Testament prophet
(Lk 7:26; Schürmann, 1969: 152-153). For Luke, the call of
John the Baptist is the beginning of the epoch of fulfillment,
for if the speeches of Acts are considered, one can see how
closely Luke links John to Jesus (Acts 1:22; 10:37; 13:24-25;
Plummer, 1901: 85).

Coming after the infancy narrative, the identification
"the son of Zechariah" is redundant in the Gospel of Luke
as we now have it (see Lk 1:13,53). It has been suggested
that if Lk 3:1ff. were at one time the beginning of an earlier form of the Gospel it would make perfect sense so to
identify John (Schürmann, 1969: 153, n. 38; Müller, 1984:
46). Such an identification is found only in Luke (Fitzmyer,
1981: 459). However, the mention here of Zechariah does
not point to the existence of an earlier form of the Gospel
without the infancy narrative. Rather it provides a bridge
back to Lk 1 (Schürmann, 1969: 153; Nolland, 1989: 140).
Moreover, it was common in the Old Testament to mention a prophet's father's name when introducing his ministry (Hos 1:1; Joel 1:1; Zech 1:1; Ernst, 1977: 138-139).

Who was "John son of Zechariah"? Material concerning
John the Baptist may be found in twenty-eight pericopae in
Luke-Acts (Webb, 1991b: 60-70). There is no reason to
doubt that John did come from a family of devout priests as
the Lukan infancy narrative indicates If his father Zechariah
was a priest, then John's destiny likewise lay in the priesthood. To abandon this role would be unheard of in the
society of his time (Kazmierski, 1996: 23; Malina, 1979: 126-
138; but see also Hendrickx, 1996: 36-39). In fact, other
sections of Luke confirm the infancy narrative in that they
show that John had priestly concerns. He engaged in the
rituals of baptism, fasting, and prayer all from the point of
view of ritual and moral purification (see, e.g., Lk 5:33a;
3:3b).

But John comes on the scene as more than simply a rural priest. He appears in the wilderness of Judaea as a radically alienated character. In addition to the wilderness habitation itself, his alienation is indicated not least by his food and clothing: "Now John was clothed with camel's hair, with a leather belt around his waist, and he ate locusts and wild honey" (Mk 1:6, here omitted by Luke, but referred to in Lk 7:25,33). This asceticism became proverbial: "For John came neither eating or drinking" (Mt 11:18 par. Lk 7:33, "For John the Baptist came eating no bread and drinking no wine"). Most of all, he sharply attacked the Jerusalem social and religious establishment for its impiety and injustice (Mt 3:7-10).

How can we account for John's Jeremiah-like separation from the normal securities and meanings of traditional life? First, John's general cultural setting is significant. There was a long-standing tradition of alienation among the prophets of ancient Israel (see, e.g., Jer 15:17: "I did not sit in the company of merrymakers, nor did I rejoice; under the weight of your hand I sat alone, for you had filled me with indignation"). Then, in exilic and post-exilic Judaism various groups of alienated priests appear on the scene (Hanson, 1975: 209-228, 280-286, 389-401). Moreover, in the middle of the second century B.C. there was a sharp revulsion against the later Maccabees which nourished among others the Qumran community. Qumran was the dwelling of a monastic group which consisted largely of lower rural priests alienated from the aristocratic urban priests of Jerusalem (Cross, 1958: 95-119). The case of Qumran is especially significant since it is a widely held view that John was like the people of Qumran in many respects, and that he may even have been a member of that group or a group like them. The result of the discussion following the discovery of the Dead Sea Scrolls can be summed up as follows: "It is possible that John had once been a member of the Qumran community" (Grant, 1963: 312).

Thus John was surrounded by a pervasive climate of alienation, possibly reaching into his own family. Now while this climate of alienation goes a long way in helping us to understand John's career, nevertheless it is not sufficient to account for the particular role which John chose to pursue. For there were many alienated priests in John's day who did not become apocalyptic prophets. We can only assume that John did have a "call" that transformed him from being simply an alienated priest into an alienated prophet of the apocalyptic cursing and blessing of God.

But even here John is not altogether without a parallel, for in this period there were many prophets, some of whom had messages similar to John's. They, like John and the Qumran community, also often led their followers into the wilderness, which had profound symbolic significance for Judaism as the place of both death and rebirth (Hollenbach, 1974: 169-179; Davies, 1974: 75-104).

Despite the scarcity of particulars about John before his public appearance, it may be concluded that he came from a family of rural priests which, according to some scholars, had Zealot leanings. These sympathies were most likely the result of the alienation the lower rural priesthood commonly felt toward the political-social-economic-religious Jerusalem establishment. At some indeterminable point John left his family and took up a desert existence and finally appeared in public as an apocalyptic prophet (Hollenbach, 1979: 852-856).

In the light of recent studies (Horsley, 1984; 1985; Horsley-Hanson, 1985), it can be seen that John fits quite well the type of "oracular prophet," which is distinguished from that of the "action prophet." These are in turn distinguished from "social bandits" and "popular kings" as well as sicarii and zealots. These types must be seen in two primary settings: (1) the specific socioeconomic conditions of first century Palestine, the essence of which is the aristocratic-peasant structure, and (2) the specific cultural traditions of

Israel, the essence of which are the traditions derived from
the Hebrew scriptures that remain popular in the oral traditions of the non-literate population.

The aristocratic-peasant social structure is characterized
primarily by the exploitation of the peasants by the aristo-
crats through heavy taxation and brutal treatment. These
conditions were perennial, but they were exacerbated in times
of devastating crises such as famines and wars. Thus variet-
ies of social disturbance were the result. This was especially
the case at the time of Herod's death in 4 B.C., Pontius
Pilate's rule (A.D. 26-36), and just before and during the
great revolt (A.D. 66-70).

The cultural traditions of Israel help us to grasp the
various social types present in first-century Palestine. We
are especially interested in the prophetic types (Horsley, 1985;
Horsley-Hanson, 1985). The "action prophet" both announced
the messages of God and led a popular movement with the
expectation that God would intervene in liberating action.
The prototype of the tradition was the Exodus from Egypt.
Moses, Joshua and the Judges were the main prototypes, as
on a lesser scale were perhaps Elijah and Elisha. In first-
century Palestine there were several such figures, one of whom
is mentioned in Acts 5, namely, Theudas (A.D. 44-48).
Josephus' accounts of these and similar movements establish a distinctive pattern: a popular prophet preaches a message
of liberation that captures the imagination of the common
people, who then march out *en masse* to a holy site expecting a miraculous deliverance from God as in the days of
old.

The "oracular prophet" did not lead such movement,
but rather only pronounced words of judgment or redemp-
tion, as did the classical prophets of the eighth and seventh centuries B.C. The two cases in the first century A.D.
about whom we have some information are John the Baptist and Jesus son of Ananias. Josephus deals rather extensively with the latter (*Jewish War* 6.5.3 #300-309). John

the Baptist seems to fit the type of "oracular prophet," with the proviso that he adds uniquely to that model his practices of baptism, fasting, and prayer (Hollenbach, 1992: 891, 898).

Concluding we may say that John's ministry was more than just a religious phenomenon. Consequently, a full appreciation of his ministry necessitates that it be perceived as having a socio-political aspect as well. John's activity of baptizing and his proclamation of judgment and restoration triggered a movement drawn primarily from among the common people. Similar to the response made to other leadership prophets, the perception by these people of oppression and deprivation contributed to their positive and enthusiastic response to John's ministry. But John's tactics were somewhat different in realizing deliverance from those of the other leadership prophets. The tactics of both John and the other prophets were pacifist, but, while the others were corporate and activist in their approach, John's movement was dispersed and pacifist. The other prophetic movements engaged in symbolic events employing the wilderness (and in one case the Jordan River) to typologically enact deliverance, recalling motifs of Exodus/Conquest. Similarly, John's ministry was associated with the wilderness and the Jordan, and it is possible that the people coming to the wilderness to be baptized by John in the Jordan were also enacting a symbolic event in which they anticipated the repossession and cleansing of the land by the expected figure. In the case of this symbolic event, however, John's followers did not participate in it as a corporate body all at the same time.

Just as the other leadership prophets faced conflict and opposition from the ruling authorities, so did John. With respect to the others, the source of that conflict was chiefly the Roman authorities in Judaea. With John, on the other hand, the greater amount of data allows us to trace that conflict to animosity between John and Herod Antipas, and probably between John and the temple establisment as well. But behind both these sources of conflict stood the imperialist power of Rome. This conflict between John and the other leadership prophets, on the one hand, and the authorities, on the other, led to the former being executed by those authorities. That those who followed John were largely spared, in contrast to those who followed the other leadership prophets, may be explained by the difference in John's tactics as well as the difference between the ruling style of Roman governors and Herod Antipas (Webb, 1991b: 377-378; Webb, 1995: 23-38).

"The wilderness" is a unique location for the call of a prophet (see Lk 1:80). The place of a prophet's call is not generally recorded in the Old Testament. The tradition had, however, firmly associated John with the desert (Lk 7:24 = Mt 1:7; Mk 1:4). This may have come about through the application to him of Isa 40:3LXX (Marshall, 1978: 135), which has "the voice of one crying out in the wilderness," whereas the Hebrew connects "in the wilderness" with "prepare": "the voice of one crying, 'in the wilderness prepare the way of the Lord'." By *he eremos* was not meant a sandy waste, but a desolate, uncultivated region, generally uninhabited. Without specification it was vague. It could denote the wilderness of Judah west of the Dead Sea (so Mt 3:1, and possibly here in Lk 3:2 in view of Lk 1:39, 65, 80). Or it could denote the land east of the Jordan (cf. Jn 1:28; 10:40).

The relation in Lk 3:2 between "the wilderness" and "all the region around the Jordan" suggests that the wilderness of Judah is meant (Fitzmyer, 1981: 459; Webb, 1991: 170). It could, however, be less a *geographical* than a *theological* term. The forty years' journey in the wilderness came to be regarded as an ideal time when Israel saw the saving acts of God and was made his people (Hos 9:10; Amos 2:10; Jer 2:10; Acts 7:36), and as such it supplied features of the coming age (Hos 2:14ff.; 12:9; Mic 7:15). There was an expectation that the salvation of God would be immediately preceded by a journey into the wilderness in the belief that there God would give tokens of deliverance (see Mt 24:26; Acts 21:38). In the theology of Qumran retreat to, and residence in, the wilderness were not unconnected with the community's conception of itself as a community of penitents, the remnant or true Israel of God (C.F. Evans, 1990: 234-235). The location identifies John as part of a movement of eschatological renewal (see comments under verse 4 below; Nolland, 1989: 140).

Verses 3-4a: (3) He went into all the region around the Jordan,
proclaiming a baptism of repentance
for the forgiveness of sins,
(4a) as it is written in the book of the words of the
prophet Isaiah,

"He went" suggests a change of location, but this should not be seen as a leaving of the wilderness (Lk 3:4; 7:24; differently Wink, 1968: 4). The coming "into all the region" does not so much suggest entry into a new area as the scope of a wide-ranging ministry (Marshall, 1978: 135; Bock, 1994: 287; different: Schürmann, 1969: 155). The "region" is not clearly distinct from the "wilderness" (Fitzmyer, 1981: 459). Rather, John moves in the wilderness to where there is water, and he moves from relative isolation (Lk 1:80) to where there are people. He seeks people to preach, and the proximity of water to baptize. Only Luke depicts John's preaching activity as itinerant (Wink, 1968: 53), and this might suggest that for Luke ministry is an itinerant activity, but there are no specific vocabulary links to the itineration of Jesus and Christian preachers (Nolland, 1989: 140). The Fourth Gospel depicts John as a stationary desert preacher, addressing his message to all who would come to listen to him in the Jordan valley. Luke does not suggest that the Jordan was not in the wilderness (as stated by Schürmann, 1969: 155), nor does he geographically distinguish the areas of activity of John and Jesus (as stated by

Conzelmann, 1961: 19). The Jordan was the gate-way to the "promised land," ending the Exodus journey. Possibly Luke may have had this symbolism in mind. John exhorts the people to enter anew into the ancient covenant and, thereby, to inherit te "promised land" into which the Messiah will bring them (Ellis, 1966: 87-88).

Being outside structured society, the wilderness was considered a place of chaos and disorder. It was also the place of negative demons; unnecessary travel through or stay in that region would have been considered deviant behavior. The quotation in Lk 3:4-5, however, indicates that the chaotic and deviant will be brought under divine reordering and that this will be the "salvation of God" (Malina-Rohrbaugh, 1992: 301).

The verbs "to proclaim" (*kerussein*) and "to proclaim the good news" (*euangelizein*) used in Lk 3:18 are strong indications of a "Christianization" of John, that is, of John being seen through Christian eyes as part of the Gospel (Acts 10:37; 13:24), since precisely these two verbs are used in Lk 4:18-19. They warn us against any sharp separation of John and Jesus: not so much the message, as well the state of fulfillment differed (Nolland, 1989: 141-142). The phrase "proclaiming a baptism of repentance for the forgiveness of sins" is a highly compressed and Christian formulation probably taken from Mk 1:4, where it is the sole description of John's ministry (C.F. Evans, 1990: 235).

Luke calls John explicitly "the Baptist" (*baptistēs*; Lk 7:20,33; 9:19). Here he depicts him "proclaiming a baptism." *Baptisma*, a passive verbal noun meaning "the act of being baptized" must be understood of a ritual washing having a religious connotation, and the following phrases specify the connotation. It is associated with "repentance" (*metanoia*), meaning literally "a change of mind," but when used in a religious sense, it has the connotation of "conversion, reform of life" (Fitzmyer, 1981: 459). This is not only a characteristic of John's ministry, but also a key term for Luke.

The product of repentance, as far as John is concerned, is elaborated in the comments found in Lk 3:10-14. It is reflected in a concern for one's fellow humans that makes an effort to meet concrete needs. Repentance produces a life with a sense of responsibility; it is an internal attitude that aims at a product (Bock, 1994: 287). The proclamation of repentance relates John to the great prophets of Israel. They called the people back from their alienation from and rebellion against God. They urged them to turn away from everything unworthy of God (Amos 4:6ff.; Isa 55:6ff.; Jer 25:4ff.). The prophets made their appeal for repentance in relation to historical judgments of God in the political sphere or by means of natural disaster. For John, the urgency of the appeal and the absoluteness of its claim is determined by its eschatological setting. The call for repentance is repeated in Jesus' ministry (Lk 5:32) and in the early Church (Acts 2:38; Nolland, 1989: 141).

The phrase "forgiveness of sins" (*aphesis hamartiōn*), though not found as such in the Septuagint, is related to the verb *aphienai* which is used with *hamartia* (e.g., Num 14:19, "Forgive the iniquity of this people..."; Ps 25:18, "forgive all my sins"). It expresses the purpose of the "baptism of repentance" that John proclaims. Yet somehow, the connection between baptism and repentance remains obscure. The genitive "of repentance" is generally taken to mean that the baptism accompanied repentance as an outward sign or symbol of it, though it is not clear why it was necessary (C.F. Evans, 1990: 236). Actually, "repentance" and "forgiveness of sins" are two of Luke's favorite ways of summing up the effects of the Christ-event (Fitzmyer, 1981:459). Here Luke describes John's ministry in the same terms, but he will clarify the distinction between John's baptism and later Christian baptism in Lk 3:16 (compare Acts 18:25).

In the Gospels the closest analogy to the forgiveness of sins is the forgiveness of debts (Lk 11:4; cf. Mt 6:12), an analogy drawn from pervasive peasant experience. Debt threatened loss of land, livelihood, family. It was the result of being poor, that is, being unable to defend one's social position. Forgiveness would thus have had the character of restoration, a return to both self-sufficiency and one's place in the community. Forgiveness by God meant being divinely restored to one's position and therefore being freed from fear of loss at the hands of God (Malina-Rohrbaugh, 1992: 303-304).

John's baptism is probably to be situated in the general baptist movement which existed in Palestine roughly between 150 B.C. and A.D. 250 (see Bock, 1994: 288-289). A number of Jewish and Christian groups emerged in this period which practiced some form of ritual washing. Though the forms differed and the connotations attached to them varied, the washings of the Essenes, of John and his disciples (Acts 18:25), of Jesus and his disciples Jn 3:22; 4:2), of the Ebionites (a Jewish Christian group), and a number of later Gnostic groups are examples of this general movement. Luke — or any other Gospel for that matter — does not tell us what the efficacy of John's baptism was supposed to be, and we must resist the tendency to interpret it in an anachronistic fashion, e.g., attributing to it a sacramental effect characteristic of later Christian baptism. Maybe, John's baptism can best be understood in relation to the contemporary interpretation of ritual washings among the Qumran Essenes. It was considered useless to partake in the Essene ritual washing as a member of the community unless one were willing to turn from evildoing: "They shall not enter the water to share the pure meal of the saints, for they shall not be cleansed unless they turn from their evildoing; for all who transgress his word are unclean" (1QS 5:13-14). Similarly, the Old Testament idea of God's forgiveness of human sin is related by John to a ritual washing and an attitude of repentance. This also makes it plausible to explain John's baptism as a development of a purificatory rite such as that of the Essenes, rather than as a derivation from Jewish proselyte baptism, which cannot be traced back to the first century A.D. (Fitzmyer, 1981: 459-460; C.F. Evans, 1990: 235).

The formula of citation, "as it was written in the book of the words of the prophet Isaiah," is unique. However, its component parts may be found in the Septuagint: in 2 Chron 35:12 we have "as it is written in the book"; in Tob 1:1, "the book of the words" (*biblos logōn*).

Verses 4b-6: (4b) "The voice of one crying in the wilderness:
'Prepare the way of the Lord,
make his paths straight.
(5) Every valley shall be filled,
and evey mountain and hill shall be made low,
and the crooked shall be made straight,
and the rough ways made smooth;
(6) and all flesh shall see the salvation of God.'"

The citation may be seen as an example of that use of *testimonia* or proof texts to establish the gospel events as being "according to the scriptures," i.e., according to the divine plan, which constituted the earliest exercise in Christian theology (Dodd, 1965: 111-125). Luke omits Mk 1:2b, "See, I am sending my messenger ahead of you, who will prepare your way" (Mal 3:1) with which Mark begins his composite quotation from "Isaiah," but he will use that text in Lk 7:27 (=Mt 11:10). Luke also omits Isa 40:5a, "then the glory of the Lord shall be revealed." Perhaps Luke did not regard it as being fulfilled in Jesus' earthly ministry, and, unlike the Fourth Evangelist, did not see a revelation of divine glory in him (Marshall, 1978: 137). Glory does not characterize the public ministry of Jesus (cf. Lk 9:32), but is the outcome of his suffering (Lk 24:26) and will mark his return (Lk 21:27; Nolland, 1989: 144; for a survey of the debate concerning Luke's use of the text of Isaiah, see Bock, 1994: 290 293).

John's ministry explicitly fulfills Isa 40:3-5; he constitutes the first stage of the realization of the consolation of Israel announced by Isaiah and expected by the pious

(Lk 2:25, 38; Cousin, 1993: 53). Isa 40:3-5 spoke of a voice announcing the need for a perfect road from the wilderness into Jerusalem, along which the Lord God was to come and bring salvation. The use of a quotation here in Lk 3, as often elsewhere, is probably an "atomic" one, i.e., the text is taken in isolation without regard for its original context. Here the connecting links are "in the wilderness" and "the Lord," which in Isa 40:3 refers to God, but is now made to refer to Jesus as the Lord of the Christians, and consequently the Septuagint text itself has been altered from "of our God" to "his" (ways), an interesting indication of the growing tendency to blur the distinction between God and the Messiah (Leaney, 1966: 106). In this way also John, his preaching and movement, do not stand in their own right, as references to "John's disciples" (Lk 5:33; 7:18; 11:1; Acts 19:3-4) suggest that they could, but are essentially the necessary divine prelude to Jesus (C.F. Evans, 1990: 237).

A firm biblical (Ez 20:33-38; Hos 2:14-23) and contemporary (CD [=Damascus Document] 8:12-15; 1QS 9.20) tradition located the beginning of eschatological renewal in the wilderness (Mauser, 1963), sometimes in connection with the text of Isaiah which is quoted here (CD 8:12-15). The imagery is that of a coming of the Lord (to Jerusalem; cf. Isa 40:2) by way of the wilderness. Only a perfect road (straight, holes filled, humps removed) will be fit for God to travel upon. But, as said above, Luke has in mind the coming of Jesus (Nolland, 1989: 143).

The poetic imagery of verse 5 should not be over-pressed, but since Luke could easily have omitted material not needed on the way to his desired goal in the next verse it is probable that the verse has some metaphorical significance. Luke may have seen significance in the use of "to make low" (*tapeinoō*) to express the humbling of the proud (Lk 1:52; 14:11; 18:14). There may also be a metaphorical significance in the use of "crooked" (*skolios*) to typify crooked or perverse or corrupt people (Acts 2:40).

By having the quotation run until it reaches "and all flesh shall see the salvation of God" (Isa 40:5), quoted in Lk 3:6, Luke somehow makes this citation serve as an introduction to the whole of the Gospel and Acts in its universal appeal. It is echoed in the final words of Paul in Acts 28:28, "Let it be known to you then that this salvation of God has been sent to the Gentiles" (C.F. Evans, 1990: 237). In light of Lk 2:30 "the salvation of God" is to be understood in close connection to the person of Jesus, and the achievement realized in his coming and ministry. For Luke, "all flesh" echoes the universalism of Lk 2:32, "a light for revelation to the Gentiles" (Nolland, 1989: 144).

b. John's Preaching (Lk 3:7-9)

Lk 3:3 presented John the Baptist as a prophetic preacher calling for repentance and inviting people to baptism. Luke then presents a more specific picture of John's prophetic preaching actitivity. Three samples of it are given, devoted to different aspects of that preaching: eschatological (Lk 3:7-9), ethical (Lk 3:10-14), and messianic (Lk 3:15-18; Fitzmyer, 1989:103-104). Lk 3:7-9 offers a sample of John's eschatological preaching (Fitzmyer, 1981:463-464). John may have been preaching in A.D. 33/34 which was a sabbatical year (Derrett, 1995: 155-165).

Verses 7-9: (7) John said to the crowds that came out to be baptized by him,
"You brood of vipers!
Who warned you to flee from the wrath to come?
(8) Bear fruits worthy of repentance.
Do not begin to say to yourselves,
'We have Abraham as our ancestor';
for I tell you,
God is able from these stones to raise up children to Abraham.
(9) Even now the ax is lying at the root of the trees; every tree therefore that does not bear good fruit is cut down and thrown into the fire."

Lk 3:7a is a Lukan transitional half-verse introducing the preaching samples, first of all a sample of his echatological preaching. Lk 3:7b-9 is one of the clearest instances of identical wording in the Double Tradition: sixty out of sixty-three (Matthew) / sixty-four (Luke) words in the Greek text of these verses are identical (see Mt 3:7-10; Webb, 1991b: 173). So, these verses are identified as sayings-material from the Q-source.

Whereas in Mt 3:7 this preaching is addressed to Pharisees and Sadducees, it is here addressed to "the crowds" who came to John for baptism. It is almost impossible to say whether "the Pharisees and Sadducees" belonged originally to Q, or whether Matthew has introduced this specification. It should be noted that in the New Testament only Matthew joins these two hostile groups together (Meier, 1980: 389). But is the combination of these two opposing groups necessarily of Matthean origin? In fact, our text simply implies that they had come among the crowd (Mt 3:6) and not necessarily together, for that matter, if the text is supposed to be a summary. On the other hand, the Lukan context also suggests the possibility of redactional work, so that on the whole, the most that can be said is that, while the exact wording of the underlying text (*Vorlage*) is unlikely to be clear, the core of the text unmistakably refers to an audience of great numbers (Kazmierski, 1987: 27-28). Given the form of address, "You brood of vipers," it is easier to see the Matthean audience as the more original (Fitzmyer, 1981: 467; Webb, 1991b:176).

This is the first of many instances in which Luke uses the word "crowd" or "crowds" (*ochlos, ochloi*). The other Synoptic evangelists use this word frequently, but the Lukan use is disconcerting; at times Luke avoids it where the others have it, at times he introduces it where they do not have it. Quite frequently the word merely designates the crowd that is present. Sometimes the crowd is specified by a genitive, e.g., "a crowd of disciples" (Lk 6:17). But in many cases, whether it be used in the singular or plural, it designates simply the anonymous audience that witnesses the ministry of John or Jesus (Lk 3:7,10; 4:42, etc.). In this last sense the Lukan use of the word suits Luke's general emphasis on the popular, universal reaction to the ministry of both John and Jesus. Here, in the immediate context, the crowds (*ochloi*) give way to "people" (*laos*; Fitzmyer, 1981: 467).

Recently, it has been shown that Luke's presentation of "crowds" has a close affinity with crowd scenes in the ancient Greek novels. The similarities suggest that, since novels were a popular genre in the ancient world, Luke is employing a narrative technique with which his audience was familiar in order to present his picture of the crowds. (1) In both the novel and in Luke-Acts crowds are often present as the hearers of stories and teachings and as witnesses of mighty deeds. John the Baptist draws a large crowd both to hear his message and to be baptized (Lk 3:7,10,21). (2) The presence of a crowd in a novel is often used to highlight the popularity of the protagonists of the story. Luke, too, is fond of noting the eagerness of the crowds to come to Jesus throughout his ministry. (3) Not only do the crowds reveal the popularity of the protagonists, they also prevent hostile actions from being taken against those characters. For the reader of Luke's Gospel such scenes bring to mind Jesus' encounters with the Jewish leaders. Jesus' popularity among the people is said to have prevented the Jewish leaders from destroying or arresting him (Lk 19:47-48; 20:19; 22:2). (4) In the novels and in Luke-Acts not all of the actions of the crowd are favorable. Crowds are also involved in disturbances. In Luke's Gospel a crowd clamors for the death of Jesus. They join their leaders in pressing Pilate to crucify Jesus (Lk 23:18-23). (5) One final role played by the crowds in both the ancient novels and Luke-Acts which can be highlighted is their contribution to the narrative flow of the story. All this suggests that Luke is using a narrative

technique familiar to the readers of the Greek novel. By
doing so he is able to draw upon his readers' expectations
about the way crowds act and function in a narrative
(Ascough, 1996: 69-81).

Addressed to "the crowds," the Baptist's words are intended as an explanation of the repentance (*metanoia*) of
verse 3 and an eschatological motivation for it. John's "preparing the way of the Lord" (verse 4) is now seen related
to what the Old Testament prophets called "the Day of the
Lord" (Fitzmyer, 1981: 464).

Whereas Luke and Matthew differ as to the receivers of
the preaching which follows, they agree that the audience
had come to seek baptism. Luke's formulation, in contrast
to Mt 3:7, depicts many people accepting John's baptism
(see Lk 3:21, "Now when all the people (*laos*) were baptized...; 7:29, "And all the people (*laos*) who heard this...").

Lk 3:7b-9 is certainly one of the most negative of the
Baptist's sayings (Hollenbach, 1979: 860), and together with
the adjoining text (Lk 3:16-18 par. Mt 3:11-12), to the
exclusion of almost all others (Bammel, 1971-1972: 95-128),
has played a major role in the general perception of the
ministry of the Baptist (Kazmierski, 1987: 23-24).

The expression "brood of vipers" occurs only here in
Luke, but besides the parallel in Mt 3:7, it occurs again in
Mt 12:34 and 23:33. The image is otherwise unknown in
the Old Testament, Josephus, or rabbinical writings. The
viper was regarded in antiquity as a poisonous snake, and
the expression is intended to convey the repulsive, even
destructive character of those so described. So characterized, they are being warned against a smugness of certain
salvation — which will be their own undoing (Fitzmyer,
1981: 467).

Is the question "Who warned you...?" a legitimate inquiry as to how they have come to sense that the day draws
near (Schurmann, 1969: 164 n. 212)? Or is it a rhetorical
and ironic question that doubts the sincerity of those who

are coming (Marshall, 1978: 139)? The following positive response suggests the former, while the greeting that calls them vipers favors the latter. There seems to be another way to read the question. One can see it as a real rebuke that is not designed ironically, but seeks to get their attention and raise the question, "Do you really understand what my baptism is about?" The question is a call to see that John's message about wrath requires repentance, regardless of one station in life. Such a response is necessary in order to escape God's judgment. The question presents a choice and warns the audience that God's judgment is linked to their decision (Bock, 1994:304).

Luke speaks of "wrath" (*orge*) only here and in Lk 21:23. In both instances it refers to a future manifestation of God's wrath. He makes use of an Old Testament expression for God's judgment by which evil is to be wiped out; it is associated with the Day of the Lord in Isa 13:19; Zeph 1:14-16; 2:2; Ez 7:19. Since God's wrath" seems to be of little interest to Luke, we do not learn in his writings what evokes it; elsewhere in the New Testament it is provoked by idolatry, disobedience, or disbelief, that is, a smugness which can do without God (1 Thes 1:10; Rom 1:18; Fitzmyer, 1981: 468).

That Luke has produced examples of the "fruits of repentance" in Lk 3:10-14, which are lacking in Matthew, suggests that he has introduced the plural "fruits" (as opposed to the singular "fruit" in Mt 3:8) in keeping with his addition in these verses. The contrast with the singular "good fruit" in the parabolic saying (Lk 3:9 par. Mt 3:10) is therefore all the more striking since it is probably from here that the image in the saying in Lk 3:8 and Mt 3:8 finds its origin. John's original demand, then, is to be understood with the singular: his hearers are to "produce the fruit of repentance" (Kazmierski, 1987: 26-27).

The parabolic saying (Lk 3:9) suggests that those who stand under the judgment are powerless to avert it (Merklein, 1981: 33-34); what is possible, however, is to escape it by bearing "good fruit," a fruit that is described as "befitting repentance." Recourse to ethnic principle, even that based on the promise to Abraham, is to no avail. It is this last point that, according to some scholars, puts into question any interpretation of the original saying, which sees the call to produce fruit that befits repentance as a call to return to pious living as is manifest in Torah obedience. The latter is almost certainly the redactional interpretation of the evangelists. There is no longer time for that. "The ax is lying at the root of the trees"; the judgment is in fact already begun (Merklein, 1981: 33). To interpret *pros tēn rhizan keitai* as anything less than the ax chopping down the tree seems to stretch credulity (Kazmierski, 1987: 30 n. 35). The references to "fire" here and in Lk 3:16-17 may serve to depict John as a fiery reformer. The "fire" has here no special connotation, being merely part of the general description of what is done with dead wood (see Lk 23: 31); a different connotation will be conveyed in Lk 3:16-17. A Jewish exegetical tradition found in the Dead Sea Scrolls and in 2 Baruch not only connected Isa 10:33-34 closely with Isa 11:1-5 but also found a reference to the messiah in Isa 10:34 (*b'dyr* = "by a powerful one"). This tradition of messianic interpretation of Isa 10:34 informs the preaching of John the Baptist (Lk 3:9 parallel Mt 3:10) and implies that John expected the coming of the Davidic messiah (Bauckham, 1995: 202-216).

Both the certainty and the nature of the already begun judgment calls for a complete turning away from the past and an abandoning of that which historically assured Israel of salvation, namely the election of Abraham. "God is able from these stones to raise up children to Abraham" means that to have "children of Abraham" God does not depend on Jews physically descended from the patriarch. In thus addressing his fellow Jews, John implies that God can even create Israel anew (Fitzmyer, 1981: 468). For John, Israel's historic prerogative now counts for nothing. His oracle is directed not to averting the disaster; within his perspective that is no longer possible. It is an announcement of impending arrival, and points to the urgency of producing a sign of repentance which recognizes that fact. In this circumstance for them to "begin to say" that as sons and daughters of Abraham they have a means to escape from the wrath to come marks them in John's eyes as "brood of vipers," for therein is not the fruit of repentance which he seeks (Merklein, 1981: 36-37). The prophet is no longer concerned with an abuse of power, but with the source of power itself. At issue here is the means of salvation now that reliance on the means heretofore available to them as children of Abraham is no longer fruitful. That this saying sets a distance between John and his hearers is sure, since such a position would clearly place him at odds with the general assumptions about power within the Jewish community as a whole (Isenberg, 1975: 24-52; Kazmierski, 1987: 30-31).

The destruction that is announced is, however, not limited to the wielders of power or to one faction against the other. It is to encompass the whole of Israel so that those, and only those who produce the fruit of repentance, will be saved. Thus the prophet John is already seen as standing outside the community and its factions; the future of the social collectivity is the real issue, for the gist of John's message is that Israel itself no longer has the means to be the salvation-community (Merklein, 1981: 34).

c. **The Ethical/Social Teaching of John** *(Lk 3:10-14)*

This paragraph which is unique to Luke's Gospel offers a sample of John's ethical teaching, especially as it was concerned with social conduct. It is unusual in both structure and in thought, and differs markedly from Lk 3:7-9. The form of a thrice repeated question, variously introduced, with answers appropriate to each group of enquirers, is elegant. The question asked by each group, "What should we do?," differentiated in verse 10 by "then," that is, in the face of verses 7-9, in verse 12 by "Teacher," and in verse 14 by "and we," recalls the same question in Acts 2:37 in a similar context of a call to repentance and baptism, and may reflect the influence of Christian baptismal catechetical practice (C.F. Evans, 1990: 240). John does not invite the crowds to adopt his mode of life, but advocates a selfless concern for others (Bock, 1994: 309). His counsel is wholly intelligible in terms of Palestinian or Old Testament backgrounds. In a sense John's counsel is of a mixed sort: on the one hand, he manifests a real concern for others in a variety of ways, and yet, on the other, he does not seem to seek to upset the existing social structure — even in view of the coming wrath. He advocates the sharing of the fundamentals of life (Lk 3:11), the avoidance of extortion, blackmail, and intimidation (Lk 3:13-14). But he does not tell the toll-collectors to sever their relations with the occupying power, nor does he counsel enlisted soldiers to give up their jobs (Fitzmyer, 1981: 465).

Luke introduces Lk 3:10-14 into his account of the ministry of John the Baptist to concretize what is meant by repentance and to show what kind of behavior is proper. Contrary to the opinion of some scholars (Scheffler, 1990: 21-36), Luke does not tone down the harshness of the Baptist's preaching (Liebenberg, 1993: 55-67).

While Josephus' depiction of John the Baptist as a moral preacher concerned with virtue owes a great deal to the author's accommodation to his Greco-Roman milieu, it must be granted that Josephus agrees to a certain extent with Luke's special material on the Baptist (Lk 3:10-14). Here too the Baptist is presented as inculcating practical deeds of social justice. This correlation might simply be chalked up to two Greco-Roman writers (Josephus and Luke) who, independently of each other, seek to adapt a strange Jewish prophet to cultural models familiar in the wider Greco-Roman world. The similarity between the presentation of

Josephus and that of Luke has been noted (Ernst, 1989: 257).

Verses 10-14: (10) And the crowds asked him,
"What then should we do?"
(11) In reply he said to them,
"Whoever has two coats
must share with anyone who has none;
And whoever has food
must do likewise."
(12) Even tax collectors came to be baptized,
and they asked him,
"Teacher, what should we do?"
(13) He said to them,
"Collect no more than the amount prescribed
for you."
(14) Soldiers also asked him,
"And we, what should we do?"
He said to them,
"Do not extort money from anyone by threats
or by false accusation,
and be satisfied with your wages."

This passage, which is without parallel in the other Gospels, is an ethical instruction. Is it a Christian paraenesis placed on the lips of John the Baptist; or did Luke compose it himself? (Bultmann, 1972: 145; Bovon, 1991: 169).

"The crowds" refers back to Lk 3:7. The question, "What then should we do?" becomes a refrain in this paragraph (see verses 12,14). It is a characteristic Lukan rhetorical question which occurs also in Lk 10:25 (different Mk 12:28; Mt 22:36), Lk 18:18; Acts 2:37; 16:30; 22:10. It is expressive of a popular eagerness for salvation (Fitzmyer, 1981: 469), and of the need for practical personal response (Nolland, 1989: 149).

Among those who came to be baptized by John were at least three distinct social and vocational groups, and John addresses specific demands appropriate to each of them. The relatively wealthy are to share their wealth of clothing and food with the destitute. Indeed we cannot take Luke's "crowds"

literally. For not only is this one of his favorite editorial
terms (see Lk 3:7), but it does not make for good parallelism with the other specific groups that follow, the tax collectors and soldiers. Therefore, the likely addressees must
be deduced from John's actual answer; and that seems easy
enough, for although the crowds in general are said to pose
the question, the response is directed specifically to those
wealthy enough to have extra food or clothing (Ringe, 1995:
53). By implication John can be seen to be radically critical of the very wealthy: if the relatively rich are to share
their goods, a fortiori the very rich have even greater obli-
gation (Hollenbach, 1979: 870 notes 68,69). Tax collectors
are not supposed to make a killing for themselves. And soldiers are to quit taking advantage of both their possession
of force of arms and their social position which gave them
judicial advantage, in order to rob others. It is important to
note that every one of these three cases of criticism has to
do with economic matters, and each case assumes the distinction between a relatively wealthy class and a very poor
class with the latter suffering oppression by the former
(Hollenbach, 1979: 870). Luke's Gospel has an underlying
motif of disputation against wealth. The Lukan polemic
against wealth involves not just mere possesions but also
those who are wealthy, attitudes toward what is important
in life, and the genuine or true concerns that are associated
with the kingdom (Okorie, 1994: 75-94).

The Greek term for "coat" (*chitōn*) refers to the undergarment that was worn next to the skin. Two of these might
be worn for protection against the cold. Despite their apparent innocuous tone, the directives given in Luke's context are revolutionary. The haves are to share with the
havenots. In antiquity people assumed that everything was
limited. If one person got more, someone else automatically
got less. Acquisitiveness was therefore always greed, whereas
sharing coats would be a form of generalized reciprocity
(Malina-Rohrbaugh, 1992: 302). Those who refuse the di-

rective to share with the havenots will, like the rich man, see Lazarus at Abraham's side and themselves — while calling on their national, ecclesiastical, or cultural paternity — be forever removed from the presence of God (Lk 16:26; cf. 13:28). The ax is heading downstroke in any society that thinks these words are an invitation merely to distribute Christmas food baskets, handouts of castoff clothes, or money. What Luke is suggesting here is not giving alms or dole out. In a society that is polarized along lines of haves and havenots, Luke is referring to a sharing towards equality. If one who has two coats gives one to somebody who has none, he gives one half of this commodity (compare Lk 19:8) and, as a result, they are equal in this respect. Anyone who is insensitive to the broadening gulf between the prosperous and the economically disadvantaged deserves to know that the prophets did not risk their necks for petty moralizing. A call to repentance, an across-the-board review of respectable resources for injustice, prejudice, and indifference to the needs of human beings, this is what set apart true prophets from the bogus (Danker, 1988: 88).

In line with the Old Testament prophets, John asks the oppressors as part of their baptism of repentance, to cease their oppression of the poor who are powerless against them. Their changed practices will constitute "fruits worthy of repentance" (Lk 3:8; Malina-Rohrbaugh, 1992:302).

The case of the tax collectors is particularly clear and helps in understanding the others. There were a variety of ways in which both the local Jewish authorities as well as the Romans extracted money from the populace. But it was in connection with collecting customs on transported goods and various other government revenues that the specific kind of official referred to in Lk 3:12 figures, for the collection of such taxes was farmed out to local Jews by the Romans. There was a hierarchy of such officials. Zacchaeus, for example (Lk 19:1-9), was the "head of a society of publicans" (Safrai, 1974-76: 333). Now the important thing about these publicans, as we see in the case of Zacchaeus as well, was that they grew rich through collecting "more than the amount appointed" them (Lk 3:12), that is, more than they had contracted with, and paid their superior. Zacchaeus, for example, had paid for his office to some superior, probably a Roman, for tax collecting privileges at Jericho. Then he in turn was paid by others for the privilege of collecting certain taxes. At each of these levels a collector would earn his own livelihood, and usually gain also his relative wealth, by collecting more than he paid for his office. That some publicans grew very rich is seen in the case of Zacchaeus and others. Zacchaeus could give away half his income as well as restore fourfold what he had defrauded (Lk 19:8), and probably still be a rich man.

Just before the time of the Maccabees, that is, around 200 B.C., a certain Josephus put in a "bid for the tax-farming rights which the king (Ptolemy Epiphanes of Egypt) used to sell every year to the wealthy men in each city." He won the rights for Syria, Phoenicia, Judaea and Samaria. With the help of two thousand of the king's soldiers, and through arresting and killing the principal men of the cities, he "thus collected great sums of money and made great profits from farming taxes," and he "used his wealth to make permanent the power he now had... This good fortune he enjoyed for twenty-two years" (Josephus, *Antiquities* 12. 160-186).

The point is then that publicans were not only what is normally emphasized, that is, Quizlings contaminated by the contact with Gentiles, and robbers, but that they were part of the wealthy oppressing establishment. For such persons to heed John's call for repentance with its accompanying demand would entail a total rejection of their former way of life with its class involvement and class consciousness. For when he demanded that they should not collect funds beyond what they had contracted for, he was striking at the root of a large part of the tax system (Hollenbach, 1979:

870-871). The requirement that publicans refrain from collecting more than was appointed to them would have set them at odds with the social and economic structures of which they were part. It would have resulted in a radical reduction in their standard of living and necessitated serious economic and social readjustments on the part of their families. Furthermore, it would have required a complete reorientation of their motivation in accepting the responsibilities of their office. Because, once the prospect of becoming rich had been removed, few would want to continue the onerous duties of collecting unpopular taxes from resentful people. Especially so when the money directly or indirectly supported the (Roman) occupation forces and the concomitant collaborating (Jewish) bureaucracy (Farmer, 1962: II, 960).

That John was striking at the root of a large part of the tax system and that he had repentant tax-collectors among his followers, as well as numbers of poor and exploited taxpayers who had felt their oppression and were glad to hear John denounce this oppressive system, may very well have been the major reason that Antipas finally took notice of John (Hollenbach, 1979: 871-872). It is pertinent to note that the requests made of Archaelaus, upon the death of Herod were the following: "that he should lighten the yearly payments," that he "release... the prisoners," and that he remove the taxes "levied upon public purchases and sales" that "had been ruthlessly exacted" (Josephus, *Antiquities* 17. 204-205). It is also generally accepted that taxes were a large factor in causing the Great War of A.D. 66-70 (Rhoads, 1976: 80-81).

In Luke, the tax collectors are contrasted with the Pharisees in their respective relations to Jesus. The reader is skillfully distanced from the Pharisees and scribes, while being prompted to respond favorably to Jesus. Thus the characterization of the tax collectors, who grow to be models of prayer, repentance, conversion and belief in Jesus, graphically invades the reader's disposition and worldview (Okorie, 1995: 27-32).

There is a connection between tax collectors and soldiers in the sense that people like Zacchaeus could avail themselves of the assistance of military forces (Safrai, 1974-76: 333; Danker, 1988: 89). Who were these soldiers who responded to John? This is difficult to determine for a variety of reasons. We do not know where these soldiers came from, nor do we know much about the existence of Jewish soldiers during this period (Jeremias, 1969: 299-300). Of course, there had been Jewish soldiers from time immemorial, and in most recent times under the Maccabees. However, with the coming of the Romans these diminished, so that Herod's soldiers seem to have been mainly non-Jewish mercenaries (Daniel-Rops, 1962: 159). There were, of course, the Roman legions stationed in Syria except in times of stress as at Herod's death. And the procurators had auxiliaries in places like Caesarea and the fortress Antonia in Jerusalem. It is certainly not correct that at the time of Jesus there were no Jewish soldiers at all, for Herod had settled some Babylonian Jews in various places, including Batanaea, east of the Sea of Galilee. Beside these Jewish soldiers there were the Levite guard of the Temple, who were armed (Mk 14:48) and who formed the police force of the Temple (Jeremias, 1969: 209) under the authority of the chief priests. Some scholars believe that they also served to maintain law and order in all of Judaea for the economic benefit of the elite (Jeremias, 1969: 33,52,71). It may have been some of these Levites, when they came along with their priestly superiors to examine John, who were converted by his preaching (compare Jn 1:19).

However, the question of whether John's soldiers were Roman or Jewish is not the main point; they could have been either. But in either case the point is that they, like all military and police forces, served the needs of those who ruled. They could have been direct supporters of the tax collectors (Plummer, 1901: 92; Creed, 1957: 53) or simply supporters of the Jerusalem establishment. In any case they were seeking their own self-interest either directly or indirectly through their service to the ruling authorities. Such service inspired them to commit various forms of injustice and oppression. Upon these soldiers John lays very radical ethical demands. If the soldiers heeded these demands, just as in the case of the tax-collectors, it would have meant a radical revision of their own personal life style as well as a challenge to the very foundations of the social order (Hollenbach, 1979: 872-873). Given the political background of the time and Josephus' comments about John the Baptist (*Antiquities* 18,117-118), it is easy to imagine that John had been suspected of seditious activity. We cite here part of that text (18.5.2 #118) in a translation made by John P. Meier:

And when the others [namely, ordinary Jews] gathered together [around John] — for their excitement reached fever pitch as they listened to [his] words — Herod began to fear that John's powerful ability to persuade people might lead to some sort of revolt, for they seemed likely to do whatever he counseled. So [Herod] decided to do away with John by a preemptive strike, before he sparked a revolt. Herod considered this a much better [course of action] than to wait until the situation changed and [then] to regret [his delay] when he was engulfed by a crisis.

Josephus agrees to a certain extent with Luke's special material on the Baptist. This correlation might simply be chalked up to two Greco-Roman writers (Josephus and Luke) who, independently of each other, seek to adapt a strange Jewish prophet to cultural models familiar to the wider Greco-Roman world. Yet Luke's material may supply further "missing links" to Josephus' narrative. As we have seen, Luke divides the various questioners into three groups: the crowds,

tax collectors, and soldiers. The intriguing point here is
that tax collectors and soldiers might have counted among
"the others," the ordinary, not especially-religious Jews who,
according to Josephus, formed the "second wave" flocking
to John. The fact that such important props of Antipas'
financial and military power as tax collectors and soldiers
had come under the influence of John and fervently hung
on his every word may have been the *Realpolitik* consider-
ation that especially alarmed the tetrarch and moved him
to his preemptive strike. He did not care if some virtuous
elite listened to John; he did care if his tax collectors and
soldiers were taking orders from a different commander. While
Luke is, of course, pursuing his own theological purpose
with his special material, he may have inadvertently thrown
some light on the mysterious *tōn allōn* ("the others") of *Ant.*
18,5.2 #118 and specifically on the reason why, in the mind
of the fearful Herod, the adherence of "the others" to John
was a danger that could not be tolerated (Meier, 1992: 236-
237).

In every case, then, of John's ethical criticism that we
have, he strikes at this structure of injustice. He is addressing the relatively privileged and powerful groups in society
who perpetuate this injustice. John's baptism is nowhere
directly connected with fasting and prayer, but it is directly
connected with social justice. He asked the baptized to for-
sake the normal socially accepted ways of acting and living
and to take up new ways. In this sense, then, we can call
John the Baptist a social revolutionary. He was not insti-
gating political revolution, though it is clear that his movement had that potentiality and Antipas apparently saw it
that way; but he certainly was fomenting social revolution.
And for him that revolution begins not with the common
people, nor with the very wealthy, but with the relatively
privileged classes, that is, with the middle classes of society
who had some power to change affairs. Evidently at John's
time there were at least a few members of these classes who

still had some sensitivity to injustice and were vulnerable to his message. While undoubtedly some of his followers were the destitute masses, maybe most of them, nevertheless it remains true that we have not one word, either negative or positive, that he addressed to them. His criticism of the powerful, of course, implied concern for the weak. Rather, like the classical prophets he addressed only those responsible for and likely to change the sorry state of affairs reigning in his society (Hollenbach, 1979: 874-875). But, according to some scholars, the judgment of the Lukan Baptist's preaching is toned down and paraenetically employed to invoke a positive reaction of sharing (Scheffler, 1990: 21-36).

d. Promise of John the Baptist (Lk 3:15-18)

Luke completes the presentation of John's ministry with two brief sections, the first of which (Lk 3:15-18) shows that John is subordinate to Jesus and points out that the real promise and hope come with the one who is mightier than John. Luke presents this emphasis more elaborately than do Mark and Matthew (Bock, 1994: 317).

Verses 15-18: (15) As the people were filled with expectation,
and all were questioning in their hearts
concerning John,
whether he might be the Messiah,
(16) John answered all of them by saying,
"I baptize you with water;
but one who is more powerful than I is coming;
I am not worthy to untie the thong of his
sandals.
He will baptize you with the Holy Spirit and
with fire.
(17) His winnowing fork is in his hand,
to clear his treshing floor and
to gather the wheat into his granary;
but the chaff he will burn with unquenchable
fire."
(18) So, with many other exhortations,
he proclaimed the good news to the people.

It is interesting to note the shift from "crowds" or "multitudes" (*ochloi*, verse 10) to "the people" (*laos*). "The people" in Luke's Gospel are usually presented as favorable to Jesus. Here they are seen as expecting "the Messiah" (Danker, 1988: 91). Some scholars have suggested that the choice of the word *laos* may reflect Luke's concept of the Jewish people as a religious body looking for the coming of the Messiah (Marshall, 1978: 145), but others consider this unlikely and suggest that it is only a stylistic variation for *ochloi*, "crowds," in Lk 3:10, as in Lk 23:13 (Bock, 1994: 319).

Though John the Baptist does not explicitly deny that he is "the Messiah," as he does in Jn 1:20, implicitly he does just that. Among the Synoptics, only Luke at this point mentions that John's preaching brought about a reaction of popular speculation (Bock, 1994: 318). It forms part of the evangelist's comment in Lk 3:15 and is not on John's lips. The implicit denial is found rather in John's referring to Jesus as the one who is coming and is the more powerful one (Lk 3:16). In Lk 3:15 Luke at first refers to the popular reaction to John's preaching, but the rest of the verse introduces the topic of verses 15-18, his messianic preaching. That the people "were questioning in their hearts" propbably should not be interpreted as an indication that only internal private speculation was involved. The other passages about the popular view of John make it clear that thoughts about John's role were a matter of public discussion (Lk 7:19-35 [where Jesus is dealing with such speculation]; 9:7-9). "In their hearts" refers to the deep personal level at which the question was raised. The question literally meaning "whether perhaps he might be the Christ" has been seen as a statement of denial by Luke (Danker, 1988: 91), since the interrogative particle *mēpote* contains the particle *mē*, a particle that expects a negative answer (Bock, 1994: 319).

The people's interest in this topic is scarcely occasioned by the immediately preceding ethical teaching; it is more likely occasioned by John's eschatological preaching, as in the first subsection (Lk 3:7-9). Luke's comment implies that there were Palestinian Jews who expected the coming of a messiah, that is, an anointed agent of Yahweh sent for the restoration of Israel and the triumph of God's power and dominion (Fitzmyer, 1981: 197-200). From at least the beginning of the second century B.C. such an expectation had crystalized in Palestinian Judaism. It developed out of the David-tradition in Israel, especially as this was represented by the Deuteronomist: David as the zealous worshiper of Yahweh, "chosen" by him to rule over Israel in place of Saul (2 Sam 6:21) and favored not for himself alone, but insofar as his kingly role would affect all Israel. The oracle of Nathan (2 Sam 7:14-17) and the "last words of David" (2 Sam 23:1-17) reveal Yahweh's promise of a dynasty and explicitly refer to the historical David as "the anointed" (*masiah*) of the God of Jacob. That title of David is repeated in the Psalms (18:51; 89:39,52; 132: 10,17). The ideal king will be a "David" (Jer 33:15; Ez 37:23-24). But in all the promises of a future, ideal "David," the title *masiah* is strikingly absent. The title occurs but twice in all the prophetic books: once applied to Cyrus, the Persian monarch (Isa 45:1); once to the reigning king of Israel, or perhaps to Israel itself (Hab 3:13). The first clear mention of *masiah* in the sense of a *future* anointed agent of Yahweh in the Davidic line is found in Dan 9:25, "...from the time that the word went out to restore and rebuild Jerusalem until the time of an anointed prince, there shall be seventy weeks...." This Danielic usage, along with various references to "anointed figures" in the Qumran literature (1QS 9:11, etc.) that attest the Essene expectation of messiahs of Israel and Aaron, and the (probably Pharisaic) *Psalms of Solomon* (17:23,36; 18:6,8) reveal a clear Jewish expectation of the coming of a messiah (or messiahs) in the period prior to the emergence of Christianity. This evidence indicates how the Old Testament theme of a coming David as an anointed agent of Yahweh developed into an explicit expectation of a messiah, or of several of them (Fitzmyer, 1981:466,471-472).

Luke establishes the fundamental importance of what is to follow in verses 16-18 by describing it as an answer given to "all" (*pasin*), that is, all Israel, not simply all the people present on a particular occasion. John contrasts his own water baptism with the Spirit-and-fire baptism of the one who is coming, and this contrast is still heightened by John's insistence on his own inferiority to the coming baptizer. "To untie the thong of someone's sandles" was the task of a slave, forbidden by rabbis in later tradition as a service done by a disciple for his master (Fitzmyer, 1981: 473). This service was for John in relation to the coming one a privilege quite beyond reach (see Lk 7:28). Without verse 15 the statement of contrast would only be a pedestal (Schürmann, 1969: 172) upon which to place John's description of the role of the coming one (as in Mt 3:11-12). But the question formulated in verse 15 focuses attention on the contrast and especially upon the limited importance of John (Nolland, 1989: 151).

The clause here comes from the tradition shared with Matthew (=Q), but Luke omits "after me" (see Mt 3:11). This last omission is not to avoid any suggestion that Jesus had been a disciple of John (Conzelmann, 1960: 24; Schurmann, 1969: 173 n. 77), nor is it to signal Jesus' presence in the crowd (Schürmann, 1969:173). Rather, it is a natural omission after the infancy narratives (Schlatter, 1960: 477), to avoid any tension with their insistence on the presence of the savior. With "after me" gone, "one who is more powerful than I is coming" must be read in close relation to verse 15 and its suggestion that John might be the messiah (Nolland, 1989: 151).

"He will baptize you with the Holy Spirit and fire." The problem in this clause is the twofold nature of the baptism that Jesus is said to confer. As in Mt 3:11, Luke has "and with fire," which differs from Mk 1:8, "with the Holy Spirit" only. The addition "and with fire" stands in contrast to the Lukan formulation in Acts 1:5; 11:16. The pair has been diversely interpreted over the centuries; the different opinions can be summed up as follows:

(1) Jesus' baptism will confer the fire of the Holy Spirit, an inflaming, grace-laden outpouring of God's Spirit — an interpretation obviously influenced by the Pentecost scene of Acts 2 (Ellis, 1966: 53-54; Bovon, 1991: 173). This is usually considered an anachronistic Christian interpretation, out of place on the lips of John the Baptist.

(2) Jesus' baptism will confer the Spirit on the repentant, but bring the fire of judgment on the unrepentant — an interpretation based on verse 17 (Brown, 1965: 136; Schürmann, 1969: 174-175). One scholar believes that the Ananias and Sapphira account (Acts 5:1-11) is to be understood as an example of the purging work of the Holy Spirit (Nolland, 1989: 153,155). This interpretation seems to connote two different baptisms, administered to different groups; it seems to neglect the common object, "you" (*hymas*).

(3) Jesus' baptism of Spirit and fire will be a baptism of judgment, since "Holy Sprit" is to be understood as a mighty wind symbolizing judgment, aided by the fire that consumes what is swept away (Barrett, 1954: 125-126). This interpretation, though it joins properly the functions of the Spirit and fire, tends to understand the baptism too much in terms of judgment. It seems to limit the scope of John's ministry to a note of warning (Bock, 1994: 322). Or, if John's own water-baptism were intended to produce "repentance," it might at least be thought that a baptism involving God's Spirit and fire would be ex-

pected to accomplish something positive too. This
interpretation also makes a poor connection with
verse 17 (Nolland, 1989: 152).

(4) Jesus' baptism will have a dual character, accom-
plishing for those persons who would accept it at
once a purification and a refinement. Here one could
appeal to a number of Old Testament passages in
which both God's Spirit and fire play such a role:
Isa 4:4-5; 32:15; 44:3; Ez 36:25-26; Mal 3:2b-3. There
is, moreover, in the *Manual of Discipline* from Qumran
Cave 1 a text with a remarkable juxtaposition of
"holy Spirit," "water," and "refining" (by fire), which
forms a plausible matrix for John's own utterance:

Then [at the season of visitation, when the truth
of the world will appear forever]

God will purge by his truth all the needs of man,
refining [i.e., by fire] for himself some of mankind
in order to remove every evil spirit from the midst
of their flesh, to cleanse them with a holy Spirit
from all wicked practices and sprinkle them with a
spirit of truth like purifying water (1QS 4:20-21).

Here one finds "water," "holy Spirit," and "refining" all
used together in an act of God's purging his community.
John has separated elements of such an activity, ascribing
to himself a refinement by water and to Jesus, the more
powerful one, a refinement by the Spirit and fire. This view
sees in both Spirit and fire the means of eschatological
purgation experienced by the penitent as purification in the
refiner's fire and by the godless as destruction by wind and
fire (Dunn, 1972: 87; Fitzmyer, 1981: 474; Nolland, 1989:
153). It has been noted, however, that in all this one has
to keep in mind that what John's words might have meant
in Stage I of the gospel tradition is one thing, and that his
words as used by the Christian evangelist, Luke, at Stage
III of that tradition, may convey a further connotation.

In Stage I, the work of the Spirit prophesied by John the Baptist would be separation. "The baptism with the Holy Spirit and fire" which John prophesied was to be a deluge of mesianic judgment that all would experience. All would be sifted and separated by a powerful blast of the Spirit of God: the unrighteous would be consumed in fire, and in this way the righteous remnant would be gathered togther and the nation purified (Menzies, 1991: 139).

In Stage III of the tradition, it is difficult to say that Luke would not have had in mind his own understanding of the Spirit poured out by the Risen Christ (Acts 2:33) and of fire related to that Spirit. Obviously, in this way the Spirit of Pentecost would be understood to accomplish the refinement and purification in its own fuller way (Fitzmyer, 1981: 473-474). In Luke's perspective, then, John's prophecy finds initial fulfillment at Pentecost and continuing fulfillment in the Spirit-empowered mission of the Church. However, the final act of separation, the destruction of the unrighteous in the fire of messianic judgment, still awaits its fulfillment. While it is likely that John viewed the baptism of the Spirit and the consuming activity of the fire as different aspects of one and the same apocalyptic event, Luke has separated these aspects chronologically in view of the ongoing mission of the Church (Menzies, 1991: 144).

In Lk 3:16, John's baptizing ministry is contrasted with the activity of the expected figure, whose ministry is also described using the image of baptizing. In Lk 3:17, the imagery changes to an agricultural picture in which a farmer is poised at the treshing floor. The picture is most frequently understood to portray a farmer who is about to winnow the harvested grain, previously piled upon the threshing floor, by tossing the grain into the air and allowing the wind to separate the wheat from the chaff. On the basis of this understanding, the expected figure's ministry includes the separation of the repentant from the unrepentant, with the emphasis being on the judgment of the latter (Marshall, 1978:

148; Fitzmyer, 1981: 474; Bovon, 1991: 173; Bock, 1994: 324).

However, another possibility exists for understanding the picture being presented: the winnowing has already taken place, and the farmer is now poised to remove the already separated piles of wheat and chaff from the threshing floor. This alternative interpretation has implications for how the expected figure's ministry and John's own ministry are perceived (Webb, 1991a: 104-105).

The picture painted in Lk 3:17 (= Mt 3:12) is quite specific in its employment of agricultural imagery, and this imagery requires clarification to be fully appreciated. The major difficulty lies in ascertaining what precisely are the actions being performed by John's expected figure. The expression "his winnowing *ptuon* is in his hand, to clear his treshing floor" has commonly be interpreted to portray the process of winnowing, as was said above. This interpretation is based on the assumption that *ptuon* refers to the instrument used for tossing the grain into the air and that the verb *diakatharizō* or *diakathairō* refers to the action of tossing itself. However, a closer examination of the evidence does not support this interpretation. First of all, the significance of the verb *diakathairō* is "to cleanse thoroughly," "to clean out," or "to prune," but there is no evidence that it signified "to winnow." It would appear that those who support this interpretation understand the verb to signify the "cleansing" of the wheat from the chaff. But it is interesting to observe that it is not the grain that is the object of cleansing in John's description, but rather the threshing floor. By contrast, John's portrayal does not employ the verbs commonly used to specify the action of winnowing (*likmaō, diaspeirō, diaskorpizō*), that have the basic significance of "to scatter" and are frequently used with reference to winnowing (*likmaō*: Isa 17:13; 30:24; 41:16; Amos 9:9, etc.; *diaspeirō*: Isa 41:16; Jer 15:7; *diaskorpizō*: Ez 5:2,10). Thus, neither the action of cleansing nor the object cleansed actually indicate that winnowing is the activity being described.

But does not the *ptuon*, "winnowing shovel," in the hand of John's expected figure indicate the process of winnowing? Gustav Dalman's work on Palestinian agricultural practices does not support this description. Two tools were evidently used on the threshing floor, a winnowing *fork* (*thrinax*) and a winnowing *shovel* (*ptuon*). The actual winnowing of the grain, that is, separating the wheat from the straw and chaff by throwing it up into the wind, was accomplished by means of the winnowing fork and not the shovel (Dalman, 1964: 116). The shovel was used to heap up the grain before winnowing as well as to gather the wheat and straw into piles after the winnowing was accomplished. It was also used for the final clearing of the threshing floor and for moving the wheat in the granary (Dalman, 1964: 116-124,201,253-254). Therefore, the fact that the word *ptuon*, "winnowing shovel," is used in Lk 3:17 rather than *thrinax*, "winnowing fork," provides further evidence that the activity being described here is not winnowing (Webb, 1991a: 105-107).

A parallel close to Lk 3:17, because it combines the terms *ptuon* and *diakathairō*, is found in the *Letters* of Alciphron:

I had just finished cleaning (*diakatheranti*) the threshing floor and was putting away my winnowing shovel (*ptuon*) when my master came suddenly upon me, saw what I had done, and proceeded to commend my industry (Alciphron 2.23.1).

In this example, just as in Lk 3:17, the object being cleansed is the threshing floor, presumably after the winnowing had been completed, and the instrument used for this cleansing is the winnowing shovel.

This analysis indicates that Lk 3:17 is portraying a scene quite different from that of winnowing. Rather, the winnowing has already taken place, and the wheat and chaff already lie separated on the threshing floor. The owner has now in his hand the winnowing shovel, the tool appropriate for the next stage of the process. He is poised with shovel in hand to clean the threshing floor. There are only two substances on the theshing floor from which it needs to be cleaned: the wheat and the chaff. Therefore, the statement, "to clear his threshing floor," describes the action as it is performed with respect to the threshing floor. Similarly, the next two statements, "to gather the wheat into his granary" and "but the chaff he will burn with unquenchable fire," refer essentially to the same action, but now it is described with respect to the wheat and the chaff respectively. Thus, the statements concerning the wheat and chaff amplify the statement concerning the threshing floor and explain why the winnowing shovel is in the owner's hand in the first place (Webb, 1991: 108; see also Schürmann, 1969: 177-178; Nolland, 1989: 153, but without the exegetical support provided by Webb).

So, in John's description of the threshing floor, the wheat and the chaff have already been separated. This alters the perception of the ministry to be performed by John's expected figure. Instead of separating the two groups, the repentant and the unrepentant, the expected figure's ministry is actually to take these two groups to their end whether to the "granary" or to the "fire," that is, whether to blessing or to judgment. This understanding of the imagery of Lk 3:17 also indicates a different perception of John's own ministry. It is John's ministry that "winnows" the "wheat" from the "chaff," that is, his ministry separates the repentant from the unrepentant. But they remain together until the expected figure arrives, who will clear his threshing floor with the winnowing shovel, that is, he will take the repentant and unrepentant to their respective ends, whether blessing or judgment. This interpretation presents a similar understanding of both John's ministry and that of the expected figure as presented in Lk 3:16, though there the imagery of baptism is employed (Webb, 1991a: 109-111).

Lk 3:18 is a kind of summary statement (compare Lk 4:14-15,43) and the phrase "with many other exhortations" suggests that John preached about much more than what is presented here (Bock, 1994: 325). The key word is the phrase "proclaimed the good news" (although some scholars find it hard to understand the verb here as meaning "announced the good news"; [Fitzmyer, 1981: 475]). In the Greek this phrase is one verb (*euangelizomai* ; see Lk 1:19; 2:10; 4:18,43; 7:22; 8:1; 9:6; 16:16; 20:1; and often in Acts). Luke uses the noun only at Acts 15:7; 20:24, for from his perspective the Christian message is not a static statement of belief that people can control, as in clever theological debate; rather, it breaks out in various patterns of expression as human beings are confronted with God's rescuing action. The central meaning of *euangelizomai* is not "preach good news" but "make a proclamation." If the context indicates that God's saving action is involved, the term connotes "proclaim good news." Since John shows the people how to avoid God's wrath, his mesage is good news, despite the fact that some of his words sound like judgment. That oppressors must ultimately render account is good news to the disadvantaged (Danker, 1988:93).

e. The Imprisonment of John (Lk 3:19-20)

Luke concludes the overview of John's ministry by recounting his arrest in a short summary note (Bock, 1994: 327). The Lukan Gospel is unique in reporting the imprisonment of John the Baptist, recounting it even before Jesus is baptized. In the baptism which is the next episode, John is not even mentioned. This episode of the imprisonment of John thus concludes the ministry of the Baptist and serves to remove him from the scene before Jesus appears. This distinction is reflected later in Lk 16:16 and Acts 13:25. But Luke makes no mention here of John's death, because of the tradition that he will make use of in the pericopes of

Lk 7:18-30 (Fitzmyer, 1981: 476). Luke's sympathies clearly lie with John in his encounter with Herod Antipas who shuts him up in prison. From a literary point of view, however, Luke himself shuts up John in prison at this stage (Erickson, 1993: 455).

Verses 19-20: (19) But Herod the ruler, who had been rebuked
                    by him
                    because of Herodias, his brother's wife,
                    and because of all the evil things that Herod
                    had done,
             (20)   added to them all by shutting up John in prison.

Verses 19-20 constitute a single summarizing sentence that completes Luke's account of John and his ministry. John dared to speak words of power to moral weakness that was masked by an offensive and irresponsible display of power. Imprisonment was the result of John's challenge to the moral character of the Jewish political leadership (Bock, 1994: 328). Josephus (*Antiquities* 18.5,2 #119) recounts that John was taken to the fortress Machaerus in chains. Originally built by Alexander Janneus on a precipitous, solitary peak on the east side of the Dead Sea, it was magnificently restored by Herod the Great. Its ruins can still be seen today (Fitzmyer, 1981: 478).

The tetrarch put away his first wife, and, in violation of Lev 20:21, married his niece Herodias, formerly married to his half brother. Luke broadens the reproof by adding a reference to "all the evil things that Herod had done" (Nolland, 1989: 156). Luke, keenly aware of political dimensions, places this notice in the context of world judgment (Danker, 1988: 94).

Assuming that Luke used Mark's Gospel in composing his own, we encounter here some striking peculiarities of Luke's editorial activity. Firstly, he moves the account of the jailing of John from where it occurs in Mark, that is, well into the story of Jesus' Galilean ministry (Mk 6:14-29), to a position preceding the beginning of that ministry.

This in itself is not so surprising, for Mark's own description of the arrest of John by Herod is actually a flashback (Webb, 1991b: 374 n. 57), and is not intended to be taken as having occurred in sequence with the events narrated just ahead of it. Mk 1:14 in fact implies that John's arrest happened not long after Jesus' baptism. Nor does John disappear from Luke's Gospel after Lk 3:20. He appears again — in prison — to express his doubts about Jesus' identity (Lk 7:18-23), and, in spite of that, he is praised by Jesus (Lk 7:24-35). The fact remains nonetheless that in Luke, John's imprisonment, somewhat like the rejection of Jesus in Nazareth (compare Mk 6:1-6 and Lk 4:16-30) is moved to a position preceding the commencement of Jesus' ministry in Galilee.

But the notable thing is that the jailing of John is moved to a position that precedes even Jesus' baptism. If we did not know the other Gospels we would undoubtedly have the impression that John did not baptize Jesus. Is that the impression Luke wanted to convey? What solutions have been proposed as explanations of Luke's handling of the text at Lk 3:19-20? Hans Conzelmann's explanation is connected with his theory of the "middle of time" (*die Mitte der Zeit*) based on his interpretation of Lk 16:16, "The law and the prophets were in effect until John came [i.e., according to Conzelmann, "until and including John came"]; since then the good news of the kingdom of God is proclaimed, and everyone tries to enter it by force." Here he finds the principle which leads Luke to extract John from the baptism of Jesus, thereby placing John in the final moments of the age of the old covenant and letting the new age begin without him, even if this would leave the reader to wonder who baptized Jesus (Conzelmann, 1960: 18-27).

But this explanation has not stood up to scrutiny. Among others, Walter Wink showed how taking the Lukan birth narrative into account (something Conzelmann refused to do) makes all the difference. From the very beginning of

Luke's Gospel, John is seen as participating in the initiation of the age of the gospel. He is even said to "proclaim the good news" to the people (Lk 3:18, but see reservations mentioned above), which does not square with Conzelmann's exclusive interpretation of Lk 16:16 (Wink, 1968: 42-86). If we reject the idea that Luke removes John from Lk 3:21 because he intends to send him back to the old era of the Law and the Prophets, how else can we solve the puzzle? Besides many other proposals, one has recently suggested that Luke attempted to get John off stage in order to make room for the entrance of Jesus (Craddock, 1990: 50-51). Others believe that Luke neither wanted nor needed to say anything more about John's fate. All interest is now directed toward the one whom John announced as "one who is more powerful than I" (Lk 3:16; Bovon, 1991: 174). Again others do not consider Luke's literary maneuver at Lk 3:20-21 as particularly unusual. They call it a "current narrative technique" (Ernst, 1989: 100-101), a "chronological anticipation" (Nolland, 1989: 156), a literary device for "rounding off" the section of John (C.F. Evans, 1990: 244). But some interpreters insist that it is not just a matter of literary neatness. Luke wants to keep John in a clear secondary place and thus puts him in prison as early as possible (Goulder, 1989: I,279).

Recently some scholars have proposed that John's rebuke of Herod Antipas at Lk 3:19 is inserted as an example of John's "other exhortations" mentioned in Lk 3:18. Further, Herod's reaction serves as a contrast to the people's response in Lk 3:10-15. Taken separately, each of these two suggestions is acceptable. But together they clash, since the "other exhortations" are made in the process of proclaiming the good news to the people. The message delivered to Herod in Lk 3:19 hardly qualifies as an example of proclamation of the good news. Thematically, John's preparatory ministry comes to an end before Jesus' ministry begins, even though they belong to the same epoch (Webb, 1991b: 64-65; Fitzmyer, 1989: 105-106).

The most plausible of the suggested motives for the redaction at Lk 3:19-21 is that of Luke's reluctance to give the impression that John is somehow superior to Jesus. If John baptizes, is that not evidence that he stands in some degree of power and authority over those who seek to be baptized by him? In most cases, yes. But certainly not in the case of Jesus. Nor is Luke the only gospel writer to struggle with this possibility. All four of them do (Erickson, 1993: 460-461). Why the evident veneration of John (Lk 7:28), on the one hand, and a nearly paranoid scramble to keep him in his place, on the other? The discussion of this issue has for many years been influenced by the conviction not only that some of John's original disciples did not pass over into the circle of Jesus' followers (Lk 7:18-23), but also that an actual baptist sect or sects existed long beyond the first century, and in this connection studies on Acts 18:24-19:7, dealing with the ministry of Apollos and John's disciples at Ephesus have played an important role (Scobie, 1964: 187-202; Erickson, 1993: 461-465). One solid result emerging from these discussions of Luke's purpose in Acts 18:24-19:7 is the conviction that John's latter-day disciples presented difficulties for Luke's own Christian community. While Luke and his people revered the memory of John the Baptist and valued his ministry highly, Luke wished to do what he could in his Gospel and Acts to suppress the confusing interpretations that the later baptist sects were placing upon John and his baptism. The similarity between John's message and Jesus' led to some confusion and competition among their respective followers concerning whether John or Jesus was the "coming one." Luke had already begun to address this problem in the infancy narrative, but here again the issue arises. In adition to the confusion because of the similarity of their messages, there was the rather uncomfortable fact that Jesus was baptized by John, suggesting, at least in that event, that John was the figure of greater authority (Ringe, 1995: 53).

Doubtless, the displacement of the narration of John's imprisonment to a point preceding Jesus' baptism serves to round off the material on John and to get him off stage in preparation for the appearance of Jesus ready to embark on his ministry. But the further removal of John from the baptism itself must be explained as part of Luke's antibaptist polemic. Rather than to give false impressions or to provide grounds for attacks by unfriendly sectarians, Luke discreetly omits to mention the fact — well known to him — that Jesus was baptized by John. Even when he comes close to conceding the fact in Acts 1:21-22 he chooses his words very carefully: he neither denies nor admits there that John baptized Jesus. But Luke's treatment is not only a cautious avoidance of material open to dangerous misinterpretation. It functions also as a warning to the faithful not to be misled by false claims on the part of baptist sectarians (Erickson, 1993: 465-466).

Compared to Mark and Matthew, Lk 3:1-20 exhibits the following characteristic features important for the interpretation of the following pericope:

(1) The person and activity of John does not have the same meaning for Luke as for Mark and Matthew. Instead of as "Baptist" (Mk 1:4; Mt 3:1), he is introduced in Lk 3:2b as "son of Zechariah." The baptism of the people by John is, in contrast with Mk 1:5b and Mt 3:5, not described by Luke. On the other hand, the baptismal and penitential preaching by John is quite extensively presented in Luke (Lk 3:7-9 par. Mt 3:7-10; Sp[ecial]Lk 3:10-14). In addition, and in line with the outdoing parallels between Jesus and John in the infancy narrative, Luke stresses more explicitly the subordination of John to Jesus. The note about the influx of people from Judaea and Jerusalem to John in the desert (Mk 1:5a par. Mt 3:5) is absent from Luke. Later, people will come from these regions to Jesus (Lk 5:17; 6:17).

Moreover, by the omission of "after me" (see Mk 1:7 par. Mt 3:11) it is right away excluded that the "coming one," namely Jesus, would be the follower or supporter of John.

(2) Luke presents the people in a more positive way than Mark and Matthew. He emphasizes first of all their readiness for repentance and conversion by the thrice repeated question "What should we do?" (Lk 3:10,12,14). Then Luke highlights the people's messianic expectation by their question, "whether he might be the Messiah" which is considered redactional, and which prepares the reader for the baptismal epiphany. John's answer in Lk 3:16 (par. Mk 1:8; Mt 3:11) is a first reference to the one who will baptize with the Holy Spirit (compare Acts 1:5; 11:16), on whom, according to the following baptism account, the Holy Spirit descends (Lk 3:22; par. Mk 1:10; Mt 3:16), and who becomes thereby the one who is anointed with the Holy Spirit (compare Lk 4:18; Acts 10:38). Only Luke mentions that the penitent people expect the messiah.

(3) Thereby it has become clear that, according to Luke's presentation, the penitential preaching of John and the people's readiness for conversion form the background for the people's messianic expectation and John's testimony about Jesus (Lk 3:15-18) in which Lk 3:1-20 reaches its climax. Luke has, of course, the announcement of Jesus as "the one who baptizes with the Holy Spirit" in common with Mark and Matthew. But it carries special weight for Luke since it is twice repeated in Acts 1:5 and 11:16, which are both presented as a word of the Lord in a context which refers to the descent of the Spirit on the community. Moreover, John's statement in Lk 3:16 is even more clearly formulated as preparation for the baptism event by the key word connection

"Holy Spirit" in Lk 3:16 (par. Mk 1:8; Mt 3:11) and in 3:22 (different Mk 1:10 and Mt 3:16: Spirit [of God]). Both the question of the people and John's answer thus refer to the descent of the Spirit on Jesus and his giftedness with the Holy Spirit (Feldkämper, 1978: 32-33).

2. Jesus' Baptism (Lk 3:21-22)

Verses 21-22: (21) Now when all the people were baptized,
and when Jesus also had been baptized
and was praying,
the heaven was opened,
(22) and the Holy Spirit descended upon him
in bodily form like a dove.
And a voice came from heaven,
"You are my Son, the Beloved;
with you I am well pleased."

Jesus' baptism is merely reported as part of a general baptism. Just as Zechariah and Anna were said to be at prayer at the moment when they received a revelation (Lk 1:10; 2:37), so here Jesus also is praying. In fact, it is already clear that, in Luke's Gospel, prayer signals an important event about to take place and the reader would do well to pay special attention. In this case, prayer becomes a window to the divine presence (Ringe, 1995: 54).

In all three Synoptic Gospels the baptism account (Mk 1:9-11; Mt 3:13-17; Lk 3:21-22) does not only intend to present Jesus at the beginning of his public ministry but also and especially to interpret *who he is* (Lentzen-Deiss, 1970: 195ff.; Fitzmyer, 1981: 480). Since the pericope does not occur as an erratic unit at the beginning of the gospel, the close connection of the baptism and temptation accounts has always been recognized, and its meaning is further unfolded by its context, one should raise the question how the Lukan version of Jesus' baptism is situated in its context.

In contrast to Mark and Matthew, Luke reports the event

of Jesus' baptism in a single sentence which exhibits his favorite tripartite structure: introductory formula (*egeneto*, "it happened," not translated in English; see Hendrickx, 1996: 45-46), time indication ("when all the people were baptized, and when Jesus had been baptized and was praying"), and the main clause ("the heaven was opened... with you I am well pleased"). All the clauses of verse 21 are subordinate to verse 22 (Marshall, 1978: 152). The time indication and the connecting main clause consist of three members that are connected with each other by means of "and." From a detailed analysis of this grammatical structure one can draw a number of conclusions for the interpretation of the baptism pericope (Lentzen-Deis, 1970: 250; Feldkämper, 1978: 39).

First, more than in Mark and Matthew, the capital statement of the Lukan baptismal pericope is found in the heavenly manifestation: the opening of the heaven, the descent of the Spirit, and Jesus' designation as Son by the voice from heaven. The opening of the heaven has a subordinate function as basis for the descent of the Spirit and the hearing of the voice from heaven.

Secondly, in contrast to Mark and Matthew, the heavenly manifestation is linked not to Jesus' baptism but to his prayer (Fitzmyer, 1981: 481). The baptism is over (aorist participle) while Jesus' prayer is still going on (present participle). The focus of the account is no longer Jesus' baptism alone, but the accompanying prayer which was ongoing after the baptism This places the opening of the heaven and the subsequent phenomena at the heart of the scene's activity. In fact, the realignment of the narrative is so complete that Lk 3:21f. is no longer an account of Jesus' baptism at all, but a portrayal of what God does as Jesus prays. Being the first example of Jesus at prayer, it is not unreasonable to expect that this account will exhibit some relevance to the function of Jesus' prayers elsewhere in Luke (Crump, 1992: 110-111).

Thirdly, in contrast to Mark and Matthew, in Luke Jesus'

baptism is not geared towards the heavenly manifestation, but to the baptism of the people. Like the whole people, Jesus submits himself to baptism and thus enters into solidarity with the people. He identifies himself with the people (Bock 1994: 337). The reference to the baptism of the people is, of course, also found in Mark and Matthew, but its link to Jesus' baptism is by far not as clear as in Luke.

Fourthly, the statement about Jesus at prayer occupies an intermediate position between, on the one hand, the statement about Jesus' solidarity with the people, and, on the other hand, the statement about his prominence and special relationship with God. In order to undertstand better the particular character of the Lukan baptism pericope and the inserted prayer notice we compare now their individual text elements with the corresponding Markan and Matthean elements.

First we list the elements missing in the Lukan text compared to the Markan/Matthean parallels:

The indications of place: Mark and Matthew refer to "Nazareth" (Mk) "of Galilee" (Mk/Mt) as the place of origin of Jesus and "the Jordan" as place of Jesus' arrival (Mt), respectively his baptism (Mk). Luke does not mention these places in his baptism pericope, but refers then in the context, contrary to Mark and Matthew, to the "Jordan" (Lk 4:1) as the place from where Jesus comes, and "Galilee" (Lk 4:14 par. Mk/Mt) as the place of Jesus initial activity (Conzelmann, 1960: 18-22).

The Baptist: Mark and Matthew say explicitly that Jesus is baptized by John the Baptist, and in addition to this Matthew brings a dialogue between John and Jesus before the baptism takes place (Mt 3:14f.). Therefore, according to Luke's interpretation, John has no importance for Jesus' baptism [although, strictly historically speaking, Jesus' baptism by John may have meant that — for the time being? — Jesus joined the movement of John]. According to Luke, it is God not the Baptist who acts. (Wilckens, 1961: 107f.).

The emergence from the water: here Luke passes over a trait that is mentioned in both parallel texts: "just as he was coming up out of the water" (Mk 1:9) and "just as he came up from the water" (Mt 3:16). Thereby a reference to the baptismal ritual (as entering and coming up out of the water) as well as the correspondence between Jesus' coming up out of the water (*anabainō*) and the descent of the Spirit from heaven (*katabainō*) is lost. Moreover, in Luke's version, the descent of the Spirit is not linked to Jesus' baptism.

Jesus' vision: What happens after Jesus' baptism is depicted by Mark and Matthew as a vision, as indicated by the use of the verb *eiden,* "he saw," which is characteristic for the description of visions. This is omitted by Luke, thereby creating the impression of a real event (Lentzen-Deis, 1970: 44, 285). It is indeed generally recognized that Luke has objectified the various events associated with Jesus' baptism, the point being that this was not merely a subjective, visionary experience on Jesus' part, but a real, observable event (Crump, 1992: 111).

Then there are the elements which are found in Luke only:

The baptism of all the people: Luke has omitted the notice where Mark and Matthew mentioned it (Mk 1:5; Mt 3:6). At that stage Luke said that the crowds came to John to be baptized (Lk 3:7). Luke now begins the baptism pericope with a note about the baptism of all the people, without describing it any further. He uses his favorite term *laos,* as he did in Lk 3:15,18. Lk 7:29, shows that thereby Luke means the people in contrast to their leaders. The expression "all the people," which is also a favorite of Luke's, does not mean here the whole of Israel, but the great number of people present, although some scholars, referring to Acts 13:24, "before his coming John had already proclaimed a baptism of repentance to all the people of Israel," do defend the meaning "the whole of Israel" (Lohfink, 1975: 36,38); but in Acts 13:24, "all the people" is further defined by "of Israel." This is not the case in Lk 3:21 (Feldkämper, 1978: 42 n. 33). Luke wishes to emphasize the close association of Jesus with "all the people," a characteristic expression, that is in accordance with the angel's declaration (Lk 2:11), anticipates Jesus' genealogy (Lk 3:23-38), and forecasts the style of his entire life as one in intimate contact with publicans and sinners (Lk 5:27-32; 15:1f.; Danker, 1988: 95).

Jesus' prayer: This is the first of many scenes in which Luke — and usually Luke alone — depicts Jesus at prayer. The confession of sins by the people at their baptism is also somehow to be understood as prayer (Mk 1:5 par. Mt 3:6; Jeremias, 1925: 137f.). But any prayer of this sort is absent from Jesus. On the other hand, one cannot interpret Jesus' prayer here, in analogy with Lk 11:13, as a prayer of petition for the Spirit. Firstly, in Lk 11:13 occurs the term *aitein*, which is the proper term for prayer of petition, unlike in Lk 3:21 where we have *proseuchomai*. And secondly, what happens after Jesus' baptism in answer to his prayer is not only the descent of the Spirit but also Jesus' designation as Son by the voice from heaven.

Finally, our discussion of the prayer notice in Lk 3:21 leads to a question which is of no small importance for the theme of Jesus' prayer according to Luke. Towards the end of the sequence of pericopes which Luke substantially follows, Mark presents his first prayer notice in Mk 1:35 [not found in the parallel Lk 4:42]: "In the morning, while it was still very dark, he got up and went out to a deserted place, and there he prayed." In view of Luke's interest in the motif of prayer it is surprising that he does not make mention of Jesus' prayer in the parallel verse. Is there an acceptable explanation for this? Jesus' "going out" (Mk 1:35) in the early morning must have been motivated by his regular habit as a pious Jew to pray in the morning in a deserted place. Simon seems to have known about both this habit and the place where Jesus used to pray — since how could he otherwise have found him (Mk 1:36f.)? On the other hand, Jesus himself gives at the end of the pericope a motive for his going out: to preach also in other places — "for that is what I came out to do" (Mk 1:38). "Come out" in verse 38 unmistakably refers to "went out" in verse 35. Therefore, "going out" does not only mean leaving the house or the city, but also — at least by way of allusion — Jesus' coming with a definite goal and a special mission. Jesus' habitual prayer in the early morning and his commission to proclaim the gospel are, therefore, also closely related in this episode.

The same situation is found in Luke. In the latter, however, the prayer notice is not found at the end of the sequence of pericopes, but at the very beginning. Thus Luke has linked Jesus' mission and activity, which have their origin in his baptism, with Jesus' prayer, even more than Mark. What for Mark is an episode which expresses something that is generally valid, Luke has made into a principle. In Luke, Jesus prays right at the beginning in relation to his mandate and mission in which his future activity is already included. It is not easy to establish whether Luke has consciously inserted the prayer notice of Mk 1:35 in Lk 3:21 and then omitted it in the later parallel text. We limit ourselves here to the following observations: Once one has recognized that the sequence of pericopes in Lk 3:23-4:44 as a unit is closely linked with the Lukan baptism account (Lk 3:21-22) and the prayer notice mentioned there, one does no longer miss the prayer notice at the end (Lk 4:42). It is not simply omitted but has found another, in Luke's composition more important place, namely, at the beginning of the whole sequence of pericopes. There it is found in close relation to the gift of the Spirit and Jesus' Sonship.

The Holy Spirit: Unlike in Mark ("the Spirit") and Matthew ("the Spirit of God"), Luke uses the expression "the Holy Spirit," which is very often found in his Gospel (thirteen times, as compared to four in Mark and five in

Matthew). Even if this expression may have turned somewhat pale by stereotype use, in Luke's understanding of the
Spirit, the expression has nevertheless a particular meaning. First, Luke has understood the Spirit as prophetic Spirit
(de la Potterie, 1958: 231). In the case of Jesus' baptism
this is confirmed by the context. Second, for Luke, Spirit
and power are often synonymous (Lk 1:17; 4:14; 24:49; Acts
1:5,8). Hence "the Holy Spirit" may be understood as em-
powerment and sending for a prophetic mission.

The bodily form of the dove: By the expression "in bodily
form" Luke stresses more than Mark and Matthew the reality of the descent of the Spirit (Grundmann, 1965: 108; de
la Potterie, 1958: 234f.). In a similar manner he underlines
the reality of the resurrection body in Lk 24:36-43 (Jesus
eating in front of his disciples). It is possible that the expression "in bodily form" (*sōmatikōi eidei*) echoes Mark's and
Matthew's "he saw" (*eiden*). This would then be an indication that Luke has transformed the visionary event into a
"real" event.

Finally, we consider the elements common to the three
Synoptic Gospels:

The baptism of Jesus: Whereas the baptism is the main
affirmation in Mark (*ebaptisthē*) and in Matthew the object
of theological reflection expressed in the conversation between John and Jesus, in Luke it serves rather as indication
of the situation. The emphasis is not on the baptism itself
(Grundmann, 1965: 106; Schürmann, 1969: 191).

The opening of the heaven: Matthew and Luke describe
the opening of the heaven with the verb *anoigein*, "to open,"
instead of Marks *schizein*, "to tear apart" (compare Isa 64:1,
"O that you would tear open the heavens and come down...").
But while in Matthew the opening of the heavens enables
the visionary to gaze into heaven (Lentzen-Deis, 1970: 44),
in Luke it makes possible the descent of the Spirit and the
hearing of the voice from heaven (Schürmann, 1969: 190).
The heaven is here the starting point of the revelatory event.

The descent of the Spirit on Jesus: Like Mark and Matthew, Luke mentions the descent of the Spirit. Since, however, according to Lk 1:35, Jesus' existence is marked by the Spirit from the beginning, Luke cannot possibly understand the descent of the Spirit in Lk 3:22 as an event that takes place at that very moment, but rather as statement and demonstration of what Jesus was already from the beginning (Schürmann, 1969: 192; Rese, 1969: 148; Lentzen-Deis, 1970: 265,270).

Like a dove: In all four Gospels it is stated that the Spirit descended on Jesus like a dove (see Jn 1:32). The phrase "like a dove" can be understood to apply to the descending Holy Spirit either adjectively (dove-like Spirit) or adverbially (dove-like descent). A survey of the gospel texts (Mk 1:10; Mt 3:16; Lk 3:22) and a review of interpretations proposed since 1970 leads to the conclusion that the adverbial sense (dove-like descent) is to be preferred (Huber, 1995: 87-101; different: Crump, 1992: 111). The precise significance of the dove has been the subject of much discussion (Lentzen-Deis, 1970: 170-183; Fitzmyer, 1981:483-484; Bock, 1994: 338-339). The meaning of this feature cannot be determined either from the baptism account itself or from any other text of the New Testament. Likewise there are no texts in ancient literature in which the dove is clearly referred to as a symbol of the Holy Spirit. The association of the dove with divinities was widespread in ancient religions, and there are faint reflections of this in the Old Testament, but this does not justify the assertion that "in the hour when God acknowledged his Son the dove could be the recognizable and almost exclusively suitable phenomenal form of the Holy Spirit" (TDNT VI, 69; C.F. Evans, 1990: 247).

But there is a defendable interpretation based on texts in Jewish literature in which the dove occurs simultaneously as Israel- and as messenger-symbol. We can conclude from these data that we are dealing here with a twofold symbol which expreses that the Spirit empowers Jesus for his (prophetic) mission to the new Israel. The context may confirm and emphasize this interpretation for the Third Gospel (Lentzen-Deis, 1970: 269). The recently published Qumran text called *A Messianic Vision* provides a clear precedent for the creative application of Gen 1-2 or picturing the Spirit as hovering over people. According to some scholars, the fragment unlocks the symbolic meaning of the dove (Allison, 1992: 58-60).

The voice from heaven: What is said by the voice from heaven is the same in the three Synoptics, except for the fact that Matthew, unlike Mark and Luke, does not use the direct address ("you are..."), but the proclamation form ("this is..."). Nevertheless Luke differs from Mark in that for him not the visionary but the praying Jesus is addressed. The much discussed tradition-historical question of whether the title "Son" originated from the Ebed-Yahweh presentation (Isa 42:1), from royal messianism (Ps 2:7), or from another tradition (e.g., Ex 4:22f. [Israel]; Gen 22:2,12,16 [Isaac]) falls outside the scope of this commentary. For our purpose it is enough to know that these and other background images are combined to assert that Jesus is the Son of God in a unique way. In order to establish which nuances the statement of the voice from heaven has for Luke, we will compare it with similar texts in the Third Gospel (Feldkämper, 1978: 45-46).

(i) "My Son": We referred already to Lk 1:35. Because of the occurrence of "Holy Spirit" and "Son of God," this verse is parallel to Lk 3:22. According to Lk 1:35, the existence of the Son is entirely brought about by the Spirit, that is, since the child promised to Mary will be brought about by the Spirit, he is Son of God. His existence brought about by the Spirit is tantamount to his (prophetic) mission (Voss, 1965: 97; Feldkämper, 1978: 46). Designating Jesus as "Son of God" is an honor declaration of the highest sort, a status emphasized throughout the infancy narrative and programmatically stated in the summary of that narrative in Lk 2:52. Since the culture expected people to act in accord with their birth status, little would have been expected of Jesus as the son of Joseph. Nor would he have had legitimacy ("authority") to speak and act in public. But if his true status is Son of God, his public statements and actions are fully legitimated. It should also be noted that public declarations in which a father acknowledged paternity were of utmost importance in honor-shame societies (Malina-Rohrbaugh, 1992: 304).

The words of the voice from heaven are fundamental to any understanding of Jesus as Son of God. There appears to have been a very significant progression or development in the Church's understanding of "Son of God." In its initial, Old Testament sense, the term identifies Jesus as an Israelite within Israel. It supplies a common ground upon which Jesus and his people both stand, and from which the issues that arise and finally separate him from them can come into focus. By the time the history has unfolded to its end, however, the Church is confessing Jesus to be the Son of God in a unique sense, normative also for anyone else's participation in the sonship. Now "Son of God" expresses the concepts of messiahship and incarnation. The decisive turning point seems to have been Jesus' passion and resurrection. Thus the New Testament Church, in confessing Jesus to be the Son of God, expresses both its continuity and its discontinuity with the Old Testament. We still need to understand better, however, the historical process by which "Son of God" achieved its full role in New Testament thought (Bretscher, 1968: 311).

(ii) "The Beloved": Jesus is designated by the voice from heaven as the Beloved Son. Like Mk 12:6, Luke uses the expression in the parable of the wicked tenants (Lk 20:13), but in the transfiguration account he substitutes "my Chosen" for it (Lk 9:35; compare Mk 9:7 and Mt 17:5, "the Beloved"). In Acts 15:25 the delegates of the community,

Barnabas and Paul, are called "beloved"; together with them the Apostolic Council sends "chosen representatives" to Antioch. "Beloved" and "chosen" seem to be parallel expressions in Acts 15:25. Finally, "beloved" (Lk 20:31, different in Mk and Mt) as well as "chosen" are used in relation to "sending." We conclude, therefore, that "Beloved" and "Chosen" are interchangeable, and that "Beloved" (Lk 3:22), which has been taken over from the Markan tradition, has not lost the original meaning it had in the text of Isa 42:1 ("chosen"). Jesus at prayer is thus the beloved Son, in sofar as he is chosen and empowered for his mission (Feldkämper, 1978: 46-47).

(iii) "With you I am well pleased": These words are probably to be understood as an allusion to Isa 42:1, the beginning of the first Servant Song (Fitzmyer, 1981: 486). But there are problems in so regarding it (Stendahl, 1968: 107-115). *Eudokein/eudokia*, "to please, good pleasure," are not favorite words of Luke [both occur twice in Luke over against 3/1 in Mt and 1/0 in Mk], but from the two occurrences in Lk 2:14 and 12:32 one may draw some conclusions concerning the meaning of these words in the Third Gospel. Whenever Luke uses these words (Lk 3:22; 10:21; 2:14), God is the acting subject. Almost always people are the object of God's good pleasure; only in Lk 3:22 it is Jesus. But we should take note of the following: Wherever the text deals with God's *eudokia* towards people, Jesus too occupies a place in the relationship between God and people. Lk 2:14 states that by the birth of Jesus, the Savior (Lk 2:11), "peace" has become a reality (Schürmann, 1969: 113) for the people who enjoy God's good pleasure. According to Lk 10:21, it pleases God to make the "littlle ones" beneficiaries of the revelation through the Son (Lk 10:22 parallel Mt 11:27). In Lk 12:32 the "little flock" is assured of the kingdom according to God's pleasure. According to Lk 22:29 — like Lk 12:32 a verse that is found in Luke only — it is again the Son (see: "my father") who acts as media-

tor of the kingdom. The verb *eudokein* is a word of election. It combines will and affection, especially in conjunc-
tion with the "beloved," and denotes the installation to a
particular function and status of one who is a special object
of delight (C.F. Evans, 1990: 249). All the texts that speak
of the "good pleasure" of God deal with the allocation of
God's salvation — peace, revelation and kingdom —through
Jesus. On the basis of this Lukan context, Lk 3:22 too can
be understood only in the sense that the Father is well pleased
in Jesus, so that and because he is chosen, designated and
sent as the Son for the allocation of God's salvation to the
people, to *his* people (Lk 3:21: "the whole people"; Feldkämper,
1978: 47-48).

We may summarize the wording of the voice from heaven
as follows: What is said here is to be interpreted not in
terms of titles but relationally, and in a twofold sense. On
the one hand, Jesus is in an exclusive and outstanding sense
the beloved and only Son of God. As such he is, on the
other hand, also chosen by the gift of the Spirit, that is,
commissioned and empowered for his mission. Thereby in
his baptism the Son is to be seen not by himself but in
relation to the whole chosen people: in the pre-synoptic
tradition as well as in Luke, the Son at his baptism is seen
as the one chosen by God *for* the people, and messenger
sent by God *to* the people (Miyoshi, 1974: 136).

Summing up the prayer notice in Lk 3:21, we can say
that:

Firstly, according to Lk 3:21, Jesus prayed at one of the
most important moments of his life, that is, at the beginning of his public ministry. Mark had already called our
attention to Jesus' prayer in Mk 1:35. At least indirectly,
he pointed out that by his prayer Jesus did not merely follow a pious Jewish custom, but that for Jesus prayer and
proclamation were closely related (compare Acts 6:4, "But
we will devote ourselves to prayer and to the ministry of
the word"). In Luke, Jesus' prayer receives already greater

importance than in Mark by the mere fact that prayer is the very first activity mentioned in Jesus' public ministry. The reference to Jesus' prayer is found at the beginning of a section that is to quite an extent the result of Lukan redaction (Lk 3:21-4:44). Thus, Jesus' prayer introduces what is described in the following pericopes. Thereby the impression could be created that among Jesus' activities prayer is the first and, therefore, the most important, but nevertheless also only one among many other activities. But a careful analysis of the text seems to indicate that Luke intends to affirm more than this.

Secondly, one of the particular features of the Lukan baptism pericope is that, next to Jesus' prayer, Luke mentions also that Jesus was baptized together "with all the people." Literarily, Luke expresses this by means of the repetition of the verb "to be baptized" and the chiastic structure of the clause. Thus Luke depicts Jesus at the beginning of his ministry as being *in solidarity with the people.* who are ready to convert — although he himself does not need repentance (see Lk 23:40f.). The act of *baptism*, in which Jesus showed himself to be in *solidarity with the people*, is a theme that pervades the whole of the Third Gospel and is, therefore, an important feature of Luke's Christology. The act of solidarity with the people who are ready to be baptized is, then, an expression of a constant, basic attitude of Jesus. Something similar is true of Jesus' *prayer* in the baptism pericope. Therein he expresses his *solidarity with God.* Jesus' close relationship to his Father is stressed through the observation that while he was praying, the heaven was opened. Luke's accounts of Jesus at prayer usually indicate a crucial moment, and his language is emphatic on this point — the revelation that follows did not take place during Jesus' baptism (Danker, 1988: 95). Jesus' solidarity with the people and his attitude towards God are presented by Luke in the act of commonly received baptism. His prayer is, therefore, the expression of Jesus' attitude to God as well as of his solidarity with the people.

Thirdly, in Lk 3:21, Jesus' prayer is closely related to his endowment with the Spirit and the acknowledgement of his sonship by the voice from heaven, that is, by the Father. The heavenly manifestation should be interpreted as the *answer to Jesus' prayer*, not in the sense of an answer to a petition, for Jesus' prayer cannot be understood here as petition. Instead of explicit or implicit petition, Jesus' prayer should be understood here as a *fundamental orientation to* and a *radical readiness for* God, a readiness to hear his word and readiness for his mission. It should be emphasized, therefore, that Jesus' prayer in Lk 3:21 is not an isolated act, but an attitude that is related to his person and mission as a whole, and thereby to each and every saving act he performs. Thus Jesus' whole activity is sustained by prayer. His prayer mediates salvation (Feldkämper, 1978: 48-49).

3. The Genealogy of Jesus (Lk 3:23-38)

The three Synoptics associate the temptation with the baptism in a number of ways that indicate the two should be viewed as closely related. While in Mark and Matthew the temptation story follows right after Jesus' baptism, Luke separates them only by a genealogy, which serves to trace the ancestry of Jesus, the Son of God (Lk 3:22), back to Adam, the son of God (Lk 3:38; Page, 1995: 92).

It is important to note that Luke offers the genealogy of Jesus immediately before narrating the tests or temptations of Jesus. As all other biblical genealogies, Lk 3:23-38 is patrilineal. Matthew's and Luke's genealogies move in opposite directions: Matthew begins with Abraham and ends with Jesus, whereas Luke starts with Jesus and traces his ancestry back to Adam, who is designated "son of God." Luke expresses this ascending order, a form more widespread in the Hellenistic period (Kurz, 1984: 169-170), by introducing Jesus as the "son of Joseph" and then simply adding the genitive form of the article before the name of each succeeding ancestor (Bailey and VanderBroeck, 1992: 183-187). A number of commentators have considered Luke's genealogy as awkwardly placed or have even stated that it has only minimal relation to what follows (Fitzmyer, 1981: 498). But when one considers the social function of genealogies in antiquity that opinion must be revised (Rohrbaugh, 1995: 187). Like any other text in the New Testament, Lk 3-4 emerged from a Mediterranean society in which honor was the central social value which permeated every aspect of public life. While anthropological studies identify a wide variety of social purposes for genealogies, like establishing kinship, they are above all honor claims. They seek to establish social status (ascribed honor) and thereby provide the all-important "map" for proper interaction (Hanson, 1989: 75-84). The best known example is that of Josephus who begins his autobiography with a lengthy claim to come from Jerusalem's finest royal and priestly stock (*Life* 1.1-6).

In publicly acknowledging a boy to be his son, that is a member of the genealogical tree, a father not only accepted responsibility for him and made him his heir, he determined his status (honor) in the community as well. Genealogies thus documented what rituals of naming and circumcision acknowledged. It is significant, therefore, that the genealogy in Luke follows immediately on the baptism scene in which God acknowledges both paternity ("my beloved son" — ascribed honor, honor as precedence), and pleasure ("in whom I am well pleased" — acquired honor, honor as virtue) in regard to Jesus.

The genealogy of Jesus is a stunning claim to honor out of keeping with the actual circumstances of Jesus' birth which may explain the strange phrase "as was thought" (Lk 3:23: *hos enomizeto*). The genealogy declares him to be no less than the "son of Adam, son of God" (Rohrbaugh, 1995: 188,196 n. 15). But the claim that one born in the lowliest of peasant circumstances has been raised to Son of God must be challenged. In counteracting this challenge Luke avails himself of several strategies. He claims that the conclusions which would normally be drawn from the genealogy are wrong (Lk 3:23: "as was thought"). He tells a birth story designed to show that the power of God has been at work from the beginning in such a way as to alter the apparent genealogy of Jesus (Lk 2:1-38). He narrates the obligatory (in Hellenistic biography) single childhood event portraying the character of the person (Lk 2:41-52; Malina, 1990: 54-64). In the baptism scene he describes how, in an act of bestowing honor, God, who has the power to do so, has claimed paternity, named the child and publicly ritualized his fictive status (Lk 3:21-22; Gordon, 1977: 101). Finally, he gives us a genealogy in which he seeks to confirm what he has been claiming all along: Jesus' honor status is not what it appears to be. In the genealogy he provides the necessary public record an ancient audience would expect for the honor claims he has made, and thus it should be clear that the connection between Lk 3:23-38 and Lk 4:1-13 is both direct and crucial to Luke's rhetorical strategy. The claim must be verified. It must be tested by an adversary no ordinary village carpenter (if indeed that is really what Jesus was) could expect to match. Luke, therefore, will go immediately from the honor claim made in the genealogy to the first of the honor tests (Lk 4:1-13; Rohrbaugh, 1995:188-189,196 ns 16,17).

Verses 23-38: (23) Jesus was about thirty years old when he began his work.
He was the son (as was thought) of Joseph son of He'li.
(24) son of Mat'that, son of Levi, son of Mel'chi, son of Jannai, son of Joseph,
(25) son of Mattathias, son of Amos, son of Nahum,
son of Esli, son of Naggai,
(26) son of Ma'ath, son of Mattathias, son of Sem'e-in,
son of Jo'sech, son of Jo'da,

(27) son of Jo-an'an, son of Rhe'sa, son of Ze-
      rub'ba-bel,
      son of She-al'tiel, son of Ne'ri,
(28) son of Mel'chi, son of Ad'di, son of Co'sam,
      son of El-ma'dam, son of Er,
(29) son of Joshua, son of El-i-e'zer. son of Jo'rim,
      son of Mat'that, son of Levi,
(30) son of Sim'e-on, son of Judah, son of Joseph,
      son of Jo'nam, son of E-li'a-kim,
(31) son of Me'le-a, son of Men'na, son of Mat'ta-
      tha,
      son of Nathan, son of David,
(32) son of Jesse, son of O'bed, son of Bo'az,
      son of Sa'la, son of Nah'shon,
(33) son of Am-min-a-dab, son of Ar'ni, son of
      Hez'ron,
      son of Per'ez, son of Judah,
(34) son of Jacob, son of Isaac, son of Abraham,
      son of Te'rah, son of Na'hor,
(35) son of Se'rug, son of Re'u, son of Pe'leg,
      son of E'ber, son of She'lah,
(36) son of Ca-i'nan, son of Ar-pha'xad, son of Shem,
      son of Noah, son of La'mech,
(37) son of Me-thu'se-lah, son of E'noch, son of
      Jar'ed,
      son of Ma'ha'la-le-el, son of Ca-i'nan,
(38) son of E'nos, son of Seth,
      son of Adam, son of God.

Jesus began his ministry at about thirty years of age according to Lk 3:23, while Jn 8:57 alludes to his age as not yet fifty. Recently one has opined that the evangelists based their respective deductions of Jesus' age on the requirements that candidates for national office be at least thirty years of age but not yet fifty (see CD 14:7-10; 1QSa 1:13-21; Buchanan, 1995: 297).

Much ink has been used in discussing patterns in the list, and in comparing it to the genealogy of Jesus provided in Matthew's Gospel. Suffice it to say that there is no convincing design or numerial pattern of the generations, and that there are some points in common, but even more dif-

ferences between the the two genealogies (Ringe, 1995: 56).
It has been suggested that Luke gives the descent through
Mary, and Matthew through Joseph. But such interpreta-
tion of Luke's list is based on slender patristic evidence.
The fact is that no satisfactory solution has yet been found
(Danker, 1988: 97; Johnson, 1991: 72).

Apart from verse 23, Lk 3:23-38 is a simple list of names
proceeding without additional notes or elaboration. Is this
list a Lukan construction, or was it shaped in some prior
tradition which Luke has incorporated? While it is true that
genealogies belong to indigenous Jewish tradition, it cannot be assumed that the list as we have it in Luke was
taken over without modification or redaction from the Palestinian Jewish-Christian Church. There are two indications
which seem to support this view. Firstly, there is the repetition of names in the list after David, some of which appear to be anachronisms, possibly suggesting that the list
had its own history. Among these repetitions are: variations
of Mattathias (five times), Jesus (twice), Joseph (three times),
Simeon (Semein), Levi (twice), and Mel'chi (twice). Thus,
the Lukan list should most probably be considered in light
of the generally midrashic use of this literary form in Judaism. Secondly, the genealogy is incorporated into a framework similar to that of Mark, that is, between the account
of Jesus' baptism and his temptation. This is to say that
Luke was not led to include the genealogy at this point
merely because of the sequence found in his sources. Moreover, the break in the Markan sequence at this crucial point
would seem to suggest that Luke had some specific purpose
in mind for the genealogy as well as for its position (Johnson,
1988: 229-230).

From a form-critical point of view, what is the meaning
of the phrase *hōs enomizeto*, "as was thought," in verse 23?
This phrase is generally taken as a parenthesis, an editorial
comment by Luke, that is, an indication of his awareness of
the difficulty of tracing Jesus' descent from Joseph while at

the same time holding to the tradition of the virgin birth. Yet nowhere in Lk 3—24 is there any hint of the idea of the virgin birth. Some scholars think that perhaps the "as was thought" is best taken as an indication of Luke's uncertainty concerning the historical value of the list, or his realization that the genealogical descent of Jesus was already a matter of polemics. In any case, verse 23 in its present form is Lukan, and a strong indication that the genealogy — perhaps in a somewhat different form — originated at a time prior to Luke. But, by the same token, this Lukan phrase also points to the probability that the hand of Luke was at work also in other parts of the genealogy. At least it is almost certain that, whatever the purpose of Luke in including this pedigree, the list has some function within Lukan theology (Johnson, 1988: 230-231).

What is this function? Two methods of approach have been frequently attempted. First, the *apocalyptic approach* which starts from the intriguing fact that the genealogy contains seventy-seven names, which are seen as seventy-seven world-weeks, at the end of which the messianic week begins (C.F. Evans, 1990: 251-252; Johnson, 1988: 231-233). But, as stated above, no numerical pattern attributed to the genealogy is convincing. Second, *Christ as the second Adam*. It is customary also to maintain that Luke has in mind a typological relationship of Jesus to Adam since he leads the genealogy back not to Abraham, as in Matthew, but to Adam, son of God (Beare, 1972: 42). This, it is said has the function of illustrating Luke's general concern to portray the universal character of Jesus' ministry. Those who argue that the Adamic connection is not really significant (Johnson, 1988: 233-235) seem to miss the big picture. The key feature of the genealogy is that it goes past Abraham to Adam. The significance of that perspective alone is significant and is not to be ignored. Luke touches here again the note of universality sounded by Lk 3:6: the significance of Jesus is not only for the "children of Abraham," but for all the descendants of Adam, all the nations of the earth (Gen 12:3; Johnson, 1991: 72). Indeed, the genealogy implies that Jesus' mission is directed not only to the sons of Abraham, as in the case of John (Lk 3:8), but to all people (Ernst, 1977: 155; O'Fearghail, 1991: 23 note 89). The point of the genealogy is to show that Jesus has his place in the human race created by God. Outside of Jesus, Adam is the only one related to the title "son of God" in Luke (Bock, 1994: 348-349).

The most compelling argument for finding significance in the present position of the genealogy is the fact that the motif of Jesus as Son of God is found in both the baptism pericope and the genealogy. There is nothing in the genealogy to suggest that its function is solely to emphasize the Davidic descent of Jesus, as is commonly assumed; moreover, there is nothing in the Gospel of Luke as a whole to suggest that the title, son of David, was especially important for Luke. But the fact that the Lukan genealogy runs *backwards* from Jesus to God is significant since there is no known parallel in the Old Testament or in rabbinic texts for a genealogy to begin with or to culminate with the naming of God. Thus it is not impossible that Luke saw in the genealogy one way of understanding the ascription of the Son of God title to Jesus. It seems best to conclude that the situation of the Lukan genealogy was determined not merely by necessity, or by the order of Luke's sources, but also by the desire to link together two pericopes which deal with the title Son of God (Johnson, 1988: 237,239).

Perhaps the most surprising aspect of the Lukan genealogy is its rejection of the royal line of Judah. Rather than enumerating the royal succession from David to the exile, as does Matthew, Luke proceeds from David to his third son born in Jerusalem, Nathan (2 Sam 5:14; 1 Chron 3:5; 14:4). Luke's rejection of the royal line in favor of David's son Nathan also suggests the importance for his Christology of the motif of the prophet as applied to Jesus since it is highly probable that Luke was aware of the identification in certain Jewish circles of David's son Nathan with the prophet of the same name (Johnson, 1988: 240-252; Nebe, 1989: 53,57).

The genealogy rounds out the introductory material of the first three chapters. Jesus' identity has been established and his vocation determined by angelic announcement, prophetic precedent, a heavenly voice, and a catalog of ancestors. A number of themes have been introduced that will be developed and elaborated as the narrative unfolds. But before the account of Jesus' public ministry can begin, Luke has one more story to tell. It will make clear the specific space within the panorama of divine vocation, human longing, and socio-political reality that Jesus' ministry will occupy. Framed by assurances that the presence and power of the Holy Spirit still surround Jesus and direct his path (Lk 4:1,14), the story relates Jesus' own time in the wilderness — an experience like that of John, of the prophets of old, and of Israel itself on its God-directed exodus journey (Ringe, 1995: 57-58).

4. The Testing/Tempting of the Son of Adam/Son of God (Lk 4:1-13)

All three Synoptic Gospels contain a temptation account, and scholars distinguish two "primary" versions of the tradition of Jesus' temptations in the wilderness (Gibson, 1995: 118). Strictly speaking, there are four narratives of the temptation — a brief Markan narrative and the Q narrative which lies behind both the Matthean and Lukan accounts (Stegner, 1990: 5). In other words, Mk 1:12-13 contains only a brief remark about this event and lacks dialogue and detail. On the other hand, Mt 4:1-11 is so close to Lk 4:1-13 that most commentators see a written source shared by Matthew and Luke and most speak of Q here (Creed, 1957: 61; Fitzmyer, 1981: 507; Tiede, 1988: 98; C.F.

Evans, 1990: 256; Bovon, 1991: 188; Page, 1995: 89-90). Indeed, within the parameters of the Two-Source theory, there should be little doubt that the story of the threefold temptation of Jesus in Matthew and Luke formed part of Q (Tuckett, 1992: 479). However, a key point of agreement with Mk 1:12-13 — the association of testing with the wilderness and with the period of forty days — suggests that Luke is also aware of material like that of Mark. Some scholars, then, see both Mark and Q as contributing to Luke (Schürmann, 1969: 218-219; Bultmann, 1972: 254; Shelton, 1991: 58).

Q is composed predominantly of sayings forms. Some are compiled into coherent speeches and clusters of thematically related pronouncements, while others are strung together rather loosely. The pericope of the temptation narrative, however, stands out as anomalous in this compilation of speeches and sayings. While most of the Q materials are simple sayings or short "speeches," the temptation narrative is a three-part dialogue with a relatively detailed narrative framework. More importantly, it is a true *narrative*, albeit one in which speech plays a central function (Kloppenborg, 1987: 246-262). But, unlike Kloppenborg, we do not necessarily see the temptation narrative as belonging to the last stage of the redaction of Q (Humphrey, 1991: 43).

Admittedly there is no other narrative piece with a three-part debate in Q. But there is at least one other term of comparison, namely, Wis 2:17-18:

> Let us see if his words are true,
> and let us test what will happen at the end of his life;
> for if the righteous man is God's son,
> he will help him
> and will deliver him from the hand of his adversaries.

Wisd 2:17-18 is a narrative in which there are two parties in conflict, the righteous person and the "ungodly," the

latter being of the party of the "devil" (Wis 2:24). The motif
of testing is clear. And clear also are three challenges. The
first challenge is to see if the righteous person's words "are
true." That is, of course, the essence of the first temptation
(Lk 4:3-4). The second challenge of the ungodly toward the
righteous person is to "test what will happen at the end of
his life." That is, however, the essence of the second temptation in which Jesus is asked to throw himself down from
the pinnacle of the temple to his probable death. The third
challenge of the ungodly pertains to the righteous person's
being truly a "son of God," a challenge echoed in the third
temptation where Jesus is challenged to change his allegiance
from serving God to serving the devil; the emphasis here is
placed on the "*If* you are God's son," like in Wis 2:18, that
is, if you are really righteous before God and his true servant. These comparisons suggest that an entirely appropriate term of comparison for the temptation narrative in the
Q-version underlying Lk 4:1-13 and Mt 4:1-11 can be found
in the testing of the righteous man in Wisdom 2.

Recently, it has also been pointed out that the stories of
the temptations/testing of Jesus in Q (Lk 4:1-13) and the
testing of Solomon by the Queen of Sheba (1 Kgs 10:1-13;
2 Chron 9:1-12) are remarkably similar in terms of character, setting, plot, and resolution (Paffenroth, 1996: 142-143).
According to many scholars, the temptations are focused not
on Jesus as miracle-worker, but on Jesus as obedient and
faithful, that is, as "righteous" in the full wisdom sense, to
the Father. Miracle-working is a very minor motif in the
first temptation; and it is absent in the second and third
temptations, where Jesus' relationship with God is the focus
(Humphrey, 1991: 46-47).

The temptation or testing of Jesus in the wilderness
constitutes the last of the pericopes introducing Jesus' public ministry in the Gospel of Luke. It is closely linked to
the baptism scene (Lk 3:21-22) and the genealogy (Lk 3:23-
38) since he is now tempted/tested as son of Adam/Son of

God (Lk 3:22,38). It has been suggested that the temptation of Jesus is part of a ritual process in Lk 3:1-4:13 that
transforms Jesus from a private person to a public prophet
(McVan, 1991: 34). But a prophetic identity in the temptations is quite concealed and partial. By the end of the
section, Lk 3:1-4:30, Jesus emerges more properly as the Spirit-
anointed divine son, prophet, and messiah (Brawley, 1992:
419-420). Lk 4:1-13 is also related to Jesus' inaugural speech
in Nazareth (Lk 4:16-30), and both set the tone for the
whole of Jesus' public ministry (Fitzmyer, 1981: 506).
There is no agreement among scholars concerning the main
thrust of the temptation narrative. Is Jesus tempted to prove
himself by signs (Dupont, 1957: 303)? Is Jesus presented as
the true Israel (Robinson, 1962: 54-60), faithful to God in
the wilderness where Israel of old had failed, an interpretation rejected by some contemporary scholars (Flusser, 1989:
110)? Or should we go back to the garden of Eden and see
Jesus as a New Adam meeting the tempter at the tree of
the knowledge of good and evil (Feuillet, 1959: 627-628)?

In the final analysis Jesus is tempted neither as second
Adam, nor as true Israel, but as Son. There is a touch of
Adamic typology and considerable exodus typology, but that
is because the experiences of Adam and Israel are paradigmatic cases of the testing of God's son. Jesus' experience is
congruent to the experience of his followers, and his example is paradigmatic for them. The parallels between Jesus'
experience and that of believers are inescapable. Jesus' temptations are not uniquely messianic, though it is clear that
his sonship is of a uniquely exalted kind. His temptations
are supreme instances of every person's temptations (Lk 3:38:
"son of Adam"). The narrative presents moral challenge as
well as Christological affirmation (Nolland, 1989: 182).
Although some argue that these tests are unique to Jesus
and should not be read as exemplary (Fitzmyer, 1981: 518;
S. Brown, 1969: 17), many scholars think that the story
was certainly also told for its exemplary features in order to

encourage Christians facing temptation and to indicate to them how to recognize and overcome it (Marshall, 1978: 166; Bock, 1994: 383-384). It has also been suggested that we have here an inner-church dispute in which Christians preoccupied with miracles are shown to have been seduced by the devil (Fridrichsen, 1972: 121-128). The individual temptations have also been subjected to widely divergent interpretations (Nolland, 1989: 178).

Whether ultimately derived from the visionary experience of Jesus himself, or the product of Christian midrashic interpretation of his messiahship and lordship, the temptation narrative sets his earthly ministry in the context of a supernatural conflict between the sole representative of God and his kingdom and the representative and ruler of the kingdom of evil (C.F. Evans, 1990: 255).

The temptations are clearly an aftermath to the baptismal identification and anointing of Jesus (Nolland, 1989: 178). The programmatic aspect of the temptation scene in each Gospel is obvious and has often been noted. It is the last of the preparatory scenes in the Lukan Gospel introducing the public ministry and encapsulates a programmatic aspect of it. Closely related to the foregoing baptism and genealogy, it depicts Jesus as being tested precisely in his character as Son of God (Fitzmyer, 1989: 151).

> To argue that Jesus disclaims a political style of messiahship is to miss the point. The question addressed by the temptation narrative is this: How will Jesus carry on his politics? Will it be as one obedient to God or as one who is self-serving? (Danker, 1988: 100). The temptations or tests, therefore, concern not so much the *goal* of Jesus' mission as well the *means* to reach that goal.

Verses 1-2: (1) Jesus, full of the Holy Spirit, returned from the Jordan
                    and was led by the Spirit in the wilderness,
              (2) where for forty days he was tempted by the devil.

> He ate nothing at all during those days
> and when they were over, he was famished.

In the introductory verses, Luke adds two significant details whose purpose is to connect the pericope of the temptations to that of the baptism. This was necessary because he had inserted the genealogy between them. The first significant detail is "full of the Holy Spirit," a form which appears in the New Testament only here and in Acts 6:5; 7:55; 11:24 (Dupont, 1966: 213). Though in the Greek the definite article is omitted here [literally: "full of a Holy Spirit"], the phrase obviously refers to the descent of the Spirit on Jesus while he was at prayer after his baptism (Lk 3:22). Thus endowed, Jesus' designation as "Son of God" is now going to be tested, as it will be throughout his ministry. The phrase "full of the Holy Spirit" prepares the reader for Lk 4:14,18. As already seen in the infancy narrative, the Holy Spirit plays a very important role in Luke-Acts (Fitzmyer, 1981: 227-231).

The second detail which Luke adds is a favorite verb of his to express that Jesus "returned" (*hypostrepho*) from the Jordan," that is, from the site where he had been baptized (Lk 3:3,21-22). The Jordan is not mentioned in either Mk 1:12 or Mt 4:1. In Luke, the connection between baptism and temptation, broken by the genealogy, is restored by "from the Jordan" (C.F. Evans, 1990: 257; Shelton, 1991: 59). The verb *hypostrepsen* can mean either "returned," as found in NRSV, or "withdrew, turned aside." Since Luke has not mentioned earlier that Jesus came from Nazareth (unlike Mk 1:9) or from Galilee (unlike Mt 3:13), there seems to be little ground to adopt the first meaning here. "Departed" or "withdrew" seems to be preferable. Its meaning will be specified in Lk 4:14 (Fitzmyer, 1981: 513).

By "he was led by the Spirit," literally, "he was led about in the Spirit," Luke not only notes Jesus' Spirit-giftedness, but also states that his experience in the wilderness was under the guidance of the Spirit. Luke uses the imperfect tense for continuous action. In Matthew, Jesus is led *to* the wilderness and stops there; according to Luke, Jesus travels *through* the wilderness, walking under the guidance of the Spirit. Matthew writes that Jesus was led "by the Spirit" — the Spirit led him as one person leads another. Luke prefers to say "in the Spirit" as an interior influence, an inspiration (Dupont, 1966: 213-214). At the baptism, Jesus was acknowledged by God as the messiah (Lk 3:22) and is equipped with the Spirit for his special role. The first thing the Spirit does is to lead Jesus into the wilderness, where his messianic calling is put to the test (Page, 1995: 94). Indeed Luke emphasizes the Spirit's indwelling and leading Jesus at the beginning of the ordeal; and when the tests are concluded, Luke alone remarks that Jesus returned to Galilee "in the power of the Spirit" (Lk 4:14; Garrett, 1989: 37). "The wilderness" is the Judaean desert, possibly understood as a place of contact with God (Hosea 2:14-15), but more probably as a dwelling place of wild beasts and demons (Lev 16:10; Isa 13:21; 34:14; Tob 8:3). Jesus, therefore, faces the double aspect of the wilderness (Fitzmyer, 1981: 514; different Mauser, 1963: 146-149).

"Forty days" [contrast Mt 4:1, "forty days and forty nights"; see Deut 9:9], is to be taken as a round number, a symbolic number for a long period of time rather than a specific calendar measurement (Ringe, 1995: 58), but may recall Deut 8:2, "the Lord your God has led you these forty years in the wilderness." For the correspondence between forty days and forty years see Num 14:34 and Ez 4:6.

Unlike Mt 4:2, Luke avoids here the religious language for fasting: "he ate nothing" (Nolland, 1989: 178-179). He uses the verb *nesteuo* elsewhere for the religious practice of fasting (Lk 5:33-35; 18:12; Acts 13:2f.; Marshall, 1978: 170). Forty days is a long time to be isolated and to go without food. Such disciplines frequently accompany rites of passage in various world religions, where fasting and isolation often function as the first stage of a ritual that is supposed to reveal the identity and vocation of the person engaging in it. In this case, however, the wilderness period is not part of a "vision quest," for the revelation is said already to have happened (Ringe, 1995: 58-59). Unlike in Matthew, where "forty days" is predicated of Jesus' fast, in Luke it is predicated of the temptations or the Spirit's leading: Luke emphasizes the duration of Jesus' fast and/or that Jesus was led by the Spirit all the time (Fitzmyer, 1981: 514).

Jesus "was tempted by the devil," literally, "being tempted by the devil," with the present participle indicating the simultaneity of the temptations and the Spirit's guidance. Luke probably thinks of the devil as tempting Jesus throughout the entire forty days (Schweizer, 1984: 82; Stein, 1992: 146; Page, 1995: 92). "The devil" (derived from the Greek *diabolos*, that underlies the adjective "diabolic") means adversary. The term is descriptive rather than nominal, but in the course of usage it has been understood to refer to a specific being as the focal point of evil (Danker, 1988: 100). Luke derived the phrase from Mk 1:13 except for his substitution of "devil" for Mark's "Satan." Luke does not avoid the name "Satan" (Lk 10:18; 11:18; 13:16; 22:3,31), but in the temptation account he consistently refers to Jesus' adversary as the "devil."

Lk 4 somehow relates the devil to the kingdom of God. The devil is mentioned for the first time in the Gospel at the beginning of the temptation story (Lk 4:2); and again for the first time in the Gospel, towards the end of the chapter, Jesus formulates his mission: the proclamation of the good news of the kingdom of God (Lk 4:43). It looks as if through the confrontation of Jesus and the devil the space is created in which the proclamation of the kingdom will take place. In fact, the theme of confrontation or conflict runs through the whole of Lk 4: between Jesus and the devil (Lk 4:1-13), between Jesus and the people of Nazareth (Lk 4:16-30), between Jesus and evil in its various forms (Lk 4:33-37, 38-39; Rijkhoff, 1990:30-31).

It is important to be clear on the verb *peirazo*. It is part of the context of honor-shame so important in the Mediterranean culture. Its focus is testing, not tempting, seduction, and in the present context, the verb is best translated "test," rather than "tempt" (Garrett, 1989: 127). The verb is used in the Septuagint of both God testing humans (Gen 2:1-19; Ex 16:4; 20:20; Deut 8:2; 13:2ff.) and humans testing God (Ex 17:2; Gerhardsson, 1966: 25-35).

Jesus "was famished." He had no food for forty days and he was hungry and helpless. Poverty, hunger, and powerlessness all go together. This is the state of the poor who like Jesus are threatened by starvation. They are in involuntary fasting. Hungry people like Jesus are vulnerable for exploitation. Food is a very valuable instrument for exploitation of those who are poor and hungry. The affluent have not been remiss in employing such means. The "food aid" of rich nations to poor nations often has hidden strings attached to it like trade concessions and foreign policies. One of the great temptations for the poor is to get the chance to accede to the elite, to be able to have a hold on the handle of power. Jesus was offered that — to be ruler not just of a piece of the world, but the glory of all the kingdoms of the world and all this authority/power (Fuliga, 1994: 176,179).

Verses 3-4:   (3)   The devil said to him,
                    "If you are the Son of God command this stone
                    to become a loaf of bread."
               (4)   Jesus answered him,
                    "It is written. 'One does not live by bread alone.'"

Something of the complexity of Luke's use of the "Son" terminology has been seen at Lk 3:22. For Luke it is essentially a relational term: the Son is privileged to share the family honor and resources, and lives in filial submission to his Father. The devil suggests that Sonship is a privilege to be exploited. If one realizes that the assertion of sonship is acknowledged by the devil, then the temptation can be taken in a variety of ways (see Marshall, 1978: 170-171; Bock, 1994: 372-373). Jesus is tempted to order his own affairs and provide for his own needs, rather than being nourished in filial dependence on the Father. But, as Jesus replies, there is no need to stop attending to God to start seeking for oneself. Rather, one should seek God's kingdom (Lk 12:31). The desire for bread should not determine the Son's use of possibilities and privileges that are his (Nolland, 1989: 179).

In verses 3-4, Luke speaks only of a single stone and single loaf of bread, while Matthew employs the plural. It is often noted that "these stones" may remind one of "these stones" in Mt 3:9, parallel Lk 3:8. A second difference is that, according to Luke, Jesus is called upon to address himself to the stone and give it a command. In Matthew's account, there is simply question of a desire. Here Luke's construction is better and can be attributed to a revision. Concerning the first point, the number of stones, it is again Luke's version that has been revised. The singular "stone" is more plausible and better adapted to the situation. Going from the plural to the singular is more understandable than the reverse; for in both Matthew and Luke Jesus is alone and one loaf would be sufficient. To focus more on the personal satisfaction of Jesus would have facilitated a relationship to Eve's temptation and those that Christians have to undergo. Satisfaction of hunger, however, takes second place (Dupont, 1966: 214).

What is so wrong about changing a stone into bread? In the context of Jesus' own hunger, making bread could hardly be seen as evil. In the context of a people for whom famine was a frequent experience, and whose poor members experienced scarcity even in years of good harvests, the ability to make bread from the abundant stones scattered on the west bank of the Jordan could be a lifesaver. Also, Moses is said to have been the instrument for a similar provision of bread for Israel on their wilderness journey (Ringe, 1995: 59). No onlookers were present on the scene, but to Greco-Roman listeners, accustomed to the use of donations of grain ("bread and circuses") for political advantage, the implications were obvious. What Jesus was tempted to do for himself he could do for others. The question is: to what end? Some exploration of that will be made at the multiplication of the loaves (Lk 9:12-17). In societies where bread and money form an equation, the meaning of this temptation is inescapable (Danker, 1988: 101). But concern for "bread," that is, for material goods, while recognized as genuine and real, is not to become the overriding concern in the Christian life (Tuckett, 1992: 498).

Later Jesus will feed five thousand. The fast of forty days has ended ("and when they were over, he was famished"). Now he must eat or die. If he could demonstrate such power to meet the basic needs of the masses (Lk 9:10-17), surely he could generate an instant following. Moses had cried to God and God had sent manna to the people of Israel; how much more ready should God be to perform mighty works on behalf of Jesus? People would recognize him as the New Moses, the prophet of the end time (Deut 18:15), the deliverer of Israel, and flock to him. Jesus' response to the devil differs in Matthew and Luke. Matthew gives a more complete quotation from Scripture; this is typical of his Gospel. As it was customary to cite only the first words of a text, the rest being understood, it is likely that "but by every word that comes from the mouth of God" is an addition of Matthew to his source, not an omission of Luke.

Jesus refuses. Is it because such acts violate the nature of the "Father" revealed to him at baptism? Or is it because of that sticky "if you are the Son of God," with its taunt to prove his sonship by a miracle? For whatever reason, Jesus turns the temptation aside by means of Deut 8:3. He will not live by bread alone, but "by every word that comes from the mouth of the Lord." He will live by what God says, and God had said at his baptism, "You are my Son; the Beloved" (Wink, 1986: 17). The choice of texts used by Jesus is significant. They come from Deut 8:3; 6:13,16, passages which relate to Israel in the wilderness, tempting God and being tested by him, and which occur in the context of the *Schema*, the authoritative claim by God upon Israel's worship and loyalty. The temptation of Jesus — and his followers — is to be seen as antitypical of the experience of Israel. But where Israel failed, Jesus shows the way to victory (Marshall, 1978: 166).

Verses 5-8: (5) Then the devil led him up
and showed him in an instant all the kingdoms
of the world.
(6) And the devil said to him,
"To you I will give their glory and all this authority;
for it has been given over to me,
and I give it to anyone I please.
(7) If you, then, will worship me,
it will all be yours."
(8) Jesus answered him,
"It is written. 'Worship the Lord your God,
and serve only him.'"

The second temptation in Luke is placed third in Matthew's account. Most scholars hold that Matthew more faithfully reproduces Q and they usually cite the order of the temptations as an example (Stegner, 1990: 6). Matthew describes the setting as a "very high mountain," the usual setting for the literary theme to which the description belongs. Luke, however, envisioned the scene in a different manner. Instead of a high mountain from which one could see the entire world, he preferred to say that the devil showed the world to Jesus "in an instant." For the sake of plausibility Luke substituted a temporal context for a geographical site. He realizes that no mountain is high enough to see all the kingdoms (Creed, 1957: 63; Dupont, 1968: 55; Schürmann, 1969: 210; Fitzmyer, 1981: 515-516). In the same way as

God showed Moses the land of Israel in a moment of time (Deut 34:1f.), the devil showed Jesus the kingdoms of the earth (Young, 1995: 29).

Thereby Luke also makes it understood that it is a purely fleeting vision. He specifies that the vision has been produced instantaneously (not that it lasted only an instant) to emphasize that it was a supernatural vision. In Mt 4:9 the devil's promise ("all this") is concerned simply with possession; in Lk 4:6 attention is drawn to the idea of power — "all this authority/power." Taken in this political sense the word *exousia* is proper to Luke's Gospel (Lk 20:20; 23:7; 12:11; 22:25). He alone uses the Greek word in other places for the "power" of Satan (Lk 20:18) and of darkness (Lk 22:53; Dupont, 1966: 214).

Presumably the order of the temptations that Luke adopted is related to the meaning which he attributes to the story. To account for this order, most exegetes refer to the importance of geographical considerations for Luke: the climactic scene takes place in Jerusalem (Fitzmyer, 1981: 507; Nolland, 1989: 179). The pattern of Luke's Gospel is: Galilee, the journey from Galilee to Jerusalem, and Jerusalem (Ringe, 1995: 61). This pattern is so rigorously followed that Luke suppresses any mention of Caesarea Philippi (compare Lk 9:18 to Mk 8:27; Mt 16:13) and the appearances of the Risen Christ in Galilee. This explanation seems correct, but is incomplete. It neglects the more profound significance of the holy city in the works of Luke (Bachmann, 1980: 138ff.). In Luke's Gospel, Jerusalem is essentially the city where the prophecies of the messiah's sufferings and glory must find their fulfillment. After the temptations, the first passage to speak of Jerusalem in relation to Jesus is found in the account of the transfiguration (Lk 9:28-36). Of the three Synoptics, Luke alone tells us the subject of the conversation between Jesus, Moses and Elijah: they "were speaking of his departure, which he was about to accomplish at Jerusalem" (Lk 9:31). Following this episode Jesus does in fact journey toward Jerusalem: "When the days drew near for him to be taken up, he set his face to go to Jerusalem" (Lk 9:51). The rest of Luke's account recalls this announcement in notices found only in his Gospel (Lk 9:53; 13:22; 17:11; 19:11).

Before the transfiguration, not only the temptation account, but also two episodes of the infancy narrative point towards Jerusalem — the presentation in the Temple (Lk 2:22-40; Hendrickx, 1996: 211-243), and the loss and finding of Jesus (Lk 2:41-52; Hendrickx, 1996: 243-267). In the former, the prophecy of Simeon is the first announcement of the Passion (Lk 2:34-35); the latter is possibly the first prefiguration of the final Passover.

Thus we have found Luke's reason for ending the temptation narrative with the one that took place in Jerusalem. Jerusalem is the city where Jesus must accomplish "his departure," where he must suffer his Passion. It is appropriate that the temptations ended there and the devil retired from him there. It is there that the devil will reappear, no longer to "tempt" Jesus, but in order to provoke the ultimate test (Dupont, 1966: 216). Thus, coupled with Luke's geographical perspective and interest in Jerusalem, his order of temptations suggests that Luke changed the sequence of the scenes from the original Q (Fitzmyer, 1989: 152-154).

The devil offers Jesus authority (*exousia*) over the kingdoms of the world and their glory (Lk 4:6a). Matthew mentions the kingdoms of the world and their splendor/glory, but says nothing about "authority/power." In Lk 4:6a the plural pronoun (*their* glory) must refer back to "kingdoms" (Mt 4:8), suggesting that Luke has himself inserted the noun *exousia* and its modifiers, but without adjusting the possessive pronoun to match its new antecedent (Garrett, 1989: 127). Luke has apparently added the devil's clarification that he may give it to anyone he pleases (Lk 4:6b), since it seems unlikely that Matthew would have omitted so significant a saying by the devil (Dupont, 1968: 57; Fitzmyer, 1981: 507;

Garrett, 1989: 128). On the other hand, Luke often adds
explanatory statements (e.g., Lk 6:19b; 8:37; 9:34b,38,48;
11:18). Therefore, one can hardly doubt the Lukan origin
of the commentary found in Lk 4:6 (Mahnke, 1978: 130,
323, n. 52).

As "situation in life" of Lk 4:5-7 some scholars refer to
the concrete dangers that threatened the Lukan community, as well as adaptation to the political realities of the
Roman Empire (Ernst, 1977: 159; Schweizer, 1984: 84). The
statement highlights Luke's understanding of the devil as
"the ruler of this world" (cf. Jn 12:31). That he is ruler
specfically of the human world is indicated by Luke's use
of the term *oikoumene* ("inhabited world," human population), where Matthew has *kosmos* (Mt 4:8). Luke's use of
oikoumene may well be a reference to the Roman Empire,
in that Rome was basically regarded as the world of that
day (Bock, 1994: 375). The devil's influence is co-exten-
sive with the influence of evil in the fabric of human affairs. Perhaps we should think particularly of the hunger
after power and glory to which Jesus' way was such an
antithesis (Lk 22:24-29). The devil's role in this situation
does not relate specifically to devil worship. It is likely,
therefore, that the worship of the devil to which Jesus is
enticed is the temptation to pursue his mission in the ways
of the world, to gain glory for himself in this world by compromise with the forces that control it, and to become indebted to the devil in the manner that every successful
person of the world is (Nolland, 1989: 180). The parallel
between Lk 4:5-7 and Rev 13:7b-8 is striking, and not to
be dismissed lightly as some scholars do. In Revelation, the
beast from the sea is allowed to make war on the saints
and to conquer them:

> *It was given authority* over every tribe and people
> and language and nation, and *all the inhabitants of
> the earth will worship it,* everyone whose name has
> not been written from the foundation of the world

in the book of life of the Lamb that was slaughtered (Rev 13:7b-8).

The devil in Luke's account, like the beast from the sea in Revelation, "has been given authority" over the inhabited world. In Revelation the beast from the sea delegates his authority to a second beast, the "beast from the earth," or "false prophet," who works great signs; in Luke's account the devil *offers* to delegate authority to Jesus, and *suggests* to him that he work great signs. Had Jesus followed these instructions, he would have become a false prophet, like Simon Magus (Flusser, 1989: 115), serving the devil and working magical signs that redound to the devil's glory rather than to the glory of God (Creed, 1957: 63). Having thus convinced Jesus into serving him rather than God, the devil would have foiled the divine plan for Jesus' life and retained for himself the authority and glory which are due God alone.

The issue of authority (*exousia*: "authority, power, dominion") appears to be a key factor in the struggle with the devil. But what does "authority" mean for Luke, and why does it have anything to do with the devil? The pericope about the centurion whose servant Jesus healed (Lk 7:2-10, parallel Mt 8:5-13) illustrates the meaning of the word in a neutral context. Here the centurion tells Jesus that it is unnecessary to trouble himself:

> But only speak the word and let my servant be healed. For I am also a man set under authority, with soldiers under me; and I say to one, "Go," and he goes, and to another, "Come," and he comes, and to my slave, "Do this," and the slave does it (Lk 7:7b-8).

The centurion is "set under authority," that is, subject to a higher power, and himself authorized by that power to command the forces under him. The soldiers "go" and "come" and "do this or that" because they recognize that their commander has been granted the authority needed to make and enforce such commands (see Lk 20:2,8).

The idea that God had authorized the devil's actions ("it has been given over to me" means "God has given it over to me") characterizes two of the three reports about Satan found in the Hebrew scriptures. In the Book of Job, Satan is a member of the heavenly court who explicitly requests and receives permission to test the faithful obedience of God's servant Job (Job 1:11-12; 2:5-6). In the fourth vision of Zechariah, Satan is one who stands near God's throne and accuses Joshua, the high priest of the returned exiles (Zech 3:1). In the other Old Testament appearance of Satan (1 Chron 21:1, in which there is no explicit or implicit indication that God has given authorization), Satan incites David to error by persuading him to carry out a census of the people. These texts illustrate three of the activities most often ascribed to Satan or the devil in subsequent literature: he tests (*Testament of Job* 4:4-9, where the concept of testing is clearly present, even if the technical terms are not), he accuses (*Jubilees* 1:20; 48:15), he leads astray (*Jubilees* 11:4-5; 22:16-17; *Testament of Job* 2:2-3:5; CD 12:2b-3). Even though Satan often seems to be God's opponent more than a divine functionary, the devil was still supposedly exercising authority that had been divinely delegated at some previous point in time (*Apocalypse of Abraham* 13:9-13; 23:11-13). The devil claims brokerage rights over all the kingdoms of the inhabited world and promises them to Jesus. In the world of politics all normally have their price. Will Jesus opt for the standard success criteria or will he choose God's directions? If Jesus renounces the offer, he must feel the destructive weight of the system. Caiaphas and Pilate, connivers in distribution of power, will crush him. And the long history of the institutionalized church illustrates how difficult it is to keep distorted political ambition from contaminating the mission of the people of God. Not government or administration as such is here challenged by the evangelist, but any attempt to reduce God's revolutionary action in Jesus to power grabs in the name of religion is here given its proper ancestry (Danker, 1988: 102).

That the devil had forces under his own authority became increasingly popular in the Hellenistic and Roman periods (see Lk 11:14-23; 13:10-17; *Jubilees* 10:7-13; Kirchschlager, 1981: 45-54). Luke accepts this view, identifying Satan with Beelzebul, the ruler of demons (Lk 11:15,18,19). Thus Satan's "kingdom" includes the demonic realm. Luke portrays Satan as a strong one, who is "well-armed" and who trusts in his many possessions, that is, the humans inhabited by Satan's minions, the demons. Such unfortunate humans suffer from a variety of ailments. Clearly the prevalence on every side of demon possession, sickness, and death epitomized for Luke the oppressive power of Satan in the world. Some scholars have emphasized the "demonization" of Luke's narrative (Busse,1977: 23-24,79-80,90,114,181-182,219,285,288,297,302). But Luke also shared with many of his contemporaries the belief that the advent of the messiah and the end of the age would coincide with the demise of Satan's forces (see, e.g., Jn 12:31; Rom 16:20; Rev 20:1-3; *Jubilees* 23:29; 50:5; 1 *Enoch* 69:27-29; 1 QM 1:1; 4:1b-2a; 11:8, etc.). When Jesus exorcises or heals humans, he is said to be "plundering" Satan's kingdom, taking "spoil" from its lord (Lk 11:22; cf. 13:26). At Jesus' first exorcism (Lk 4:31-37) the demon cries out, "Have you come to destroy us?" The answer is certainly Yes (Garrett, 1989: 39-40).

The devil's statement in Lk 4:5-6 that he has received authority over the kingdoms of "the inhabited world" refers, however, not only to his authority over demons and the scattered individuals they afflict. Given Luke's horror at the prospect of misdirected worship, the devil's arrogation of divine glory — culminating in his brazen effort to persuade Jesus to worship him — must have drastic consequences. Accordingly, Lk 4:6-7 ought to be paired with the remark in Lk 10:18 about Satan's fall. There are precedents for an association between such events: in Isa 14:4-20, a taunt song for the king of Babylon that was reinterpreted sometime in or around the first century to refer to Satan (*Life of Adam and Eve [Vita]* 12:1-16:3), the king's desire for divine status causes him to "fall from heaven" (verse 13). In the narrative world of Luke's Gospel, Satan genuinely does possess the authority and glory of the kingdoms of the world, for many are indeed under his sway. But this intollerable situation cannot last indefinitely. Since God alone is to be worshiped and served, this challenge will lead to Satan's demise (Garrett, 1989: 40-41). After the first engagement with Jesus, the devil did not withdraw from the contest but bided his time; throughout Jesus' public ministry the devil worked underground — or, more accurately, *on* the ground — through human agents (Pagels, 1995: 90).

The devil offers Jesus the kingdom of David, grown to the proportions of world empire. This hope is all over Scripture. Israel burned with desire for some form of its fulfillment. Jesus could not but have internalized that desire: freedom from Roman oppression, restoration of God's nation, the vindication of Yahweh's honor. Consider Jesus' context. The heavy foot of Rome was on the people's neck, and that alien occupation was itself a denial of God's sovereignty and an obstacle to the coming of God's promised reign of justice and peace (see, e.g., the promises scattered through Isa 40-66). If Jesus' vocation was to participate in that divine reign, surely the means are secondary to the end, and the theological details can be ironed out later. But Jesus' response is the first commandment, "Worship the Lord your God and serve only him" (Deut 6:13). As tempting as such political rationales might be to an occupied and suffering people, the tradition is harsh in its linking political compromise with betrayal of the most basic commandment to worship only God (Ringe, 1995: 59-60). God is the God who demands exclusive worship. Hence neutrality is impossible. But part of the claim of God is via the claims associated with his kingdom; and any rival "kingdom" is here claimed to be demonic in origin. Above all, the kingdom *of God* is associated with the "poor," and any anxious concern about money or the like is implicitly classified as a form of demonic idolatry (Tuckett, 1992: 506).

The devil presents Jesus with well-attested scriptural expectations which everyone assumed were God's chosen means of redeeming Israel. The devil throws up to Jesus the collective messianic hopes, and by so doing brings them for the first time to consciousness as options to be chosen rather than as a fate to be accepted. Tested against Jesus' own sense of calling, they did not fit. Jesus could perceive them to be "yesterday's will of God," not what was coming out of the mouth of God. One does not need to "live by every word that comes from the mouth of the Lord" in order to be a "good Christian" — which is anyway always defined by some denomination or strong religious personality or creed. One need only to be pliant, docile, and obedient. Is it not easier to "let Jesus do it all for us," rather than embark on the risky, vulnerable, hazardous journey of seeking to find God's will in all its mundane specificity for our own lives? That harder way will certainly entail mistakes and failures, false starts. When Jesus is depicted as leaving the wilderness and moving "with a sure, fierce love towards Galilee" (Moon, 1972: 20) he does so not so much knowing *who he is and what he will do*, as *who he is not and what he will not do*. The rest will emerge through listening, through being true to the baptismal voice as the vital force of his being (Wink: 1986: 18-19).

Luke has made two important changes in his account of the second temptation. As already seen above, the first concerns the scene: the vision is not one that could be had from a high mountain; it is of a different order. This revision is the result of Luke's concern for plausibility. The other change is found in the words of the devil promising to give Jesus total power over the inhabited world, in twenty-eight words in Luke as against eight in Matthew [in Greek]. Luke's interest in the devil, as against Matthew's focus on Jesus can be explained by the fact that in Luke's perspective Satan is the principal actor in the drama of the Passion (see below). The full significance of these revisions will become clear when they can be compared to Luke's conclusion to this episode (Dupont, 1966: 214-215).

After the devil's promise Luke gives an explanatory clause, "for it has been given over to me, and I give it to anyone I please." The idea was familiar to Judaism and to the early Church. The world is subject to the power of "the prince of this world."

The scriptural quotation of Jesus' response is preceded in Matthew by some words in direct address: "Away with you, Satan." Exegetical opinion is divided as to whether this was in the common source of Matthew and Luke. However, since Luke does not end the temptations at this point, he could not have Jesus reply with an order for Satan to leave.

Verses 9-12: (9)   Then the devil took him to Jerusalem,
                     and placed him on the pinnacle of the temple,
                     saying to him,
                     "If you are the Son of God,
                     throw yourself down from here,
              (10)   for it is written,
                     'He will command his angels concerning you,
                        to protect you,'
              (11)   and
                     'On their hands they will bear you up,
                     so that you will not dash your foot against a
                        stone.'"
              (12)   Jesus answered him,
                     "It is said,
                     'Do not put the Lord your God to the test.'"

The struggle may begin in the wilderness but it must eventually be brought to the city, the seat of authority and power (Fuliga, 1994: 181). Indeed, the setting of the third temptation is on a lethal height in the temple complex (Young, 1995: 27). It has been pointed out that it is more likely that an author would change "the holy city" (Mt 4:5) into "Jerusalem," rather than the other way around. The use of *Hierousalēm* could also express Luke's special interest in the city of Jerusalem which has for him a highly saving historical meaning (*Hierousalēm* occurs sixty-three times in Luke-Acts over against twice in Matthew, none in Mark, none in John). The same Lukan interest may account for Luke's having situated the third and last temptation in Jerusalem. So, Jesus ends up on the pinnacle of the temple, but the exact locale is uncertain (Nolland, 1989: 181; Bock, 1994: 379). Most scholars take it to refer to the royal colonnade of the temple on the south side of the outer court. This overlooked a deep ravine and was high enough to cause giddiness (Josephus, *Antiquities* 15. 411f.; Marshall, 1978: 172-173). The selection of the temple as the site of the temptation likely relates to its significance as the dwelling place of God. What the devil is asking Jesus to do is to put God to the test, and the temple is the most natural place to do this (Gerhardsson, 1966: 56-58; Page, 1995: 96).

To the first test Jesus had replied that he would live "by every word that comes from the mouth of the Lord" (Deut 8:3, the continuation of "one does not live by bread alone"). The devil now takes Jesus on his word and cites such a word: "*It is written*, 'He will command his angels concerning you' and 'on their hands they will bear you up, so that you will not dash your foot against a stone'" (Ps 91:11-12). The devil, twice repulsed with Scripture texts, now tries a text himself. Put God to the test. Trust God's promises, "If you are the Son of God, throw yourself down" from the pinnacle of the temple in Jerusalem (Wink, 1986: 17). As with each of the other temptations we have here a private transaction between Jesus and the devil. It is wrong, therefore, to create a crowd of observers to help explain the temptation, as is regularly done (Nolland, 1989: 181). In his account of the third temptation, Luke gives fuller quotations from Scripture than Matthew. It is striking that in Matthew all of the responses of Jesus are a little longer, while Luke lingers on the interventions of the devil. The devil's role is developed at length in the second temptation and a more complete statement is ascribed to him in the third. Matthew's attention is concentrated on the words of Jesus; Luke's is focused on the devil and his discourse. The text of the third temptation in Luke does not give any indication of his purpose in leaving this temptation as the final one. In the present text here is nothing that emphasizes the importance of where this test took place: Jerusalem, the Temple (Dupont, 1966: 215).

Jesus again refuses: "Do not put the Lord your God to the test." He quotes from Deut 6:16. At Masah the people confronted God (Moses) about the preservation of their lives (Ex 17:3). But the faithful person does not seek to dictate to God how he must express his covenant loyalty and fulfill his promises. That would be to put God to the test (Nolland, 1989: 181). To live by what one has heard from God does not mean biblical proof-texting (the devil can quote the word of God!). It means listening to what God says to us about the specific life-tasks to which we are called. The word of God must be found and heard among all the turmoil of voices of Scripture, tradition, creed, doctrine, experience, science, intuition, the community; but God's word is none of these alone, or perhaps even all of them together. Jesus is being nudged by God toward a new, unprecedented thing, for which no model existed. No one else could have helped advise him. Scripture itself seemed to be loaded in the opposite direction — toward messianic models of power, might, and empire (Wink, 1986: 18). That is exactly what we got in the second test (in Luke; in Matthew the sequence of the second and third tests is different and, according to most scholars original).

Verse 13:   When the devil had finished every test,
             he departed from him until an opportune time.

The conclusion of the account differs coinsiderably in Luke and Matthew. The latter, whose text is identical with Mk 1:13b, ends the account by showing us Jesus ministered to by angels. Luke ends by anticipating that the devil will retire only "until an opportune time." [This phrase occurs in only one other place in the New Testament, in Acts 13:11]. Matthew speaks to us of Jesus; Luke speaks to us of the devil. Luke shows that he envisions another scene and warns the reader that the devil will reappear, that the temptations in the desert are not an isolated event.

Luke's concern to bind together certain remote episodes should alert us to what he wished to indicate as the end of the history of temptations. Since the devil has retired only "until an opportune time," when will he reappear? The answer is that Luke explicitly presents the devil as an actor in the Passion. The Passion of Jesus is part of a cosmic drama in which ultimate goodness and ultimate evil struggle for victory (Senior, 1989: 32; Neyrey, 1985: 31-33). The Passion account begins with the betrayal by Judas. At this point Luke adds a significant detail: "Then Satan entered into Judas" (Lk 22:3). This is the devil's re-entrance (Ringe, 1995: 61). Behind his enemies, Jesus recognizes the adversary who incites them and he declares this at his arrest. Luke alone adds to Jesus' response to those who come to arrest him: "But this is your hour, and the power of darkness" (Lk 22:53b). The "hour" of the enemies of Jesus is actually that of the power of darkness; they are merely instruments (Dupont, 1966: 215).

Luke concludes his account of the testing with the remark that when the devil had finished all the tests he withdrew from Jesus for a while (Lk 4:13). The remark has generated controversy ever since Hans Conzelmann claimed that it marked the beginning of a "Satan-free" period to last for the duration of Jesus' ministry (Conzelmann, 1960:

16,80-81,132,156-157,200). In order to make such a claim, Conzelmann took the phrase *syntelesas panta peirasmon* absolutely ("the devil had finished *every* temptation") rather than in context, that is, as referring to every temptation in the forty days just described (Conzelmann, 1960: 28). This unbalance, combined with an equally extravagant emphasis on the ambiguous temporal expression that is variously translated "for a while" or "until an opportune time" (*achri kairou*), led Conzelmann to focus too much attention on its implications for the events immediately preceding. In other words, Conzelmann did not ask why Jesus' successful endurance of the devil's tests should have caused the devil to withdraw. Since the remark about this withdrawal serves primarily as a conclusion to the testing narrative, and only secondarily as an introduction to Jesus' subsequent ministry, this is a critical question.

Luke's editorial attention to the devil's departure may in the first place have been prompted by his familiarity with a stereotyped pattern of mythical events. This hypothesis is supported by two roughly contemporaneous texts from outside the New Testament in which a righteous or Spirit-filled individual "conquers" (*nikan*) the devil by successfully enduring his onslaught thereby causing the devil shame and to depart. In the *Testament of Job*, a document dating from sometime between the first century B.C. and first century A.D., Job's staunch endurance of Satan's attack causes the devil to concede defeat (*Testament of Job* 27:2-6). In Lk 4:13 also, the notice about the withdrawal apparently points in the first place backwards, to underscore Jesus' victory. It is true that Luke does not explicitly refer to the testing as a struggle or use the word "conquer" in Lk 4:13, but in Lk 11:22, Luke changes Mark's *dēsai*, "bind" (Mk 3:27), to *nikēsai*, "overcome." Luke's attention for the withdrawal of the devil is plausibly explained by the assumption that he knew of such tradition (Garrett, 1989: 131).

But does the phrase "until an opportune time" or "for a

while" also point forward, to Satan's later resumption of activity at the Passion? This was the argument of Conzelmann, who concluded that the interim between the wilderness confrontation and Satan's entry into Judas in Lk 22:3 was therefore free from Satan's attacks (rejected by Marshall, 1978: 174). Some even argue that Lk 4:13 signals an end to temptation or testing (*peirasmos*) not only during Jesus' earthly ministry but during the time of the Church as well (though they say that Satan does pursue other forms of attack; S. Brown, 1969: 6-19). Of course, one can agree with Conzelmann's premise that the phrase *achri kairou* points ahead while rejecting his subsequent inference that Jesus' ministry was therefore Satan-free. It is likely that in saying that Satan withdrew "until an opportune time" Luke was indeed hinting that the devil was not yet finished with Jesus. This does not, however, imply that Luke deliberately created the myth of a bounded interim period utterly free from Satan's activity and presence. Conzelmann loads more weight onto Lk 4:13 than it can bear: the statement is primarily significant for what it says, not about the absolute quality or precise duration of Satan's resultant absence, but about Jesus' victory, of which Satan's withdrawal was both consequence and proof. Jesus is the "stronger one" who has conquered the "strong one" (Lk 11:22). He has thereby demonstrated that his own authority (Lk 4:32,36) is greater than the devil's, with the result that when accosted the demons suddenly recognize and obey Jesus (Lk 4:34,41), making exorcisms possible. To emphasize this new position of authority, Luke has Jesus immediately preach a sermon about "release to the captives" (Lk 4:18) and follow this up with a series of illustrative healings and exorcisms. A number of scholars hold that Acts 10:38 alludes back to Lk 4:18 (itself a quotation of Isa 61:1), which is significant since Acts 10:38 explicitly describes Jesus lifework as one of "healing those oppressed by Satan" (Busse, 1977: 184). But Satan, even if he has temporarily ceased to attack Jesus directly, is not completely absent. Luke probably sees

Satan as making his presence felt in other ways during Jesus' ministry, for example, in the people's frequent testing of Jesus (Garrett, 1989: 41-43).

Unlike Mark and Matthew, who affirm that angels "waited on" or served Jesus in the wilderness (Mk 1:13; Mt 4:11), Luke leaves Jesus in the care of the Holy Spirit alone, both there and in his whole ministry. In Luke, the angel's care for Jesus comes only on the Mount of Olives (Lk 22:43), when a time of renewed and even harsher human testing is about to begin (Ringe, 1995: 61).

The superhuman struggle between the Son of God and the devil is located at the level of human beings and takes the form of a rabbinical dialogue or debate between protagonists who hit each other with verses from the Bible (Bultmann, 1972: 254,256 Bovon, 1991: 196). Alongside the imitation of the Scriptures that draws its inspiration from the narrative forms, and biblical prophecy looking for fulfillment, there is here a third usage of the Scriptures. The latter are seen here as a norm that applies not just now and then but permanently. The future tense used in the citations is the future not of prophetic promise but of concrete obedience.

Both parties accept the scriptures as law. Jesus recalls the passages that fit the circumstances and shows his adversary how to use them properly. Against the devil's misuse of Scripture Jesus appeals to Moses. The Scriptures serve as an explicitly cited norm for the decisions and actions of Jesus, who is presented as a hero of faith and obedience. The devil's formal fidelity but real infidelity to the Scriptures is met by the faithful fidelity of Jesus, a fidelity characterized by trust and dedication. Thanks to the passages he chooses, Jesus outlines a behavior, based on faith, that the people should have demonstrated at the exodus: reliance on the word of God (Deut 8:3), determination to adore God and God alone (Deut 6:13), refusal to put God to the test (Deut 6:16).

This is an obedience that is not so much moral as theological. The Son of God chooses to use neither the miracle-working power which he possesses (he refuses to transform a stone into a loaf of bread) nor the political power that is his inheritance (he renounces the kingdoms of this world) nor the immunity attested by the princely escort at his disposal (he does without the help of angels' wings). The story of the temptations is messianic but also ethical and theological and can be read as christological as well as paraenetic. It leads us to the Scriptures as well as to other areas by reason of new events and experiences. Here on this still unknown terrain of spiritual experience and testing, Jesus, the principal protagonist, who is located, if we may so put it, in his own time and context, refers to Scripture as norm of faith and life. This is one of the more important things Luke is saying in his account of the temptations (Bovon, 1993: 30-31).

JESUS' MINISTRY IN AND AROUND GALILEE (LK 4:14-9:50)

I. The Beginning of the Ministry in Nazareth and Capernaum

1. Return to Galilee (Lk 4:14-15)

While appearing in Luke's text at the point corresponding to Mk 1:14-15, Lk 4:14-15 is not simply to be regarded
as a free redaction of these verses. Luke has made use of
Mk 1:14,28 and 39 to produce a generalizing summary of
the sort that Luke uses in Acts (Fitzmyer, 1981: 522). It has
been proposed that Lk 4:14-15 reflects a special source parallel to Mk 1:14,28,39 (6:1) (Schürmann, 1969:221-224), but
recently one has been able to offer plausible alternative explanations for most of the features of the text in which
the use of such a source was found reflected, thereby supporting Lukan redaction (Delobel, 1989: 113-133, 306-312;
Fitzmyer, 1981: 521; Nolland, 1989: 185).

Verses 14-15: (14) Then Jesus, filled with the power of the Spirit,
returned to Galilee.
and a report about him spread throughout all
the surrounding country.
(15) He began to teach in their synagogues
and was praised by everyone.

In contrast to Mk 1:14-15, these verses omit a significant element. There is no mention at the outset of Jesus'
kerygmatic proclamation of the kingdom and the gospel or

of his call for repentance. The two verses serve as a generalizing introduction to the accounts of concrete ministry in Nazareth and Capanaum: Jesus has this kind of ministry throughout Galilee (Lk 4:44 later generalizes it further to all Judaea and also serves to mark the boundary of the section commented on by verses 14-15). The ministry involved is characterized as one of mighty works and synagogue teaching, both in the power of the Spirit (Nolland, 1989: 187-188).

This summary is marked by three distinctive Lukan features. First, a leitmotiv is presented in the phrase "filled with the power of the Spirit." The period of Jesus is thus inaugurated. Since the Spirit will later be presented as an inspiring and formative agent in the early Christian community, Luke takes care to present Jesus' ministry as guided by the same Spirit's "power." There is continuity between the period of Jesus and the period of the Church. Second, though verse 15 does not read like a logical continuation to verse 14, Jesus' activity is first of all described as "teaching." This implies that this activity too is being conducted under the power of the Spirit. This is important for the entire purpose of Luke-Acts: Jesus must be seen "teaching" those things about which Theophilus is being given assurance (Lk 1:4). Third, the note of Lukan universality appears in the summary in that Jesus is "praised by *all* the people" (Fitzmyer, 1981: 522).

Lk 4:14 serves a double purpose. It closes the parentheses around the previous account by the reference to Jesus as "filled with the power of the Spirit," just as earlier he was said to be "full of the Holy Spirit" and "led by the Spirit" in the wilderness (Lk 4:1). At the same time, Lk 4:14-15 introduces the following section. The action is set in Galilee, and the specific incidents are narrated against the background of Jesus' growing fame and his practice of beginning his teaching in the Galilean synagogues (Ringe, 1995: 66).

Luke has not explicitly mentioned Jesus' departure from Galilee. The use of "returned" (*hypestrepsen*) refers rather to his coming from the baptism (and the temptations). These have a fundamental role for the ministry in the power of the Spirit now to be exercised. As to the reason why Jesus returned to Galilee, it has been suggested that he went there to take the place of John the Baptist after the latter had been arrested by Herod Antipas. Luke expresses the role of the Spirit with Jesus variously (Lk 3:22; 4:1,14,18; 5:11; 10:21). The meanings are not identical but each identifies Jesus as a pneumatic figure: not ruled by the Spirit but operating in the sphere of the Spirit and with the power of the Spirit at his disposal (Schürmann, 1969: 222; Nollland, 1989: 186).

The report (*phēmē*, the source of our English term "fame") about Jesus went out into the whole region. Jesus' ministry drew quick attention and Lk 4:15 will erxplain why. This is the first of several notes about how people initially responded to Jesus (Lk 4:22, 28,32,36-37). The response was varied. But initially it was certainly favorable. Luke also notes such reports about Jesus elsewhere (Lk 5:15; 7:17). Jesus' work received a lot of attention (see Acts 26:26; Bock, 1994: 391-392)...

The source of the public interest was Jesus' synagogue preaching. The origin of synagogues, which rabbinic sources ascribed quite unhistorically to Moses, is still shrouded in mystery. The word *synagoge* is not used in the Old Testament for a building or place of assembly. It first appears in this sense in the first century A.D. in Josephus, Philo and the New Testament. Some hold that synagogues arose during the Babylonian exile (587-538 B.C.), when the temple could no longer be a focus of worship. Others think that they emerged in Palestine during the time of Ezra to give effect to his requirement that the people should be taught the law. Again others believe that they emerged in the Diaspora in the Hellenistic period to provide worship for those who lived far from the temple, and were transplanted thence to Palestine. Finally some others again think that they were copied from secular assemblies in the Greco-Roman world and given religious character. While synagogue worship stood alongside temple worship, by which it was not influenced, it was primarily lay, and was shaped by the central place in Judaism of the law and the prophets, and of their reading and exposition. Synagogues either had schools attached to them or were themselves used as schools. When the temple was destroyed they survived (C.F. Evans, 1990:264-265; cf. Prior, 1995: 102-110).

Primarily because of his teaching, Jesus "was praised by everyone." The imperfect verb (*edidasken*) is deliberate to establish the sense of repeated action; Jesus was making a circuit of local communities before he came to his own. The verb "to praise" (*doxazō*) is used of a positive response to Jesus' work in Lk 5:25-26; 7:16; 18:43; 23:47. The "everyone" is important for it sets up the contrast to Jesus' townspeople rejection of him (Johnson, 1991: 78).

2. Jesus' Preaching at the Synagogue of Nazareth (Lk 4:16-30)

It is widely recognized that this pericope in Luke is extremely important for Luke's overall literary plan, functioning as a programmatic summary of the story that is to follow in his two-volume work: the rejection of Jesus in his hometown prefigures the rejection of Jesus in the passion, and that of the gospel by the Jewish nation, the Gentile mission being alluded to in the notes about Elijah and Elisha (Lk 4:25-27; Conzelmann, 1960: 31-38; Fitzmyer, 1981: 526; Tannehill, 1986: 61), though some doubts have been expressed recently about whether there is really any allusion to the Gentile mission in the references to Elijah and Elisha (Koet, 1989: 42-52; Tuckett, 1996a: 227 note 61).

1. Introduction

Structure of the Pericope

Lk 4:16-30 definitely fits its immediate context within the overall composition or macrostructure of the Gospel (Busse, 1978: 13-15; Scheffler, 1993: 27). It is a self-contained and relatively independent text unit as is clearly shown by the inclusion formed by the beginning, "When he came to Nazareth, where he had been brought up" (Lk 4:16) and the conclusion, "But he passed through the midst of them and went on his way" (Lk 4:30). The beginning of the pericope is demarcated by the redactional note in Lk 4:14-15, and its end is demarcated by the note in Lk 4:31-32. It is fixed in place, the synagogue (Lk 4:16,20,28), and time, a sabbath (Lk 4:16). After the Nazareth incident the scene shifts to Capernaum, on a different sabbath (Lk 4:31) and in another synagogue (Lk 4:33). Lk 4:31-32 marks the transition from the Nazareth scene to what happened in Capernaum (Lk 4:33-43; Chiappini, 1990: 229-237; Prior, 1995: 150-151).

The main line of the account is very clear: "He," that is Jesus, last mentioned in Lk 4:14, came to Nazareth and went to the synagogue on the sabbath as his custom was. He was given the book/scroll of Isaiah and read a passage from it. Then he applied the text to himself. The synagogue public reacted with amazement. His further discourse led the synagogue public to great anger. They wanted to throw him down from the hill outside the city. But he walked away from them (Noorda, 1989: 219).

The interaction between Jesus and his audience consists of three phases:

The *first phase* of the interaction pattern appears in Lk 4:16c-20. This phase consists of two parts: (1) Lk 4:16c-20a, Jesus' actions, and (2) Lk 4:20b, the audience's reaction. Tightly linked to the preceding, the actual action starts in Lk 4:16c. Jesus remains the main actor until 4:20b. One can arrange Lk 4:16-20 in a way that shows the first part to be mirrored in the second, with the mirror, so to speak, being at the critical point of contact between the two parts (Tiede, 1980: 35; Prior, 1995: 151). The quotation in Lk 4:18-19 is framed by two parts displaying a concentric pattern.

A He stood up to read,
B and the scroll of the prophet Isaiah was given to him.
    C He unrolled the scroll and found the place where
      it was written:
        Isa 61:1; 58:6.
    C' And he rolled up the scroll,
B' gave it back to the attendant,
A' and sat down (Busse, 1977: 36; Talbert, 1984: 54-55; Kyo-Seon Shin, 1989: 117).

The *second phase* of the interaction is described in Lk 4:21-22. Jesus' reaction to the people's expectation is found in his statement of Lk 4:21b. The audience reacts with a question (Lk 4:22).

The *third phase* is found in Lk 4:23-29. Jesus' reaction to the question of the audience, consisting of two parts, each one introduced by "he said" (Lk 4:23,24), is a description of the reaction of the listeners. When the audience rises to cast Jesus down from the hill, he abruptly ends the interaction.

In Lk 4:30 the pericope comes to an end. This verse has a double function. As said above, it constitutes an inclusion with Lk 4:16 and describes Jesus' final reaction to his audience in Nazareth. The repetition of the proposition *dia* (*dielthon dia*) stresses the fact that Jesus walks right through the audience and thereby definitely ends the interaction (Koet, 1989: 27-28; compare Prior, 1995: 151-154).

Programmatic Character

Lk 4:16-30 has a definite programmatic character (Fitzmyer, 1981: 529; Nolland, 1989: 195), and, in a sense, the whole of Luke-Acts is indeed found in Lk 4:16-30 (Radl, 1988: 43). Jesus' opening sermon in the Nazareth synagogue interprets his ministry as a whole and anticipates his later rejection (Tannehill, 1986: 61). It has also been maintained that the setting of the sermon and its consequences (i.e., its emplotment) lead to viewing Jesus' additional sermons in Lk 4—10, that is, the "Sermon on the Plain" (Lk 6:20-49), the parable discourse (Lk 8:4-21) and the mission discourse (Lk 10:1-16), as descriptive for the narrative sections that follow them (Staley, 1993: 282). In fact, almost every scene in Luke-Acts can be related to Lk 4:16-30, especially the Galilean ministry (Gowler, 1991: 180-181).

The pericope stands as the cornerstone of *Luke's* entire theological program. This conclusion is quite generally accepted and stems from two observations. Firstly, most scholars think that Luke alters Mark's chronology in order to place this pericope at the outset of Jesus' ministry (Fitzmyer, 1981: 526; Johnson, 1990: 80-81; Diefenbach, 1993:73-74). Luke feels compelled to present the Nazareth passage at the beginning of Jesus' ministry because he sees it as programmatic for all of Jesus' ministry (Shelton, 1991: 69). Secondly, the pericope combines the major theological themes of Luke-Acts: the work of the Spirit, the universality of the Gospel, the grace of God, and the rejection of Jesus (Menzies, 1991: 161-162). But scholars can agree wholeheartedly on the programmatic nature of the passage and still fiercely disagree on the nature of the program (Schreck, 1989: 399).

Lk 4:16-30 is also programmatic in another way. The Isaiah quotation in Lk 4:18-19 is a characterization of Jesus' prophetic activities. According to Luke, Jesus' visit to the synagogue in Nazareth is his debut. It is a preview of his mission and of the mission of his disciples (compare Lk 4:18-19 with the description of Jesus' mission in Lk 4:43 and the mission of the twelve in Lk 9:1-2; see 10:1; Koet, 1989: 55).

Finally, it has been said that Lk 4:16-30 is programmatic for the Lukan version of Jesus' passion (Busse, 1977: 28-29). The attempt to hurl Jesus from the cliff makes the reader suspect that Jesus will in all probability be killed by his opponents because of his ministry. However, in view of a broader discussion of Luke-Acts, the treatment that Jesus received at Nazareth alludes to both the final passion and the rejection he suffered during his ministry before his passion (Scheffler, 1993: 109-110).

Source Criticism

The fundamental source-critical question here is whether or not Lk 4:16-30 is to be considered basically dependent upon Mk 6:1-6a. Majority opinion has continued to affirm dependence upon Mark (Schreck, 1989: 404-407; Prior, 1995: 82-83). But a significant minority of authors have, in recent times, argued in favor of the pericope's dependence upon a non-Markan source in addition to, or as an alternative to, Mark (Schreck, 1989: 407-410). Finally, a number of authors who have recently treated the question have remained uncommitted (Schreck, 1989: 410-411).

Those who accept dependence, in whole or in part, upon Mk 6:1-6a are able to recognize the Markan material taken over by Luke. Among the motifs which Lk 4:16-30 has drawn from Mark's account of the Nazareth visit can be listed:

(1) Jesus' visit to his own hometown (Mk 6:1; Lk 4:16,23);
(2) teaching/speaking in the synagogue on the sabbath (Mk 6:2; Lk 4:16);
(3) the synagogue audience's reaction of astonishment/wonderment (Mk 6:2; Lk 4:22);
(4) the question about Jesus' origins (Mk 6:3; Lk 4:22);
(5) Jesus' response: the saying about the prophet (Mk 6:4; Lk 4:24);
(6) the impossibility/refusal to work many miracles in Nazareth (Mk 6:5; Lk 4:28-29);
(7) rejection (Mk 6:3; Lk 4:28-29).

Moreover, by his transportation of the scene forward from the Markan order, Luke has made the Nazareth visit a programmatic proclamation of Jesus' message and mission, thus taking over, by position and function as well as by content, motifs from Mk 1:14-15. Among these one can cite:

(1) Jesus' return to Galilee (Mk 1:14; Lk 4:14);
(2) Jesus' proclamation of the Gospel (Mk 1:14-15; Lk 4:18);
(3) Jesus' announcement of fulfillment (Mk 1:15; Lk 4:21; Schreck: 1989: 411).

Nothwithstanding some significant and provocative recent challenges to the majority opinion, most authors are unwilling to claim that Luke's Nazareth account is basically independent from Mark. The prevailing opinion continues to be that Lk 4:16-30 is best explained solely as Lukan redaction of Mk 6:1-6a (Shelton, 1991: 65-66; Scheffler, 1993: 31-37). But recently scholars have been reminded that this question should be clarified by a recognition that Markan creativity is most probably responsible for more or less the whole of Mk 6:1-6a and that the conclusion that Mark is responsible for virtually all of Mk 6:1-6a has a powerful bearing on the source criticism of Lk 4:16-30 (Catchpole, 1993: 232-234).

Internal Coherence

A question not unrelated to the assessment of Lukan redaction in Lk 4:16-30 concerns the problem of internal coherence (Prior, 1995: 90-100). It has even been said that Luke has given us an impossible story (Leaney, 1958: 52). If one takes the story as it stands, then a presumably favorable, highly attentive reaction on the part of the synagogue audience (Lk 4:22) suddenly turns into open hostility and a prelude to mob violence (Lk 4:28-29). In the past some commentators explained the crowd's rejection of Jesus as

resulting from his (assumedly purposeful) provocation beginning with the "offensive" proverb, "Doctor, cure yourself" (Lk 4:23). It is undeniable that Jesus himself takes the
initiative by speaking again after the caesura of agreeable
reaction in Lk 4:22. However, there is nothing "offensive"
or insulting in the words of the proverb itself. Even the
first cryptic saying about the prophet (Lk 4:24) might be
positively received. It seems then that it is rather the ensuing commentary in Lk 4:25-27 that the assembly must have
found inacceptable.

After opening up the touchy subject of the lack of reception accorded a prophet in his own country (Lk 4:24),
the hometown's messiah's words about the works of Elijah
and Elisha accomplished at a time — not unlike Jesus' own
— when many in Israel were suffering and found no relief,
are utterly provocative (Schreck, 1989: 427-428). Of course,
some obscurity may be intentional, or at least suitable to
complex situations. Mob scenes at Nazareth (Lk 4:28-29),
Corinth (Acts 18:12-17) and Ephesus (Acts 19:23-41) are
not explained as logical performances (Cadbury, 1958: 334).
Luke's redaction of the scene is far from casual. He must
certainly have realized that the psychological straightline
was thereby disturbed but he took this in his stride (Lohfink,
1975: 46). The suggestion that we are dealing in Lk 4:16-
30 with a conflation of sources is a recourse of desperation,
and is dismissive of the literary skills of the author (Prior,
1995: 99).

The overwhelming majority of interpreters continue to
hold that the initial reaction of the crowd to Jesus' speech
in Lk 4:22 is to be understood positively (differently, e.g.,
Jeremias, 1958: 45) and that supposed incoherences within
the scene are both attributed to and explainable within the
framework of the Lukan redactional decision, in particular
Luke's fundamental decision to transpose the scene out of
its Markan order to make it a programmatic introduction
to Jesus' public ministry as well as to that of the Church.

From all the above, it should be clear that we are not dealing here with any real synagogue sermon that the real Jesus preached in the real Nazareth, but rather with a narrative that Luke has constructed for a purpose. Luke built, of course, on the Synoptic tradition (Sanders, 1987: 166, 386).

Liberationist Approach

With the rise of liberation theology has come a corresponding increase of exegetical interest in Lk 4:16-30 and especially in Jesus' prophetic announcement with its themes of "good news to the poor," "release (*aphesis*) to captives," and "liberty (*aphesis*) (for) those who are oppressed" (Lk 4:18). A perusal of the literature verifies the ample number of studies explicitly concerned with this proclamation as well as with the larger social issues of wealth and poverty in Luke-Acts. M.V. Abraham is one of the most recent representatives of the liberationist approach to the passage in his rejection of any spiritualized or allegorical interpretation as well as in his upholding of the consensus view that *aphesis* must be understood as implying total liberation of the whole person (Abraham, 1988: 71-72; see further Scheffler, 1991: 284-296).

2. Analysis of Lk 4:16-30

Verse 16-17:   (16)   When he came to Nazareth, where he had
                      been brought up,
                      he went to the synagogue on the sabbath
                      day, as was his custom.
                      And he stood up to read,
              (17)   and the scroll of the prophet Isaiah was given
                      to him.
                      He unrolled the scroll and found the place
                      where it was written:

Nazareth is thrice referred to in Luke's infancy narrative (Lk 2:4,39,51) and then for the last time in Luke here in

Lk 4:16, and further in Luke-Acts only in Acts 10:38. Ancient Nazareth was a relatively small village on a broad ridge between the Beth Netopha basin to the north and the Great Plain to the south. While Nazareth had clearly been occupied earlier, in the Middle Bronze Age and the Iron Age, recent interpreters conclude that a more substantial village was "refounded" in the second century B.C. (i.e., prior to the Hasmonean takeover in Galilee). This implies that the village was less than two-hundred years old in the first century A.D., but that it continued to be attractive to settlers. Estimates of the population of the village have come down recently, from an earlier estimate of 1600-2000 to a maximum of 480 at the beginning of the first century A.D. Nazareth was only three or four miles from the city of Sepphoris. Like other villages in Galilee, Upper and Lower, Nazareth was brought under the rule of the Jerusalem temple-state by the Hasmoneans about a hundred years before Jesus' birth. Assuming that the pre-Hasmonean villagers were descended from former Israelites, they already lived according to Mosaic covenantal traditions. It is unlikely, however, that Jerusalem priestly authorities and scribal retainers had mounted a serious program to "resocialize" Galilean villagers in order to bring local practice into conformity with the official Judaean Torah. All of the villages of western Lower Galilee were ruled and taxed from Sepphoris. Because of its proximity to Sepphoris, Nazareth would have been unusually sensitive to administrative pressures from the regime based there, whether that of Herod or Antipas, or others. Relations between villagers and their rulers were generally not harmonious. It is curious that most treatments of ancient Nazareth do not mention events in and around Sepphoris in 4 B.C. (about the time Jesus was born), that is, the popular insurrection led by Judah son of Hezekiah and the brutal Roman repression of the revolt with massive show of military force. These events not only manifest the conflict between Herodian rule and the Galilean peasantry that had been building toward an explosion but indicate the trauma that would have left a persistent wound in the village communities around Sepphoris for generations. The tensions between Sepphoris and the nearby villages such as Nazareth continued, escalating again into popular insurrection of villagers against their urban rulers at a later date (Horsley, 1996: 108-112).

With the emphasis on Nazareth as the place "where he had been brought up" (*tethrammenos* [perfect passive participle]) — which may be considered as a summary of Jesus' infancy — Luke prepares for the conflict between Jesus and his co-citizens (Ernst, 1977: 169; Kyo-Seon Shin, 1989: 111).

"Where he had been brought up" refers back to the infancy narrative, especially Lk 2:39-40,51-52, and prepares for Lk 4:23-24, "in your hometown...in the prophet's hometown." "As was his custom" refers back to Lk 4:15, that is, to his synagogue teaching habits (Busse, 1977: 31,56), not to his earlier practice in Nazareth, nor generally to his practice of attending the synagogue (different: Fitzmyer, 1981: 530; Kyo-Seon Shin, 1989: 113), and makes the Nazareth account into a concrete exemplification of Jesus' Galilean synague ministry (Nolland, 1989: 195). Likewise in Acts 17:1-3 we are told that Paul went to the synagogue, as he used to do.

According to Lk 4:15, Jesus had already been active in the synagogues of Galilee (plural). The singular use "synagogue" in Lk 4:16 clearly indicates that only the synagogue of his hometown is meant. Thereby it becomes clear that Jesus is rejected by the inhabitants of Nazareth, for in the other synagogues in Galilee (Lk 4:14-15), as well as in Capernaum (Lk 4:31-37), he receives a positive reaction (Kyo-Seon Shin, 1989: 114).

The expression " on the sabbath day" is found five times in Luke and thrice in Acts. Luke may be implying that Jesus was invited by the president of the synagogue assembly to read and expound a Scripture text, as happened to Paul and Barnabas in Antioch in Pisidia (Acts 13:15).

Luke's account is generally consistent with the format of the ancient synagogue service, as far as we know it. But it is foreshortened to eliminate everything that would keep Jesus from center-stage and that would detract from a sense of his total command of the situation (Haenchen, 1974: 294; Nolland, 1989: 194-196). A synagogue service had various elements: recitation of the *Shema* (Deut 6:4-9) which is a public confession of the Jewish faith, prayers (including some set prayers like the *Shemoneh Esreh* [Eighteen Benedictions]), a reading from the Torah (*seder*), a reading from the Prophets, instruction on the passages, and a benediction.

The exact nature of the synagogue service — including how fixed it was in this period — has been the subject of much discussion (Prior, 1995: 110-115). Although some claim that the synagogue readings were precisely fixed in an annual cycle that began in the month Nisan, our mid-March to mid-April (Goulder, 1978: 52-53), and others speak of a Jewish lectionary with a fixed cycle of readings every three years, such a schedule in this period seems unlikely. The Hebrew Scripture would be read in a standing position in one- to three-verse units. Then the text was translated into Aramaic, the local language, an oral procedure that often involved targumic renderings of the text (i.e., Aramaic paraphrases of the Hebrew Old Testament). The Torah was always read, and often a reading from the Prophets followed. After the reading came an invitation for someone to instruct the audience. Based on texts already read or on new texts, this instruction could be done by any qualified male in the audience, provided ten males were present.

Jesus "stood up" apparently to indicate that he could speak about a passage. He gave such a lesson from the Prophets, what was called the *Haftarah* (a reading from the Prophets). Jesus "was given" and "unrolled" the scroll to the place from which he would give instruction (Bock, 1994: 403-404). Some interpret the "finding" of the text as providential. Others wonder whether the clause means that he found the passage through divine guidance or that Jesus deliberately selected the text. Was it a regularly appointed text or did he choose it? Did Jesus himself add the allusion from Isa 58:6 to the reading from Isa 61? Or did this connection arise from Jewish or early Christian exposition of Isaiah or from Luke's own understanding? There seems to be no reason to take the phrase "he found the place where it was written" to mean a chance happening upon Isa 61. It sounds as if Jesus deliberately sought out the passage (Fitzmyer, 1981: 532).

Verses 18-19: (18) "The Spirit of the Lord is upon me,
because he has anointed me
to bring good news to the poor.
he has sent me
to proclaim release to captives
and recovery of sight to the blind,
to let the oppressed go free,
(19) to proclaim the year of the Lord's favor."

The quotation of Isa 61:1-2 and 58:6 is only one of several instances in which Luke relates the ministry of Jesus to the pronouncements of Isaiah. No other book of the Hebrew Bible is used as extensively in the New Testament. There are no fewer than 590 references in the New Testament to Isaiah, from 63 of its 66 chapters, with 238 from Isa 1—39, 240 from Isa 40—55 (Second Isaiah), and 111 from Isa 56—66 (Third Isaiah). Of these 590 references 78 are found in Luke (Sanders, 1987: 75; Prior, 1995: 130). Isa 61:1-2 may be regarded as a succinct statement of election traditions in which the oppressed and suffering are promised vindication and deliverance (C.A. Evans, 1987: 78).

It is not difficult to see why this text was congenial to Luke. The references to "the Spirit," "evangelizing," and "the poor" are all clearly of a piece with Luke's interests (Tuckett, 1996a: 231-232). Some scholars have understood these verses as a summary of the Gospel. "The Spirit of the Lord is upon me" refers back to Lk 3:22, "and the Holy Spirit descended upon him," as well as to Lk 4:1, "Jesus, full of the Holy Spirit, returned from the Jordan and was led by the Spirit ...," and Lk 4:14, "Then Jesus, filled with the power of the Spirit, returned to Galilee." The anointing by the Spirit has taken place at Jesus' baptism. In Isa 61 the anointing is clearly that of a prophet (see 1 Kgs 19:16; Acts 10:38, "how God anointed Jesus of Nazareth with the Holy Spirit and with power" (Nolland, 1989: 196). Clearly Luke is responsible for this positioning of references to the Spirit (Shelton, 1991: 67).

The quotation from Second Isaiah is actually a conflation of Isa 61:1a,b,d; 58:6d; 61:2a. There is no other example of a similarly mixed citation in Luke-Acts (Tuckett, 1996a: 232). It is a midrash-like text (Kyo-Seon Shin, 1989: 154). Two phrases are omitted: Isa 61:1c, "to bind up the broken-hearted" (at the end of verse 18); and Isa 61:2b, "the day of vengeance of our God." The latter is considered by many a deliberate suppression of a negative aspect of the Deutero-Isaian message (Fitzmyer, 1981: 532). The conflation of Isa 61:1 and 58:6 could surely not be read in any scroll of the synagogue collection; it represents a Christian "splicing" of separate passages to form a doubly emphatic testimony of the messianic "release" offered by Jesus (Dillon, 1979: 253). Though Luke uses *aphesis*, "release," (and *aphiemi*, "to release") almost exclusively to refer to forgiveness of sins, it is evident from such passages as Lk 4:38-39 and Lk 13:16, as well as from a series of healings and exorcisms following (and fulfilling) the Nazareth sermon, thast Luke also conceived of these miraculous deeds as a form of "release" (Garrett, 1989:141-142; Ringe, 1985: 65-80).

The citation in Lk 4:18-19 diverges from Isa 61:1-2 (LXX) at several points. It may be possible to determine whether the alterations point to a particular theological interest and, if so, whether this tendency corresponds to distinctive aspects of Luke's theological program expressed elsewhere.

Luke 4:18-19	*Isa 61:1-2 LXX*
The Spirit of the Lord is upon me	The Spirit of the Lord is upon me
because he has anointed me	because he has anointed me
to preach good news to the poor	to preach good news to the poor
he has sent me	he has sent me
	to bind up the brokenhearted
to proclaim release to captives	to proclaim release to captives
and recovering of sight to the blind	and recovering of sight to the blind
to let the oppressed go free	[to let the oppressed go free (Isa 58:6)]
to proclaim the year of the Lord's favor	to proclaim the year of the Lord's favor
	and the day of vengeance of our God.

Luke has clearly followed the Septuagint. He did not himself translate the Hebrew, or he would not so consistently have come up with the same translation as the Septuagint when so many possibilities exist (New, 1993: 90-93). As the comparison above indicates, the citation in Lk 4:18-19 deviates from the text of Isa 61:1-2 (LXX) at four points:

(1) The phrase "to bind up the brokenhearted" has been omitted;

(2) an excerpt from Isa 58:6 (LXX), "to let the oppressed go free," has been inserted into the quotation;

(3) the verb *kalesai*, "to call," has been altered into *keruxai*, "to proclaim";

(4) the final phrase of the Septuagint text, "and the day of vengeance of our God, has been omitted (for more details, see Kyo-Seon-Shin, 1989: 117-134).

Many scholars have indicated that the historicity of the general outline of Luke's account is credible. Jesus entered into the synagogue of Nazareth, read from the scroll of Isaiah, applied the passage to himself, and encountered resistance (Hill, 1971: 179).

However, it is unlikely that the variant form of Isa 61:1-2 found in Lk 4:18-19 stems from Jesus himself. It is difficult to imagine a synagogue reader taking such liberties with the text (Perrot, 1973: 327). Although considered of little consequence by some (Fitzmyer, 1981: 532), the insertion of the phrase from Isa 58:6 into the text of Isa 61:1-2 is particularly striking; for, although skipping verses was permissible in the *haphtara*, it is unlikely that such a rearrangement of the text would have been tolerated (Busse, 1978: 48-49; Bock, 1987: 107-108). We are, therefore, justified in concluding that it is improbable that Jesus himself, during the course of the *haphtara*, in a synagogue service, inserted Isa 58:6 into the text of Isa 61:1-2 and made the other alterations recorded in Lk 4:18-19.

The question that remains is, of course, whether the interpretative reproduction of the *haphtara*, in the form in which it is presented in Lk 4:18-19, stems from Luke or is carried over from pre-Lukan tradition. This calls for an analysis of the alterations of the text from Isaiah and the theological motivations that have produced them (Menzies, 1991: 165-166).

*The omission of "to bind up (iasasthai, literally 'to heal')
the brokenhearted."* First, it has often been suggested that Isa 61:1d has been omitted to make room for the insertion of Isa 58:6c, that is, that structural concerns motivated the omission (Busse, 1978: 34). But in view of the ambiguous

nature of the arguments from structure and the varied conclusions they have produced, it is unlikely that structural
elements played a significant role in the omission of Isa 61:1d
(Menzies, 1991: 166).

A second, more probable view is that Isa 61:1d is omitted because of Luke's prophetic understanding of the Spirit
(Rese, 1969: 214). This view accords quite well with an
analysis of Luke's redactional activity, although it has not
gone unchallenged in an unpublished PhD dissertation (Max
Turner, Chicago 1980). This dissertation questions especially
the view's basis, namely, that Luke adopts the typically Jewish
idea that the Spirit is the Spirit of revelation rather than
the source of inspired speech. But this distinction was alien
to rabbis, who commonly described the prophet simply as
one who "speaks in the Holy Spirit." The prophet was not
simply a person who received; he/she was the mouthpiece
of God. Revelation and proclamation go hand in hand, and
both are attributed to the Holy Spirit. While some passages
focus on the Spirit's role in the revelatory act, others, such
as Isa 61:1, focus on the prophet's Spirit-inspired utterance.
Numerous other texts indicate that the proposed distinction was not maintained. But the decisive objection is that
Luke himself connected the two. He explicitly describes Spirit-
inspired speech as prophetic activity in the infancy narratives and in Acts 1—2; and the idea is implicit in Lk 4:18-
19 (Isa 61:1-2). On the basis of the above we may conclude
that Luke was responsible for the omission of Isa 61:1d in
Lk 4:18 and that the motivation for this alteration came
from Luke's prophetic understanding of the Spirit. This
conclusion accords well with Luke's redactional activity elsewhere and offers a plausible explanation of an omission that
is otherwise difficult to explain (Menzies, 1991: 169-171).

*The insertion of Isa 58:6 (LXX), "to let the oppressed go
free" (literally, "to send away those who have been crushed in
release [aphesei]").* The text of Isa 58:1-12 originated apparently later than Isa 61:1-3. The temple had already been

rebuilt which would suggest a time between 515 and 450. B.C. (Albertz, 1983: 192; Kyo-Seon Shin, 1989: 124-127). The insertion was most probably made as a result of the verbal linkage that *aphesei* provides with the preceding clause, "to proclaim release [*aphesin*] to captives and recovering of sight to the blind." Some scholars suggest that the linkage was made by Luke because he interpreted *aphesis*, "release," to refer to the forgivenes of sins which Jesus, inspired by the Spirit, proclaimed (Rese, 1969: 146). Others think that the linkage was motivated by jubilary concerns, that is, concerns related to the jubilee year (Sloan, 1977: 39-40; Ford, 1984: 56-59).

Since some scholars believe that Luke does not develop jubilary themes elsewhere (but see Ringe, 1985: 33-98), some conclude that the linkage of Isa 61:1-2 with Isa 58:6 points to the traditional origin of the quotation. Yet, several other factors indicate that the insertion is to be attributed to Luke. Firstly, although some scholars maintain that Luke does not develop jubilary themes elsewhere, he does display special interest in the term *aphesis* (ten times in Luke-Acts over against once in Matthew and twice in Mark), generally understood as "release from sin." Secondly, the suggestion that Isa 58:6 was linked with Isa 61:1-2 in order to heighten a distinctive jubilee emphasis is unconvincing. There is no evidence of such a linkage in the literature of intertestamental Judaism, and it is by no means certain that the jubilary motif is emphasized in other parts of Luke's narrative, whether traditional or redactional. This indicates that the linkage of Isa 61:1-2 with Isa 58:6 was made by Luke and, not in order to heighten the jubilary emphasis, but rather as a result of his interest in *aphesis* as a *description of the liberating power of Jesus' preaching* of which an important aspect was forgiveness of sins (Menzies, 1991: 171-173).

As a result of the insertion the term *aphesis* receives considerable emphasis. The context in which the quotation appears, namely Jesus' healing ministry (Lk 4:23d and 4:31-

44), does not allow for a purely "religious" interpretation. The fact that the rest of the Gospel depicts the poor as the literally poor and the blind as literally blind makes such an interpretation highly improbable. Indeed, it is a moot point whether Luke (within the parameters of his thinking) could have used *aphesis* in an exclusively religious sense at all. In the text under discussion the use of *aphesis* together with the more general *tethrausmenoi*, "oppressed," is indicative of Luke's comprehensive view of suffering (Scheffler, 1993: 39).

The alteration of kalesai, "to call," to keruxai, "to proclaim." Since Luke never uses *kalein* in reference to preaching, it is quite probable that this alteration reflects his emphasis on preaching as the pre-eminent activity inspired by the Spirit (Rese, 1969: 146). However, noting that the preference for *kerusso* is not unique in Luke, it has been maintained that the change points as firmly to a traditional source as it does to Luke (Bock, 1987: 106). But the force of this point is lessened by Luke's frequent duplication of words in quotations from the Old Testament. Thus the alteration of *kalesai* (LXX) to *kēruxai* corresponds to Luke's handling of Old Testament citations elsewhere and strongly suggests that the alteration reflects Luke's hand (Holtz, 1968: 40; Menzies, 1991: 173)

The omission of "the day of vengeance of our God" (LXX). It is a matter of discussion whether any particular theological interest should be attached to this omission for, strictly speaking, it does not represent an alteration of the Septuagint text. Nevertherless, the quotation is broken off abruptly in the middle of a sentence. Thus, it is quite likely that the phrase was omitted from the citation in order to emphasize the grace of God (Grundmann, 1961: 121). While this emphasis on the salvific dimension of Jesus' work may have been taken over from the tradition, it is equally compatible with Luke's perspective, and therefore, indecisive in determining whether the quotation stems from a traditional source or Luke's hand. However, in view of the conclusions cited above, it is most probable that the entire quotation, as it stands in Lk 4:18-19, reflects Luke's redactional stamp (Menzies, 1991: 174; Tannehill, 1972: 64,66). It should be noted that the words omitted here from Lk 4:19 are substantially found in Luke's eschatological discourse: "for these are the days of vengeance, as a fulfillment of all that is written" (Lk 21:22).

By moving the account forward in the chronology of his Gospel Luke links it with that of Jesus' reception of the Spirit at the Jordan (Lk 3:21-22) and, as a result, highlights the significance of Jesus' Spirit-anointing for his entire ministry. The verb *chrio*, "to anoint," occurs only here in the Synoptic Gospels, within the quotation of Isa 61:1-2, and in Acts 4:27 and 10:38 in passages that are either directly or indirectly related to Isa 61:1. In Luke-Acts the verb "to anoint" is reserved for Jesus. The other two New Testament occurrences are 2 Cor 1:21 and Heb 1:9 (Kyo-Seon Shin, 1989: 61-62).

Scholars do not agree as to whether Lk 4:16-30 highlights Jesus' prophetic or messianic office. If one "framed" the unit as form criticism does, as an individual piece of tradition, then a prophetic emphasis is likely. However, to call this Luke's redactional point, because he is responsible for the additions, ignores the literary flow of the passage. Framing the text in this larger border, the answer becomes more complex. Everyone recognizes that the allusion to anointing in Lk 4:16-30 is, within the larger Lukan story, an allusion to the baptism. This means that to understand the literary force of this declaration, the reader is to recall that event, which cited Ps 2:7 and Isa 42:1 (Bock, 1987: 99-104). Although the interpretive force of these remarks is disputed by scholars who argue that the baptismal statement is merely regal and non-messianic (Fitzmyer, 1981: 482), the question remains of whether a baptism taking place in as eschatological a context as John the Baptist's ministry and carrying regal inplications would only suggest a non-messianic, regal connection. The citation of Ps 2:7 alone might not suggest a messianic understanding in the sense of *the* messiah, but placed in an eschatological frame, it seems hard to avoid that conclusion. In light of the baptism account and the additional background of Luke's infancy material, it seems that one should conclude that Jesus is both prophet and messiah, proclaiming and bringing salvation (Bock, 1994a: 614-616; O'Toole, 1996: 498-522). The theme of Jesus as proclaiming and fulfilling the sabbatical/ jubilee year can be seen throughout Luke's redaction of the Gospel tradition and his record of the early Church (Finkel, 1984: 4-10).

The idea of being anointed to carry out a divinely-commissioned task is central to the Old Testament (Pilgrim, 1981: 67; Kyo-Seon Shin, 1989: 90-91). Because of the "anointing," Jesus is sometimes thought to be presented here as messiah (Leaney, 1958: 118). In Acts 10:38 Jesus' baptism is interpreted as an "anointing," and it is likely that the use of Isa 61:1 here alludes to Jesus' baptism and the descent of the Spirit upon him.

But in what sense is the "anointing" to be understood? This passage certainly contains no reference to a Davidic dynasty or a royal function of Jesus. However, the idea of prophets as anointed servants of Yahweh does emerge in late pre-Christian Palestinian Judaism, e.g., in the Qumran literature. Moreover, the "herald" of good news in Isa 52:7 appears in Qumran as "an anointed with the Spirit." Whether the "anointing" of Jesus is to be understood of the "prophetic" sort or the "heraldic" sort, it gives a nuance to his "anointing" which is not that of the political, kingly sort. This, too, makes it intelligible why Jesus is compared to Elijah and Elisha in Lk 4:25-27. Elisha in particular is introduced as "the prophet"; implicitly, Jesus is suggested to be such, too (Fitzmyer, 1981: 529-530). But it has been pointed out that ultimately the concepts of eschatological prophet and the messiah merge (Marshall, 1978: 183). There are, in fact, numerous Jewish texts which connect the Spirit with the anointing of both kings and prophets. Particularly striking are those texts that describe the king, upon being anointed with the Spirit, as prophesying (1 Sam 10:1f.,9f., etc.), and these elements are believed to have merged also in Lk 4:18-19 (Tiede, 1980: 46; Tuckett, 1982: 346; Bock, 1987: 110-111). One has recently called attention to the fact that Isa 61:1-2 refers to a non-messianic prophetic figure while Isa 58:6 refers to a messianic liberation figure. Clearly, then, Jesus is presented as incorporating both the prophetic and the messianic (Prior, 1995: 137).

The quotation from Isaiah defines with precision the significance Luke attaches to Jesus' anointing with the Spirit. Firstly, Jesus' reception of the Spirit at the Jordan was the means by which he was equipped to carry out his mission. Secondly, by altering the text of Isa 61:1-2 (LXX), Luke brings the quotation into conformity with his distinctive prophetic theology of the Sprit and thus highlights preaching as the primary product of Jesus' "anointing" and the pre-eminent aspect of his mission. According to Luke, the Spirit-inspired preaching of Jesus effects salvation (Rese, 1969: 147). Luke, more than any other of the Synoptic Gospels, views Jesus' entire ministry as well as his "anointing," as Lk 4:18-19 indicates, in prophetic terms. Luke often depicts people referring to Jesus as a prophet (Lk 7:16,39; 9:8,19; 24:19; Acts 2:30). Jesus refers to himself as a prophet (Lk 4:24) and he accepts the fate of a prophet (Lk 11:49-50; 13:33). He is explicitly identified as the prophet like Moses in Acts 3:22; 7:37.

This analysis of Lk 4:18-19 confirms analyses of Lk 3:21-22 and 4:1,14: according to Luke, Jesus' Spirit-anointing, rather than the source of his unique filial relationship to God or his initiation into the new age, was the means by which he was equipped to carry out his divinely appointed task (Menzies, 19891: 176-177).

Luke's use of the verb *euangelizomai*, "to bring good news," can be summarized as follows: (1) in Lk 4:18 Jesus appears as the subject of the verb, as in Lk 4:43; 7:22; 8:1; 20:1 (compare Lk 16:16); (2) the christological-soteriological use of *euangelizomai* with Jesus as object (to proclaim the good news about Jesus Christ) is found especially in Acts (5:42; 8:35; 11:20); (3) *euangelizomai* in the passive is found in Lk 7:22 and 16:16. In both cases Jesus is the subject and the verb should here be understood as a *terminus technicus* of Jesus' activity (Kyo-Seon Shin, 1989: 63). *Kerusso*, "to proclaim," is for Luke synonymous with *euangelizomai* (Kyo-Seon Shin, 1989: 65-66).

Isa 61:1-2 is often understood against the background of a cluster of images of liberation, as they are found in the institution of the sabbatical year (Ex 21 and 23; Deut 25), its development into the jubilee year (seventh sabbatical year; Lev 25), and the eastern amnesty decrees (compare Jer 34 and Neh 5). Restitution of land, remission of debts, liberation and ransoming of slaves presupposes that every Israelite is equally dependent on Yahweh who is the ultimate owner of the land. The mutual relations of debt among Israelites are, therefore, relative and temporary in nature. The restitution of the jubilee year restores the true relations. Even if it is highly uncertain that these stipulations were ever put into practice, they maintain the conviction that Yahweh is king over all Israel with all its consequences for the mutual relations among the Israelites. Against this background the "I"-figure of Isa 61:1-2 should be understood as the prophet and herald of Yahweh who as the latter's anointed in his name proclaims good news to the poor and freedom to captives and oppressed.

Summing up the above, we may say that throughout the history of Israel, from the early sabbath year laws in the Covenant Code (Ex 21-23) to the interpretation of the late Second Temple period (the era after the return from the Babylonian exile) traditions associated with the jubilee year appear to affirm two things. The first is that God is sovereign over Israel, both in actual fact and in eschatological hope. The second is that the structure of economic and social life must embody the people's affirmation of God's sovereignty. In other words, God's reign and humankind's liberation go hand in hand (Ringe, 1985: 32).

The combination of Isa 61:1-2a and a line from Isa 58:6 via the key word *aphesis* does indeed evoke the jubilee/sabbatical year. Both texts concern a time pleasing to the Lord (see *dektos* in Isa 58:5 [LXX] and Isa 61:2 [LXX]). Moreover we find that the poor are mentioned in Isa 58 as well as in Isa 61 (see Isa 58:7 and 61:1). We saw how the intention of the jubilee year was profoundly social in character: restoration of the land through redistribution was a central element. This element is worded in rather general terms in Isa 61:1-3 (Koet, 1989: 33). However, the association of Isa 58, a prophetic critique of the type of religious practice that is contradicted by acts of injustice, with Isa 61, addressed to Jewish exiles returning from Babylon to devastated Jerusalem in 538 B.C., intensifies the social dimension of the prophetic message. It provides a striking corrective to any religious practice which is carried on without concern for the poor, and especially so when the religious activity continues in the very act of oppressing them. It suggests that in addition to Jesus' message being good news for the poor, it is bad news for the rich. The only chance for the rich is to share their bread with the hungry, to bring the homeless poor in their houses, to cover the naked, and to satisfy the desire of the afflicted (Isa 58:7-10). This is in keeping with a major thrust of Luke-Acts (Prior, 1995: 134-135).

The adjective *dektos* occurs five times in the New Testament, twice in Luke (Lk 4:19,24), in Acts 10:35; 2 Kor 6:2; and Phil 4:18. Only in Lk 4:24 does it refer to human acceptance; in the other four occurrences it refers to acceptability by God (Kyo-Seon Shin, 1989: 68). So Luke uses the term *dektos*, "acceptable," thrice: Jesus announces "the acceptable year of the Lord," but he himself will not be "acceptable" to his countrymen, while in Acts 10:35 the circle of those who are "acceptable" is expanded to include people of all nations. "The "acceptable year of the Lord" is a summary statement of Jesus' saving activity, to which refer the "gracious words" of verse 22: "grace" is said to be God's favor, the gift of salvation.

Yet the "acceptable year of the Lord" (Lk 4:19) announced by Jesus is not a single year but rather the time of fulfillment, and among the many scriptural motifs and practices fulfilled are the customs concerning sabbatical/jubilee years. The jubilee was a time of redistribution of wealth so that everyone was put back on an equal footing (Karrunkal, 1988: 183). The jubilee year motif with its radical call for justice played a vital part in the teachings of Jesus and it has even been suggested that Isa 61 may have been used in the Old Testament in the proclamation of the jubilee year, and that Luke used Isa 61 at the beginning of Jesus' ministry as suited to presenting Jesus' programme after the fashion of a jubilee year (Monshouwer, 1991: 90-99). But it should be noted that Luke does not use terminology peculiar to the jubilee (no sowing, no pruning, no rest for the land, no day of atonement, and so on). Neither does he develop peculiarly jubilee concepts in the course of his writing (Prior, 1995: 139).

The jubilee vision of Isaiah, then, is interpreted not literally as a kind of legal prescription, but as a symbol or vision of the new age. Clearly this is not just another jubilee year on the calendar of ancient Judaism. This is God's jubilee, which Luke, after describing the beginning of Jesus' and the disciples' journey to Jerusalem (Lk 9:51-10:42), identifies with God's kingdom to come (J.A. Sanders, 1993: 85). The jubilee provides the background for Jesus' exorcisms and healings, and for his concern for the poor and oppressed throughout the Gospel of Luke. *Aphesis*, "release," must be understood as implying total liberation of the whole person as well as of the society and environment in which he/she lives.

The four parallel lines:
- to preach good news to the poor,
- to proclaim release to captives,
- and [to proclaim] recovering of sight to the blind,
- to let the oppressed go free

which are, as it were, summed up in the last line, "to proclaim the year of the Lord's favor" (C.F. Evans, 1990: 271), are four ways of expressing Jesus' mission in terms of an overall liberating approach to whatever burdens and/or oppresses people. For some interpreters, the phrase "to preach good news to the poor" is understood as both introducing and governing the following lines. This interpretation rightly recognizes the importance of this phrase in the quotation. Yet it can also be argued that it should be taken independently, so that the poor are to be set alongside the captives and others as a separate group (Pilgrim, 1981: 67). We favor the first interpretation.

A text that is quoted remains recognizable in its new context but becomes at the same time part of the new context. We should make a clear distinction between the meaning of Isa 61 in the context of Third Isaiah and in the context of Luke. In other words, what is the point in asking what this text meant for the rural Palestinians for whom Third Isaiah was writing in the sixth or fifth century B.C. while ignoring its impact on the urban Christians of the first century A.D. who constituted Luke's audience? To allow the real Luke to speak, we must examine his message in the light of what it was actually like to be rich or poor in the Hellenistic cities of the Roman East. From a brief survey of social stratification and the experience of poverty in the provincial cities of the empire, it is clear that the urban poor suffered extreme forms of economic, social and political deprivation (Esler, 1987: 170-179).

For Third Isaiah, the "poor" were the exiles who had just returned from Babylon or, according to some scholars, more precisely the disillusioned generation of shortly after the exile, when the high expectations raised by Second Isaiah had not been fulfilled. Third Isaiah wanted to counteract their disappointment by reinterpreting the message of Second Isaiah. The codification of the Jubilee legislation was done by the exilic theologians of Israel. They assured the impoverished people in exile a place of equality in the new community on their eventual return, and proclaimed that the impoverished Israelites of any age would always have the hope of restored freedom and equal status in their community. The primary purpose of the legislation was to preserve equality among Israelites by preserving that most precious commodity, land (Kavunkal, 1988: 183).

For Luke, the "poor" were the "urban poor" in a city of the eastern part of the Mediterranean where his community was located. In the socio-economic reality of such cities the particular word used for "poor," namely *ptōchos*, means "beggar" (Esler, 1987: 164,180,183). The term *ptōchos* occurs ten times in Luke (against five in Matthew, five in Mark, and four in John; it is not found in Acts; altogether thirty-four times in the New Testament; Kyo-Seon Shin, 1989:63-64). The *ptōchoi* lived on the fringes of Greco-Roman society, since they had no place in the economy, and for their survival depended entirely on the hospitality of others (Prior, 1995: 165,167). Some scholars hold that, for Luke, the poor of Lk 4:18 (and 7:22) are the Christian community of Luke's day, who are suffering deprivation and persecution for their faith. They add that the "woes" (Lk 6:24-26) are addressed to the rich members of the Christian community who are tempted to stick to their riches, and ignore the plight of their fellow followers of the Way (Karris, 1978: 112-125).

Luke's community, living in a Hellenistic city of the Roman East, experienced difficulties both from within and without. Its membership was mixed, and included people from the opposite ends of the religious and social spectra. Prior to their embracing the Christian Way some had been pagans, and others conservative Jews. Some were from the richest echelons of society, while others were beggars. The fact that the members of Jewish origin shared table fellowship with those of Gentile origin further exacerbated the problems that the Jewish Christians were having with the synagogue. The social mix of the community also contributed to the internal tensions of the Lukan community (Esler, 1987: 220-223; Prior, 1995:180-181).

If the Lukan audience were urban Christians located in some significant city in the eastern Mediterranean (Balch, 1991: 223), as is now quite generally accepted, the Lukan Jesus is addressing his message to the "urban poor" of Luke's time whose condition was reduced to that of "beggars." For Luke the "poor" are people who can find no security or hope in the structures of human institutions or plans of human rulers. The insertion from Isa 58 into Isa 61:1-2 may be the key to what Luke had in mind. Isa 58:6 is clearly part of a social plea in which creditors are called upon to release captives/slaves. This slavery was caused by the heavy economic pressures brought about by the newly imposed tax system that affected, among others, small family businesses (compare Neh 5). The oppressed of Isa 58:6, then, were economically ruined people. Luke was probably aware of this concrete social context of the verse, so that also in Lk 4:18 the poor and oppressed are people who are economically on the rocks.

The Lukan theme of rich and poor must leave any Christian community disturbed in the face of serious inequalities and polarization. According to Luke, a Christian ought not to possess more than is necessary, as long as others are in need. The concept of evangelizing the poor involves both theory and praxis. In addition to getting the rhetoric right, one should get involved in action and programs for and with the poor (Prior, 1996:34-41).

When the Lukan Jesus speaks of sight for the blind, he may be referring, in part, to his work of healing. This sense is supported by the reference to the blind receiving their sight as the first of a list of Jesus' healing activities in his reply to John the Baptist (Lk 7:22). As a physical ailment, blindness need have no special importance; one type of physical ailment can stand for all. This would mean that Jesus' healing ministry is to be seen as one aspect of his overall liberating approach to whatever burdens and oppresses people. This interpretation may be supported by the fact that in the healing of a crippled woman in a synagogue (Lk 13:10-17), Jesus addresses her, saying, "Woman, you are set free from your ailment" (Lk 13:12). Moreover, in the light of the suitability of the verb *thrauein*, "to oppress" (Lk 4:18), to describe physical illness and subjection to an oppressive power (physical sickness: Wis 18:20; oppression by an alien power: Ex 15:6; Num 24:17), physical illness must be understood as the scourge of evil, from which Jesus is set to deliver people (Catchpole, 1993: 237). It has been pointed out that Isa 61:1-2 is connected with a series of other passages in Isaiah, with the granting of light or sight as one of the connecting themes. Some of these other passages have also influenced Luke-Acts, and it is likely that they would affect the author's understanding of what it means for Jesus to be sent to give sight to the blind. The command to "let the oppressed go free" in Isa 58:6 is followed by the promise of light rising in the darkness (Isa 58:8,10). The reference to "a light of the nations" and "salvation to the end of the earth" in Isa 49:6 is quoted in Acts 13:47, but "a light to the nations" is also mentioned in Isa 42:6-7, where it is followed by a reference to opening the eyes of the blind: "I have given you as a covenant to the people, a light to the nations, to open the eyes that are blind, to bring out the prisoners from the dungeon, from the prison those who sit in darkness." In these and other Isaian passages that may have influenced Luke-Acts, the reference to opening eyes is connected with turning from light to darkness, and so clearly is not limited to enabling blind people to see physical objects (Tannehill, 1986: 66-67). But this should in no way weaken the first interpretation given above.

It has been suggested that the quotation of Isa 61:1-2, applied to the work of Jesus in Lk 4:18, specifies the proclamation of recovery of sight to the blind as part — indeed, the center — of the Isaian scenario. While we fully agree with the first part of the affirmation, we cannot help but feel that the chiastic presentation of the Isaian quotation in support of the second part of the affirmation is somehow artificial (see Meynet, 1982: 33; Hamm, 1986: 458-459). This does not mean, of course, that we would deny that, like the other evangelists, Luke too is aware of the symbolic dimensions of physical seeing.

The expression "the year of the Lord's favor" or "the acceptable year of the Lord" is found only here in the New Testamnent (a similar text is found in 2 Cor 6:2) and means the time in which the Lord shows favor. It is further specified as "a day of salvation" in Isa 49:8. The language is based on the institutions of the Sabbath Year and the Jubilee described in Lev 25. Their hallmark was freedom (Lev 25:10; Jer 34:8,15,17), since they involved the emancipation of slaves, the suspension of debts, the restoration of property and the return of the land to fallowness, in short a redistribution of wealth that put everyone on equal footing.Thus a jubilee year was indeed an acceptable year to all types of oppressed persons. Luke portrays Jesus as proclaiming the inauguration of such an era (Ford, 1984: 55). The Talmud's statement, "This is the time of salvation," shows that it is given an eschatological nuance. Thus, as said above, verse 19 is a summary of the previous statements (C.F. Evans, 1990: 771; Kyo Seon Shin, 1989: 100-104).

Verses 20-21: (20) And he rolled up the scroll,
                  gave it back to the attendant,
                  and sat down.

> The eyes of all in the synagogue were fixed
> on him.
> (21) Then he began to say to them,
> "Today this scripture has been fulfilled in
> your hearing."

Jesus rolled up the scroll and handed it back to the synagogue attendant. Then he "sat down," a phrase which might
simply mean that he resumed his seat in the congregation,
but here it no doubt refers to taking up the posture of a
teacher (Marshall, 1978: 184; Danker, 1988: 107; Nolland,
1989: 198; Bovon, 1991: 207). The reading of the Isaiah
passage evoked expentancy. The verb *atenizein* occurs twice
in Luke and ten times in Acts. In most instances it expresses a steadfast gaze of esteem and trust — the nuance
intended here. It is part of the audience's initial reaction of
admiration or pleasant surprise (Fitzmyer, 1981: 533). The
interpretation of the last part of verse 20, saying that the
people in the synagogue stared at Jesus, wondering how he
could read without having received formal instruction, is
misguided.

Jesus "began to say to them" may simply refer to a transition from reading to preaching (Plummer, 1901: 123). But
perhaps Luke wishes also to stress that these are the opening words of Jesus' public ministry (see Lk 3:23, "when he
began his work [ministry]"; Acts 10:37, "beginning in Galilee after the baptism that John announced"; Schurmann,
1969: 231; Marshall, 1978: 185; Danker, 1988: 107).

The sequence of verses indicates that Luke is "summarizing" the events. Luke only notes Jesus' brief declaration
here, but the following verse stating that the crowd was
impressed with the message of gracious words, indicates that
Luke implies that Jesus said more than he recorded (Bock,
1994: 412).

The first word we hear from the adult Jesus is "today"
(Schweizer, 1984: 89). The adverb *sēmeron* occurs 41 times
in the New Testament, of which twenty times in Luke-Acts.

Occurring at the beginning of the sentence, "today" is emphatic (Fitzmyer, 1981: 533; C.F. Evans, 1990: 272). Luke mentions several times the "today" (*sēmeron*) of salvation (Pilgrim, 1981: 66; Kyo-Seon Shin, 1989: 69-70): "to you is born today (NRSV: this day) in the city of David a Savior" (Lk 2:11); "today this scripture has been fulfilled in your hearing" (Lk 4:21); "for I must stay at your house today" (Lk 19:5); "today salvation has come to this house" (Lk 19:9); "today you will be with me in Paradise" (Lk 23:43). The "today" of Jesus is also addressed to all the readers of the Gospel and assures them that the era of salvation is present (Marshall, 1978: 185). Ever since that day in Nazareth this is true for anyone who reads or hears this message. The age of God's reign is here; the eschatological, that is, final and decisive, time when God's promises are fulfilled and God's purpose comes to fruition has arrived; there will be changes in the conditions of those who have waited and hoped. The time of God is today, and the ministries of Jesus and the Church, according to Luke-Acts, demonstrate that this "today" continues. Throughout Luke-Acts, "today" is never allowed to become "yesterday" or to slip again into a vague "someday." The statement is meant as an explanation of the Isaiah quotation. This is evident from the phrase "this scripture" (see Lk 4:17, "where it was written"). The word "today" is a categorical and synthetic expression implying authority for the fulfilment of the divine design announced through the prophets. It indicates the exceptional character of the event, shows its place above all other events and manifests it as the unique moment that was awaited for centuries (Kavunkal, 1988: 182).

The meaning of "to fulfill" is of crucial importance in this context. There are three ways in which the verbs *plēroō*, "to fulfill," as well as *pimplēmi* and *teleiō* and their compounds can be used in Luke-Acts in a metaphorical sense: (1) to indicate the end of a certain period; (2) to describe the realization of certain prophecies or obligations from the

Scriptures or on the basis of the Scriptures; (3) to clarify a
certain state of mind, especially the fullness of the Spirit
(Koet, 1989: 36). In Lk 4:21, "to fulfill" is concerned with
the realization of what is announced in the Isaiah quotation. The fulfillment of Scripture implies that the spirit of
the Lord rests upon Jesus. Also the other elements of the
quotation are fulfilled in Jesus' ministry and are a kind of
preview of Jesus' activity (Tuckett, 1982: 347; Koet, 1989:
37). A comparison of the present verse with Lk 24:44, "These
are the words that I spoke to you while I was still with you
— that everything written about me in the law of Moses,
the prophets and the psalms must be fulfilled," surfaces several parallels and is very enlightening (Kyo-Seon Shin, 1989:
70-72, 104-108).

   "In your hearing" is an Old Testament expression (Deut
5:1; 2 Sam 3:19). The fulfillment of the Scripture takes place
as the audience *listens* to the message. One has noted the
subtle joining of eyes (Lk 4:20b) and ears (Lk 4:21b) with
the activity of the synagogue crowd mentioned in the following verse: "all spoke well of him" (*emarturoun*, literally,
"bore witness"). If the text in Lk 4:21 concerns only the
fulfillment of the Scripture in Jesus, then the addition of
"in your ears" would be superfluous. Considering the use of
"ear" elsewhere in Luke-Acts, it is quite possible that at his
debut Jesus alludes to the choice that the listeners have (and
will have later on): would they follow him, take his message
seriously and repent with the ultimate prospect of receiving
the Spirit (Acts 1:8)? Or should they refuse to listen and
thereby resist the Spirit (cf. Lk 4:28-29; Acts 7:54-57; Koet,
1989: 39)?

Verse 22:   All spoke well of him
            and were amazed at the gracious words that came
               from his mouth.
            They said, "Is not this Joseph's son?"

Lk 4:22 serves to connect the two halves of the narrative,
Lk 4:16-21 and 4:23-30 (Siker, 1992: 79). "All spoke well

of him," literally, "All bore witness to him," can be taken in the sense of "to praise" with a dative of advantage (Acts 13:22; 14:3;15:8; 22:5), or in the sense of "to bear witness against," i.e., "to condemn" (see Mt 23:31). Most commentators adopt the first, positive meaning (Marshall, 1978: 185; O'Fearghail, 1984: 62-65; Tyson, 1986: 32-33; Kyo-Seon Shin, 1989: 73-74). One has also pointed out the typical Lukan interest in positive testimony to Jesus from those who stand somewhat apart from his mission (Nolland, 1979: 219-229). And some scholars propose that *martureō* should be understood in the sense found in many inscriptions, namely, as indicating favorable testimony rendered by persons who lived with the person in question. The opening of the Nazareth pericope which so soon after Lk 2:40-52 reminds the reader that Nazareth, which Jesus was visiting, was the place where he had grown up (Lk 4:16) seems to point in that direction (O'Fearghail, 1984: 66).

But a number of scholars adhere to a negative interpretation. Some of them point out that the connection between the Nazarene rejection and the Samaritan rejection (Lk 9:52-55) is instructive. These two incidents stand in parallel positions at the beginning of Luke's major divisions of Jesus' public ministry (Weatherly, 1994: 122-125). It has also been noted that both incidents are followed by parallel examples of "faith" among Jews and Samaritans (the lepers in Lk 5:12-16 and Lk 17:11-19; Tiede, 1980: 62). This factor suggests that neither Nazareth nor the Samaritan village is intended by Luke to characterize the response of their entire people. The rejection at Nazareth is treated by Luke as typical only of one part of the nation's response to Jesus (Weatherly, 1994: 126-127).

A few regard the pronoun *autoi* as neuter (Fitzmyer, 1981: 534), and translate then: "All acknowledged it" (literally, "were testifying to it"). The verb *thaumazō* ("to be amazed") which occurs thirteen times in Luke and five times in Acts can express astonishment (coupled with criticism, doubt or censure) or also admiration (coupled with pleasure). The common interpretation rightly understands it positively as admiration (except in Lk 11:38, speaking of the Pharisees; Lohfink, 75: 44 note 92; Kyo-Seon-Shin, 1989: 74-76). So, the reaction of the people in the synagogue is one of positive astonishment (compare Lk 4:15).

The term *logos* occurs thirty-two times in Luke and sixty-five times in Acts. In Lk 5:1, Jesus' word is identified with the word of God (Kyo-Seon-Shin, 1989: 76-78). The expression "gracious words" (literally, "words of grace") is most probably a positive paraphrase of Jesus' words (Koet, 1989: 40). "Gracious words" is not to be understood as "words about God's mercy and grace" (i.e., omitting the words of judgment in the continuation of Isa 61:2, as held by Jeremias, 1958: 44-45), but words endued with the power of God's grace. "Grace" is the divine influence that is present in the words and that gives the words their quite tangible impact. They are the message of salvation (O'Fearghail, 1984: 68; Nolland, 1989: 198-199).

In connection with "from his mouth" one should recall the importance of "the mouth of the prophets" in the Old Testament (de la Potterie, 1958: 231-232). The expression is also reminiscent of Deut 8:3, "in order to make you understand that one does not live by bread alone, but by every word that comes from the mouth of the Lord," the first part of which is quoted in Lk 4:4 (but fully cited in Mt 4:4; Schweizer, 1984: 90). This may suggest that Luke — not the crowd (Bock, 1994: 414-415) — saw Jesus' words as divine words, bringing life and salvation (Schürmann, 1969: 234-235; Marshall, 1978: 186).

The rhetorical question, "Is not this Joseph's son?" reflects the townspeople's common understanding of who Jesus is (compare Lk 2:48-49). Whereas in itself the query could be one of cynical indignation or one of pleasant surprise or admiration, the context suggests the latter (Fitzmyer, 1981: 535; differently, Marshall, 1978: 186). The question has, therefore, been interpreted in a positive sense (Catchpole, 1993: 239) and is certainly not particularly hostile since Luke also refers to Joseph as Jesus' father (Lk 2:27,41,47; 3:23). Some suggest that the people in the synagogue are using the question to evade the message (Tiede, 1980: 37-38). Those who interpret this question as having a negative meaning are most probably too much influenced by the Markan parallel (Bajard, 1969: 165).

Verse 23:   He said to them,
             "Doubtless you will quote to me this proverb,
             'Doctor, cure yourself!'
             And you will say,
             'Do here also in your hometown the things we
               heard you did at Capernaum.'"

Jesus puts into words his interpretation of the question in Lk 4:22b. His reaction reflects what he supposes to be the inner thoughts of the people in the synagogue (Hill, 1971: 168). Jesus knows the thoughts of his audience also in Lk 5:22; 6:8; 7:39-40; 9:47 and 11:17 (Giblin, 1985: 25 note 16; Stein, 1991: 158).

There are proverbs in classical literature similar to the proverb in Lk 4:24 which have the meaning that a doctor should care first for his own family, neighbors and surroundings. It can be described in the following way: One must not refuse to do to one's own relatives the favors that one does to others, or, one must not benefit others, while refusing the same benefits to one's relatives (Noorda, 1982: 463). The metaphor, "Doctor, cure yourself," is thereafter transformed in plain language: "Do here also in your hometown the things we heard you did in Capernaum." In Lk 4:23 Jesus puts into words the claim of his fellow citizens. In the following verses he will contrast this claim with his prophetic role. It is not the duty of a prophet to benefit his own people. On the contrary, a prophet calls people to repentance. In Lk 5:31-32 Jesus compares himself with a doctor and he relates this with his mission to call sinners to repentance (Koet, 1989: 42 and note 64). The verb *therapeuo* that occurs fourteen times in Luke and five times in Acts is used both for exorcisms (Lk 6:18; 8:2) and for ordinary physical healing (Kyo-Seon Shin, 1989: 79-81).

According to Luke, there are two ways by which people impede the mission of Jesus. On the one hand, they want to reserve Jesus for themselves, monopolize him (Lk 4:23, the inhabitants of Nazareth; Lk 4:42, the people of Capernaum; Lk 8:19-20, Jesus' relatives); on the other hand, they refuse to accept Jesus, or want him to leave their territory (Lk 4:29, the inhabitants of Nazareth; Lk 9:53, the Samaritans; Lk 19:29-39, the city of Jerusalem and its spokespersons, the Pharisees). The Pharisees' advice belongs to the second category. As can be gathered from the above, both reactions were exhibited in the Nazareth scene: the first in the desire of the Nazarenes to keep Jesus for themselves as part of their group (Lk 4:23); and the second in their refusal to accept Jesus, and their violent expulsion of Jesus from their domain (Lk 4:29). Recently, one has defended that the heavy emphasis on healing in Lk 4:18-19 makes the address "doctor" appropriate and that the tone of the hypothetical request in Lk 4:23 must be adjudged entirely positive (Catchpole, 1993: 242).

Verse 24:   And he said,
             "Truly, I tell you,
             No prophet is accepted in the prophet's hometown."

"Truly, I tell you" (literally, "Amen, I tell you") is the first occurrence of this asseverative phrase, containing the only Semitic word that has been retained in the Lukan Gospel from the earlier tradition (Lk 4:24; 12:37; 18:17,29; 21:32; 23:43). There is no uniform reason underlying the use of this formula in this Gospel (Fitzmyer, 1981: 536).

The proverb, "Doctor, cure yourself," is checked by another. The doctor is also a prophet, and "the acceptable year of the Lord" has been rejected by the people in the synagogue because the prophet is not "acceptable in his own hometown" (Tiede, 1988: 109; Danker, 1988: 107). The use of the word "acceptable" (Greek: *dektos*) in verses 19 and 24 points up the relation between sharing in the time of salvation that Jesus announces and the acceptance of Jesus himself. People can only share in the "acceptable year of the Lord" if they accept the one who announces and brings it (Tannehill, 1972: 58; Bovon, 1991: 209).

In the Septuagint, *dektos* can in general be used in two ways: (1) in a cultic context, it bears a meaning derived from *dechomai*: "acceptable," "welcome"; (2) in Second and Third Isaiah it gets a more active meaning: "favorable," "pleasing" (Isa 49:8; 61:2). So, considering the background in Isaiah, *dektos* in Lk 4:19 may approximately mean "pleas-ing," "bringing benefit/salvation," and it may carry the same meaning in Lk 4:24. When the meaning of *dektos* in Lk 4:24 leans towards "pleasing," "of benefit," then Jesus is indicating in this proverb that a prophet certainly does not exist to please or to benefit his fellow citizens. Thus Jesus' statement is an adequate reaction to their claim. The an-swer that Jesus gives in Lk 4:24 is elaborated with the ref-erences to Elijah and Elisha (Koet, 1989: 43-44). Some schol-ars think that "the prophet's hometown" picks up "in your hometown" of the previous verse (Stein, 1991: 158). But, while the Greek word *patris* means home*town* in verse 23, in verse 24 it may shift its meaning to become home *coun-try*, and is illustrated by the stories of Elijah and Elisha going outsidse the coundaries of Israel (Tucket, 1996: 52).

Verses 25-27: (25) But the truth is,
There were many widows in Israel in the time of Elijah,
when the heaven was shut up three years and six months,
and there was a severe famine over all the land;
(26) yet Elijah was sent to none of them except to a widow at Zarephath in Sidon

(27) There were also many lepers in Israel
in the time of the prophet Elisha,
and none of them was cleansed
except Naaman the Syrian."

Lk 4:25-27 has been considered the interpretive key to
the whole pericope. In Lk 4:25-27 the themes of "prophet,"
"acceptable," "country/hometown" (*patris*), anticipated in
Lk 4:16-24, are developed and resolved (Siker, 1992:83).
The link between Lk 4:23-24 and 25-27 is probably first of
all that Elijah and Elisha provide examples of prophets who
do not fulfill the desire of those wanting healing for their
own homeland. They even healed Gentiles instead of Israelites (Tannehill, 1986: 70). And they were sent by God!
So, to those who say that a doctor/prophet should (first of
all) benefit his own kin, Jesus replies that apparently God
does not think that way. Elijah and Elisha are also scriptural models for Jesus' healing ministry. Jesus' raising of
the son of the widow of Nain (Lk 7:11-17) clearly recalls
Elijah's raising of the widow's son, and some scholars think
that the healing performed for a foreign officer in Lk 7:1-
10 parallels Elisha's healing of Naaman (Crockett, 1969:
181-182). But maybe Lk 17:11-19, the healing of ten lepers, one of whom was a Samaritan, is an even closer parallel (Bruners, 1977: 103-122; Hamm, 1986: 470; C.A. Evans,
1987: 78).

Many biblical scholars hold that the references to Elijah
and Elisha serve to announce the salvation of the Gentiles
and the non-salvation of Israel. Elijah and Elisha rescue the
widow and the leper outside of Israel, not in Israel. Luke is
seen to have used this as a pre-indication of God's turning
away from Israel in favor of the Gentiles. Elijah and Elisha
thus become prototypes; they announce the end of God's
bond with Israel (Grundmann, 1966: 123; Fitzmyer, 1981:
537). It has also been said that the theme of Acts 28:17-
28, in which Paul quotes Isa 6:9-10, is brought to clear
expression at the begining of Jesus' public ministry, his ser-

mon at Nazareth (Lk 4:16-30). But does the representation of Elijah and Elisha as prophets to the Gentiles fit in with the representation found in 1-2 Kgs and other places in the Old and New Testament, with earlier and later Jewish literature in which they are mentioned, and with the context of Lk 4:16-30? (Koet, 1989: 44). It should also be noted that Elijah and Elisha scarcely fit a situation of mission. Elijah is involved in 1Kgs 17:8-16 as a refuge, and engages in no public activity whatsoever before his return to Israel in 1Kgs 18:1. Elisha, for his part, makes no move at all to contact Gentiles in general or Naaman in particular — the initiative comes exclusively from the side of Naaman himself (2Kgs 5:4; Catchpole, 1993: 248; on 2Kgs 5, see Conroy, 1991: 32-47).

The stories in 1-2 Kgs show that Elijah and Elisha are intent upon restoring God's covenant with Israel. Elijah is presented as a prophet of the covenant between Israel and God. The episode with the widow (1Kgs 17 referred to in Lk 4:25-26) is an example of how there was knowledge of God and his Torah outside of Israel. This is not meant as a rejection of Israel. On the contrary, it is a chance for the prophet to stay alive during the famine so that he can later restore the covenant between God and Israel (see 1Kgs 18:31: during the famine Elijah is fed by the widow). Elijah's image as depicted in Sir 48 is that of the protector of the covenant and the commandments. His aim is to bring about reconciliation between generations and between the tribes of Israel (Koet, 1989: 44-48; compare Kyo-Seon Shin, 1989: 91-99).

The stories of Elijah and Elisha are closely connected. We find many of the themes in the Elijah stories repeated in the stories of his disciple. The story to which Luke refers in Lk 4:27 (2Kgs 5:1-19), and in which Elisha is depicted as a miracle worker, is nevertheless first of all an illustration of a lesson to the king of Israel. Elisha greatest concern is the restoration of the covenant between Yahweh and Israel, especially the relationship between the king and the people (2Kgs 5:1-19; see also 2Kgs 10). In Sir 48:12-16 Elisha is characterized as someone who was intent upon converting the king (Sir 48:12) and the people (Sir 48:15; Koet, 1989: 46,48).

In the New Testament Elijah is associated with reconciliation and restoration and the keeping of the covenant (e.g., Rom 11:1-4; Jas 5:17-18; Lk 1:17). The image of Elijah in rabbinical literature is the elaboration of his portrait in the Old Terstament. His eschatological task is always the same: he comes to rescue Israel, to bring good news and to restore Israel by gathering the dispersed people (Koet, 1989: 48-49).

Thus the characterization of Elijah as an enthusiast for the maintenance and restoration of God's covenant with Israel is found in the Old Testament as well as in rabbinical literature. In the Gospel of Luke, Elijah's concern for the unity of Israel and the restoration of the covenant is a well-known concept. To interpret the references in Lk 4:25-27 as a prefiguration of God's turning away from Israel in favor of the Gentiles is in direct opposition to the image of especially Elijah but also of Elisha found in the texts discussed above. The references are to be seen as a characterization of Jesus' task as a prophet and as an answer to the demand of the audience. The prophet Elijah was of no advantage to Israel, but to the widow of Zarephath. This, however, was a way of bringing Israel back to the knowledge of the Lord (Koet, 1989: 49-50).

Applying this now to our pericope, we see that in Lk 4:25-27 a contrast between Israel, on the one hand, and the widow of Zarephath and the Syrian Naaman, on the other hand, is highlighted. The contrasts are mentioned to stimulate Israel to convert. In Lk 4:23 Jesus expressed the (future) demand of his listeners in his own terms. In Lk 4:25-27 he makes clear the task of a prophet and answers his listeners' claim by explaining that a prophet is not directly an advantage to his own people, but rather exhorts his people to conversion. The references to Elijah and Elisha illustrate this further (Koet, 1989: 50).

The references to Elijah and Elisha are also a further explanation of the Isaiah quotation which is primarily a message of salvation for Israel. They are a further elaboration of the role of the prophet and his task of converting the people of Israel, as implicitly indicated in the Isaiah quotation. God gives his blessings to a Gentile widow and to Naaman for the sake of the conversion of Israel. Jesus' explanation of the Scriptures concurs with the argumentation in Isa 49 as well as in 1—2 Kgs. The Gentiles are saved with Israel (see Lk 2:32, "a light for revelation to the Gentiles, and for glory to your people Israel"). This will become an important theme in Acts (2:21; 10:34-35; Koet, 1989: 51). Any suggestion that the references in Lk 4:25-27 announce a turning away from the Jews in favor of an exclusive mission to the Gentiles is unwarranted. The Lukan reference highlights the universal call to conversion and repentance, addressed to both Jews and Gentiles alike. The Gentile interests of Elijah and Elisha are best understood as stimuli to Jews to conversion (Prior, 1995: 143). The line of thought may be best described as a warning, a salutary warning to Jews that their position is not so special that they cannot be bypassed by God (Catchpole, 1993: 249). They are not "indispensable to God who is able to raise children of Abraham from stones (Lk 3:8).

As in Jas 5:17, Luke uses "three and a half years" instead of the three years stated in 1Kgs 18:1. Three and a half years may function more as a stereotyped number of a period of distress (Dan 7:25; 12:7; Rev 11:2; 12:6,14) than an exact period of time (Stein, 1992: 159; Marshall, 1978: 190). But since this symbolism seems to play no role in Luke's presentation, its use should most probably be attributed to an earlier stage of the tradition (Fitzmyer, 1981:

537-538; Nolland, 1989: 194). "Elijah was not sent" is an example of the "divine passive" and means "God did not send" (Stein, 1992: 159; Bock, 1994: 417).

It has been stated that the widow of Zarephath and Naaman represent both extremes of the social spectrum: the widow, one of the urban poor on the brink of death by famine (1Kgs 17:12), and Naaman, the rich and powerful army commander of the king of Aram (2Kgs 5:1-5; Esler, 1987: 180). But others would rather see Naaman as representing another category of needy and marginalized people, namely, lepers (Bock, 1994: 418). Both the widow and Naaman are marginalized people, though for various reasons. This no doubt prefigures Jesus' special attention for the marginalized throughout his ministry. Throughout the Old Testament "widows [and orphans]" are a byword for the exploited and oppressed. In the Gospel of Luke we may refer to Lk 20:47, where Jesus warns the people for the scribes who "devour widows' houses."

Verses 28-29: (28)   When they heard this, all in the synagogue
                            were filled with rage.
                 (29)   They got up, drove him out of the town,
                            and led him to the brow of the hill on which
                            their town was built,
                            so that they might hurl him off the cliff.

Jesus' words are treated as having been highly provocative. The reaction of the crowd in the synagogue is the culmination of their resentment against a prophet whose words they failed to appreciate and who had done nothing to justify his claims (Marshall, 1978: 190). The words "when they heard" will be echoed in Acts 7:54 in the story of Stephen. Simeon had talked about the sign to be spoken against, so that the thought of many hearts would be revealed (Lk 2:34-35). Nazareth is a commentary on this prophecy (Danker, 1988: 110).

That they "drove him out of the town" foreshadows the locale of the crucifixion itself (Lk 23:26; Fitzmyer, 1981:

538). It is difficult to know exactly what Luke meant since Nazareth is built on a slope and no clear "brow" or cliff is nearby. He may have intended to refer to the martyrdom of Stephen or in general to the customary practice of throw-ing a person down from a height before stoning (Acts 7:54-60; Nolland, 1989: 201). But others, pointing out that Luke's mention of "the hill" suggests a greater height than that prescribed for precipitation before stoning ("twice the height of a man" according to the Mishnah, tractate Sanhedrin 6:4) suggests that a lynching is meant (Schweizer, 1984: 91; C.F. Evans, 1990: 275; Bock, 1994: 419).

Verse 30:   But he passed through the midst of them and went
              on his way.

That Jesus "passed through the midst of them" is often considered miraculous, but there is no need to interpret it so. The evangelist's intention is to state that it is not yet time for the opposition to succeed (Fitzmyer, 1981: 539). Johannine parallels (Jn 7:30; 8:59; 10:39) express the point that Jesus' hour had not yet come (Marshall, 1978: 190; Nolland, 189: 201). Attempts to account for the departure of Jesus on psychological grounds, such as "the majesty of Jesus' bearing," fail to do justice to the theological perspec-tive (Danker, 1988: 110). But the shadow of rejection hangs over Jesus' ministry from the beginning.

"Jesus went on his way" is the first occurrence of the significant verb *poreuesthai* in the Gospel proper. It has been used in the infancy narrative (Lk 1:6,39; 2:3,41) in a more general sense. But now it is predicated of Jesus with the nuance of his "proceeding" on his way — a way that will eventually lead him to Jerusalem, the city of destiny (Ernst, 1977: 174-175; Fitzmyer, 1981: 539).

3. Jesus' Ministry in Capernaum (Lk 4:31-44)

Introduction

After the programmatic scene of Jesus' teaching in the Nazareth synagogue, Luke introduces the reader to the first characteristic incidents of his Galilean ministry outside of his hometown. The four following episodes (Lk 4:31-37, 38-39, 40-41, 42-44) illustrate concretely what had been reported about Jesus in Nazareth concerning his Capernaum activity (Lk 4:23). These four episodes are derived by Luke from his Markan source. He has omitted Mk 1:1-20, to make use of it later (Fitzmyer, 1981: 541). The events in Lk 4:31-44 are bound closely together by unity of place and time. The narrator presents a rapid sequence of events happening in the same place and during a brief time (a Sabbath day, the following evening, and the next morning. There are indications of connections with preceding material. The narrator is beginning to fill out the summary report about Jesus' activity in Lk 4:14-15 by narrating specific incidents (Busse, 1977: 31; Tannehill, 1986: 82).

a. Teaching and Healing in the Capernaum Synagogue (Lk 4:31-37)

The first of the four episodes is parallel to Mk 1:21-28. Luke's version is clearly dependent on Mk 1:21-28, which he follows rather closely (Tiede, 1988: 111; Johnson, 1991: 85). In both Mark and Luke the narrative occupies a prominent position, for it is the first miracle they record. Both Gospels connect the exorcism with the authoritative teaching of Jesus in the synagogue; thus, the scene in the synagogue is programmatic of Jesus' ministry of teaching and healing (Twelftree, 1993: 57; Page, 1995: 139). There is little doubt that Jesus performed exorcisms as they were understood in his time. It was just a natural thing to do for an itinerant charismatic healer and teacher in his social-historical envi-

ronment; and he was not the only one to do it as is abun-
dantly documented. The story reported in Lk 4:31-37 is a
typical case of exorcism (Rousseau, 1993: 141, 143).

In Luke in particular, the exorcism of a demon possessed person in the Capernaum synagogue is preceded by
two verses that contain a generic statement about Jesus'
sabbath teaching and the reaction of the people of Capernaum
to it. By placing the stories of the temptations (Mk 1:12-
13; Lk 4:1-13) and exorcism in proximity to one another,
Mark and Luke suggest that Jesus' power over the demonic
realm is the consequence of the defeat of the devil in the
wilderness. The differences between the two texts are of a
redactional nature (for details, see Schramm, 1971: 85-91;
Fitzmyer, 1981: 542), and there is no need to call on another source beside Mark (Busse, 1977: 71, 74). Lk 4:31-32
and 4:33-37 are linked together by means of the keywords
"authority" (*exousia*) and "word" (*logos*) found in verses 32
and 36. But a new starting point is clearly noticeable in Lk
4:33 with the change of subject from Jesus to the possessed
man (Kirchschlager, 1981: 28).

Verses 31-32: (31) He went down to Capernaum, a city in Galilee,
and was teaching them on the sabbath.
(32) They were astounded at his teaching,
because he spoke with authority.

The geographical note at the beginning is composed of a
verb of movement and a precise indication of place (Morgen,
1992: 237). "*He* went down" (different Mk 1:21, "*they* went
to," that is, Jesus and his disciples, just called in Mk 1:16-
20) is appropriate since in Luke Jesus comes from Nazareth
which would have been about six hundred meters higher
than Capernaum. Since Luke has transposed the scene of
the calling of the first disciples to Lk 5:1-11, he must depict Jesus going alone to Capernaum (Busse, 1977: 72;
Fitzmyer, 1981: 544; Nolland, 1989: 205).

Capernaum, located on the northwest shore of the
Sea of Galilee, has not traditionally been considered a city.

There is no evidence as yet for a city wall, court, or any large administrative institution or apparatus such as have been found in other urban centers in lower Galilee. The population is now estimated at 12-15,000. It was a fishing village, and it has been said that around the sea of Galilee fishing was big business (Overman, 1988: 162). The impression left by Mark and Matthew that Capernaum was the residence of Jesus, and for some time his headquarters, disappears in Luke, where it is just one of the cities of Galilee. Luke now specifies it as such for the benefit of his Gentile Christian readers: "a city in Galilee" (C.F. Evans, 1990: 277). But this notice is also important in that it places Nazareth and Capernaum side by side as Galilean cities and characterizes Jesus' public ministry as a city-mission (Busse, 1977: 70). Capernaum was the center of Jesus' activities by the lake (Van Der Loos, 1965: 378).

As in Nazareth, Jesus has come into the Capernaum synagogue to teach (Bock. 1994: 429). To stress the habitual character of Jesus' activity, that is, his ongoing ministry of teaching, in the Greek Luke uses the imperfect of the verb "to be" and the participle "teaching" (Johnson, 1991: 83).

Jesus' words elicited astonishment, for "he spoke with authority" (more literally, "his word was with/in authority"), that is, he spoke as one who had firsthand knowledge of God. Luke alters the text of Mark in that he changes the latter's "he taught them as one who had authority" into "for his word was with authority" (RSV), thereby making the "word" the subject of the clause and stressing it as if it were an independent entity (Marz, 1973: 39).

The "authority" (*exousia*) with which Jesus spoke refers to his ability to elicit conviction from his hearers, an authority that was rooted in the "power (*exousia*) of the Spirit" (Lk 4:14), with which he had been "anointed" (Lk 4:18). The word *exousia* will occur in verse 36 and there will be associated with Jesus' exorcising commands (Fitzmyer, 1981:

544). Luke speaks not only of Jesus' "teaching" (Mk 1:22,27) but also of the "word" (of God) which then continues on through Acts (Schweizer, 1984: 98). "Word" (*logos*), for Luke, is more than instruction or teaching (*didachē*). One can be an eyewitness of this word (Lk 1:2), for it is attested with powerful actions (Lk 4:36; 5:1; 7:7; 22:61; 24:19; and often in Acts). Capernaum will soon see the deeds that back the words of Jesus. And a few years later a proconsul on Cyprus will be "astonished at the teaching about the Lord" (Acts 13:12) when a magician called Bar-Jesus (Elymas) becomes blind for a time under the indictment of Saul, "also called Paul" (Acts 13:4-12; Danker, 1988: 110-111). Unlike in Mk 1:22, in Luke the authority of Jesus' word in his sabbath teaching is recognized without any negative comparison toward the scribes (Fitzmyer, 1981: 544; Tiede, 1988: 112). For Luke the concern is not with a formal characteristic such as an absence of appeal to a binding tradition (as was presumably done by the scribes). The authority of Jesus' word is an intrinsic quality visible in its effects (Nolland, 1989: 205). It is already clear in the Markan account that a close relationship is being established between "teaching... as one having authority" (Mk 1:22) and "he commands even the unclean spirits... and they obey him" (Mk 1:27). Luke develops this by treating the two as different aspects of a single phenomenon (Leaney, 1958: 120). Luke does not allow a separation of word and deed. In both the saving act of God in Jesus is visible as powerful effect (Marz, 1973: 39; Nolland, 1989: 205-206). Verse 32b is so important that it can be treated as a "redactional subtitle for the following episodes" (Robinson, 1964: 40 note 247; Busse, 1977: 69).

Verses 33-37: (33) In the synagogue there was a man
who had the spirit of an unclean demon,
and he cried out with a loud voice,

(34) "Let us alone! What have you to do with us,
Jesus of Nazareth?
Have you come to destroy us?
I know who you are, the Holy One of God."

(35) But Jesus rebuked him, saying,
     "Be silent, and come out of him!"
     When the demon had thrown him down
        before them,
     he came out of him without having done him
        any harm.
(36) They were all amazed and kept saying to one
        another,
     "What kind of utterance is this?
     For with authority and power he commands
        the unclean spirits,
     and out they come!"
(37) And a report about him began to reach every
     place in the region.

This is the first of twenty-one miracle-stories in Luke's Gospel. Luke repeats (Lk 4:31-37; 8:26-39; 9:37-43) the three Markan exorcisms (Mk 1:21-28; 5:1-20; 9:14-29 (omitting Mk 7:24-30) and adds another very brief exorcism account (Lk 11:14) which he shares with Mt 12:22 (Nolland, 1989: 204).

The present account has all the characteristics of the typical exorcism story: (a) The demon recognizes the exorcist and puts up a struggle; (b) the exorcist utters a threat or command; (c) the demon departs, making a scene; and (d) the spectators' reaction is recorded (Bultmann, 1972: 210).

The exorcism stories are but one of the four kinds of miracle stories in Luke; there are in addition, healing stories (sometimes not easily distinguished from exorcisms), resuscitations, and nature miracle stories. Though it is customary to label such gospel episodes as "miracle" stories, one has to beware of the connotation that this Latin-derived title brings with it a connotation that is not necessarily conveyed by the Gospel accounts. The Lain *miraculum* means "a thing causing wonder"; its Greek equivalent would be *thaumasion*, which is found only in Mt 21:15 in the New Testament. In Luke one finds on occasion the term *paradoxa*, "remarkable things" or *ta endoxa*, "glorious things" (see Lk

5:26; 13:17). But this element of wonder and surprise (especially at what might seem to be out of the ordinary) is not per se the reaction that these accounts usually evoke.

Behind the New Testament miracles is the Old Testament idea of *mopet*, "portent, prodigious sign," usually translated in the Septuagint as *teras*. Yet it is often a symbolic action authenticating a prophet's mission and not necessarily preternatural (see Ez 12:1-6). The Greek *teras* is never used alone of Jesus' miracles in the New Testament; but in Acts 2:22,43 Luke uses the Old Testament expression *terata kai semeia*, "wonders and signs" (see Deut 28:46; 13:2; 29:2), along with the normal Greek word used in the Synoptics for them, *dynameis*, "powers, powerful deeds." Contrast the Johannine use of "signs" (*semeia*) and "works" (*erga*). The Lukan use of *dynameis* is found in Lk 10:13; 19:37. This Synoptic designation for Jesus' miracles better reveals the character of these deeds; and in this very episode, Lk 4:31-37, there will be mention of power (Lk 4:36). They are not meant in the Gospels as apologetic proofs of Jesus' mission (though Luke does refer to them in this way in Acts 2:22) or of his divinity. They are rather the powerful manifestations and means whereby the dominion of God is established over human beings in place of the "dominion of Belial," freeing them from the evil to which they have been subjected. They also reveal that a new phase of saving history is at work. Jesus' *exousia*, "authority," makes his teaching carry weight, and his *dynamis*, "power," reveals that God's dominion is being established in him.

In the worldview of the first-century Mediterranean area, causality was primarily personal. It took a person, human or nonhuman, to effect change. This was true not only at the level of human society but at the levels of nature and the cosmos as well. Things beyond human control, such as weather, earthquakes, disease, and fertility, were believed to be controlled by non-human persons who operated in a cosmic social hierarchy. Each level in the hierarchy could control the ones below:

1. "Our" God, the Most High God
2. "Other" Gods or sons of God or archangels
3. Lower non-human persons: angels, spirits, demons
4. Humankind
5. Creatures lower than humankind.

Demons (Greek) or unclean spirits (Semitic) were thus personified forces that had the power to control human behavior. Accusations of demon possession were based on the belief that forces beyond human control were causing the effects humans observed. Since evil attacks good, people expected to be assaulted (see Lk 13:16). A person accused of demon possession was a person whose behavior (external symptom) was deviant or who was embedded in a matrix of deviant social relationships. A deviant situation or behavior required explanation and could be attributed to God (positive) or to evil (dangerous). Such attribution was something the community would be concerned to clarify in order to identify and expel persons who represented a threat. Freeing a person from demons, therefore, implied not only exorcizing the demon but restoring that person to a meaningful place in the community as well (Lk 8:39).

In antiquity, all persons who acted contrary to the expectations of their inherited local status or role were suspect and had to be evaluated. Accusations of demon possession leveled at Jesus (Lk 11:5) were essentially the judgment that because he could not do what he did of himself, an outside agency had to be involved. It could be God, as Jesus claimed, or the demonic forces claimed by his opponents. [In Jn 8:44,48, Jesus and the Judaeans trade the charge of demon possession back and forth].

Though it is now common to call the casting out of demons "exorcism," this is not a word the New Testament uses of Jesus. Jesus' power over demons is essentially a function of his place in the hierarchy of powers (and is used as evidence of that by the Gospel writers). He is an agent of

God, imbued with God's holy/clean spirit, who overcomes the power of evil (Malina-Rohrbaugh, 1992: 312-313).

This, then, is the real implication of the present scene. It concretely illustrates Jesus' teaching and power over evils that beset unfortunate human beings. In the Lukan context that authority and power are rooted in Jesus' anointing with the Spirit (Lk 3:22; 4:18). Because of that he is now recognized to be not only "Jesus of Nazareth," but even "the Holy One of God" (Lk 4:34; Fitzmyer, 1981: 542-543). Against the background of Jesus' authoritative teaching Luke presents the story of his exorcism of a demon in the synagogue.

A second important figure enters the scene: "there was a man." This man is further described as having "the spirit of an unclean demon" (compare Mark's "with an unclean spirit"), an expression found only here in the New Testament. The spirit of the man is caused by a "demon," who as such is a neutral figure for Luke's Hellenistic readers, and is therefore described as "unclean," and therefore negative. Luke does not provide a description of the demoniac's symptoms, apart from reporting what he shouted at Jesus and saying that the man was thrown down (Lk 4:35) when the demon left. On this slender basis, it has been speculated that the man was suffering from hysteria or epilepsy, but there is too little evidence to be confident about either diagnosis. It is clear from other New Testament accounts of possession that the condition was often associated with physical or psychological illnesses (Page, 1995: 140-141).

There is most probably a deliberate contrast between the characterization of the demon as "unclean" and the description of Jesus as "the Holy One of God" (Mk 1:24; Lk 4:34; Page, 1995: 140). Luke intensifies the man's/spirit's cry by adding "with a loud voice." In Luke there is no longer room for such a reaction *after* the command to leave the man (compare Lk 4:35 and Mk 1:26; Kirchschläger, 1981: 35-36). It is important to observe that nowhere in the Gos-

pels is a demon-possessed person charged with moral de-
fects. Emphasis is placed on the oppressed, depressed, or otherwise debilitated condition of the victim (Danker, 1988:
111).

The traditional heart of the story lies in the verbal exchange between the possessed man and Jesus, and here Luke
agrees with Mark almost verbatim (Tiede, 1988: 112). The
demon cries out and challenges Jesus. Such cries by demons
who meet Jesus are common (Mk 3:11; 5:7; Mt 8:29; Lk
4:41; 8:28; Bock, 1994: 431). Luke begins the direct speech
with an exclamation that expresses displeasure or surprise
(Fitzmyer, 1981: 545) or fear. Except for *ea*, Lk 4:34 corresponds exactly in wording to Mk 1:24. The Greek particle
ea ("Ah!" as in RSV; not an imperative, "leave/let us alone!,"
as in NAB and NRSV; see Busse, 1977: 81; Kirchschläger,
1981: 37; differenly in Schurmann, 1969: 247 note 194;
Nolland, 1989: 206). With this exclamation the demon
expresses his resignation in the face of Jesus' authority (Compare Lk 10:17ff.; Busse, 1977: 81). "What have you to do
with us?" literally, "what to us and to you," is frequently
found in the Septuagint and represents a denial that the
parties have anything in common (Nolland, 1989: 206-207).
Similar expressions appear in Judg 11:12; 2Sam 19:22; 1Kgs
17:18, all of which involve situations of conflict. A comparison with these Old Testament texts demonstrates that
the demoniac here uses accepted language of opposition (Van
Der Loos, 1965: 379). The wording also closely parallels
the initial question posed by the Gerasene demoniac in Lk
8:28. Jesus is here addressed as "Jesus of Nazareth" (Twelftree,
1993: 63-66; Page, 1995: 141).

The note of conflict comes in the question of whether
Jesus has come to destroy. Such conflict between forces of
good and evil is common (Lk 8:28; 10:8-9,17-19; 11:14-
23). The question, "Have you come to destroy us?" clearly
serves well the early Church's purposes. The destruction of
evil was expected in the messianic age (e.g., *Assumption of*

Moses 10:1,3) The early Church took up the theme (Lk 10:18) and Jesus is portrayed in the Gospels as one who destroys evil powers (Lk 11:20ff.; Twelftree, 1993: 66).

It is debated what "us" refers to. It has been suggested that it refers not just to the spirit, but to all in the synagogue audience, as the spirit attempts to alienate the audience from Jesus by raising the threat of destruction (Van der Loos, 1965: 379-380). But this interpretation seems far-fetched. Most scholars opt for a reference to Jesus' power over all evil spoirits and see here an allusion to all evil forces that Jesus will overcome (Schürmann, 1969: 247; Fitzmyer, 1981: 545-546; Nolland, 1989: 207; Page, 1995: 141). It has also been argued that "us" is a reference to both the demon and the man (Danker, 1988: 111-112; differently in Fitzmyer, 1981: 545). Thus the man, possessed by evil, is potentially subject to destruction. Luke knows that the possessed can be harmed by demons (Lk 8:28; 9:39,42; 11:14; 13:10-17). But in this case, Jesus will extract the evil force without harming the man (Lk 4:35). The power exerted involves Jesus' total control of evil (Bock, 1994: 432-433).

The demon's claim to know who Jesus is may represent an attempt to gain power over him through knowledge of his name (Marshall, 1978: 193; C.F. Evans, 1990: 279). By speaking this name the demoniac opposes power to power; his knowldge of the true name must adjure the power of his opponent (Van Der Loos, 1965: 380). Indeed many scholars believe that these confessions by demons are based on the notion, common in the world of magic, that to know the identity of one's opponent is to have power over him or her (Hull, 1974: 67; Page, 1995: 142-143). At the same time the demon recognizes in his conqueror the Son or "Holy One of God." As suggested above, the word "holy" contrasts with "unclean" in verse 33 and highlights the conflict (Danker, 1988: 111).

Jesus' reply is the same as in Mark: Jesus rebuked the

demon. The Greek word *epitimaō* underlying the rendering
"rebuked" is used by Luke in the technical sense of "exor-
cize" (Lk 4:39,41; 8:24; 9:42; Danker, 1988: 112). It has
been shown that in the Septuagint this technical usage
denotes the pronouncement of a commanding word whereby
God or his spokesperson brings evil powers into submission.To
use this verb of the demon reveals the lordship of Jesus;
that is what is connoted by the authority and power in-
vested in the command that he utters (Fitzmyer, 1981: 546).
Jesus' call for silence is in harmony with the passage's note
of conflict (Bock, 1994: 434; Theissen, 1983:144).

By the command "come out of the man" Jesus distinguishes between the man and the demon that possessed him.
The demon's destructive power is engaged in a last effort to
overpower the man, throwing him down before the onlookers, but out he must come, and Luke notes that the man
was not harmed. At this point Luke omits "with a great
cry" (Mk 1:26). The cry, which could denote a sign of struggle,
is here deleted. Any struggle was *before* the word of rebuke
(see "cried with a loud voice" in Lk 4:33). This highlights
Jesus' complete mastery over the demon (Danker, 1988: 112).

"Before them" is a Lukan addition to the description of
the departure of the demon that enables all present to see
what has happened (Johnson, 1991: 84). It may also be Luke's
way of insisting on the reality of the miracle and making
the healing all the more conspicuous (Busse, 1977: 83;
Fitzmyer, 1981: 546; Schweizer, 1984: 99; C.F. Evans, 1990:
281). The demon's action should not be understood as a
final threat. After Jesus' word the demon had no more power.
In fact, Luke insists that the demon went out "without having
done him any harm" (Kirchschläger, 1981: 38). Besides the
powerlessness of the demon Luke also emphasizes Jesus' mercy
for the afflicted man. The departing demon is not allowed
to harm him (Busse, 1977: 83; Johnson, 1991: 84).

The miracle story culminates in the reaction of the spectators. The beginning of this verse reads literally: "And fear

came on all..." The "amazement" (*thambos*; see Lk 5:9; Acts 3:10, each time in reaction to a miraculous event) that falls on all those present, expresses "fear and trembling" because of the unexpected confrontation with the divine. This "fear" is also expressed in the ensuing conversation among the onlookers, as is skilfully suggested by the alliteration of the Greek text, *sunelaloun pros allēlous legontes*, literally, "they spoke to one another saying." This is expressed more concretely in direct speech in verse 36b. Luke anticipates the answer by formulating the question, "What kind of utterance is this?" or "What is this word?" He formulates similar questions in Lk 1:66; 7:49; 8:25; 9:9. The tendency to define things more precisely appears especially in Lk 5:21, "Who is this who is speaking blasphemy?" compared with Mk 2:7, "Why does this fellow speak this way?" The reference to Lk 4:32, "because he spoke with authority," or "his word was with authority," is obvious in verse 36c, "for with authority and power he commands...." Grammatically it is a distinct possibility that the subject of the verb to command" is "the word" rather than Jesus himself (Kirchschläger, 1981: 39-40).

As a result of the exorcism the fame, literally, the "sound" or "echo," of Jesus spread into the surrounding area. Only here does Luke use the word *ēchos* for information about Jesus. In Lk 21:25; Acts 2:2 (and Heb 12:19) it has another meaning. It has been pointed out that the word *echos* is related to the word *katēchēthēs*, "instructed" in Lk 1:4 (Danker, 12988: 112). Elsewhere Luke uses *phēmē* (Lk 4:14; "fame") or *ho logos* (Lk 5:15; 7:17). By substituting "every place in the region" for Mark's "the surrounding region" Luke makes the expression "in the surrounding region" recede into the background. What is important is not the "spreading throughout all the surrounding region" (cf. Mk 1:28), but the fact that *each place* in the region received the report (Kirchschläger, 1981:41). Luke is certainly thinking of the region of the lake of Genesareth around Capernaum. The exact location is al-

ready given by Lk 4:14 and 31. He implies that Jesus' reputation goes even beyond the regions that he himself visits
(Fitzmyer, 1981: 547). For Luke this spread of Jesus' reputation helps account for the crowd that appears with its sick
folk in Lk 4:40 (Johnson, 1991: 84).

Two angles of investigation might help us get inside
stories such as this one, in order to better understand how
these stories function in the Gospel narrative.

The first direction we might take is to ask *what condi-*
tion is being attributed to demon possession, and *what is said to*
happen to the person in the course of the story. In this story
for example, the man is described as shouting angry and
accusatory words. "What have you to do with us?" should
be understood as an accusation that Jesus is a threat to what
is making the person not an integrated "I," but a fragmented
"we." Were we to hear somebody shouting like that, we
would think immediately of mental illness or a severe personality disorder: Something is making the person "not him-
or herself." Our concern would be for the person to get
care in the short term, and treatment over the long haul,
to attempt to bring the broken parts of the personality back
together into the sort of integrated whole that we recognize as healthy human life. That is exactly what the exorcism narratives are attempting to communicate. In the language of the world from which the Gospels emerged, demons are recognized in conditions of physical and mental
suffering, not where there is moral wrongdoing. In these
stories, as in the world from which they came, the symptoms indicating demon possession were seen as frightening
(as such symptons are to many people today as well). The
person seen as "possessed" migh be avoided or ignored —
not acknowledged until an outburst forces people to notice
— or physically removed to the margins of society. But what
is recognized to be needed is healing, or perhaps for the
person to be freed from captivity or enslavement to the alien
and self-alienating forces that are in control. What is not

called for is judgment or punishment. Thus, in Lk 5:31-17, the "demon" is simply said to be silenced (resulting in the cessation of the principal symptom), and after provoking something like a seizure in the person, to leave the person unharmed and restored to an integrated whole.

A second way to get inside such stories is to look at *what claims the narrator makes about Jesus*. In Lk 4:31-37, it is while the person is shouting as a fragmented self that "they" are said to recognize Jesus, to realize that he represents a threat, and to identify him as "the Holy One of God" (Lk 4:34). As a power beyond the realm of everyday human interaction (the demon has been able to conquer and take over a human being), the demon can recognize that greater-than-human-power in Jesus. The narrator thereby makes a claim about Jesus' own identity as involving more than simply the human authority of, for example, a great teacher. Power is at issue, and Jesus is not only recognized as moving in the realm of greater-than-human power that so often has destructive manifestations. He is also able to control even that sort of power when it functions to harm a person (Lk 4:35). Just as the people were astounded at the authority of his teaching (Lk 4:32), so now they are amazed at this other sort of authority and power that he manifests (Ringe, 1995: 72-73).

b. The Healing of the Mother-in-Law of Peter (Lk 4:38-39)

Verses 38-39: (38)   After leaving the synagogue he entered
                     Simon's house.
                     Now Simon's mother-in-law was suffering
                     from a high fever,
                     and they asked him about her.
             (39)   Then he stood over her and rebuked the fever.
                     and it left her.
                     Immediately she got up and began to serve them.

The second story in this section of the Gospel does not deal with the disintegrative power of "demons," but with the physical ravages of disease — a fever. From a form-critical viewpoint, the scene is another miracle-story, but this time one belonging to the category of healings. Sometimes it is not easy to decide whether the healing is strictly such or borders on an exorcism (Fitzmyer, 1981: 548).

Jesus' ministry to diseased women is the subject of several passages in the Synoptic tradition. In fact, there are six healings involving females in the Synoptic tradition (Dewey, 1993: 183). In each instance we are given further evidence of Jesus' outright rejection of various taboos inhibiting his ability to heal those in need. In Lk 4:38-39 we see Jesus' willingness to heal a diseased woman even on a sabbath. That this healing is paired with that of a man (Lk 3:31-37) may be the evangelist's way of saying that Jesus was willing to perform such an act on the sabbath for both men and women. Though there were precedents for rabbis taking the hand of another man and miraculously healing him, there are no examples of rabbis doing so for a woman, and ceretainly not on the sabbath, when the act could wait until after sundown (Witherington III, 1990: 76-77).

The location of the story in the Markan narrative between the exorcism in the synagogue on the sabbath and the crowd gathering for healing at the door at sundown, the end of the sabbath (Mk 1:21-28,32-34), places the healing on the sabbath, and thus Jesus' act of touching the woman, is work breaking the sabbath rest. However, the story itself makes no mention of this being a sabbath healing, and as an independent oral unit, it was not necessarily connected with the sabbath. If the story is not a sabbath healing, Jesus' behavior is not subversive. In Matthew's narrative order, the story does not occur on the sabbath (Mt 8:14-15); in Luke's version, the story is in the same narrative placement as Mark, but Luke treats it as an exorcism, curing by word, command, which was not considered work on the sabbath. Thus Matthew and Luke avoid even the inference of sabbath breaking which is present in Mark's narrative (Dewey, 1993: 185).

In Luke, the time is still the sabbath as in the previous story, but the setting has shifted from the public arena of the synagogue to the privacy of Simon's house (Ringe, 1995: 74). Luke depicts Jesus' entry (*eiserchomai*) into houses throughout the course of his ministry. He only rarely speaks of Jesus' entry (*eiserchomai*) into the synagogue (Lk 4:16. 6:6) or temple (Lk 19:45). When Jesus enters a village or city (Lk 7:1;9:52; 10:38; 17:12; 19:1), it often leads to a mission to houses (Lk 7:1; 10:38; 19:1). Unlike in Mark and in Matthew, *eiserchesthai eis ton oikon*, "to enter into the house," is a virtual technical term in Lukan literature to denote the act in which the guest enters into and accepts the hospitality offered by the host. In contexts of hospitality, the independent use of *eiserchomai* carries essentially the same meaning (Matson, 1996: 55).

Luke has not yet introduced Simon into the narrative (see Lk 5:4). This may have been caused by his shifting the order of the stories he found in Mark. But the fact that Simon appears in the narrative without introduction also suggests that he is known to the implied reader of Luke (Tyson, 1992: 27; Bock, 1994: 435-436). Luke also eliminates mention of Jesus' other companions that are listed in Mk 1:29 (Johnson, 1991: 84). "Simon's house" (in *Capernaum*) naturally suggests that Simon is the owner of the house. This detail is taken by Luke from Mk 1:29, but it seems to conflict with Jn 1:43 which speaks of *Bethsaida* as "the city of Andrew and Peter" (Fitzmyer, 1981: 549). That the narrator later identifies this same Simon as the owner of a fishing boat in a commercial fishing business (Lk 5:3) adds to Simon's status as a person of some economic means on the pages of Luke's Gospel (Matson, 1996: 56)

Unlike Mark, Luke speaks of a "*high* fever." Some scholars suggest that this would correspond to distinctions made in the medical language of the time and that thereby Luke would indicate a particular type of fever (Marshall, 1978:

195); but others rather think that Luke wants to insist on
the seriousness of the illness and the condition of the woman
(Kirchschlager, 1981: 60), and that it will take a powerful
deed of Jesus to cure it (Fitzmyer, 1981: 550).

Luke accords the household a strategic role in the healing of Simon's mother-in-law. Whereas in Mark the disciples explicitly make request on her behalf (Mk 1:30), in
Luke this role belongs to the members of Simon's household: "and they asked him about her," meaning that they
requested Jesus to heal her (Schürmann, 1969: 251;
Kirchschläger, 1981: 60). Luke's earlier omissions leave the
"they" without possible antecedent. Presumably the members of the household are intended (Nolland, 1989: 211-
212). The possibility should be considered that with the
plural "they asked" Luke refers to the fact that it is the
Christian community of yesterday and today that must pray
for the healing and salvation of the sick and sinners (cf. Jas
5:14-15; Acts 8:15). It would be mistaken to overlook this
typically Lukan perspective and to translate this
communitarian plural by an anonymous "one asked him."

The expression "he stood over her" is not used anywhere else in the New Testament (but see 2Sam 1:9LXX.
The translation is correct provided it is understood that "bent
over" is implied, not "stood over threateningly." Jesus placed
himself *above* her. To be *up* implies to be powerful, to be
down powerless (Ps 37:14; Ez 32:18). Even in present-day
exorcisms one "talks down" to the "demon." Jesus mimes
the common and biblical power-relation between "up" and
"down" (Deut 28:13). Standing *epano*, "over," he threatens
(2 Sam 1:9) the demon, not the woman. Luke assumes popular
Jewish biblical notions in this area (Derrett, 1993: 99-109).

The request by the household elicits a dramatic response
from Jesus whose *rebuke* of the fever (Lk 4:39) recalls his earlier expulsion of the demon at the synagogue in Capernaum
(Lk 4:35). The fever demon that Jesus casts out of the woman
is a living creature (Rice, 1982: 26). Thereby the exorcism

and the healing are linked; like the demon, the fever also left (Johnson, 1991: 84). Only in Luke does Jesus rebuke the fever that has seized her (in Matthew, Jesus heals the woman by simply touching her hand [Mt 8:15]; in Mark, he does so by raising her up and taking hold of her hand [Mk 1:31]). In treating the fever as produced by a demon, Luke assimilates the technique of healing to that of exorcism and there is no mistaking the features of an exorcism in the healing (Theissen, 1983: 86; C.F. Evans, 1990: 282). But it may not be a real exorcism because a vital feature is missing, namely, the departure of the demon, unless Luke implies this by the phrase "the fever left him" (Theissen, 1983: 87,185)

This rebuke of the demonic fever provides a further illustration of Jesus' powerful word (see the repeated emphasis on the *logos* of Jesus at Lk 4:22,32,36; Tannehill, 1986: 84-85). As a result, the house of Simon becomes the scene of further healings and exorcisms (Lk 4:40-41) as suggested by the immediate context in Luke (more explicit in Mk 1:33). It becomes the place for proclaiming release to Satan's captives (Lk 4:18-19; Rice, 1982: 23-28; Matson, 1996: 57). And Jesus' action is another display of the liberation which the messiah brings (Tiede, 1988: 113).

Of particular significance here is the relation of the adverb *parachrema*, "immediately," to the rest of the clause in Lk 4:39b: release from Satan's control issues "immediately" on her act of hospitality. Luke inserted here "immediately" (*parachrēma*) to emphasize the miraculous nature of the cure. The word occurs also in Mt 21:19,20; otherwise it is confined in the New Testament to Luke, who uses it ten times in the Gospel and six times in Acts (Lk 1:64; 4:39; 5:25; 8:44,47,55; 13:13; 18:43; 19:11; 22:60; Acts 3:7; 5:10; 12:23; 13:11; 16:26,33; Bock, 1994: 437 note 27). As here, it is often used by Luke in connection with miracles.

Upon being restored to a full and vigorous health, the woman resumes her normal domestic activity of the household. In a study on the taxonomy of sickness in Luke and

Acts, that is, the identification, classsification, and clustering of illnesses into culturally meaningful categories, Lk 4:38-39 has been assigned to the symbolic body-zone of the hands and feet, the zone of purposeful activity (Pilch, 1991: 200,205; Matson, 1996: 57-58).

If Simon's house becomes a locus for the healing of his mother-in-law, she reciprocates accordingly by serving Jesus and Simon's household as her guests (Lk 4:39b, "immediately she got up and began to serve them"; whereas in Mt 8:15, she serves only Jesus, not the household; Moxnes, 1991: 261-263). Healing isues in the celebration of food and drink. Luke often employs *diakoneō*, "to serve," for the preparation and distribution of food (Lk 4:34; 8:3; 10:40; 12:37; 17:8; 22:26-27[3x]; Acts 6:2; 17:22; Via, 1985:37-45).

The woman's role seems to be conforming. After her cure, she serves the men present (Mk 1:31; Mt 8:15; Lk 4:39). In Mark, the later use of *diakonos* and *diakoneō* in the instruction of the twelve (Mk 9:34; 10:43,45) and for women followers in Mk 15:41 suggests that the woman in Mk 1:29-31 is performing a ministry of service as a disciple. However, given the cultural expectations of women's roles, some scholars expect that service in the story as an independent oral narrative would be generally construed as referring to women's traditional role in cooking and serving food. The mother-in-law has been restored to her proper role in a peasant patriarchal household. The narrative basically upholds the dominant cultural values. In this story, both Jesus and the woman were presented as behaving in culture-conforming ways (Dewey, 1993: 186).

In Luke, the picture we have is of a woman getting up from her sickbed and bringing them food, and that may be the meaning intended here. The verb "serve" does refer to serving food, and thus is connected to the importance of meals in the life of early Christian communities. "Serve" is also the word Jesus uses later in the Gospel to identify the appropriate activity and posture of disciples (Lk 22:26). By portraying the woman as engaging in this act of ministry as a consequence of her having been healed by Jesus early in his ministry, Luke may already hint at the continuing life of the Christian community.

It is interesting that the first person actually to carry out the duty of ministry or service is this unnamed woman. She is not the only woman in Luke's Gospel described as "serving" Jesus and those with him (Martha's work described in Lk 10:38-42 is another well-known example). Other women will learn from Jesus (Mary in Lk 10:38-42) and even "preach" (the woman who had been cured of hemorrhages, according to Lk 8:47) — despite the fact that in Luke's Gospel and in Acts only men are officially commissioned to preach. By Lk 4:38-39, then, the evangelist not only amplifies the picture he is sketching of Jesus, but he also sets the stage for the continuing work of carrying forward the Gospel, which comes into focus in Acts (Ringe, 1995: 74-75).

c. *Healings in the Evening (Lk 4:40-41)*

Verses 40-41: (40) As the sun was setting,
all those who had any who were sick with
    various kinds of diseases
brought them to him;
and he laid hands on each of them and
    cured them.
(41) Demons also came out of many, shouting,
    "You are the Son of God!"
But he rebuked them and would not allow
    them to speak,
because they knew that he was the Messiah.

Following the Markan summary report (Mk 1:23-34) of healings and exorcisms performed by Jesus in the evening, Luke presents his third Capernaum scene in a similar way. Like the text of Mark, it has the nature of a summary (see Lk 4:14-15,31-32). The Lukan summary presents Jesus as healer and exorcist, this time allowing the demons to recognize him as the Son of God and the Messiah. Combined with the title used earlier in Capernaum, "the Holy One of God" (Lk 4:34), these titles emphasize Jesus' closeness to God in his role in salvation history (Fitzmyer, 1981: 553).

At sundown, that is, when the sabbath was past, the townspeople brought their sick to Jesus. A new feature in Luke's version is that Jesus performed his healings by laying his hands on the sick (Lk 13:13; cf., 5:13). The imposition of hands as a gesture of healing is unknown in the Old Testament and in rabbinical literature, but is found in the Dead Sea Scrolls, and in Hellenistic accounts of miraculous healings. The action points to the personal interest Jesus took in the sufferers as well as to his lack of fear of contracting ritual defilement (Marshall, 1978: 196; Fitzmyer, 1981: 553; Danker, 1988: 113).

The pericope culminates in the confession of the demons that Jesus was the Son of God (or the Christ). Mk 1:34 has only that the demons knew who Jesus was. Apart from Mary (Lk 1:35), only Jesus himself (Lk 3:22) and the demons know him as "Son of God" (Lk 4:3,9,41). Likewise, the recognition of Jesus as Messiah is the only one prior to Peter's in Lk 9:20 (Johnson, 1991; 84). Luke's addition to Mark's account, that the demons identified him as the Son of God, gives him an opportunity to equate this name with Jesus" role as the "Christ" or Messiah. Thus Luke suggests that the healings enumerated are in keeping with the program announced at Nazareth, where Jesus said that the Spirit of the Lord had annointed (= "christed") him (Lk 4:18; Danker, 1988: 113). Mentioning Jesus' titles represents an attempt by the demons to demonstrate superiority to the exorcizer by knowledge of his name, or it may be a confession of the superior power of Jesus on the part of the defeated demons (Schürmann, 1969: 253). In any case, Christians would recognize it as a true insight into the person of Jesus, who is now fulfilling the proper function of the Son of God instead of yielding to the devil's temptation to misuse his position (Marshall, 1978: 196-197).

d. *Departure from Capernaum* (Lk 4:42-44)

Verses 42-44: (42) At daybreak he departed and went into a
          deserted place.
          And the crowds were looking for him;
          and when they reached him,
          they wanted to prevent him from leaving them.
     (43) But he said to them,
          "I must proclaim the good news of the
             kingdom of God
          to the other cities also;
          for I was sent for this purpose."
     (44) So he continued proclaiming
          the message in the synagogues of Judea.

Jesus begins the new day by going out to a secluded place. Mark tells us that he goes specifically to pray. That Luke lacks this point is interesting in light of his emphasis on prayer (Lk 3:21; 5:16; 6:12; 9:18,28). The normal interpretation for this omission is that Luke wanted to focus only on the issue of mission here and so will refer to prayer in Lk 5:16 (Creed, 1957: 72). But not all scholars agree with this interpretation (Bock, 1994: 439-440). According to a recent commentary, the omission of "he prayed" (found in Mk 1:35) is not surprising, as attached to the incident it might suggest that Jesus was still uncertain of the nature and range of his mission, whereas he has been certain of it since his baptism (See Lk 4:16-30). The omission is repaired in Lk 5:16 by an addition to a generalizing summary from Mark, where it more aptly suggests that retirement from crowds for solitary prayer was a constant feature of the ministry (C.F. Evans, 1990: 284). The exorcism and healing stories continue to prepare the readers for, and to provide previews of, what Luke will narrate in the rest of the Gospel. They portray Jesus as not only proclaiming the good news, release, and liberty that is our first encounter with God's reign, but also as doing deeds to make that proclamation a reality. The concluding verses of this section remind us, by means of summary statements, of the dual direction of Jesus' ministry — deeds of healing and exorcism that make clear Jesus' power (Lk 4:40-41), and preaching of the message, which is "the good news of the kingdom of God" (Lk 4:42-44). Jesus' earlier departure from Nazareth may have been under threat, but he leaves Capernaum compelled only by the clarity of his vocation: "I must proclaim the good news of the kingdom of God to the other cities also; for I was sent for this purpose" (Ringe, 1995: 75). This statement reproduces the program announced at Nazareth, for the same terms (*euanggelizō, apostellō*) are used in Lk 4:18. "I was sent" picks up "He has sent me" in the Isaiah quotation in Lk 4:18.

The expression "the kingdom of God" is used here for the first time in Luke. He is to use the expression some thirty-five times. While very frequent in the Synoptic tradition it is comparatively rare in the rest of the New Testament (C.F. Evans, 1990: 284-286). Luke is the only New Testament author to use the phrase "the kingdom of God" as object of verbs expressing proclamation (Lk 4:43; 8:1; 9:2,60; 16:16; Acts 20:25; 28:23,31; Schweizer, 1984: 99). To these passages one should add the summary notices owing to which the text speaks of "*about* the kingdom of God" (*[ta] peri tes basileias tou theou*; Lk 9:11; Acts 1:3; 8:12; 19:8). The first (Lk 4:43) and last (Acts 28:31) occurrences of "the kingdom of God" form an inclusion for Luke's two-volume work (Wolter, 1995: 541,543). But is has been noted that the kingdom of God thematic is absent from Luke's special material (German: *Sondergut*; Pittner, 1992: 2).

In Lk 4:43 the earthly Jesus declares that the proclamation of the kingdom of God is the program of the mission God gave him. The verse receives its importance, on the one hand, from the fact that Lk 4:43-44 link Jesus' proclamation in the synagogues of Nazareth and Capernaum with is wider activity, and, on the other hand, from the conceptual linking with the Isaiah quotation in Lk 4:18-19 (*euangelizesthai, apostellein, kērussein*). Thereby Jesus' proclamation in his hometown becomes exemplary of his entire proclamation. That is, in sofar as Luke in Lk 4:43 explicitly qualifies the christological substance of the Nazareth pericope (that the promise of Isaiah [Lk 4:18-19] is fulfilled in Jesus [Lk 4:21]) as proclamation of the kingdom, he links the kingdom of God to the mission of the earthly Jesus: The kingdom does not bring us Jesus, but Jesus brings us the kingdom (Wolter, 1995: 549).

God's political action is to be seen in a remarkably dramatic manner. Some hint of it appeared in Lk 1:33, but now, in the light of Jesus' encounter with demonic forces and in view of his program announced in Nazareth, it is clear that the kingdom of God is a major assault on the forces of evil and the realization of Isaianic expectation. In practical terms this means that the people of God are to implement justice, which is the foundation of God's throne (Ps 97:2). So intimately is the reign of God connected with the person of Jesus that Acts 8:12 describes Philip as making a proclamation "about the kingdom of God and the name of Jesus Christ" (Wolter, 1995: 543). This king is no tool to be manipulated by nationalistic interests! A divine necessity rests on him: He "must" preach the good news of this news. The kingdom of God is not a demonstration of patronizing power. Jesus renounced that in his rebuff of the devil (Lk 4:8). Luke's entire narrative may be read as affirming Jesus' way of enacting the roles of Son of God and Messiah. Jesus is exercizing the reign of God correctly (Tiede, 1988: 114). The reign proclaimed by Jesus is God in outreach to claim what is properly God's: the poor, the estranged, the outcast — all who by established religious or social custom have been excluded from association with God (Danker, 1988: 114). Luke's real concern is not when the kingdom of God will come, but who will qualify to be admitted to it (Maddox, 1982: 106).

Luke's reinterpretation of the kingdom of God concept consists in his detaching the kingdom from its construction through Israel and binding it exclusively to the interpretation through Jesus. For Luke, the essence of the "kingdom of God" was determined by the totality of the proclamation of Jesus. With this new interpretation Luke managed to reassure his readers of continuity with the normative beginnings of Christian history and with the promises of salvation intended for Israel (Wolter, 1995: 541-563).

The concluding geographical reference to "Judaea" is a remarkable departure from Mark's "Galilee" (Mk 1:39). Galilee is important to Mark as a locality, but not to Luke. In Luke, Galilee is significant primarily because of the witnesses who are gathered from that region, whereas Jerusalem is the central locale for much of the decisive action described in Acts. Reference to "Judaea" suggests activity that takes in all of Judaea (Lk 1:5; 6:17; 7:17; Danker, 1988: 114; Tiede, 1988: 115).

4. The Call of Peter and His Companions (Lk 5:1-11)

The four preceding episodes (Lk 4:31-37, 38-39, 40-41 and 42-44) provided a view of a ministry conducted by Jesus alone, teaching and healing in Galilee. Luke now presents Jesus again in Galilee, on the shore of the Lake of Gennesaret, associating himself to Simon to whom he promises a new career. Peter is followed by two others. Luke also used Lk 5:1-11 as an introductory paradigm for what is to follow in Lk 5:12-6:16. Literarily, these passages are tied together by the term *egeneto* (see Hendrickx, 1996: 45-46) in Lk 5:1,12,17; 6:1,6,12 (Stein, 1992: 168).

The delimitation of the present pericope is obvious: verses 1 and 12 begin in practically the same way (*egeneto de*, "and it happened"; *kai egeneto*, "and it happened"; in both cases translated by "now" in NRSV). It is, therefore, obvious that the pericope ends with verse 11. Scholars are practically unanimous in accepting this, with the exception of Meynet (1979:34), who attaches Lk 5:12-16 to the pericope of the call of Peter. To him the question "Who is this?" is decisive for the delimitation of the pericope. But this question does not occur in Lk 5:1-16, as Meynet himself admits. The pericope is framed by preaching in the cities (Lk 4:43; 5:12). The two framing pericopes mention that Jesus withdraws into deserted places (Lk 4:42; 5:16). Internally too the pericope displays a serried structure. On the other hand, the writer intends us to read this pericope in relation to the preceding, because he starts the pericope with "he," and we have to return to Lk 4:34 to know who "he" is. (This is true of the Greek text; NRSV supplies "Jesus"; Bouwman, 1986: 116)..

This pericope and the one following it precede any mention of controversy that Jesus' ministry of teaching and healing will eventually evoke; they belong then to the "beginnings" of his (mainly) Galilean ministry. Lk 5:1-11 serves as a foil to the Nazareth pericope (Lk 4:16-30). Both are Lukan transpositions and create a literary contrast: in contrast to Jesus' experience of rejection at Nazareth is his own reception of outcasts. The acceptable year of the Lord (Lk 4:19) has indeed arrived (Danker, 1988: 115). From another viewpoint, this episode telling of the promise made to Simon foreshadows the choosing of the Twelve (Lk 6:12-16), of whom Simon will be the leader.

The two dialogues (Lk 5:4-5 and 8,10b) are the most important parts of the pericope. If one takes the two dialogues together, they appear to form a chiasm: Jesus - Peter x Peter - Jesus. In a chiasmus the emphasis is on the innermost pair, in this case therefore on Peter. The intermediate verses 6-7 are the core of the account. In them the transformation takes place: the sinner becomes a fisher of people (Bouwman, 1986: 119).

Lk 5:1-32 seems to be built around the theme of the forgiveness of sins. Beside Peter, who thinks that because of his sinfullness he is unworthy of the company of his Master (Lk 5:8), stands the leper who, because of his illness that was often considered a divine punishment for sin, doubts whether Jesus would be willing to cure him (Lk 5:12). Next appears the paralytic who needs forgiveness as well as healing (Lk 5:17-26). Finally we have the call of a tax collector who because of his occupation was considered to be a sinner (Lk 5:27-32; Feldkämper, 1978: 57).

The present pericope is a Lukan transposition (Fitzmyer, 1981: 71), for it is influenced by Mk 1:16-20, as is especially felt in verses 2 and 11 (Claudel, 1988: 120-121). But it is not a mere parallel to the Markan pericope. By transposing the scene from its Markan setting, Luke has eliminated the oft-noted implausibility of the Markan story about the call of the four disciples — the first thing Jesus does in that Gospel after his baptism and desert experience (Mk 1:9-11, 12-13). In the Lukan context, Jesus has been seen preaching and healing, and Simon (at least) has witnessed one of his mighty deeds (Lk 4:38-39). The preceding Lukan scenes thus provide a psychologically plausible setting for the call of Simon: Peter's call occurs only after those summoned to be disciples have had experience of both Jesus' teaching and healing (Fitzmyer, 1981: 560, 549; Perkins, 1994: 84). Luke has sketched an outline of the "good news" that is Jesus' agenda for teaching and action before anyone is invited to follow him, so that those who do become disciples should have a fairly clear idea of the design of Jesus' project. According to Luke, those who join Jesus in his mission should know what they are getting into (Ringe, 1995: 76).

In view of the disciples' place in the Gospel narrative and that of the early Church (Lk 8:51; 9:28,54; Acts 3:1; 4:13; 8:14ff.; 12:2), and especially Peter's place as the leading apostle and missionary of Jew and Gentile (Lk 9:20; 22:31; Acts 2:14,37; 5:29; 10-11; 15:14), Luke will hardly have been content to produce, either here or earlier, Mk 1:16-20, which is very terse and in which Peter appears only as one person in two pairs of brothers. As Paul is to be given a special call (Acts 9:1ff.), so must Peter be (C.F. Evans, 1990: 287). Nevertheless, Lk 5:10c, "Do not be afraid; from now on you will be catching people," gives no decisive information regarding the historical question of Peter's rank (Pesch, 1976: 44-59).

Apart from its new setting provided by the transposition, three main things are different: (1) Jesus is not a mere passer-by; he preaches from Simon's boat to the crowd on the lakeshore (verses 1-3); (2) Simon lets down his net for a miraculous haul of fish at Jesus' command (verses 4-10a); (3) Jesus promises Simon a new career, which results in his (and two of his companions') abandoning everything to follow Jesus (verses 10b-11). The whole episode is thus composed by Luke from transposed and redacted Markan material and other material from Luke's special source ("L"; Fitzmyer, 1981: 560). Scholars usually agree with a segmentation of the texts into three segments, but those who practice narrative hermeneutics or semiotics often present the following segmentation, different from the one just mentioned: (1) Jesus proclaims the word of God (Lk 5:1-3); (2) the miraculous catch of fish (Lk 5:4-7); (3) Simon's call to discipleship (Lk 5:8-11; McKnight, 1978: 277; Geninasca, 1978: 194; Tannehill, 1986: 203).

The similarity of the story of the call of Peter to details in Jn 21:1-11 has often been noted and ten points of similarity have been singled out:

1. The disciples have fished the whole night and have caught nothing.
2. Jesus' directive to cast their nets (in John: from the shore; in Luke: from the boat).
3. The directions are followed, and a large catch results.
4. The effect of the haul of fish on the nets.
5. Simon Peter reacts to the haul (a clearly Johannine touch makes the Beloved Disciple precede Peter)
6. Jesus is addressed as "Lord."
7. Other fishermen take part in the haul but say nothing.
8. The theme of following Jesus ends each acount (Brown

appeals to Jn 21:19,22, that, however, belongs to a subsequent event).

9. The catch symbolizes a successful missionary endeavor.
10. Some vocabulary overlaps, especially the name "Simon Peter," which appears only here in Luke.
11. The absence of any mention of Andrew in either account (cf. Mk 1:16; Brown, 1970: 1090; Brown et al., 1973: 116-117; Fitzmyer, 1981: 560-561; but see also the similarities noted by Bovon, 1991: 122; Bock, 1994: 449 note 2).

On the other hand, six points of dissimilarity have been noted:

1. In John Jesus is not recognized at first.
2. In John Jesus is on the shore, not in a boat.
3. In John Simon Peter and the Beloved Disciple are in the same boat;
4. In John Peter leaves the hauling of fish to the others.
5. In John the fish are caught close to shore and dragged to it.
6. In John Peter rushes through the water to the Lord; in Luke he begs the Lord to depart from him (Plummer, 1901: 147; Fitzmyer, 1981: 561).

Moreover, there are few precise verbal contacts between the two pericopes and a good number of those that can be established are of little importance (Claudel, 1988: 123). Whereas Plummer concluded to two miracles of a similar nature performed by Jesus — one to illustrate Simon's call; the other, the recall of the chief apostle, present-day commentators regard the Lukan and Johannine scenes as accounts of the same miracle. A long history of modern criticism has not brought the issue of the relationship between Lk 5:1-11 and Jn 21:1-14 to rest. The hypothesis that Luke's pericope is a transposed Easter story, hence the tradition-historical priority of Jn 21, frequently posited but seldom given substantial analytical support, has lost ground in recent discussion (Pesch, 1969: 86-110; Dillon, 1978: 63). Maybe it is best to hold that the two pericopes represent a piece of the Gospel tradition that has come independently to the two evangelists; Luke has made it part of his story of the call of Simon, but John has made it into a story of the appearance of the risen Christ (Fitzmyer, 1981: 561).

As the story stands now in Luke's Gospel, it can be form-critically classified as a pronouncement-story, with as "punch-line" verse 10d, "from now on you will be catching people," a Lukan redactional modification of the more original metaphor of Mk 1:17, "I will make you fish for people" (Fitzmyer, 1981: 562; differently in Nolland, 1989: 223). But the story has further been described as a "commission narrative," which also emphasizes the importance and function of the pronouncement (Talbert, 1982: 60-61). Lk 5:4-9a may have been a miracle-story in the pre-Lukan tradition, but the evangelist has subordinated it to the pronoucement-story; the miracle-story is now part of the narrative leading up to the pronouncement. The commission to Simon was not originally part of the miracle-story. The association of a miracle-story with the call of Simon, such as Luke has here done, heightens the idealistic character of the scene. But this is not sufficient to question the basic historicity of a call of Simon by the historical Jesus during his ministry (Fitzmyer, 1981: 562)

Verses 1-3: (1) Once while Jesus was standing beside the lake of Gennesaret,
and the crowd was pressing in on him to hear the word of God,

            (2) he saw two boats there at the shore of the lake; the fishermen had gone out of them and were washing their nets.

            (3) He got into one of the boats, the one belonging to Simon,
and asked him to put out a little way from the shore.
Then he sat down and taught the crowds from the boat.

In Lk 5:1 the sacred space of the synagogue (Lk 4:16,33,44) gives way to the shore of the lake. The account begins and ends at the shore of the lake ("away from the shore" [Lk 5:3] — "to the shore" [Lk 5:11]). Its counterpart is "the deep water" where the story proper unfolds.

Jesus is engaged in the mission that he described in Lk 4:43, and the great catch is a symbolic portrayal of the expanding mission in which Jesus is already engaged in Lk 5:1-3 (Tannehill, 1986: 203-204). The verb *epikeisthai*, found only in Luke among the Synoptics (Lk 5:1 23:23; Acts 27:20) describes the physical pressure of the crowd on Jesus to hear his teaching described as "the word of God" (Dietrich, 1972: 32-34; Marshall, 1978: 201). We meet here for the first time in Luke *ho ochlos* (singular, "the crowd," not "the people," which in Luke is *ho laos*). This crowd forms a regular undifferentiated audience for Jesus' words and deeds. Whereas Mark — with one exception, Mk 10:1 — always has the word in the singular, for Luke it is interchangeable with the plural (see *hoi ochloi*, "the crowds," in verse 3). They are represented throughout the Gospel as favorable to Jesus until the last moment in the passion, when they are found among his opponents (Lk 23:13-24), but then only temporarily (Lk 23:27,48; C.F. Evans, 1990: 289).

This is also the first occurrence of the phrase "the word of God" (*ho logos tou theou*) in Luke's Gospel. Except for Mk 7:13; Mt 15:6 (where it is used for an Old Testament statement; some manuscripts of Mt 15:6 have *nomos*, "law"), and Jn 10:35, it occurs only in Luke (Lk 5:1; 8:11,21; 11:28) and fourteen times in Acts. In most of the instances in Acts the phrase denotes the Christian message as preached by the apostles. Here in Lk 5:1 it is used of Jesus' own preaching. Thus Luke brings out the continuity between the teaching of Jesus and that of the Church (Marshall, 1978: 201). But, as the phrase suggests, the ultimate root of this preaching/teaching is God himself, for the phrase means "God's word" or "the word coming from God" (Bock, 1994: 453-

454; C.A. Evans, 1990: 85; Nolland, 1989: 221; Stein, 1992: 168).

There is little connection between Jesus' preaching of the word of God to the crowds that in Lk 4:40 came for healing and now press about him and the following miracle, but it does illustrate his ministry as a kingdom preacher and prepares for the function to which Peter will be called. Indeed, the way in which the crowd disappears further in the story suggests that Luke has linked together two separate incidents, using a typical scene in Jesus' ministry from Mark to stress that the call of Simon took place *after* he had heard "the word of God" (Marshall, 1978: 201).

The geographical notice "beside the lake of Gennesaret" is derived from Mk 4:1, "he began to teach beside the sea," that is, of Gennesaret, not far from Capernaum (Mk 2:1; 3:19b). This is supported by the fact that later on Luke omits Mk 4:1 in his parallel introduction to the parable of the sower (Lk 8:4; Fitzmyer, 1981: 560; differently in Dietrich, 1972: 30-31). Gennesaret is the Greek name of a small, fertile, and heavily populated district west of the lake that some writers refer to as the Sea of Galilee; it lay south of Capernaum. From the district the name was extended to the lake (Fitzmyer, 1981: 565).

Increasing demand for fish in the first century led to two basic systems of commercialization. In the first system, fishermen were organized by royal concerns or large landholders to contract for a specified amount of fish to be delivered at a certain time. Compensation was either in cash or in kind (processed fish). Papyrus records indicate that complaints about irregular or inadequate payment were not uncommon. Such records also indicate that this system was highly profitable for estate managers or royal treasuries. The fishermen themselves got little. The second system made fishing part of the taxation network. Fishermen leased their fishing rights from the toll collectors of New Testament times for a percentage of the catch. Evidence indicates that such lease fees could go as high as forty percent. The remaining catch could be traded through middlemen who both siphoned off the majority of profits and added significantly to the cost of fish in the markets. Legislation in Rome early in the second century sought to curtail rising costs by requiring that fish be sold either by the fishermen themselves or by those who first bought the catch from them. Such fishermen often worked with "partners," the term used in Lk 5:7. Hence the fishing done by Peter, James and John may have been of this second type (Malina-Rohrbaugh, 1992: 313-314).

By mentioning "two boats," Luke may be thinking of the next statement implying that Jesus selected the boat *of Simon* by design (Danker, 1988: 115-116), but he certainly prepares the reader for the miracle in verse 6 and the summoning of the *second* boat in verse 7. The choice of Simon's boat focuses on the one who is to play the leader's role in the group of disciples that Jesus will form (Fitzmyer, 1981: 566; Bock, 1994: 454-455). Since the pressure of the crowd prevented Jesus from speaking to them from the shore, he decided to use one of the boats as a pulpit (Marshall, 1978: 202). Jesus sits and teaches the crowd, a posture that he often takes when he teaches.

The peculiarity of the Lukan version should be noted. The story concentrates on Peter, even to setting the scene with him and Jesus apparently alone in the boat (verses 3-4). But then a puzzling alternation of singular and plural verbs (verses 4-6) abruptly reminds us of the plurality of disciples in the tradition even while he deliberately concentrates on Peter. The same is even more striking in verses 10-11: The sons of Zebedee suddenly appear in verse 10, after an episode in which they have not been mentioned, only then to have Jesus address his vocational demand to Peter only. Yet finally they all — plural — leave everything and follow Jesus. The pattern is clear: reminiscence of sources in which a plurality of disciples were involved, but concentration on Peter (Dillon, 1978: 64).

Verses 4-9a: (4) When he had finished speaking, he said to
                    Simon,
                    "Put out into the deep water and let down
                    your nets for a catch."
              (5) Simon answered, ""Master, we have worked
                    all night long
                    but have caught nothing.
                    Yet if you say so, I will let down the nets."
              (6) When they had done this, they caught so
                    many fish
                    that their nets were beginning to break.
              (7) So they signaled their partners in the other boat
                    to come and help them.
                    And they came and filled both boats,
                    so that they began to sink.
              (8) But when Simon Peter saw it
                    he fell down at Jesus' knees, saying,
                    "Go away from me, Lord, for I am a sinful man!"
              (9) For he and all who were with him were amazed
                    at the catch of fish that they had taken;
             (10a) and so also were James and John, sons of
                    Zebedee,
                    who were partners with Simon.

"When he had finished speaking" marks the major transition in the narrative: in verses 1-3 the link with Peter is
incidental; from this point on it is central (Nolland, 1989:
222).

Lk 5:4-10a may originally have been a post-Easter story
which was anticipated by Luke in Jesus' public ministry (Brown,
1973: 83-101), although the Lukan form of the story has
little trace of the elements of an appearance-story (Fitzmyer,
1981: 561). But a number of scholars hold the opposite view
that the original setting of the miraculous catch was Jesus'
public ministry (Pesch, 1969, and 1989: 153-154; Dietrich,
1972: 54-56).

In verse 4 the crowd disappears; the action changes,
and so does the space. The distance from the shore increases. The scene moves to a place which is suitable for
fishing, and there it stays until verse 11 (Delorme, 1971-

1972: 338-338). Verse 4 ushers in the transition to a new phase of the account: the teaching of the crowd is followed by an appeal to a few (Van Der Loos, 1965: 670-671). When he had finished his teaching, Jesus ordered Simon (singular) to sail out into the deep water where the men accompanying Peter were to lower the nets for a catch; the second command, "let down" is in the plural, since that action would involve all in the boat. There is no mention here of Andrew as in Mk 1:16f.; James and John are mentioned later. All the attention is concentrated on Simon (Marshall, 1978: 202-203). His name occurs six times (Lk 5:3,4,5,8,10ab).

In verses 5-7 follows the description of the catch itself. Simon addresses Jesus as *epistata*, "master." In secular Greek, the word was used for a whole series of people, for instance, for administrators in Roman occupied Egypt. In the New Testament the word occurs only in the Gospel of Luke (Lk 5:5; 8:24,45; 9:33,49; 17:13; C.A. Evans, 1990: 85; Stein, 1992: 169; the Synoptic parallels use *didaskalos*, "teacher," or *rabbi*) in which the word is used only by disciples (or "near-disciples," the only apparent exception being Lk 17:13). The word connotes a relation of authority. "Boss" is too trivial but renders its content better than "master" (Bouwman, 1986: 118). Since for Luke *didaskale*, "teacher," is an objective description while *epistata* involves a personal recognition, the latter is mostly on the lips of disciples (except Lk 17:13; Nolland, 1989: 222). The word is used in the context of a group placing itself under a master — this is also the case in Lk 17:13 — and may reflect a communal consciousness attributed by Luke to the disciples (Dietrich, 1972:38-43). In any case, the word "master" expresses an attitude of obedience which is intensified by the fact that notwithstanding an unsuccessful night's fishing trip Simon is prepared to cast the nets (Marshall, 1978: 203), "if you say so," more literally, "upon your word" (*epi de tōi rhēmati sou*; Tiede, 1988:118). "If you say so" points to the intrinsic authority of Jesus' words (Nolland, 1989: 222).

Simon is presented as speaking from two perspectives. First, Simon the *fisherman* speaks as he relates that they were unsuccessful on the previous evening. Though night was the best time to fish, the previous night had been fruitless. So Jesus' request that they go out and cast their nets during daytime had two strikes against it. The description of the pre-miracle conditions is common to this kind of account and is intended to draw attention to the the action's greatness when the miracle reverses the situation. The greatness of the miracle is then attested in several ways: "many fish," "the nets were beginning to break," and "they began to sink" (Nolland, 1989: 222).

Second, Simon the *man of faith* responds. Despite the fisherman's professional view of the situation, at Jesus' powerful word (see Lk 7:7,14) Simon orders his companions to cast the nets. This part of the verse shows that Simon is in charge of the group. Peter's responsiveness to the word reflects the proper reaction to God's messenger (Lk 1:38; 6:46; 8:21; 11:28; Bock, 1994: 456).

The huge catch of fish is obviously meant as something extraordinary, manifesting Jesus' power in preparation for the promise to be made to Simon (Fitzmyer, 1981: 567). "Their nets were beginning to break" seems to mean "were about to break." They did not break actually, for Simon and his partners were still able to fill two boats with fish. Fishing boats usually worked in pairs (Grundmann, 1966: 128). The fact that Peter is unable to haul in his catch without the assistance of his companions (Lk 5:6-7) indicates that the symbolic referent has a community dimension right from the start (Sweetland, 1990: 23. Luke focuses all attention on the immensity of the catch to explain why Simon Peter reacts as he does (Danker, 1988: 116). Simon "fell down at Jesus' knees." The body-language is clear. In verses 8ff. Simon is the central figure. As the story approaches its climax, Simon is given his full name "Simon Peter." The presence of the name here may simply lay stress on the person of Simon (Dietrich, 1972: 44-45) or reflect the consciousness that Simon's call and his naming by Jesus were connected (Grundmann, 1966: 128), or draw attention to the identity of Simon with Peter, the leader of the Twelve (Marshall, 1978: 204).

His action of falling down at Jesus' knees would be more appropriate on land than in a boat, as would his words, "Go away from me" (Brown, et al., 1973: 115). Besides, "Go away from me, Lord, for I am a sinful man!" is hardly the response that one would expect from a fisherman with a full boat. But then neither would it seem likely that the story would conclude with all of these fishermen leaving their boats and the catch and "everything" when they had just made such a catch (Tiede, 1988: 118). Simon and his companion(s) signal for help. The partners in view are probably James and John (Creed, 1957: 75).

"Go away from me" (*exelthe ap' emou*) should not be understood as "get out of the boat," but rather, "leave my vicinity" (cf. Lk 8:37, "Then all the people of the surrounding region of the Gerasenes asked Jesus to leave them; for they were seized with great fear"). The response of fear before the revelation of transcendent power is a staple of religious phenomenology: Simon's response is appropriate to a theophany (Nolland, 1989: 222; Dietrich, 1972: 46-47). What is remarkable here is that Simon repeats the command of Jesus to demons in Lk 4:35: "come out of him" (*exelthe ap' autou*; Johnson, 1991: 88).

Simon's reaction to the power shown in the miraculous catch of fish relates Jesus to a realm or sphere to which he himself does not belong. He is "a sinful man." His reaction is similar to that in Isa 6:5, "I am a man of unclean lips." Simon's self-description is not to be proleptically understood of his coming denial of Jesus (Lk 22:54-60), and the point is certainly missed if Simon's confession is traced to aware-

ness of the sinlessness of Jesus. Luke says plainly that the
confession was prompted by astonishment over the catch of
fish (Danker, 1988: 117). The term "sinful person" does not
necessarily denote one of a mass of people classified by the
Pharisees as outcasts, not entitled to God's favor (against
Danker, 1988: 116). "Amazement" (*thambos*) is to be understood as religious awe before the Holy (see Acts 3:10; Johnson,
1991: 88).

Simon, the sinner, kneels down before his "Lord" (*kurios*)
using a title that is normally reserved for the risen Christ,
but that is used here by the evangelist because of his
hindsight, as he writes from the perspective of his post-
Easter situation (Fitzmyer, 1981: 200, 567-568), thereby
establishing a clear link between the confession of the
Christian community and the history of Jesus (Danker,
1988: 117).

Verses 9-10a constitute a flashback in which the re-
dactor leads the reader back to give an explanation ("for").
He introduces "James and John, sons of Zebedee," without
explaining how Jesus got to know them. No doubt, they
are supposed to be known to the implied reader (Delorme,
1971-1972: 333). They are most probably introduced into
the story under influence of Mk 1:19 (Dietrich, 1972: 24).
Luke omits the mention of Andrew, who is less important
to him (he appears in the apostolic lists only: Lk 6:14 and
Acts 1:13) and who could not be introduced without somehow sacrificing the central focus on Simon (Nolland,
1989: 223).

Verses 10b-11): (10b) Then Jesus said to Simon, "Do not be afraid;
                       from now on you will be catching
                       people."
             (11)   When they had brought their boats to the
                       shore,
                       they left everything and followed him.

Then the calling of Simon follows. In Mk 1:17 and Mt
4:19 it is clearly stated that Jesus' call applied to the four

men present, while it follows from Lk 5:11 that not only
Simon but also the others followed the call (Van Der Loos,
1965: 672). Jesus' response begins with: "Do not be afraid,"
familiar in epiphany scenes (Pesch, 1969: 139). The expression "from now on" is Lukan (Lk 1:48; 12:52; 22:18,69; Acts
18:6). Luke does not use the expression strictly chronologically. Rather, it denotes a fundamental change in the state
of affairs (Pesch, 1969: 140). *Zogrein* used with *esei* means
literally "catching alive" or "to take alive" and is used in
this sense in the Septuagint (Grollenberg, 1965: 330-336).
This certainly suggests a rescue operation, that is, Peter and
his companions shall be in the business of rescuing human
beings. Luke thus interprets the original saying — whatever its exact original meaning may have been — by changing
the verb to make clear its positive focus (Witherington III,
1990: 130). Lk 5:10c should be considered as having been
formulated by Luke on the basis of Mk 1:17 (Pesch, 1976:
44-59).

Luke heightens the sense of a new beginning by writing,
"they left everything" (Nolland, 1989: 223) instead of Mark's
"they left their father Zebedee in the boat with the hired
men" (Mk 1:20). The stress is clearly on "everything, as subsequent texts will confirm. Luke thereby wants to emphasize
the totality and radicality of the call. They left behind their
job, their families, and all their possessions to follow Jesus.
The break was complete. Luke's description also allows us to
glimpse something of what this may have meant economically. Fishermen belonged to the middle class. From Luke's
version we can probably infer that the three fishermen were
fairly prosperous, especially by the fact that they formed a
partnership, an obvious business venture (Lk 5:7,10). Hence
the call to leave everything will have meant a considerable
change in their social status (Pilgrim, 1981: 87-88).

The final words of the pericope "and followed him" are
the first occurrence of *akolouthein* in the Lukan Gospel, where
it will often be used of Christian discipleship (Lk 5:27-28;

9:23,49,57,59,61; 18:22,28,43; Marshall, 1978: 206; Fitzmyer, 1981: 569; C.F. Evans, 1990: 292). According to some scholars, "following" here is not so much an image of Christian discipleship but the apostolic being-with-Jesus (Lk 1:2; Acts 4:13) that prepares them for their mission (Pesch, 1969: 141; Schürmann, 1969: 272; Nolland, 1989: 223-224). But before the term "disciple" is too readily restricted to an elite group among Jesus' followers, thus separating us from its challenge, we should note that the same response is later attributed to the tax collector Levi (Lk 5:28), whose name does not appear in the list of the twelve "chosen" apostles in Lk 6:14-15. Willingness to leave "everything" behind — one's family, possessions, status, economic security, and identity itself — in order to join in Jesus' ministry of the good news of God's reign characterizes all of Jesus' followers. It has implications for the nature and the norms of the new community being formed around Jesus, that form the basis of the Church (Ringe, 1995: 78).

In its present location in the Gospel, Lk 5:10b makes it clear that the abundant catch of fish is symbolically related to Simon's future catching of people. Thus the apostolic sending of Peter and his success in missionary endeavor of which we read in Acts is grounded in the pre-Easter intention of Jesus (Schürmann, 1969: 264; Nolland, 1989: 223). Indeed, since Simon's own fishing has caught nothing and all the fish are caught through an acceptance of the power of Jesus, it is apparent that Simon as a fisher of people will have his success also through the power of Jesus. Of himself, he is a sinful man, and he needs Jesus to make him a catcher of people. Luke certainly means that Simon's partners, James and John, will also catch people; but in directing the Lord's promise to Simon alone, Luke is preparing for the important role that Simon will have among the Twelve in the Acts of the Apostles (Brown, et al., 1973: 118-119).

In Lk 5:11, the evangelist uses the Greek word for "to follow" for the first time. In the Synoptic Gospels, this word appplies almost exclusively to following Jesus. In contemporary philosphical writings the term often described the relationship of teacher and disciples. Luke emphasizes how those following Jesus left "everything." More is involved here than leaving material goods behind. Geographical mobility and the consequent break with one's social network (biological family, patrons, friends, neighbors) were considered seriously deviant behavior and would have been much more traumatic in antiquity than simply leaving behind material wealth (Malina and Rohrbauch, 1992: 313).

Various allegorical interpretations, in which, for instance the boat, the net and the sea are said to depict the Church, the faith and the pagan world respectively, though ingeniously thought out, have no foundation in the account itself (Van Der Loos, 1965: 674).

5. Healing of a Leper (Lk 5:12-16)

With the pericope of the healing of a leper (Lk 5:12-16) Luke picks up the thread of the Markan sequence which he had been following in Lk 4:31-44 (Stein, 1992: 171). It was interrupted to accommodate the transposed story about the call of Simon and his companions (Lk 5:1-11). Luke's version clearly depends on Mk 1:40-45 — although a number of differences can be pointed out (Fitzmyer, 1981: 571-572) — and is parallel to Mt 8:1-4.

As the pericope stands in the Lukan Gospel, it is a simple miracle story of healing. It concentrates on the miracle that Jesus performs on behalf of a poor social outcast of a Palestinian Jewish town by using the power that Luke has already attributed to him (Lk 4:14). In contrast to Mark, Luke omits the mention of Jesus' emotion (Mk 1:41: "moved with pity" or "moved with anger"; Mk 1:43: "sternly warning him"). The result is that all the emphasis in the Lukan form of the account is on Jesus' will. He does touch the leper, but his all-powerful word gives utterance to an act of his will (Fitzmyer, 1981: 572).

For quite some time biblical scholars have noted that what the Bible calls "leprosy" is probably not — or not only — the disease we know as leprosy caused by the bacillus myobacterium leprae first discovered by Gerhard Hansen, and therefore commonly called Hansen's disease. Regarding the New Testament, it has been observed that not only are there no clinical descriptions of *lepra* in the New Testament, but the use of the word *lepra*, in itself, is strong evidence that the New Testamnent "leprosy" was not modern leprosy. In the Greco-Roman world, modern leprosy was called *elephas* and was described just as moderns know it by Celsus, Pliny the Elder, and Galen. Medical historians conjecture that it was probably brought into Palestine by the followers of the Ptolemies and the Seleucids who had in turn contracted it from the armies of Alexander the Great after their return from India. Though the medical evidence strongly militates against this condition being identified as "real" leprosy, there can be no certitude as to the exact disease under discussion. As the most accurate translation or paraphrase of the word *lepra/sara'at*, one has therefore suggested "a repulsive, scaly skin disease" (Pilch, 1981: 108).

One should read Lev 13—14 as background for the understanding of the episode. The condition which Leviticus calls "leprosy" clearly included a complex variety of diseases, according to the diagnosis of modern medicine. But the social effect was always the same: exclusion from the community. The fears of contamination were probably most like those associated with the fears of contagion from AIDS in our time. To be healed meant to be restored to friends and family and community as well as to be rid of the disease (Tiede, 1988: 119-120). Lev 11—16 deals with the notions of clean and unclean. Four major categories are treated: clean and unclean animals (Lev 11:1-47); childbirth or uncleanness similar to that of menstruation (Lev 12:1-8); unclean skin, garments, walls leprosy (= repulsive scaly skin condition; Lev 13:1-14:57); unclean bodily discharges (seed; blood; Lev 15:1-

33). The "theological" reason for the discussion in Lev 11—16 is located in Lev 11:44: "Be holy, for I am holy." In order to ascertain individual "holiness" these guidelines were given so as to prevent unholy folks from "defiling" God's tabernacle (Lev 15:31; see further Num 5:2-3; 2Kgs 7:3-9; 15:5, where one finds the Old Testament reasons for the ostracism of the "leper" from cities, unwalled towns, and general intercourse with other people). None of these chapters in Leviticus offers any advice on "cure" though clearly it was believed that "leprosy" was curable since it was the priests' function to ascertain and declare the cure. The rock bottom concern, however, was not biomedical but rather sociocultural, that is, to preserve holiness, the integrity, wholeness, and completeness of the community and its members, by safeguarding symbolic orifices and boundaries on the physical body. Sometimes bodily orifices seem to represent points of entry or exit of social units, or bodily perfection can symbolize an ideal theocracy (Douglas, 1966: 4). This appears to be clearly the case in Lev 11—16 and it tallies well with Israel's political and social situation in the immediate post-exilic era in which Leviticus was finalized (Pilch, 1981: 111).

Medical anthropology points out that all healing activities include two related but distinguishable tasks: curing of disease, and healing of illness. Curing of disease is presently understood as taking effective control of disordered biological and psychological processes. Since we do not know for certain what kind of disease *sara'at/lepra* was in biblical times, and since medical anthropology argues convincingly that it was not modern-day leprosy, we seem to know now little more than we ever did about curing disease.

But healing illness is understood as the provision of personal and social meaning for the life problems created by sickness/disease. And in this area medical and cultural anthropology seem to have enhanced our understanding of what might be going on in biblical texts. Healing on the cultural level is not so much a result of the healer's efforts

as a condition of experiencing a fit between socially legitimated forms of illness and care with the cultural context of
the health care system. Cultural healing is a necessary activity that occurs to the patient, and his family and social
nexus, regardless of whether the patient's disorder is affected
or not, as long as the sanctioned cultural fit is established.
The health care system provides psychosocial and cultural
treatment and the efficacy for the illness by naming and
ordering the experience of illness, providing meaning for
that experience, and treating the personal, family, and social problems that constitute the illness. Thus it "heals" the
illness, even if it is unable to effectively "cure" the disease
(Kleinman, 1980: 360).This could very well have been the
case with the biblical "repulsive, scaly skin condition" (Pilch,
1981: 113; Malina and Rohrbaugh, 1992: 315-316).

Verses 12-13: (12) Once, when he was in one of the cities,
there was a man covered with leprosy.
When he saw Jesus,
he bowed with his face to the ground and
begged him,
"Lord, if you choose, you can make me clean."
(13) Then Jesus stretched out his hand, touched him,
and said, "I do choose. Be made clean."
Immediately the leprosy left him.

"In one of the cities" may with its definite article refer
back to Lk 4:43: this is one of the cities where Jesus is
announcing the good news of the kingdom of God. If, however, as some have suggested, there is a Semitic influence
on the expression, no definiteness need be intended: "in a
certain city." The man was "covered with leprosy" (literally: "full of leprosy"), an alteration of Mark"s "leper," so
that the leprosy can "depart" in verse 13 (Johnson, 1991:
92). Having juxtaposed Jesus and the leper, Luke establishes
contact between them with "when he saw Jesus (literally:
seeing Jesus)." "He bowed with his face to the ground" (literally: falling on his face) is reminiscent of, but not identi-

cal to, Peter's falling down at Jesus' knees. Luke adds: "and begged him" (Nolland, 1989: 227).

The words of the leper are a request and not simply a confession, despite the assertion form. Compared to Mark, Luke adds, *Kurie*, "Lord," to the leper's words. The connection with Peter's use in Lk 5:8 of the same address suggests that more is involved than a polite "Sir." While "Sir" may suit the Gospel tradition in Stage I (during Jesus' lifetime); for Luke, writing at Stage III, it may have the connotation of "Lord" (Fitzmyer, 1981: 574).

The sentence, "Lord, if you choose, you can make me clean" (RSV: "Lord, if you *will* [*theleis*], you can make me clean") is borrowed literally from Mk 1:40c. The words suggest that the afflicted man recognizes something special in Jesus, probably because of his reputation (Lk 4:37). He insinuates that Jesus can cure him by an act of will alone (Fitzmyer, 1981: 574). The statement "If you choose/will" prepares the reader for Jesus' response "I choose/will," with stress placed on Jesus' initiative (Danker, 1988: 118-119). Stress is also placed on "clean" (Lk 5:12,13,14). This is no ordinary healing, nor is touching simply a part of the healing technique, as in Lk 7:14; 13:13. Jesus is not only able to heal the man of his leprosy by his authoritative word, but in doing so to touch him without himself becoming thereby unclean (C.F. Evans, 1990: 295). Luke omits Mark's reference to Jesus' pity or anger. Thus he omits from the Markan account the words that express Jesus' inner feelings, as he does elsewhere (Lk 6:10; Pesch, 1970: 103). It is risky to try to estimate why Luke did not preserve such an intriguing feature of the tradition, but the effect of the omission is for the reader to be drawn even more sharply into the revelation of the will of the Lord. And as Jesus prays in the conclusion of the account, the reader is aware that Jesus' will is one with God's (Tiede, 1988: 121).

Since Jesus' word is one of power, the leper is cured in the instant. But Jesus does not seek fame for cures. Jesus

does not want any single dimension of his ministry to become so well known that he is defined by it: a healer, an
exorcist, a preacher. To be misperceived is to be robbed of
effectiveness in the totality of his work, as outlined in Isa
61:1-2, (Craddock, 1990: 72). His healings are but one facet
of a total ministry (Danker, 1988: 119) of liberating people
from whatever burdens and oppresses them (Lk 4:18-19).
The healing happens precisely when Jesus touches this person whom law and custom prevented from being touched
(Ringe, 1995: 78-79). By touching the man Jesus enters into
the man's isolation and shame. No long-distance relief here;
Jesus gives himself to whom he ministers. Just as one cannot forgive without appearing to condone the very sin forgiven, neither can one help a leper without entering the
colony (Craddock, 1990: 71; Tannehill, 1986: 93).

Verse 14:   And he ordered him to tell no one.
             "Go," he said, "and show yourself to the priest,
             and, as Moses has commanded,
             make an offering for your cleansing,
             for a testimony to them."

The mysterious injunction to silence (compare Lk 4:41)
is derived from Mk 1:44, though it plays no part in the
narrative and the fame of Jesus spreads (Lk 5:15; C.F. Evans,
1990: 295). Jesus' words, "show yourself to the priest," allude to the Mosaic regulation of Lev 13:49. A similar instruction will be given to the ten lepers in Lk 17:14. "The
priest" (singular) most probably refers to the one on duty
in the temple at the time, the officiating priest (Creed, 1957:
77; Fitzmyer, 1981: 575). The Torah has special commandments concerning purification of a leper (Lev 13—14). Jesus'
order to the healed one (Lk 5:14b) was in harmony with
that law. Luke's purpose seems to be Jesus' compliance with
the law, and he does not bother to add information about
the purification rite of Lev 14. The placement of the pericope
before the controversies start is influenced by Mark. Jesus
demonstrates his adherence to the law before anybody has

even questioned it. It is interesting to notice here the close connection of the law and Moses. Moses, as a law-giver, designates the whole law, and the phrase "as Moses has commanded" simply means "as the law commands."

The expression *eis marturion autois* holds several difficulties. First, we do not know the group referred to as *autois*. Another problem is that the phrase can be interpreted as "for" or "against them" or have a neutral meaning. In Lk 9:5, "shake the dust off your feet as a testimony against them," the saying has a clearly negative meaning and therefore it is most likely that Luke has understood the phrase here in the same sense (Banks, 1975: 103). Although there have, so far, been no controversies between Jesus and the leading Jewish groups, it seems best to understand the phrase with reference to those who oppose Jesus. Apparently we must here keep in mind the following pericope and the controversies starting there (Lk 5:21-24,30-39; 6:1-11). Most likely Luke has interpreted the phrase as "proof against them," that is, the Jewish leaders (Salo, 1991: 71; Ernst, 1977: 191).

Neither is it completely clear to what the word *marturion* refers. It can be interpreted as a witness of the mission and message of Christ (Creed, 1957: 77; Schürmann, 1969: 277; Marshall, 1978: 210), proof of healing of healing, or proof of Jesus' obedience to the law (Wilson, 1983: 24). The first view finds support from Luke's normal usage of the word *marturion*. In Lk 21:13ff. there is a specific authority behind the term (the risen Jesus or God). The promise given in this incident has the effect of silencing the adversaries. Also in Acts 4:33 the apostles give witness to the resurrection of the Lord Jesus. The second interpretation creates a problem in the text. Proof of healing seems difficult in connection with Jesus' command not to tell anybody about the miracle. The third view seems to be correct, since it gains support from the context. Lk 5:14b talks about two different legal customs (showing oneself to the priest after being healed and offering to God) and therefore it is easiest to understand the phrase *eis marturion autois* with reference to Jesus' showing his obedience (and the obedience of the healed) to the law, to the Jewish leaders (Salo, 1991: 71-72; differently in Bovon, 1991: 234).

Due to the difficulty of the phrase *eis marturion autois*, Luke's understanding of his tradition cannot be determined precisely. At least the author has not attempted to clarify redactionally the difficult saying. Apparently he has considered it clear enough. At any rate, it seems probable that the above mentioned interpretation accurately reflects Luke's understanding of the tradition.

Verses 15-16: (15) But now more than ever the word about Jesus
                spread abroad;
              many crowds would gather to hear him
              and be cured of their diseases.
       (16) But he would withdraw in deserted places
              and pray.

Clearly, the repetitive *logos* of the opening scenes (Lk 4:22,32,36; 5:1,15) of Jesus' Galilean ministry reflects the author's intent to project the authoritative voice of Jesus. Unlike common speech — or even the extraordinary prophetic utterances of Mary, Zechariah, Simeon or John the Baptist — Jesus' words will be the very means through which the liberating power of God is activated in human experience (Staley, 1995: 189).

Here Luke omits the mention of the leper's disregard of Jesus' injunction to silence (See Mk 1:45). He is more concerned to note the publicity of the event and the general reaction to it (Fitzmyer, 1981: 575). The summary with which the account ends contains both an affirmation and a warning. It affirms Jesus' growing renown as a preacher and a healer. But the mention of Jesus withdrawing to pray signals a major turning point at hand (see Lk 3:21; 6:12; 9:18,28-29; 11:1; 22:41). Despite all the activity, Jesus is portrayed as seeking time with God, rather than fanning his fame.

Perhaps the activity's very scope and importance required that time be spent with God (Bock, 1994: 478). In this case the time of prayer serves as an unspoken warning: Jesus will be using that time apart to prepare himself for the series of conflicts that is about to begin (Danker, 1988: 120; Ringe, 1995: 79). With Jesus withdrawing from the crowd to pray, the focus of the narrative once again turns to him. But all that has happened in this story is now caught up in the will and plan of God (Tiede, 1988: 121).

Lk 5:12-16 showed Jesus ministering to the rejected of society. Perhaps no one pictures this separation more than lepers. These people were isolated socially and physically so that others would not contract their contagious disease. Jesus overcomes the disease and overturns the man's situation. The healing is but another evidence of Jesus' power and compasion (Bock, 1994: 487-488).

II. The First Controversies with the Pharisees (Lk 5:17-6:11)

In Lk 5:17-6:11 we have five controversy stories that contrast the people's enthusiastic reaction toward Jesus here and earlier (Lk 4:31-5:15) with the negative reaction of the Pharisees and the teachers of the law (Stein, 1992: 174). In comparison with Mk 2:1-3:6, Luke structures his parallel (Lk 5:17-6:11) into a more coherent series of encounters between Jesus and the Pharisees. Accordingly, he introduces Pharisees at the very beginning, whereas Mark accounts only for scribes. Lk 5:33 carries over the setting of the call of Levi to the question of fasting and produces an incongruity in that Pharisees refer to themselves in the third person. Lk 6:7 mentions the Pharisees in setting the scene for the healing of the man with the withered hand, whereas Mark refers to them only in the conclusion. By themselves these last two bits of editorial activity seem insignificant. But together with Lk 5:17 they confirm Luke's intent to present the complete block of material as consecutive confrontations between Jesus and the Pharisees (Brawley, 1987: 85).

1. The Healing of a Paralytic (Lk 5:17-26)

This pericope is the first of the series of five controversies that Luke has introduced into his Gospel, deriving them from his Markan source. Such stories about Jesus' altercations with Pharisees and scribes have come into the Gospel tradition in various groupings. The present group is undoubtedly even a pre-Markan gathering of such material. The series may preserve the early Church's recollection of debates that Jesus himself had with leaders of Palestinian Jewry; but even more probably they reflect controversies that early Christians had, as their community grew and took shape. It is never easy to say whether the words and replies to Jewish leaders which the evangelists have put on Jesus' lips represent his actual sayings as recalled and used in later controversy or whether later controversies gave rise to sayings attributed to him. The latter is likely and cannot be dismissed; but it may not be the full story. One has to allow for an original tradition and a further shaping of it in the light of later developments (Fitzmyer, 1981: 577-578).

The first controversy, Lk 5:17-26, deals with a dispute between Jesus and Pharisees and scribes about his power to heal and to forgive sins. The story is derived from Mk 2:1-12, but Luke has introduced a number of redactional changes into his form of the story (Fitzmyer, 1981: 578). In its present Lukan form the episode is a pronouncement-story, with the pronouncement preserved in Lk 5:23, "Which is easier, to say, 'Your sins are forgiven you' or to say, 'Stand up and walk'?" It also reflects the earlier form in Lk 5:20, "Your sins are forgiven you." The passage is conflated, composed of a miracle-story and a pronouncement-story, which has been inserted into the former. So understood, the passage would include a miracle-story (Lk 5:17-20ab,24c-26 = Mk 2:1-5a,11-

12) and the pronouncement-story (Lk 5:20c-24ab = Mk 2:5b-10; Bultmann, 1972: 66; Maisch, 1971: 21-48).

At Lk 5:17 controversy begins to play a major part in the development of Luke's story. The significance of Lk 5:17-26 centers around the theme of forgiveness of sins (Lk 5:24) and thus forms a natural prologue to the relationship of Jesus to "sinners" which is to follow (Tannehill, 1986: 104). This has also been presaged by the confession of sinfulness by Peter in Lk 5:8. The confession there introduces the "sinners" theme to the Gospel of Luke and first raises the prospect of forgiveness for the "sinner" (Neale, 1991: 109).

Verses 17:   One day, while he was teaching,
             Pharisees and teachers of the law were sitting near by
             (they had come from every village of Galilee and
                 Judea
             and from Jerusalem);
             and the power of the Lord was with him to heal.

The Lukan setting of the healing of the paralytic is remarkable for several reasons. According to Luke there is an impressive audience gathered about Jesus from throughout Israel to witness what is about to occur. In the preceding miracle in Lk 5:12-16, the leper was charged by Jesus to tell no one of his healing (except the priest). This next incident involving the paralytic, however, appears to be purposely staged by Luke as a crucial public event. A setting in which such an important group of leading Jews was gathered is extraordinary. Compare this dramatic scenario to that of Mark where we learn only that Jesus was "at home" and "many gathered around" (Mk 2:1-2) when the miracle occurred. In Mark it is only later in Mk 2:6 and somewhat incidentally that he informs us that "some of the scribes were sitting there." Unlike Mark and Matthew Jesus attracts special attention to the conflict with the Pharisees (Neale, 1991: 109-110).

The hyperbolic "every" (pasēs) performs at least two functions: (1) the mention of Galilee, Judaea, and Jerusalem generates the impression that the Pharisees and teachers of the law have some authority; and (2) the comprehensiveness of the geographical areas underlines the increasing fame of Jesus and the number of people who came to see him (Gowler, 1991: 186). Luke may have referred to Judaea and Jerusalem at this point to alert his readers that what happened here in the controversy stories foreshadowed what would happen later in Jerusalem (Stein, 1992: 175-176).

The Pharisees were an organized body with official status, who came from all the territory of the Jewish people. They were an authoritative group of some sort that would be contrasted with Jesus' authority (Brawley, 1988: 141-142). The Pharisees were one of four major Jewish groups — the other three being the Sadducees, Essenes, and Zealots (C.F. Evans, 1990: 298-299). The Pharisees were a nonpriestly or lay movement whose goal was to keep the nation faithful to Mosaic faith. In order to do this, they had a very developed tradition that gave rulings on how the law applied to a varietry of possible situations not addressed directly by Scripture (Bock, 1994: 478-479; Marshall, 1978: 212; Fitzmyer, 1981: 581). In contrast to the Sadducees, the Pharisees believed in the resurrection, the existence of angels and demons (Lk 20:27; Acts 23:6-9), predestination as well as free will, and the validity of both the written and the oral law. Politically they were more conservative than the Sadducees, but religiously they were liberal due to their acceptance of the oral law. The teachers of the law, usually called scribes, were religious lawyers who supported the development of the extrabiblical tradition. Their motive was to preserve and contextualize the biblical teaching into new settings (Bock, 1994: 479). Although one could be a "teacher of the law" or scribe and not a Pharisee, most scribes were in fact Pharisees and leaders in this sect (Stein, 1992: 175).

In order to appreciate the importance of the introduction of the Pharisees in the Gospel of Luke it is necessary to give some attention to Luke's treatment of this group. It is certainly true that the theme of conflict is one which is particularly susceptible to redaction in the Gospels, and it is often said that Luke is less harsh on the Pharisees than the other Gospel writers. It would be more accurate to say that Luke is ambivalent in his treatment of the Pharisees and this fact is evidenced in an almost bewildering array of interpretations by scholars of Luke's attitude towards the Pharisees (Carroll, 1988: 604-607). Most frequently, far from being soft on the Pharisees, Luke portrays them as the very enemies of God's purpose. At other times, however, he presents them as the "righteous." Moreover, the almost heroic representation of the Pharisees in Acts is often noted (Brawley, 1987: 88ff.) and this only increases the enigmatic nature of Luke's attitude toward the Pharisees in his Gospel.

How do Luke's Pharisees differ from those in the other Gospels? It would seem that Luke has adopted his basic body of conflict material from Mark (as does Matthew). But he is not less harsh in his portrayal of the Pharisees than Matthew, as some contend (e.g., Ziesler, 1979; 146-157; opposed by Neale, 1991: 105-108). An appreciation of the Pharisees as a crucial element in the Lukan story brings the whole issue of religious categorization in this Gospel into focus. Neale's proposal for the reason for Lukan hostility to the Pharisees is that the Gospel story itself requires such a conflict. No conflict, no Gospel story. All other proposals must, in a sense, build on this fundamental observation. To speculate about the literary function of the Pharisees in his Gospel for the Lukan community (Carroll, 1988: 606-607) or with respect to various social or economic factors (Moxnes, 1988: 17-21) is simply to build on this basic foundation. All Gospels, it would seem, must embody conflict and portray the struggle between an ideological good and evil; Luke's Pharisees fulfil this role (Neale, 1991: 108).

The honor/shame implications of Jesus' rising fame as an authoritative teacher would be significant in a limited good society. Therefore, Jesus' rise to fame is not incidental to the appearance of the Pharisees, and they should not be seen as merely innocent bystanders (Gowler, 1991: 186).

"And the power of the Lord was with him to heal" is virtually the same as saying that "Jesus, filled with the power of the Spirit, returned to Galilee" (Lk 4:14) and "the Spirit of the Lord is upon me" (Lk 4:18), but now the reader is aware that the healing that is about to take place is the work of the Lord God. Any conflict with Jesus will also be contending with God (Tiede, 1988: 123).

A person who acted outside his or her social role could be labelled in one of two ways: as a deviant or prominent. A *deviant* is a person who is perceived as acting outside his or her social role to such an extent that he or she is redefined in a new, negative way. A *prominent* would be seen as also out of place, but would be redefined in a positive way. Jesus' role as prominent also makes him a *limit breaker*, that is someone who can transcend the socially-defined limits in a given culture in some socially accepted way (Malina, 1986: 143-154). The Pharisees do not appear by coincidence; they come in response to Jesus' rising fame. Their association with teachers of the law indicates that the honor Jesus was receiving impinged upon their own honor. The problem was that Jesus was acting outside his inherited social role, which would be seen as shameful from their point of view. Jesus' inherited social role had already been mentioned by the people in Nazareth (Lk 4:22: "Is not this Joseph's son?"), and his response indicates that he expected to be labelled a deviant. Yet according to the information supplied thus far to the reader, Jesus' activity was quite honorable (Malina-Neyrey, 1991: 25-65). Those who label Jesus as a deviant are unreliable characters who themselves lose honor; those who label Jesus as a prominent are usually more reliable characters. Often a close correlation exists between reliability and acquired honor (Gowler, 1991: 192-193).

Verses 18-20b: (18) Just then some men came.
                       carrying a paralyzed man on a bed.
                       They were trying to bring him in and lay
                           him before Jesus;
                (19) but finding no way to bring him in
                           because of the crowd,
                       they went up on the roof and let him
                           down with his bed
                       through the tiles into the middle of the
                           crowd in front of Jesus.
                (20a) When he saw their faith, he said,

From "they were trying to bring him in" we learn for the
first time in the story that Jesus has been teaching indoors.
The roof of the common Palestinian house was made of
wooden beams placed across stone or mudbrick walls; the
beams were covered with reeds, matted layers of thorns, and
several inches of clay. Such a roof could have been dug
through (Mk 2:4). Luke, however, has changed —
inculturated! — the description, introducing the tiled roof
of Hellenistic houses in the eastern Mediterranean area —
making the action more intelligible to Greek-speaking Christian readers outside Palestine (Fitzmyer, 1981: 582; Stein,
1992: 176; somewhat differently in Bock, 1994: 480-481).

In Lk 5:20 we have the first occurrence of the word
pistis, "faith," in Luke. In Stage I of the Gospel tradition
"faith" would have meant a conviction that Jesus was able
to do something for the man's condition. Such a meaning
would suit most of the other passages in Luke where the
word occurs (Lk 7:9,50; 8:25,48; 17:5,6,19; 18:8,42). Luke
has also taken over from Mk 5:34; 10:52 the expression "Your
faith has made you well [RSV: has saved you]," using it not
only in his parallel passages (Lk 8:48; 18:42), but even elsewhere (Lk 7:50; 17:19), undoubtedly because it was apt for
his theology of salvation. But in Lk 17:5; 18:8 (possibly);
22:32 *pistis* may carry more of the nuance of personal commitment to Jesus, an attitude that can grow or diminish,
involving the nuance of Christian discipleship and faith in

Jesus as the risen Lord. This would reflect more of the understanding of the word in Stage III of the Gospel tradition.
It is found in this sense in Acts 6:5; 11:24, etc. (Fitzmyer,
1981: 582-583; Stein, 1992: 176). "When he saw their faith"
does not require unique spiritual discernment. After all, they
have torn a house apart. They must believe that Jesus will
be able to help the man.

Verses 20b-24b): (20b) "Friend, your sins are forgiven you."
         (21) Then the scribes and the Pharisees began
            to question,
            "Who is this who is speaking
            blasphemies?
            Who can forgive sins but God alone?
         (22) When Jesus perceived their questionings,
            he answered them,
            "Why do you raise such questions in your
            hearts?
         (23) Which is easier, to say, 'Your sins are
            forgiven you,'
            or to say, 'Stand up and walk'?
      (24ab) But so that you may know that the Son of
            Man
            has authority on earth to forgive sins."

Instead of Mark's and Matthew's *teknon*, "child" or "son,"
Luke addresses the paralytic as *anthrope*, "man," but it is
like saying "Friend." Luke may have decided to change the
address because the word *teknon* might have easily caused
Luke's audience to conclude that the paralytic was a boy
(Bovon, 1991: 238). The perfect passive form "have been
forgiven" indicates that the man's sins have been forgiven
by God (Fitzmyer, 1981: 583; Tiede, 1988: 124; Bovon, 1994:
481).

    It is not clear from the text as such whether a specific
sin was in view. Numerous texts in Judaism saw paralysis as
the product of sin (C.F. Evans, 1990: 301). But John 9:2-3
shows that one should not be quick to make a one-to-one
correpondence between specific, personal sin and disaese.

The general disorder of creation is more likely the point (Danker, 1988: 122; Bock, 1994: 482). To always associate disease with a specific sin is cruel (Tiede, 1988: 122).

The pairing of the scribes and the Pharisees is also found in Lk 5:30; 6:7; 11:53; 15:2 (Stein, 1992: 177). The first words "spoken" by the Pharisees are very important for their characterization in Luke-Acts, but the narrator has not provided any commentary on how the Pharisees should be evaluated. Is their objection to be seen as basically correct and understandable, or is it an inimical question that betrays a willful hostility to the purpose of God? The position underlying the thought that Jesus was blaspheming seems to be the idea that sin was an offense against God. Only the person offended could forgive any offense, so Jesus was implicitly attacking God's majesty (Fitzmyer, 1981: 112-114). The charge is quite serious; the scribes and the Pharisees *began* to question — no premeditated hostility is mentioned — but their status as adversaries of Jesus is beginning to be established (Gowler, 1991: 187).

The extent of Jesus' *ascribed honor* is well-established (Gowler, 1989: 58). Now Jesus gains *acquired honor* through his conflict with the scribes and the Pharisees. The contest with the devil (Lk 4:1-13), of course, is a powerful statement about the honor and authority of Jesus, but now Jesus contends with earthly authorities. The narrator notes that the scribes and the Pharisees "began to question" (Lk 5:21); any such questioning denotes initiation of a challenge to someone's honor. "Who is this [fellow]." This unspoken thought, reported by the "omniscient" narrator, is the key to the understanding of this passage (Stein, 1992: 177). The challenge, in order to make a response more likely, must be made in public and in the presence of the one challenged. The narrator creates confusion, however, by observing that Jesus perceived their questionings and said, "Why do you raise such questions *in your hearts*" (Lk 5:22). The use of *dialogizesthai*, "to question," and *legontes*, "saying," may allow for the possibility that the questioning is indeed interiorized, just as Jesus' words indicate (Marshall, 1978: 214). The result seems to be that the Pharisees do not really question Jesus directly, thus only offering an indirect affront to Jesus, not the more serious direct affront. The person who is challenged ambiguously may choose to ignore the affront, but here Jesus responds to the (unspoken?) charge by the scribes and the Pharisees (Gowler, 1991: 193-194).

The verb that the NRSV translates as "raise questions" is the same word that Simeon used in Lk 2:35 to speak of the "secret thoughts" or "questionings" of the heart that the child Jesus was destined to disclose. Now the Messiah is exercising a kind of discernment that threatens those who would choose to keep their objections to themselves (Tiede, 1988: 125).

It is worth noting the way in which Luke, in contrast with Mark, formulates the "question" of Jesus' critics:

Mk 27	Lk 5:21
Why does this fellow speak in this way? It is blasphemy! Who can forgive sins but God alone?	Who is this who is speaking? Who can forgive sins but God alone?

The second question is practically the same in Mark and Luke. It represents a confession of faithful Jews in the form of a rhetorical question. The first one is a real question that Luke changes from a "why-" into a "who-question." In Luke, therefore, Jesus' critics do not ask for the basis of his activity, but his person. We have a similar formulation in the second Lukan pericope that deals with forgiveness of sins (Lk 7:36-50):

Lk 5:21	Lk 7:49
Who is this who is speaking blasphemies? Who can forgive sins but Got alone?	Who is this, who even forgives sins?

The comparison shows that both questions of Lk 5:21 are combined into one in Lk 7:49. In the latter the reference to blasphemy and that God alone can forgive have been omitted. The Pharisees apparently admit indirectly that Jesus himself forgives sin. But both Lk 5:21 and 7:49 have the question "Who is this?" in common. That question is, therefore, very important. In that question both Lukan accounts undoubtedly reach their climax (Feldkämper, 1978: 74).

Jesus' awareness of the thoughts of the scribes and the Pharisees need not imply a "divine omniscience, particularly since none of the evangelists made anything of it. However, in Lk 7:36-50 such knowledge serves to show that Jesus is indeed a prophet, and this probably is also the sense here (Compare Lk 2:35; 6:8; 9:47; 24:38; Stein, 1992: 177; Bock, 1994: 484).

Jesus' comparison, "Which is easier to say...," implies that the scribes and the Pharisees would consider it easier to declare the forgiveness of sins, because they could not tell whether the effect had been achieved or not, than to heal the paralyzed man, which could be directly verified. Rhetorically, the statement can be compared with other such "easier" statements in Lk 16:17 and 18:24-25 (Tiede, 1988: 122). Luke understood that if God granted Jesus power to work this miracle, then God himself supported Jesus' claim that he can forgive sins (Stein, 1992: 177). Jesus will display his power (Lk 5:17e) by doing what they regard as more difficult (Fitzmyer, 1981: 584).

Lk 5:24 contains the first of the twenty-four occurrences of "Son of Man" in Luke's Gospel (Bock, 1994: 485). Luke has clearly inherited the phrase here from Mk 2:10. The "Son of Man" in Lk 5:24 can refer to Jesus as the representative person called by God to exercise authority over sin. The autholrity, however, is one unique to Jesus and as such means that the representative is unique. Jesus' "innovations" with the Son of Man concept in Lk 5:24 are, firstly, the claim to be able to identify the authoritative, heavenly-human figure (as himself!), and, secondly, the association of that figure with the right of the Son of Man to forgive sins (Bock, 1991: 109-121).

Luke clearly understands the title "Son of Man" to refer to Jesus: Proof of the authority of the former is in the power of the latter. It is important to be aware, though, that this connection we take so easily for granted rests on fuzzy beginnings. In both Hebrew and Aramaic there are idioms that can be literally translated into the phrase "The son of the human being." As is the case with idioms in many languages, however, a literal translation does little to convey the meaning. What the words "the son of the human being" actually meant in Jesus' time is unclear (Ringe, 1995: 82).

Recently, a critique of the various nontitular interpretations of the expression "Son of Man" has been presented. It discusses successively, firstly, the circumlocutional sense ("this person" = "I"), secondly, the generic sense ("people" in general), and, thirdly, the indefinite sense ("a person," "someone"). The author maintains that despite their appeal the nontitular theories lack any substantial basis and that future research will make progress only with the recognition that "Son of Man" in the bulk of its occurrences is a title rather than a nontitular idiom (Burkett, 1994: 504-521).

Verses 24c-26:	(24c)	he said to the one who was paralyzed — "I say to you, stand up and take your bed and go home."
	(25)	Immediately he stood up before them, took what he had been lying on, and went home, glorifying God.
	(26)	Amazement seized all of them, and they glorified God and were filled with awe, saying, "We have seen strange things today."

The structure of Lk 5:24 is awkward, since the verb changes from a second person plural to a third person singular. This leaves the translator with at least two options. The option chosen by most translators and commentators is to consider the phrase "he said to the paralytic" to be the narrator's tag which has been inserted into Jesus' speech. This interpretation would see the comment about the ability of the Son of Man to forgive sins as the address of Jesus to the people and religious leaders present in the room (Tannehill, 1986: 108,113,124 n. 33, and 173). Another option has been adopted by Fitzmyer (1981: 579; Nolland, 1989: 237). Due to the ambiguity of the structure and the use of the second person plural the possibility certainly exists that the narrator addressed these words to the reader. In fact, this statement may function on both levels, even if the first option is chosen by a translator. In light of the comment made to the reader in Lk 1:4 concerning the reader's relationship to the story, the comment in Lk 5:24 functions to reinforce the idea that the relationship in question is the one of gaining knowledge. This action of Jesus imparts knowledge that has ramifications for salvation as well as for the reader's understanding of Jesus (Sheely, 1992: 117).

Jesus turns to the paralytic and gives him three commands: get up, take your mat, and go home (Bock, 1994: 486). The command to return home attests to his healing and is an indication of the man's restoration to the community (Danker, 1988: 123). The healing of the man gives a clear answer to the questions of the scribes and the Pharisees: Jesus is the one upon whom God's power rests; the paralyzed man rose, took up his bed, and went home glorifying God. Then the response of the people "all of them") is given. The final comment must be integrated into the portrait of the Pharisees. The Pharisees are regarded by a number of scholars as having a change in attitude and as temporarily, at least, being unsure in their charge of blasphemy. The power and authority of Jesus were *paradoxa*, "strange things," contrary to their expectation. They too, along with the crowd, were amazed, glorified God, and were filled with awe. The suggestion that the Pharisees are not included in the crowd's praise (Marshall, 1978: 211; Tyson, 1986: 82) should be rejected; they are included among those giving praise to God, as implied by Lk 5:17 and 25 taken together (Brawley, 1987: 86; Sanders, 1987: 92; Tiede, 1988: 126). The audience was filled with awe, a reaction that Luke's readers should have as well (Schürmann, 1969: 285; Marshall, 1978: 217; Bock, 1994: 487).

Only in Luke does the man whom Jesus healed respond by standing up and glorifying God as "he went home" Lk 5:25), a phrase which in Luke appears to suggest restoration to the way things ought to be. Here is a person who has identified God at work in Jesus' activity.

Two words in the conclusion of the narrative demand attention: *sēmeron* and *paradoxa*. "Today we have seen *paradoxa*." Putting "today" at the very beginning of the onlookers' response gives it the emphasis found in Luke's own syntax. *Semeron* is a significant Lukan word whose appearance at this point draws a reader's attention to an event's place in the scheme of salvation (e.g. Lk 2:11; 4:21). *Paradoxa* presents different problems: because it appears only here in the New Testament there is no possibility of identifying a normative Lukan use. It is not frequently used in the Septuagint, but its presence is instructive. Judith 13:13; Wis 5:2; 16:17; 19:5; Sir 43:25; 3Macc 6:33; 4 Macc 2:14 appear to be its uses. The Judith and Maccabees occurrences take up the unexpectednes of an event, clearly one of its root meanings, and the Sirach passage lends weight to refuting Fitzmyer's suggestion that *paradoxos* approaches "miracle" because there it points to God's work in nature. The Wisdom passages do offer help. This group actually suggests itself as a source for Luke's use of *paradoxos* in his distinctive telling of this story. Wisdom's use of *paradoxos* proves instructive. Its basic thought is of what is unexpected. In Lk 5:26 the assembled scribes and Pharisees are reported to have glorified God. Luke places their reason for doing so firmly in a context different from that he found in his sources; in what had happened before them the opponents of this man had seen and recognized a sign of God at work (Doble, 1996: 30-34).

Jesus, the healer, brings the man back into proper relationship with God (Lk 5:20), with his fellow human beings and, most importantly, with his kinship group (Lk 5:25). The Pharisees initially objected to Jesus' pronouncement that the man's relationship to God was restored, but the visible sign of healing caused them to reconsider their position. The Son of Man does have such authority (Gowler, 1991: 197).

The healing of the paralytic in Lk 5:17-26 is a turning point in Jesus' ministry, as Jesus measures his ministry in terms of forgiveness of sins. Accordingly, the healing takes on an additional importance beyond the mere reversal of physical ills. But the event also represents a more ominous development as Luke describes the first offical rejection of Jesus. The charge of blasphemy is raised, and the lines of opposition are forming (Bock, 1994: 488).

2. The Call of Levi; the Banquet (Lk 5:27-32)

Jesus' outreach to the outcasts continues. But now he deals with the social outcast rather than with the physically handicapped (Danker, 1988: 125; Bock, 1994: 489). For Luke the sequence is one of thought from the forgiveness of sins of the paralytic to the call of sinners to repentance (C.F. Evans, 1990: 304). This story takes us from a private home to the semi-public setting of a tax collector's booth. As in Lk 5:1-11, what is left behind is the earlier way of earning a living — the basic security of an income and a place in the social hierarchy that is familiar, regardless of whether it is prestigious or lowly (Ringe, 1995: 83).

The events of Lk 5:27-32 are of great importance to Luke's portrayal of the Gospel message. In these few verses Luke sets out the basic themes of conflict, forgiveness and inclusion of "sinners" that will play an important role throughout his work. For Luke it would seem that the fact of Jesus calling a tax collector is so extraordinary that the event does not seem out of place among a series of miraculous events. It is actually a fitting climax to this list because the call itself is a miracle. Only the evocative power of the call can account for its inclusion and climactic position at this point in the narrative. Luke has purposely structured his reporting of these events to heighten the drama and impact of the relationship that Jesus bears to the "tax collectors and sinners" (Neale, 1991: 110, 111). The passage focuses on Jesus' association with sinners, an association that he initiates. This concerns a *literary* appreciation of the place of the tax collectors in Luke's Gospel.

From the *historical* perspective a wide variety of views have been proposed about the significance of Jesus' fellowship with tax collectors. They range from the view of many scholars that associations with tax collectors were indeed "characteristic" of Jesus' conduct (e.g., Jeremias, 1963: 109ff.) to the view that Jesus never actually had fellowship with tax collectors at all (e.g., Horsley, 1987: 212-217; Neale, 1991: 112-113). The common element of these various opinions is an overriding interest in dealing with the question on a historical level. It is necessary, however, to discern the difference between the "historical" facts of Jesus' supposed association with "sinners' and the ideological significance those events assume in the Gospel text. It seems that the former does little to help one fully understand the latter. Whether Jesus numbered one, two or twenty tax collectors among his followers is beside the point; what matters is that this feature is used in the Gospel of Luke to indicate a radical departure from religious convention (Neale, 1991: 113).

The present story consists in two parts that display different forms. Lk 5:27-28 is a brief story about Jesus that is also a call narrative. Lk 5:29-32 is a pronouncement story that is also a controversy account (Bock, 1994: 489-490). The figure of Levi assures the unity between the two parts

(Bovon, 1991: 246). The Lukan story is dependent on Mk
.2:13-17, but Luke has again modified the Markan material.
Topical arrangement has undoubtedly linked this controversy with Pharisees and scribes to the former one; likewise
the pronouncement about the forgiveness of sins in the former
provides the background for Jesus' association with sinners
in this scene (Fitzmyer, 1981: 587).

Verses 27-28: (27) After this he went out and saw a tax
                    collector named Levi,
                    sitting at the tax booth; and said to him:
                    "Follow me."
             (28) And he got up, left everything, and followed
                    him.

Luke marks the episodic separation from what precedes by
"after this," literally, "after these things" (as at Lk 10:1;
Luke is the only one among the Synoptics to use this construction; Nolland, 1989: 244). Jesus "went out," probably
from the house implied in Lk 5:19; but it could also mean
"one of the towns" (Lk 5:12). The sea (Mk 2:13) is not
mentioned. "He saw," not *eiden* as in Mk 2:14, but *etheasato*,
"he observed" (Fitzmyer, 1981: 589), which indicates that
Jesus consciously singled this man out (Bock, 1994: 493).
Levi — in Mt 9:9 he is called Matthew — was not the
chief tax or toll collector, like Zacchaeus (Lk 19:2), but an
agent working at a toll booth (Stein, 1992: 181), who would
have reported to someone like Zacchaeus. Jesus issues Levi
a call to follow him. Other such calls occur in Lk 9:23,59;
18:22 (Bock, 1994: 493,494).

   In Luke the phrase "follow me" is often used to describe
Christian discipleship (Lk 5:11; 9:23,49,57,59,61; 18:22,28).
It means the commitment to become a Christian, as is clear
from Lk 5:32. Luke adds "left everything" to the narrative to
clarify for his readers what it means to follow Jesus. Levi's
leaving everything, including his tax table, has become a
metaphor for the repentance of the unsavable, and any other
conlusion simply misses the point of the narrative (Neale,

1991: 115). This also ties the present account to the call of Simon, James, and John, who also "left everything and followed" (Lk 5:11). In Lk 14:33 Jesus states that one must "give up everything" to become a disciple, and there too this refers to becoming a Christian this time addressed to the "crowds" and "anyone" (Lk 14:25-26). The power of Jesus' word, noted previously on occasions of exorcism and teaching, is again demonstrated here in the power of Jesus' word to command response (Craddock, 1990: 76; Danker, 1988: 125).

Having read "left everything," one is unavoidably struck by the mention of the "banquet" that Levi gave in Jesus' honor in his own house. This is the first of several occasions in Luke when Jesus teaches from the position of a guest at a meal (Lk 7:36ff.; 10:38ff.; 11:37ff.; 14:1ff.; 19:5ff.; C.F. Evans, 1990: 305). The suture in the two elements of account, the story about Jesus and the pronouncement-story, is more apparent in the Lukan version than in Mark and Matthew (Fitzmyer, 1981: 590). "Followed him" is an inceptive imperfect and should be translated "and he began to follow him." It emphasizes the commencement and continuation of Levi's discipleship (Marshall, 1978: 219; Stein, 1992: 181).

Verses 29-32: (29) Then Levi gave a banquet for him in his house;
and there was a large crowd of tax collectors and others sitting at table with him.

(30) The Pharisees and their scribes were complaining to his disciples,
saying,
"Why do you eat and drink with tax collectors and sinners?"

(31) Jesus answered,
"Those who are well have no need for a physician,
but those who are sick;

(32) I have come to call not the righteous but sinners to repentance."

Luke clearly presents Jesus as being in the house of Levi (Matson, 1996: 81).To ask how Levi could have abandoned everything and then provide a banquet to which Jesus was invited is to miss the whole point of the passage. To ask it is to spoil the story (Fitzmyer, 1981: 589; Malina and Rohrbaugh, 1992: 317 referring to 313). Luke often likes to mention events at meals (Lk 7:36-50; 9:10-17; 10:38-42; 11:37-54; 14:1-24; 19:1-10; 22:7-38; 24:29-32,41-43; Danker, 1988: 125).

The banquet is intended to give a concrete expression of Levi's following. But the issue is not so much the party as well who is invited to it. Luke speaks of a large company of tax collectors and others, identified as sinners by the Pharisees in Lk 5:30 (Bock, 1994: 495). Luke alone designated this meal as a (great) banquet (Lk 5:29: dochē, "great feast" [RSV]; Lk 14:13). Later Luke will give a parable of a great banquet (Lk 14:15-24) that is likewise filled with outcasts. It is clear that Luke has considerably enhanced the setting of the event and in so doing raises its significance to pivotal importance for his story (Stein, 1992: 181; Ford, 1984: 71-72; Neale, 1991: 116).Whereas Mk 2:15 has "many tax collectors *and sinners*," Luke refers to "others" who are only gradually so labeled in the Lukan version (Fitzmyer, 1981: 591). Luke lets the word "sinners" come on the lips of the Pharisees (Lk 5:30; Danker, 1988: 125; Craddock, 1990: 77).

The official reaction to the banquet seems to occur some time after the event when "the Pharisees and their scribes" approach the disciples with a question. Since privacy was non-existent in village life, Pharisees and scribes could be expected to know about and comment on such a dinner (Malina and Rohrbuach, 1992: 317).

Ridicule of the Pharisees as mere "legalists" is unfair and minimizes the power of the account (Tiede, 1988: 127). They "complained" (RSV: "they murmured"; see Lk 15:2; 19:7 for a cognate verb) to express an adverse reaction to

Jesus' keeping company with "sinners" (Nolland, 1989: 245). This is Luke's first use of the term "disciple" (*mathētēs*), though disciples have been in evidence in his Gospel since Lk 5:11. The term refers to those who give up everything to follow Jesus (see especially Lk 14:26-27,33) and involves hearing and doing what Jesus says (Lk 6:47-48). From the circle of disciples the apostles are chosen (Lk 6:13), and for the most part it is the Twelve who represent discipleship, though the term is much broader (Lk 19:37; Nolland, 1989: 246; C.F. Evans, 1990: 306-307).

The hostile questioning addressed to Jesus' disciples (instead of being addressed to Jesus himself) mirrors the situation of the early Church when Christians had to face hostile questions and accusations concerning their practices and their beliefs (C.A. Evans, 1990: 97; Craddock, 1990: 78). Since the Lukan principle is that every disciple "will be like his teacher" (Lk 6:40), Acts will record a similar charge against Peter, an accredited messenger of Jesus who eats and drinks with unclean Gentiles in a house (Acts 11:3; Matson, 1996: 81). The question injects a new element of conflict into the developing drama. Its purpose at the level of the story is perfectly clear: it produces the opportunity for Jesus to silence his antagonists and demonstrates the irresistible force of his mission in the face of a bigoted opposition. Of all the issues concerned with Jesus' association with "sinners," the matter of table-fellowship is the most important and least understood. And since most of the "sinner" material in Luke is connected with fellowship at table, the issue requires close attention (Neale, 1991: 118). The meal scenes in Luke are Lk 7:36-50; 9:10-17; 10:38-42; 11:37-54; 14:1-24; 15:1-2; 19:1-10; 22:4-38; 24:29-32,41-43. These encompass all our "sinner" material (Marshall, 1978: 219).

What was the objection to Jesus eating with certain individuals? Perhaps the charge was *political* in nature, that is, Jesus' association with these individuals constituted a breach of fidelity to his nationality as a Jew (Perrin, 1967: 103).

But the political factor does not provide a very satisfactory understanding of the charge in Lk 5:30 (Neale, 1991: 119-120).

Was the issue a question of biblical or rabbinic injunction and were Jesus' actions thus considered an *attack on the law*? At the most basic level the question is: Was Jesus breaking a law by eating with "sinners"? There is nothing in the Mosaic code with respect to table-fellowship with wayward Jews or even with Gentiles (Esler, 1987: 84); nevertheless the Jews had a reputation for being unsociable at table (Esler, 1987: 78-84). But it is vital to point out that this had solely to do with table-fellowship with *Gentiles*. Could there have been issues relating to tithing as a potential source of legal conflict between Jesus and his contemporaries? On the whole, the generally low level of observance of the tithing laws during this period makes the whole question an unlikely source of conflict, and legal prescriptions with regard to tithing are unlikely to be the issue at stake in Lk 5:30 (Neale, 1991: 121-122).

What about the suggestion that Jesus was breaking the law by incurring ritual impurity in his contact with these "tax collectors and sinners?" The answer is that he undoubtedly was incurring ritual impurity. But this violated no law unless he attempted to enter the Temple in such a state. In conclusion, there seems to be no significant question of law at stake in the Pharisaic criticism in Lk 5:30 and we must look elsewhere for its significance (Neale, 1991: 122-123).

Perhaps the offence of Jesus' table-fellowship with "sinners" was based on *moral considerations*. It has in fact been maintained that the basis of offence was "exclusively moral" (Jeremias, 1971: 111). It has also been held that the offence was based on the perceived immorality of Jesus in associating with wicked people (Derrett, 1970: 278-285). But the calling of the "lost" can in no way be construed as the dissolution of ethics (Neale, 1991: 123-126).

Another way Jesus' table-fellowship has been understood

is in terms of its *religious symbolism*. The fellowship of Jesus with "sinners" has been said to represent their inclusion in the Kingdom of God (Perrin, 1967: 106-108; Smith, 1989: 466-467). According to Marcus Borg, Jesus' table-fellowship was perceived by the Pharisees as a challenge to the internal movement of reform that was intended to make Israel a holy community of priests (Borg, 1984: 84). But the significance of these events at the time they occurred does not necessarily conform with the role they now play in the Gospel story itself. The tendency of ideology to overtake an act and invest it with symbolic significance can be observed in many studies (Neale, 1991: 127-129).

That this encounter comes after the banquet is clear, because the Pharisees would not have come to such a party, as their question shows, even in the unlikely event that they had been invited (Marshall, 1978: 220; Tiede, 1988: 128). The appearance that the leaders are near or at the party is a result of literary compression (Bock, 1994: 495). They register a complaint (*egogguzon*, "they were grumbling"). Luke reserves this verb for complaints about Jesus' relationship to outsiders (Lk 15:2; 19:7; Schweizer, 1984: 111). In Luke, the complaint attacks Jesus indirectly by aiming at the disciples, while Mk 2:16 and Mt 9:11 complain only about Jesus. In addition, only Luke mentions both eating and drinking with undesirables, slightly intensifying the charge. The juxtaposition of "tax collectors and sinners" occurs again in Lk 7:34; 15:1; and implicitly in Lk 19:7. The "sinners" are the principal device by which Luke demonstrates the extent and scope of Jesus' ministry; without "sinners" the story would falter for want of a radical issue around which controversy can be built (Neale, 1991: 100).

The issue of eating and drinking is a frequent charge against Jesus (Lk 5:33; 7:33-34; Marshall, 1978: 220). The problem in the leaders' view is not mere contact with sinners, but table fellowship that seeks out and welcomes these people. Lk 7:34,36-50 and 15:1-32 also treat the theme of associating with sinners, explaining why Jesus does so (Ernst, 1977: 198; Bock, 1994: 496).

The Pharisees' question has a double answer. The first is proverbial, impersonal and defensive, the second personal, positive and programmatic of Jesus' mission. The form is the same in both ("not...but"), though not the force; and the second does not follow naturally from the first, as healing in answer to need and going out to call are different kinds of activity (C.F. Evans, 1990: 307).

Jesus responds in wording that is virtually identical in all three Synoptic Gospels. Luke's reference to the healthy fits with the picture of Jesus as a physician (Bock, 1994: 497). His reply adopts the Pharisees' perspective, and there may be a note of sarcasm in it, as the later account of Lk 18:11-14 suggests. Jesus' reply shows that he is not seeking direct confrontation, because he keeps his answer solely in terms of the sinners' need and does not yet criticize the Pharisees explicitly (Danker, 1988: 126). More than any other saying, Lk 5:32 provides a window into the purpose and mission of Jesus for Luke's story. It stands at the start of the Galilean mission and sets the tone of conflict right through to Lk 19 and the companion statement, "For the Son of Man came to seek out and to save the lost" (Lk 19:10). This tells us not only how Jesus differs from his contemporaries but also provides the *raison d'être* for his whole mission (Neale, 1991: 129).

The conventional understanding of Lk 5:31-32 has focused in how Jesus' call to the lost was a radical departure from convention and constituted a grave offense to the religious authorities. On one level, the calling of "sinners" was indeed radical since it was a term that heretofore had applied only to the irredeemably lost. This Gospel habit of portraying the "sinner" as one deserving of mercy does mark a turning point in the history of the usage of the term. Yet, this should not obscure the fact that the saying itself is perfectly orthodox in its attitude that a religious figure should seek the reformation of the lost and as such it was not a radical departure from Jewish thinking (Sanders, 1983: 21-22). On the contrary, Jesus' stated intention of seeking the lost would have been understood by all as perfectly justifiable conduct for a spiritual shepherd in Israel. One should consider here the probable relation of Ez 34 (speaking of God as the true shepherd) to Lk 5 (Neale, 1991: 131). We should note that at the end of the account Luke adds the expression *eis metanoian*, "to repentance," "in view of repentance" (Fitzmyer, 1981: 592; Tiede, 1988: 127; Bovon, 1991: 247).

The response Jesus makes to the objections (intervening in defense of his followers) combines elements from the tradition in an original way: Jesus uses the standard medical imagery of the Hellenistic philosopher (Johnson, 1991: 97). He is the physician, therefore, he must be where the sick are. His fellowship is to be one in which the service orientation of the physician defines the community as such as one of accessibility and availability (Johnson, 1991: 99). Jesus' example teaches the church community that they need to seek and associate with the outcast as a part of their mission, even though there might be some who would frown on such personal relationships (Fitzmyer, 1981: 589). Jesus has gone from forgiving sinners to openly associating with them. Mission requires more than casual contact. Jesus engages with those in the culture. They sense that he cares for them and does not just preach at them (Bock, 1994: 489).

3. The Debate About Fasting; Parables (Lk 5:33-39)

The third controversy depicts Jesus answering the criticism of unnamed opponents who find fault with him because he does not teach his disciples to fast, as do John the Baptist and the Pharisees. Jesus' reply to such criticism is followed by two similitudes (or extended metaphors) and a proverb — all three joined by the catchword bond of the "old" and the "new." The whole unit (Lk 5:33-39) raises the question of the relation of the old way of Jewish piety to that of Christians. Luke has derived this episode from Mk 2:18-22, but he has again modified the Markan form. From the form-critical point of view, the episode, as it appears both in Luke and his Markan source, is again conflated. Lk 5:33-35 is a pronouncement-story, a controversy dialogue (Bultmann, 1972: 18-19). Lk 5:36-38 are similitudes (or extended metaphors). They were joined to the pronouncement in the Markan source, and probably also in a pre-Markan grouping (Kuhn, 1971: 61-72). To these Luke has added the proverb in Lk 5:39 (Fitzmyer, 1981: 594-595; Tiede, 1988: 129).

Lk 5:33-39 moves from Jesus' associations to his lack of religious asceticism. The passage presents an encounter between differing religious lifestyles. Interestingly, Luke ties this account closely to the previous one by the reference to Jesus' eating and drinking (Lk 5:33), recalling the uniquely Lukan remark of Lk 5:30. It is more than Jesus' associations that are bothersome. Jesus' meal with sinners is the tip of the iceberg. For Luke, the first direct challenge of Jesus comes here. Jesus is emerging as a controversial figure (Bock, 1994: 508).

Unlike Mark, who separates the question of fasting from Levi's house and has unidentified people raise it, and unlike Matthew, who separates the debate from the previous one and has John's disciples raise the issue, Luke implies at least that "they" who question Jesus are persons present at Levi's banquet. This allows the banquet setting to exemplify the eating and drinking of Jesus' disciples which is set over against pious fasting practices (Nolland, 1989: 247). Here the issue is addressed to Jesus, but it is about his followers (the Church), whereas earlier the disciples were asked about their behavior and Jesus answered. In both cases the matters involve the Church (Craddock, 1990: 79).

Verses 33-35: (33) Then they said to him,
"John's disciples, like the disciples of the
Pharisees,
frequently fast and pray,
but your disciples eat and drink."
(34) Jesus said to them,
"You cannot make wedding guests fast
while the bridegroom is with them, can you?
(35) The days will come when the bridegroom is
taken away from them.
and then they will fast in those days."

In the Lukan context the unnamed opponents have to be those mentioned in Lk 5:30, since Luke has omitted the narrative setting of Mk 2:18: "Now John's disciples and the Pharisees were fasting...," but then the comparison with John's disciples and the disciples of the Pharisees seems to imply non-Pharisaic questioners (Marshall, 1978: 224; Gowler, 1991: 203). Luke adds "frequently...and pray," to the fasting. "Frequently" is intelligible as a concern not to deny entirely to Jesus' disciples a practice of fasting (see Acts 13:2-3, and the Lukan alteration of Lk 5:34, "make...fast"; Nolland, 1989: 247).

The question for Luke is not *whether* fasting is appropriate, but *when* (Tiede, 1988: 129). Further, the error lies in the assumption that fasting is a matter of rule and regulation (Danker, 1988: 127). The disciples of John the Baptist are known from Lk 7:18-19; 11:1. They seem to be a group of Palestinian Jews (but see Acts 18:25-26), who had accepted John's baptism, used some set form of prayer, and fasted regularly (see Hendrickx, 1996: 237-238). The Lukan addition "and pray" seems to suggest that John had taught his disciples certain prayer-forms (Lk 11:1). Jesus does not here enter into the question of prayer. Prayer and fasting were closely joined in Jewish thought, and the purpose of the fasting was to improve the praying (Danker, 1988: 128).

In the last clause of verse 33, Luke has reformulated Mk 2:18, "your disciples do not fast," into ""your disciples eat and drink." This provides a link with the preceding episode, were Jesus and his disciples are accused of "eating and drinking" with tax-collectors and sinners (Lk 5:30; Fitzmyer, 1981: 597,598).

The narrator groups the disciples of John the Baptist and the disciples of the Pharisees together — in regards to their practice of fasting and offering prayers — in opposition to the disciples of Jesus. This association with the disciples of John the Baptist could put the disciples of the Pharisees in a more positive light, but one could more likely conclude that the two groups were mentioned together because they both had a deficient opinion of who Jesus was. Even John himself did not yet have an adequate view of Jesus' identity, as the reader will later learn (Lk 7:18-23). Thus his disciples and the disciples of the Pharisees had not yet come to the correct affirmation of Jesus' identity, and that deficiencty was evident in their behavior (Gowler, 1991: 204).

The statement addressed to Jesus in verse 33 is a negative challenge to the honor of Jesus. He must respond in order to retain honor. "They" — probably the Pharisees — accuse the disciples of dishonorable activity, but Jesus responds with a question that remains unanswered by his opponents and pronouncements that go unchallenged by them as well. He, by virtue of his victorious response, gains honor, The Pharisees, on the other hand, since they are defeated in the repartee, lose honor (Gowler, 1991: 205).

Jesus' answer, couched as a rhetorical question (Lk 5:34), is that it would be equally unthinkable for those present at a wedding to fast during the festivities; joy, not fasting, is the appropriate attitude for the companions of Jesus. The present time is thus likened to a wedding, and the period of Jesus' ministry is seen in terms of the messianic banquet (Marshall, 1978: 222). Jesus compares his disciples to celebrating wedding guests. The disciples of John the Baptist and the disciples of the Pharisees do not celebrate because they do not recognize the bridegroom (Gowler, 1991: 204).

To fast (mourn) at a wedding is a supreme insult to the principals and their families. Fasting would signal a refusal to enter wholeheartedly into the wedding celebration (Malina and Rohrbaugh, 1992: 317-318). Jesus compares himself to a "bridegroom," for the messianic age is a time of happiness, and a wedding is the supreme example of joy (Schürmann, 1969: 296; Fitzmyer, 1981: 599). The images of the groom and wedding express God's relationship to his people and are often used to allude to messianic times (Isa 54:5-6; 62:4-5; Jer 2:2; Ez 16; Bock, 1994: 516). Hosea had described Israel as a faithless wife (Hos 2:5) and pronounced dire judgment (Hos 2:10-13). But there was to be a new betrothal in the future (Hos 2:13-14). John had called for repentance in order to make that betrothal possible. Now it is bridal and festal time, and since the Jews did not fast on sabbaths and festival days, it would be inappropriate for the disciples to fast in the time of fulfillment for Israel's marriage to God (Danker, 1988: 127-128).

Luke omits Mk 2:19b, "as long as they have the bridegroom with them they cannot fast," no doubt because it seemed redundant, and he goes straight on to the period of contrast. Lk 5:35 is almost certainly a later adaptation and application of Lk 5:34 in a christological sense. The language is no longer parabolic but allegorical. The bridegroom is now a specific bridegroom, Jesus; the wedding guests (literally, "the sons of the bridechamber") are his disciples; "while the bridegroom is with them" is now taken literally of a particular period of time, his earthly ministry (C.F. Evans, 1990: 311). A time will come in which things will be different (Marshall, 1978: 225). Those days in which the bridegroom is taken away have happened (Acts 1:11). Thus the radical newness and freedom that characterized the practice of Jesus and his disciples while he was still with them no longer characterized Luke's own times (Tiede, 1988: 130). Thus it seems that Luke anchors the custom of early Christian fasting in a saying of Jesus. But it is not apparent, even from the general context, that this is meant as a fasting of mourning for the passion and death of Christ (Fitzmyer, 1981: 599; Bock, 1994: 518). What is not clear is whether Luke thinks his Church is living in a time when the "bridegroom" has been taken away (because Jesus has been crucified), or whether with the risen Christ the celebration continues. The mention of a time when fasting will be resumed makes the former seem to be the case (Ringe, 1995: 84).

Verses 36-39: (36) He also told them a parable:
                    "No one tears a piece from a new garment
                    and sews it on an old garment;
                    otherwise the new will be torn,
                    and the piece from the new will not match
                      the old.
               (37) And no one puts new wine into old wineskins;
                    otherwise the new wine will burst the skins
                    and will be spilled, and the skins will be
                      destroyed.
               (38) But new wine must be put into fresh
                      wineskins.
               (39) And no one after drinking old wine desires
                      new wine,
                    but says, 'the old is good.'"

Lk 5:36-39 gives a deeper rationale for Jesus' reply. He goes beyond the issue of fasting and prayer, as he explains through illustrations the religious situation of his ministry (Bock, 1994: 518-519). Jesus elaborates with two parables. The word "parable" is used to refer to simple figures of speech, to analogies, and to metaphors (often called "similitudes"; Marshall, 1978: 226) extended into narratives. It seems best to wait until we meet parables in their fuller and more complex forms (Lk 8) to discuss what parables are and what they do. In this case, the parable is a rather straightforward analogy (Craddock, 1990: 80). Luke alone here identifies Jesus' words as a parable. As in Lk 4:23, the meaning is close to that of *mashal*, a proverb or riddle, rather than a metaphoric narrative (Johnson, 1991: 98).

The twin parables of the patch and the wine clarify the response to the Pharisees that has been attributed to Jesus. Both parables depend on common sense, just as the previous saying depends on one's recognition of how weddings come as a joyful interruption in life and business as usual. Common sense recognizes that no one would tear a piece out of a new garment in order to repair an old one, even though the old is still worth saving. The new one would be left with a hole in it, and the patch would not work to fix the older one either. The two would not match to begin with, and in the days before fabrics were preshrunk, the new patch would soon pull away from the surrounding garment. Both the old and the new would be ruined (Lk 5:36). In the same way, to put new wine that is still fermenting into stiff old wineskins would result in the skins bursting, ruining them and spilling the wine. Again, both valuable commodities would be lost (Lk 5:37-38).

The common-sense wisdom of the parables reinforces Luke's double affirmation in the previous saying. Both the old and the new garments, both the new wine and the old wineskins, are valuable. Similarly, traditional religious practices like fasting are valued and good too, in their appropriate time. Jesus does not put down the religious practices of the other groups (Ringe, 1995: 85).

Lk 5:33-39, sometimes titled "The Question about Fasting," does not really deal very much with fasting. While it is true that Jesus is questioned concerning the additional fasts introduced to the Jewish liturgical calendar by John the Baptist and the Pharisees, Jesus does not answer the question directly. Should we concentrate on the question or on the answer? The answer possesses greater value. A deeper meaning of the story is to be found in Jesus' reply. Why does Jesus respond to a question about fasting by telling them that the bridegroom will be taken away? Why does he speak about the patch of new cloth on an old garment and new wine in old wineskins? Jesus evokes images of life, from the wedding scene to pouring new wine in old wine-skins. What is the central point of Jesus' illustration? Jesus leads his listeners on a path of discovery. No one who has drunk old wine will desire new. The main focus of the teaching emerges in Luke's version when Jesus says, "The old wine is better" (Lk 5:39).

In spite of the traditional title, fasting is not the major issue here. Although Jesus was asked about fasting, he wanted to say something more. He explained his own mission in terms the Jewish people of the first century could understand. When asked a question about fasting, Jesus took the opportunity to teach a deeper message. The message of Jesus was intimately related to his task and to his desire for the people's salvation.

Is fasting the issue? Many Bible students tend to overlook the final words of Jesus in Lk 5:39, "And no one after drinking old wine desires new; but says, 'The old is good.'" The Jewish liturgical year included a number of specified fast days for the entire nation. On Yom Kippur, the Jewish Day of Atonement, for example, all people afflicted themselves and fasted, asking for God's mercy and forgiveness. The Pharisees desired spiritual renewal. They wanted the people to be close to God all the time. Also the movement of John the Baptist was characterized by its urgency for spiritual revival. Lk 5:33 indicates that both the Pharisees and John the Baptist instituted new fasts to intensify the spiritual awarenes of the people.

What did Jesus think? Jesus was spearheading a renewal movement within the Judaism of his day. His approach to reform was much less radical than the Pharisees or John the Baptist — at least in the matter of fasting — though all of them desired a return to the people's spiritual heritage. The fasting of John's disciples and the Pharisees was one way to call for revival. The disciples of Jesus apparently did not observe these additional fasts. Jesus answers the question about fasting with two parables. The form of these two parables and their Hebrew background are firmly rooted in the teaching of Jesus (Young: 1989: 40-42). The structure of these parables of the old garment and the wine-skins, moreover, leads up to Luke's conclusion and forceful application in Lk 5:39 when Jesus declares that the old wine is better. The emphasis on the old wine indicates that all the talk about fasting may not be the answer for the true spiritual renewal. In modern times, however, Jesus' saying about the old wine has been overlooked and sometimes emphasis has wrongly been focused on the new wine. No one should forget that when it comes to wine, the old is better than the new. Jesus seems to speak about the rich Hebrew heritage of Judaism in his day with the highest esteem.

The old wine refers to the ancient faith and practices of the Jewish people. Then the question of fasting is related more to these additional fast days, which were called by John the Baptist and the Pharisees, and certainly not to the recognized fasts of the Jewish holy days, which would be observed by everyone. New fast days were used sometimes for encouraging members of a particular religious order to express their identifcation with their movement. These new fasts were being called in addition to the accepted practice. The new fasts may be compared to new wine while the old wine is closer to the accepted practices of the ancient faith. For genuine spiritual renewal, according to Jesus, the people must return to the best of the old wine.

The purpose of Jesus was to revitalize the people spiritually by a revival through the old wine. He did not teach that Judaism should be abolished. Rather he compared the Judaism of his day to an old garment which needs mending or to old wineskins. Jesus was saying that the spiritual condition was not ideal. But certainly he did not desire to put away the noble traditions of the ancient faith. On the contrary, when he says that the old wine is better, he is upholding the finest contributions of ancient Judaism and seek-

ing wholehearted reform from within. The old wine is the
Judaism of his time. It is the best.

The old wine is good. It teaches the way of life according to the faith in the one and only God of ancient Israel.
But the old wine needs new wineskins. Men and women of
God must be renewed in order to hold the old wine. Jesus
points the people to the truth of God's love and grace on
the basis of the best in the old wine. But fresh skins are
required for the old wine.

While many New Testament scholars would deny the
truth of Lk 5:39, "The old wine is better," one has shown
the authenticity of the saying, and notes that the best expression of Jesus' opinion about Judaism in his days would
probably have been, if Jesus had said: 'Fresh skins for old
wine!'" (Flusser, 1979: 26ff.).

The saying, "The old wine is better" cannot be attributed to the early Church. In fact, it seems that Marcion
deleted it from his Bible because it spoke about Judaism in
a positive way. Jesus was telling the people something about
his purpose. He came to bring renewal and liberation through
the power of the kingdom of God. His purpose was not to
destroy the significance of Torah but to fulfill it. The old
wine of Torah is the best.

When it comes to wine, the rabbis, along with wine con-
noisseurs, would agree with Jesus. Old wine is better than
new. The rabbis related wine to the study of Torah. The
more one studies the Scriptures, the more proficient one will
become. Knowledge of Scripture will change people's lives.
Concerning old wine and the study of Torah, the rabbis taught:
"One does not feel the taste of wine at the beginning, but
the longer it grows old in the pitcher, the better it becomes;
thus also the words of Torah: the longer they grow old in the
body, the better they become" (*Sopherim* 15:6).

Jesus desired to see new wineskins — that is, a revital-
ized people — enjoying the best of he old wine. The old
wine is the best. A spiritual renewal is needed. The new

fasts may contribute something toward this goal, but the future of the spiritual renewal will be linked more to Jesus and his disciples as they teach about God's reign than to the new innovative fasts being called for by John the Baptist and the Pharisees. Jesus desired the revitalization of the faith — a renewed people, spiritually preparted for the best of the old wine (Young, 1995: 155-158).

Jesus speaks, moreover, about the bridegroom. In fact, the whole passage surrounds the image of the bridegroom. Why do Jesus' disciples not fast? The bridegroom is with them. The day will come when the bridegroom is taken. In Hebrew the term "taken" used in this context is a euphemism clearly understood to refer to death.

The bridegroom is for a wedding, the occasion of supreme joy in Jewish thought and custom. Great joy is reserved for the wedding ceremony. The exact opposite is the case for a funeral. The grief expressed at a funeral is the supreme act of mourning. Jesus combines the two strongest emotions of men and women: the great joy of a wedding and the solemn mourning characteristic of a funeral.

When Jesus said, "But when the bridegroom is taken away from them," the people were probably puzzled. The word "is taken away" was another way of saying, "when he dies" or "when he is killed." The term "bridegroom" could be associated with the coming of the messianic Redeemer (cf. Mt 25:6). The time will come when he will be taken; then his disciples will fast. In the puzzling saying of Jesus, one sees both joy and sadness interrelated. But how can one associate the joy of a wedding with the death of the bridegroom? Perhaps the answer to this question is related to the messianic task as defined by Jesus himself.

Jesus quite possibly alludes to Isa 53:8, where the same word refers to the death of the suffering servant (doubtful according to Marshall, 1978: 226). Joy is associated with the coming of the messiah. But when the messianic idea is connected to the suffering servant in the words of the prophet

Isaiah as Jesus taught in his prophecies concerning his death, a reference to the death of the bridegroom is not out of place. Both of the diverse feelings of joy and mourning may be associated with the coming of the messianic figure in the teachings of Jesus. At least in Isa 53:8, we read, "*He was taken away* from rule and from judgment...for he was cut off from the land of the living." Is it possible that Jesus made a veiled mention of his death as the bridegroom?

The bridegroom is here. Now is not the time for fasting. He brings renewal. He is fulfilling his mission. Renewed wineskins are being prepared for the finest old wine. But the day will come when the bridegrom will be taken. He will die. This also will be part of his mission.

The twin parables of the "Garment" and ther "Old Wine" make no sense when they are separated from their original setting of the first century. The message of these parables must in the first place be heard as a dialogue within Judaism. Some of the new efforts at reform such as innovative fast days will not contribute to a deeper level of interaction with the ancient faith. Jesus is an insider promoting renewal and reform from within the system. According to Jesus the old wine is the best! We as Christians have tended to view the Judaism of the time of Jesus in a negative way. The teachings of Jesus, however, evaluate Judaism positively. When we prefer new wine, the message of Jesus is distorted. The followers of Jesus should be for Judaism and enjoy the fine taste from the best of the old wine. A greater understanding of the Jewish roots of early Christianity will enhance our appreciation of the theological depth of Jesus' message (Young, 1995: 158-160).

4. Debates Concerning the Sabbath (Lk 6:1-11)

There is little introduction to the next event. Luke moves right into the action (Bock, 1994: 522). That Luke locates these stories quite generally — "on a sabbath" (Lk 6:1) and "on another sabbath" (Lk 6:6) — is not only to say that these are two examples of conflicts over Sabbath observance but also to underscore that what is important is not where or when these events occurred but the kind of events they are: they are Sabbath stories. This is to say that these incidents from the life of Jesus present him in conflict with Jewish leadership over practices that were central to the piety and identity as God's people. So very much of what it meant to be the faithful community was tied to table customs and Sabbath observance. In this section of controversy stories (Lk 5:17-6:11), two have dealt with Jesus' eating habits (he ate with sinners; he ate when others fasted). Now we have two that deal with Sabbaths. In the first, Jesus defends the actions of his disciples (Lk 6:1-5); in the second, his own action, which, we may assume, was for the early Christians, an argument for their own behavior from the precedent of Jesus (Lk 6:6-11; Craddock, 1990: 81-82).

According to the the two stories, which may reflect the shape of controversies between the early Christian community and the neighboring synagogue as much as any reminiscences of Jesus' time, the Pharisees ask about the limits on one's Sabbath activity, while Jesus presses for a discussion of the purpose and intent of Sabbath-keeping (Ringe, 1995: 86). The question thus arises whether more was intended here than a protest against an over-rigid legalism in favor of humanitarian action (cf. Lk 14:5), and whether the intense opposition aroused (cf. Mk 3:6) was to something more than the performance of the right action on the wrong day (cf Lk 13:14; C.F. Evans, 1990: 313).

The theme of the old and the new from Lk 5:27-39 provides the perspective from which to approach Lk 6:1-5 and 6:6-11. The situation created by the presence of Jesus opens up new freedoms and possibilities that cannot be contained within the constraints of Pharisaic piety but that nevertheless correspond to the true purpose of God for his people (Nolland, 1989: 255).

1. Plucking Grain on the Sabbath (Lk 6:1-5)

For Luke, the plucking of grain is next to last in a series of stories leading up to Jesus' appointment of twelve disciples (Lk 6:12-16) and his Sermon on the Plain (Lk 6:20-49). In this position it helps to provide the narrative context in which he can conclude with a speech to "a great crowd of his disciples and a great multitude of people" (Lk 6:17) with an appeal which asks: "Why do you call me 'Lord, Lord' and do not do what I tell you?..." (Lk 6:46). These observations support the general consensus that Luke's version of the story is especially "christological," with its quick movement to the final saying that the Son of Man is lord of the Sabbath (Neirynck, 1975: 230; Banks, 1975: 116; Robbins, 1989: 131).

Some scholars have considered the story too unrealistic to be considered an authentic report of Jesus' behavior, and parodied the narrative "Pharisees did not organize themselves into groups to spend their Sabbaths in Galilean cornfields in the hope of catching someone transgressing" (Sanders, 1985: 265). But the careful conclusion has been advanced that it still does not seem possible to eliminate completely a genuine confrontation between Jesus and the Pharisees (Freyne, 1980: 321). In fact, the Pharisees' likely presence in Galilee has been strongly defended recently (Witherington, 1990a: 61-66).

Verses 1-5: (1) One sabbath while Jesus was going through the grainfields,
his disciples plucked some heads of grain,
rubbed them in their hands, and ate them.
(2) But some of the Pharisees said,
"Why are you doing what is not lawful on the sabbath?"
(3) Jesus answered, "Have you not heard what David did
when he and his companions were hungry?
(4) He entered the house of God
and took and ate the bread of the Presence,

> which it is not lawful for any but the priests to
>   eat,
> and gave some to his companions?"
> (5) And he said to them,
> "The Son of Man is lord of the sabbath."

In Lk 6:1-5 the evangelist fairly closely follows Mark's account. The changes can be assumed to be redactional (Salo, 1991: 86). From the rhetorical point of view, the story has been classified as judicial rhetoric. According to the parts of judicial speech, the story can be divided into: (1) introduction (Lk 6:1); (2) statement of the case (Lk 6:2); (3) refutation — example as precedent (Lk 6:3-4); (4) conclusion — judgment as rationale (Lk 6:5; Robbins, 1989: 108-110). In contrast to the Markan version, the Lukan version does not develop the rhetoric "in" the story with special rhetorical features. Rather, Luke tells the story with "special touches" in a style characteristic of abbreviated composition in *chreiai*, [A *chreia* is a brief statement or action with pointedness attributed to a definite person or something analogous to a person — Aelius Theon].

According to Deut 23:26, one was permitted to pluck grain from a neighbor's field provided that one did not presume to put a sickle to the standing grain (Fitzmyer, 1981: 608). Thus it could not be the cause of controversy. Rather, the issue is the proper observance of the Sabbath. Plucking ears of grain could be regarded as part of harvesting — an implication which Luke made even clearer by adding the expression "rubbed them in their hands." From the Pharisaic point of view, this meant working on the Sabbath, and, as such, it formed a challenge to the Torah, which explicitly commands the Sabbath to be observed, even during harvest time (Ex 34:21). Unfamiliar with halakic details, Luke added "plucking" to "rubbing." The disciples' action was considered inappropriate only to those who were more stringent in their Sabbath observance (Lk 6:2: "*some* Pharisees"; Safrai, 1990: 3-5). Luke makes it clear that the disciples were acting against the Sabbath commandments as understood by the Pharisees (Salo, 1991: 87; Robbins, 1989: 129). But the narrator notes that it is "some" of the Pharisees who challenge the actions of Jesus' disciples, which may be a mitigating factor for any negative evaluation of the of the group as a whole (Sanders, 1987: 172; Ziesler, 1979: 146-157; Salo, 1991: 87). Mark tends to treat the Pharisees as a fixed group; Luke is more ready to differentiate (Nolland, 1989: 256).

The ubiquitous Pharisees' objection is registered against a plural "you," i.e., the disciples, but Jesus takes responsibility for his disciples' actions (Nolland, 1989: 257). The relationship between a Master and his disciples establishes the social framework for the story (Daube, 1972:1-15; Bovon, 1991: 262). A person who is a disciple has accepted the social position of subordinance for the purpose of learning through imitation and instruction. It is the responsibility of the Master to teach and encourage good actions and thoughts and to correct and discourage bad actions and thoughts (Robbins, 1984: 63-65). So, though the charge is laid against the disciples Jesus answers in defense of them. Thus, the declaration that he is "lord of the Sabbath" is not only a christological claim, but legitimates the community practice of the first Christians who handed on stories such as these (Johnson, 1991: 101).

The argument concerns the difference in opinion about the way in which one must keep the Sabbath holy. The brief appearance of the Pharisees in Lk 6:2 consists only of one statement, and Jesus' pronouncement forcefully puts them in their place. Their role as the opposition of Jesus and his disciples is clear, and Jesus' speech gives emphasis to their deficiency. The question "Have you not read?," i.e., in the Scriptures, stresses the fact that Jesus knows and that the Pharisees, at least "some," do not, and the use of *oude*, "not," heightens the irony (Fitzmyer, 1981: 608).

Yet the juridical appearance of this scene is of secondary importance. The analogy is quite imprecise: (a) There is no allusion to the Sabbath in David's action (1Sam 21:1-6); (b) David's error was to eat forbidden food, "the bread of the Presence," i.e., the loaves set out in Yahweh's presence (Ex 25:30) and which after one week were to be eaten only by the priests (Lev 24:9), but the disciples' error was to work on a forbidden day. The analogy rests solely on the fact that both actions were illegal in one form or another (Wilson, 1983: 33; Salo, 1991: 88). Jesus explicitly affirms that David's action was illegal (Lk 6:4), so he does not deny the Pharisees' charge (Lk 6:2, "it is not lawful"). Since there is no attempt to evade the charge of illegality, it seems that an analogy is being made between the two leaders, Jesus and David. The parallel uses of *poieo* in Lk 6: 2-3, as well as the direct juxtaposition of David's authority (Lk 6:4) with Jesus' authority (Lk 6:5), drive home the point that Jesus has even greater authority than David.

The concluding saying, "The Son of Man is lord of the Sabbath" (Lk 6:5) is clearly the point of the passage (Ringe, 1995: 87). In fact, as Son of Man, one more factor has been added to his power (Lk 4:14,36; 5:17) and authority (Lk 4:32,36; 5:24): he is the lord of the Sabbath (Lk 6:5). Therefore, with this authority he stands above the law and claims the right to determine what is and what is not acceptable behavior on the Sabbath. Luke is fond of the term "Son of humanity," for it gives him opportunity to define Jesus as one who identifies wholeheartedly with the human race (see Lk 3:23-38) and with all the fragility that such identification implies. At the same time, Jesus' is recognized by Luke's readers as the exalted Son of humanity, and they know that he has every right to refer to himself as "lord of the Sabbath" (Danker, 1988: 131). The title "Son of Man" is part of the christological buildup of the Gospel (Fitzmyer, 1981: 610; Nolland, 1989: 257).

Some scholars have advanced the opinion that we have here an example of Jesus clearly breaking the Old Testament Sabbath law. The law that David broke could only have been the Torah. The text also would place Jesus above the law (Blomberg, 1984: 54). They interpret the pericope as challenging the law as a whole. Nowhere, they say, does Luke make a distinction between the law and its application (Turner, 1982; 104; Wilson, 1983: 35). These treatments of Lk 6:1-5 are not adequate. Luke produces a great number of positive statements concerning the Sabbath (Lk 4:16,31; 13:10; Acts 13:14ff.,42,44) or even a direct saying about fulfilling the Sabbath law (Lk 23:56). On ther other hand, direct and explicit attacks on the Sabbath law are missing from Luke-Acts. It seems that in Lk 6:1-5 the Sabbath Torah itself is not challenged (Klinghardt, 1988: 229). The challenge is not against the law, but against its interpretation by "some" Pharisees (Wilson, 1983: 41-42; Salo, 1991: 90). The narrator's direct concern is not the juridical aspect of Sabbath observance, but is instead the person and character of Jesus. The Pharisees' role is to highlight that authority (Gowler, 1991: 207-208).

The Pharisees, as before, do not addresss a direct objection to Jesus about one of his own actions. They instead challenge Jesus' disciples about plucking grain, rubbing it in their hands, and eating it on the Sabbath. Maybe we should note here that the disciples are not represented as acting out of danger of starvation, but naturally out of a freedom they possess as Jesus' disciples (C.F. Evans, 1990: 314). Because of the corporate nature of honor, Jesus must respond to this challenge addressed to his followers (Daube, 1972-1973: 1-15). A direct affront to the honor of Jesus is not made, but the indirect challenge is accepted, and Jesus gains honor at the Pharisees' expense.

Jesus' claim to authority over the Sabbath is indeed unusual. An honorable person tries to avoid any resemblance of self-aggrandizement. As in Lk 5:24, though, the term "Son of Man" lends at least a small amount of detachment to the claim to authority, and this extraordinary pronouncement by Jesus is left unchallenged by the Pharisees (Gowler, 1991: 208-209).

Jesus' closing remark, "The Son of Man is lord of the Sabbath," centers on *kurios*, "lord," which comes at the start of the citation. A literal rendering according to word order is, "Lord is of the Sabbath the Son of Man." The passage has its fullest development in Mk 2:27-28, "The Sabbath was made for humankind, and not humankind for the Sabbath; so the Son of Man is lord even of the sabbath." Many see Mark's point to be humankind's authority over the Sabbath, with the "Son of Man" as a reference to humans in general, since the phrase can have this meaning in Aramaic (Creed, 1957: 84-85; Bock 1994: 485-486, 924-930). A later rabbinic statement is close to this remark in force; nonetheless, many regard Jesus' remark as a likely interpretation of an ancient view: "The Sabbath is given over to you and not you to the Sabbath" (*Mekilta de Rabbi Ishmael, tractate shabbata* 1 on Ex 31:14; Marshall, 1978: 232). The point of Mark's text, which Luke does not have, is that the Sabbath is not to be a master over God's people, but is a service to them. It was created for them and not as a burden against them. Luke does not have Mark's remark about the Sabbath and God's people. Rather, Luke has a more exclusive christological focus. Mark's intermediate argument is not made, but the deeper issue about Jesus is emphasized. The Son of Man is an authoritative representative on behalf of his people, much as a king would be (Fitzmyer, 1981: 610; Marshall, 1978: 232-233; Danker, 1988: 131). Jesus, as this representative, has authority as Son of Man to evaluate and interpret tradition and law. This is why authority is stressed by the placement of *kurios* in the emphatic first position (Bock, 1994: 526-527).

Historical questions surrounding the observation of the Sabbath have been widely examined, but the cultural aspects surrounding the idea of sacred time should be noted. The Sabbath, according to the Pharisees in Luke-Acts, is sacred time that is related to other purity regulations. Virtually every society utilizes some sort of purity system, where the clean is distinguished from the unclean. These distinctions not only display the core values of a society, but also provide clarity and consistency for accepted social behavior (Neyrey, 1988: 72-82). Most of the conflicts between Jesus and the Pharisees in the Gospel of Luke are concerned with purity rules (Gowler, 1991: 23). The way that Jesus neglects these social conventions represents — to the Pharisees — a flagrant rejection of how God had ordered the world, and, more specifically the purity regulations laid down by God's law. Jesus is contravening their entire God-ordained *Weltanschauung*. Thus the Pharisees' objection is quite understandable; their mistake is that they do not recognize who Jesus is (Gowler, 1991: 209-210).

2. Healing a Man with a Withered Hand on the Sabbath (Lk 6:6-11)

The illustration of the old and the new (Lk 5:27-39) continues here with a further instance of Jesus' action as lord of the Sabbath (Lk 6:5). As he has provided on the Sabbath for the needs of his disciples, so now on the Sabbath he meets the need of the man with the withered right hand (Nolland, 19879: 260). Lk 6:6-11 is a conflict story in which the healing is entirely subordinate (C.F. Evans, 1990: 316).

Verses 6-11: (6) On another Sabbath he entered the synagogue and taught,
and there was a man there whose right hand was withered.
(7) The scribes and the Pharisees watched him
to see whether he would cure on the Sabbath,
so that they might find an accusation against him.
(8) Even though he knew what they were thinking
he said to the man with the withered hand,
"Come and stand here." He got up and stood there.

(9) Then Jesus said to them,
    "I ask you, is it lawful to do good or to do
    harm on the Sabbath,
    to save life or to destroy it?"
(10) After looking around at all of them, he said to
    him,
    "Stretch out your hand." He did so, and his
    hand was restored.
(11) But they were filled with fury
    and discussed with one another what they might
    do to Jesus.

The next healing occurs on another Sabbath, which does
not necessarily mean the next Sabbath, but simply makes
clear that the event would be seen in the light of Sabbath
traditions. The introduction also temporarily separates this
event from the previous controversy (Lk 6:1) and reveals a
topical concern about Sabbath controversies that links these
events (Bock, 1994: 527-528).

Lk 6:6-11 shows interesting alterations to the tradition
Luke used at this point (Mk 3:1-6). Right at the beginning
the author employs a redactional phrase *egeneto de en heterōi
sabbatōi*, "[it happened] on another Sabbath," presumably
wanting to emphasize that we are also, in this pericope,
dealing with issues related to the Sabbath observance. Thus
the story recited in Lk 6:6-11 is to be viewed as an extension of the issue raised in Lk 6:1-5 (Danker, 1988: 132).
The fact that Jesus as the Son of Man is lord of the Sabbath is taken out of the realm of simple assertion (Lk 6:1-
5) by the present story in which Jesus demonstrates his power
to heal on the Sabbath and thereby confounds his opponents (Marshall, 1978: 233; C.F. Evans, 1990: 316).

The author wants redactionally to heighten Jesus' teaching
mission by adding the verb *didaskō* (Bovon, 1991: 265-266;
Danker, 1988: 132). What does the story tell about the link
between Jesus' healings and his preaching? In short, the
healing and the teaching are of a piece in Jesus' rejection
of the rabbinic halakah on the Sabbath that prevented the

people from fulfilling God's commandment of love (cf. Mk 2:27; Twelftree, 1993: 169).

He also stresses the importance of the healing for the man by talking about his right hand, not just a hand (see below; Salo, 1991: 91). The action takes place "on... Sabbath," which brings to mind the all-important Nazareth scene (Lk 4:16-30), and the addition of "another" in Lk 6:6 to the phrase "one Sabbath" of Lk 6:1 recollects the immediately previous scene (Lk 6:1-5). Other word repetitions occur such as the use of "synogogue" (Lk 4:16-30,33,38) and "to teach" (Lk 4:15,31-37; 5:3,17). The attentive reader will remember the important events that have occurred in synagogues and on the Sabbath day, and this scene will function either to resonate with, to develop, and/or to contradict what has gone before in similar situations. Thus the comparisons between how the characters are portrayed in such similar times yield much information about them. The people in Nazareth that Sabbath day, for example, rejected Jesus' message, but other people received him — even when he exorcized a demon from a man in the Capernaum synagogue (Lk 4:31-37). The reader wonders, How will the characters respond to him in this synagogue on the Sabbath? (Gowler, 1991: 210).

The mention of the man with a withered hand telegraphs the action that is to follow. Because of the previous episodes (e.g., Lk 4:31-41; 5:12-26) the mere mention of the man's condition serves as a proleptic reference to the healing that will surely follow. The narrator increases sympathy for the man by noting that it was his *right* hand that was debilitated (Lk 6:6). The reference heightens the man's unfortunate position (Fitzmyer, 1981: 610; Nolland, 1989: 260; Ringe, 1995: 87). Medically speaking, the man's hand was probably paralyzed (Van Der Loos, 1965: 438-439; Tiede, 1988: 132). [The importance of the right hand can be seen throughout Luke-Acts (e.g., Lk 1:11; 20:42; 22:50; Acts 2:25,33-34). The right hand, for a number of reasons, is closely connected to one's honor (Malina and Neyrey, 1991: 9]. But the description also suggests that the situation is not extreme. Sympathy for the man's disability is also increased by the obstacle created by the scribes and the Pharisees (Lk 6:7), that must be overcome by decisive action (Gowler, 1991: 210-211).

The narrator ominously introduces the scribes and the Pharisees: they closely watch Jesus because they want to find an accusation against him (Lk 6:7). They are on a fact-finding mission (Schürmann, 1969: 306 note 48; Nolland, 1989: 260; Bovon, 1991: 268). The term *paratēreō* is used by Luke of hostile observation in Lk 14:1 and 20:20 (Johnson, 1991: 102) No action of Jesus immediately precipitates this animosity, and this reference is the first mention of any *explicit* hostility against Jesus. Indeed, the conclusion that the hostility from the scribes and the Pharisees here is premeditated (Danker, 1988: 132) is to be preferred to the conclusion that no a priori hostility could be attributed to the Pharisees (Brawley, 1987: 86). The situation is clear; the scribes and the Pharisees are the opponents of Jesus. How far will their opposition go? (Gowler, 1991: 211-212). "To find an accusation" or "to find a charge" (*katēgoreō*) is understood by Luke in its full forensic sense of a legal charge brought against someone (see Lk 11:54; 23:2,120,14; Acts 22:30; 24:2,19; Johnson, 1991: 102).

The contrast between Jesus and the Pharisees bears the brunt of this scene's characterization of them. Debate about the Sabbath is not merely academic, argues Luke. Involved ultimately is the question whether human beings are more important than the security of any establishment where interest in rules and regulations in a situation takes precedence over the importance of meeting needs (Danker, 1988: 132). This issue is as relevant now as it was in Jesus' time.

The Torah does not provide material concerning healing on the Sabbath, but the picture rabbinic Judaism gives seems to be that healing on the Sabbath was permitted when life was in danger [m Yoma 8:6: "...whenever there is doubt whether life is in danger this overrides Sabbath"], but otherwise it was not allowed. In extremes only was the priority of Sabbath keeping to be disturbed (Nolland, 1989: 261). The key to the formulation of the alternatives is rightly found in Jesus' conviction that the love of God is inseparately linked to love of neighbor (Schürmann, 1969: 308). That which honors God cannot dishonor my neighbor. That what leaves my neighbor in his suffering can only be evil (Busse, 1977: 140). Not even on the Sabbath (or perhaps especially not on the Sabbath) can there be a comfortable neutrality that is content to define one's responsibilities negatively in terms of what is not to be done (Nolland, 1989: 261). The spirit of the Sabbath ordinance is that people should be preserved from exploitation by others and have the opportunity to ponder the goodness of God. Since the Sabbath is the day on which God's goodness is especially to be noted, there is no better occasion for Jesus to display that goodness. The Church cannot avoid the summons to hear and then respond promptly to the groans of humankind (Danker, 1988: 133).

Clearly in Luke's Sabbath healing accounts the sick ones did not have a fatal illness, and in every situation the healing could have waited until the next day. The scribes and the Pharisees opposed healing on the Sabbath, and this coincides with the picture we get from rabbinic literature. Luke has understood that Jesus' healing miracle on the Sabbath was not accepted by some Jewish circles, although we cannot be sure how much he knew about the Jewish reasoning at this point (Fitzmyer, 1981: 606; Salo, 1991: 91-92).

Jesus knew their thoughts — a sure sign that he is a prophet (Lk 2:34-35; 5:22; 7:39) — and took the initiative. The man with the withered hand did not even have to ask for help; Jesus told him to rise and to stand in their midst. The unfortunate man is made to take a position center-stage (Fitzmyer, 1981: 611). Jesus and the man stand in the midst of those who are seeking to accuse him. "The middle" is the place of confrontation between Jesus and his Pharisaic investigators (Nolland, 1989: 261). The conflict reaches its climax when he returns their unspoken challenge (Lk 6:9). No answer is given; their silence betrays their opposition — although Luke does not explicitly mention their silence in contrast to Mk 3:4. Luke follows the tradition in allowing Jesus to give only two alternatives from which to choose. The contrast is not doing good versus doing nothing, but rather good and bad deeds, saving or destoying life. Apparently the implication is that healing belongs to the sphere of good deeds, which one should be allowed to do on Sabbath. On the other hand, not to heal in a time of need means acting in a bad manner, and such conduct is condemned. From Luke's, and his readers," point of view, Jesus actually fulfills the Sabbath law by healing and being a savior (Schürmann, 1969: 309).

The narrator also mentions that Jesus looked "around at all of them" (Lk 6:10). This subtle technique of composition continues to create the heroic image of Jesus standing defiant in front of those who would accuse him. Faced with their shameful silence, Jesus himself supplies the answer to the question by restoring the man's hand to health. The actions of Jesus also unambiguously proclaim his superiority to the scribes and the Pharisees.

The narrator concludes his account by saying that the scribes and the Pharisees "were filled with fury and discussed with one another what they might do to Jesus" (Lk 6:11). The threat of negative sanctions is a creative use of ambiguous foreshadowing; suspense is heightened, but ambiguity reigns for a a number of reasons. First, no mention is made of what specific actions the scribes and the Pharisees could take. Second, the optative mood projects the sense of possible action. No clear plan of opposition is certain. Third, *anoia*, "fury," could possibly mean just "folly" or "lack of understanding" (Tannehill, 1986: 176; Fitzmyer, 1981: 611, dismisses this possibility as unlikely). Therefore, even their contemplated act of revenge does not close the door on the Pharisees. There may still be hope. Thus far, however, their devotion to a particular view of God's order has blinded them to the identity of Jesus. Their blindnes serves as a warning to those who are similarly devoted to things other than the person of Jesus, then and now (Gowler, 1991: 212-213).

We mày conclude that Luke does not want to picture the breaking of the Sabbath law, but rather lets Jesus discuss with the Pharisees the true essence of observing the Sabbath — and this message could well be directed to the Christian Jews (Pharisees). To do what benefits a person is acceptable even if it goes against the current Jewish *halakah*, their understanding of the implications of the law.

In Lk 6:6-11, compared with Mk 3:1-6, Luke has seemingly redactionally reduced the criticism against the Pharisees. Jesus does not show his anger toward his critics or criticize their "hardness of heart" (Mk 3:5). Nor do the Pharisees hold a meeting with the Herodians against Jesus in oder to kill him. Instead, Luke's scribes and Pharisees end up angry, and thus show their disapproval of Jesus' action on the Sabbath. Notably, they do not make a decision to kill Jesus, but only discuss at length (the verb is in an imperfect indicating duration) what they should do with him (Salo, 1991: 93). Luke prefers to tone down the notice of specific opposition depicted in Mk 3:6 (Fitzmyer, 1981: 607, 611; Schweizer, 1984: 113; Tiede, 1988: 133; Nolland, 1989: 262).

III. The Preaching of Jesus (Lk 6:12-49)

Lk 6:12-49 is accepted as a unit by a large number of commentators because of several indications, both literary and thematic. Let us first pay attention to the *literary mo-*

tifs. Perhaps the best literary index pointing to the unity of this section is provided by two uses of the verb *erchomai,* first in the opening verse of the narrative (Lk 6:12) and then again in the first verse of the following section (Lk 7:1). This latter verse, as in many instances in the Lukan writings, functions as a sort of bridge-sentence (Marshall, 1978: 243; Danker, 1988: 88,90), containing indications both of closing one section and opening another. In both instances the verb is in compound form and significantly the prefixes give contrasting meanings to the verb forms when placed side by side. In Lk 6:12 the verb form is *exelthein* which implies the idea of moving away from the scene of action hihterto described. In Lk 7:1 the verb form is *eiselthen* which, in the context, along with its complement of place (*Kapharnaoum*), implies the idea of reverting to a familiar scene and mode of activity that was left off at some point. The effect created by the verb forms that frame the entire section is like that of a theatrical aside [An aside in the theater context can be defined as something spoken in such a way as to be audible only to the person addressed, especially by an actor, which the others on stage are not supposed to hear.] (Malipurathu, 1994: 24-25 and note 58). That Luke intended to mark off Lk 6:12-49 by the deliberate use of the two verb forms discussed above may also become evident from a comparison with the other two Synoptic authors (Malipurathu, 1994: 26-27). This effect has a certain relevance especially in the context of the discussion regarding the intended audience of the beatitudes and woes and of the sermon in general.

Another literary index to the unity of Lk 6:12-49 may be seen as coming from several mutually linked occurrences of words from the root *akouein,* "to hear" (Lk 6:18,27,47,49; 7:1; Tiede, 1986: 65; Flender, 1967: 25). The first occurrence of it in Lk 6:18 (*akousai*) seemingly sets the tone for the subsequent uses. Here it is positively implied that the large crowds gathered at the foot of the mountain were there to listen to him (Goulder, 1989: 344). The linking phrase in Lk 6:27a, "But I say to you that listen" — a typical Lukan transitional formula made necessary because of the presence of the woes in Lk 6:24-26 (Dupont, 1958: 189) — calls the attention of the listeners (*tois akouousin*) and is obviously in reference to the crowds who had come to listen to him (Lk 6:18; Lambrecht, 1985: 214). The two occurrences in Lk 6:47 (*akouon*) and in Lk 6:48 (*akousas*), occurring as they do in the context of the parable of the two housebuilders, effectively highlight two kinds of attitudes in relation to receiving the message of Jesus that can possibly result from the act of hearing. These certainly refer back to Lk 6:18 and 27 (Fitzmyer, 1981: 629,637). Finally, when the substantive (*akoas*) occurs to indicate that all these things were said in the *hearing* of the people (Lk 7:1), it appears to sum up the implications of the four occurrences of the verbal forms in the section (Kahlefeld, 1962: 60; Malipurathu, 1994: 28).

Many exegetes think that besides such literary indications, some of the *thematic motifs* apparently present in the sequence of events described here can also be used to demonstrate the essential unity of the section. Naturally one has to admit that considerations based on contents are less persuasive than those based on literary indications, because the former are not verifiable in the same manner as the latter are. But a solid case can be made for an Israel symbolism (the Twelve [new Israel]; representatives of "old" Israel; the crowds as representative of all Israel, etc.; Malipurathu, 1994: 30-32; Geldenhuys, 1951: 205; Kilgallen, 1988: 85) and there is a possible allusion to Sinai typology suggested by the sequence of pericopes: top of the mountain, foot of the mountain, waiting crowds, proclamation of God's word in their presence (Malipurathu, 1994: 33-36; Conzelmann, 1960: 46; Ernst, 1977: 207; Marshall, 1978: 236; Lambrecht, 1985: 33; Danker, 1988: 78-79).

At the end of the previous section, Lk 5:17-6:11, it has

become clear that the powerful presence of Jesus has begun to generate feelings of uneasiness in the minds of the Pharisees and the scribes (Fitzmyer, 1981: 613). At this stage the evangelist moves a step forward with his story to introduce the idea of Jesus' choosing a special group of disciples, whom he subsequently names apostles (Lk 6:12-16), and of his teaching the crowds in their presence about the implications of casting one's lot with him (Lk 6:17-49). The proclamation activity of Jesus, which until now has been mostly referred to only without detailing its contents (Lk 4;15,31-32,44; 5:1,4,17; 6:6) now gets a programmatic development in the Sermon on the Plain (Ernst, 1977: 205; Lambrecht, 1985: 11-13; O'Fearghail, 1991: 194). Moreover, the mission of Jesus set out in the Nazareth pericope (Lk 4:16-30), that effectively serves as the frontispiece of the public ministry in Luke, is now shown as concretely unfolding: Jesus' address begins with the good news to the poor (Malipurathu, 1994: 13-14).

When we examine the larger section dealing with Jesus' ministry in Galilee (Lk 4:14-9:50), we become aware of a certain intention to project the Sermon on the Plain as a basic summary of Jesus' teaching (Lk 4:32: *didachē*), or as his *didachē* par excellence. In the narative prior to the sermon (Lk 4:14-6:19), Jesus' teaching activity is repeatedly referred to through the direct use of the verb *didaskō* (Lk 4:15,31,32; 5:3,17; 6:6) and by statements to the effect that people flocked to listen to him (Lk 5:1,15; 6:18: *akouō*). The references to the favorable reaction of the crowd upon hearing his word (Lk 4:15,22) can also be added here. All the above instances of using the word *didaskō* are cases of using it absolutely, i.e., without an object (see especially Lk 4:15; Fitzmyer, 1981: 522). When reporting on the crowds coming to Jesus in Lk 5:1 and 15, nothing is specified of what was said in their hearing. The mention of the large crowds in Lk 6:18 is clearly in view of the sermon. This omission of reporting the content of Jesus' teaching seems to be due to the nature of what was said on the occasion of the Sermon on the Plain, conceived of as the essential core of all his teachings. Interestingly, the word *didaskō* does not occur in the section dealing with the Galilean ministry after the sermon (Lk 7:1-9:50). The next occurrence of it is only in Lk 11:1, where the disciples request Jesus to teach them to pray. These observations suggest that the evangelist deliberately presents the Sermon on the Plain as the quintessential teaching of Jesus (Malipurathu, 1994: 21-22).

So, in the face of rising opposition, the rest of Lk 6 narrates Jesus' organizing of disciples (Lk 6:12-16), a summary about his teaching and healing (Lk 6:17-19), and an example of his ethical-religious teaching (Lk 6:20-49; (Bock, 1994: 537). According to some scholars the commonly acknowledged unit Lk 6:12-49 is also framed by the name *Petros* (Lk 6:14) and the closely related word *petra*, "rock" (Lk 6:48; O'Fearghail, 1991:45; Dietrich, 1972: 94), but this seems to be rather forced because the word *Petros* in verse 14 is a proper name and it occurs not really at the very beginning of the section (Malipurathu, 1994: 29).

Luke's account of Jesus' ministry now moves into a new phase. The beginnings in Galilee were described in various traditional scenes of teaching and healing centered about two episodes that Luke had transposed for programmatic effect, the visit to Nazareth (Lk 4:16-30) and the role of Peter, the fisherman (Lk 5:1-11). The account of the beginnings was followed by a block of controversy-stories in which Jesus was portrayed offsetting Pharisaic and scribal criticism of himself and his disciples (Lk 5:17-6:11); they ended with the mention of talk among them about what to do with Jesus (Lk 6:11).

Now Luke's story moves a step further, as it presents Jesus fashioning for himself a small group of special disciples (Lk 6:12-16) and giving samples of his preaching to the crowds. The section begins with another Lukan transposition. Two scenes that are dependent on the Markan order are taken up (Mk 3:7-12 and 3:13-19) but are now reversed, becoming respectively Lk 6:17-19 an 6:12-16. The result is that the discipleship of the Twelve (Lk 6:12-16) is now directly contrasted with the opposition and debate of the scribes and the Pharisees in the preceding episode (Lk 6:1-11). The choosing of the Twelve is a foreshadowing, not only of their mission in Lk 9:1-6, but also of their role in Acts 1:2,8,26; 2:14 (Fitzmyer, 1981: 613-614).

Having given us a sketch of the general character of the ministry of Jesus and depicted his relationship to his opponents, Luke proceeds to describe the relationship of Jesus to his disciples. First of all he narrates the call of the twelve apostles (Lk 6:12-16). Then he describes how Jesus came down from the mountain where he had chosen them, to be met by a large crowd drawn from all over the country who sought healing for their sick (Lk 6:17-19). In their presence he taught his disciples the implications of discipleship (Lk 6:20-49; Marshall, 1978: 236). The two subunits in the part preparatory to the sermon, i.e., those comprising Lk 6:12-16 and 6:17-19, appear as clearly defined single units (Malipurathu, 1994: 46).

1. The Call of the Twelve (Lk 6:12-16)

It is debated whether this pericope links up with Lk 5:1-6:11 (Nolland, 1989: 264) or Lk 6:17-49 (Fitzmyer, 1981: 613). It has been noted that Lk 6:12-49 is composed of a group of pericopes framed by two temporal indications (Lk 6:12 and 7:1; Garcia, 1993: 3). It may be preferable to call it a bridge. This text is a third call text (the first two being Lk 5:1-11 and 5:27-32), only here we have a call within the call (Bock, 1994: 537).

Most commentators consider the narration of the selection of the apostles (Lk 6:12-16) as the point at which the evangelist turns his attention to the preparation of the immediate setting of the great sermon (Schürmann, 1969: 310-

386; Ernst, 1977: 206; Marshall, 1978: 236; Fitzmyer, 1981: 613; Schweizer, 1984: 113-128). The typically Lukan expression in Lk 6:12, *egeneto de en tais hēmerais tautais exelthein auton eis to oros*, "now during those days he went out to the mountain," appearing as words of introduction to the momentous event of the call of the apostles — different from the Markan formulation of the same introductory rubrics in Mk 3:13 — besides evidently implying a change of scene (O'Fearghail, 1991: 45), is also intended to signal the transition from the controversy stories to a new phase of activity. The withdrawal to the mountain and the events at the top signal the shift of narrative focus. The reversal of the Markan order by Luke in presenting the two units leading up to the sermon proper (Mk 3:-12 = Lk 6:17-19; Mk 3:13-19 = Lk 6:12-16) shows that the evangelist is trying to gain an audience for the sermon (Conzelmann, 1960: 45; Ernst, 1977: 206; Marshall, 1978: 237). The reversal of the Markan pericopes brings about the effect of creating a wider context and a meaningful situation for the discourse that follows. Besides, the rather short introduction proper of the sermon given in verse 20a is fully understood only if we read it in relation to the preceding two pericopes (Malipurathu, 1994: 17-20).

The background for this scene is the previous collection of stories about Jesus' continuing power to heal and his authority to teach, and at the same time stories of many-sided objections raised to his work and to his lifestyle by the religious authorities. Against that background, Luke reports the establishment of the administrative structure that will make possible the ongoing life of this movement that Jesus is beginning. Jesus' withdrawal to a mountain top to pray again signals the importance of what follows. Out of the whole group of people who have "left everything and followed" Jesus, and who apparently are with him on the mountain, an inner circle of "twelve" are chosen and named "apostles," or "sent-ones" (Ringe, 1995: 88).

Verses 12-16: (12) Now during those days he went out to the
mountain to pray;
and he spent the night in prayer to God.
(13) And when day came, he called his disciples
and chose twelve of them, whom he also
named apostles:
(14) Simon, whom he named Peter, and his brother
Andrew,
and James, and John, and Philip, and
Bartholomew
(15) and Matthew, and Thomas, and James son of
Alphaeus,
and Simon, who was called the Zealot,
(16) and Judas, son of James,
and Judas Iscariot, who became a traitor.

Before choosing the Twelve, Jesus withdraws and spends the
entire night in prayer. This third prayer notice (Lk 6:12;
see Lk 3:21-22; 5:12) is again found in Luke only. But it is
possible that it depends on a Markan example. The motifs
— prayer, location (mountain), and time of prayer (night)
are also found in Mark's and Matthew's acount of Jesus'
walking on the water (Mk 6:45-52; Mt 14:22-33; Marshall,
1978: 237). Luke has passed over this pericope as part of
the so-called "great omission," but may have taken over the
motifs mentioned above, as a comparison of Mk 6:46 and
Lk 6:12a suggests (Schürmann, 1969: 312 note 4). The expression "he spent the night in prayer" occurs only in Lk
6:12 in the New Testament (Bock, 1994: 540). But Mk 6:45-
56 (par. Mt 14:22-33) may suggest that Jesus spent the whole
night in prayer, as can be derived from the expressions "when
evening came" (Mk 6:47 par. Mt 14:23), that is, after sunset, and "early in the morning" (Mk 8:48 parallel Mt 14:25;
Feldkamper, 1978: 84-85). Still the fact remains that nowhere else is such a sustained period of prayer attributed to
Jesus. The purpose of the prayer becomes evident from Jesus'
next action. As he prays he receives the guidance of the
Spirit for the choice he is to make. In the future, prayer
will always be important in Christian appointments to of-

fice (Acts 1:24; 6:6; 13:2-31 14:23; Nolland, 1989: 271-272; C.F. Evans, 1990: 319).

The link between the motifs of the mountain and prayer can be traced to a well-known association in the Old Testament. Luke did not only take over these motifs but "absolutized" them. In the Third Gospel — in contrast to Mark and Matthew — Jesus never goes unto a mountain without praying there: Lk 6:12; 9:28; 22:39-46 (In the other Mount Olivet passages, Lk 19:21,37, Jesus is not *on* but *at* Mount Olivet). The mountain is, therefore, for Luke in effect "the place of prayer" (Conzelmann, 1960: 44; Schürmann, 1969: 312f.), though not the only or the preferred one (compare Lk 3:21; 5:16; 9:18; 11:1). It is the locale for God's presence, of nearness of the revealing God (Fitzmyer, 1981: 616). From the twofold mention of prayer (intention and execution), the emphasis on duration ("all night"), and the stress on its theocentric character (the mountain; prayer to [of] God, it is clear that Luke has attributed great importance to Jesus' prayer in this passage (Feldkämper, 1978: 85-86).

The mention of Jesus' nocturnal prayer on a mountain is undoubtedly the beginning of a new series of pericopes (Fitzmyer, 1981: 616). In between Lk 6:11 and 6:12 occurs a change of place (in Lk 6:6-12 Jesus is in the synagogue, but in Lk 6:12 he is on a mountain. The scribes and the Pharisees (Lk 6:7), who since Lk 5:17 were present at all controversies, are for the time being mentioned for the last time in Lk 6:11, and they disappear from the scene until Lk 7:30,36. This creates the impression that the two pericopes, Lk 6:6-11 and 6:12-16, are to be treated as separated from each other (Dietrich, 1972: 83).

But there are also indications that the new pericope should be read and understood in connection with the previous. The indication of time "in these days" (*en tais hēmerais tautais*) — as distinct from "in those days" — is clearly related to the previous (Grundmann, 1966: 137; Craddock, 1990: 83;

Danker, 1988: 134; Marshall, 1978: 237-238). And the pronoun *auton*, "he," refers to the redactional "to Jesus" at the
end of Lk 6:11. In the whole section Lk 6:12-49 the name
"Jesus" does not occur. Thereby all statements in that section refer to Jesus whom the religious leaders want to harm.
The rejection of Jesus by the authorities thus constitutes
the dark background for Jesus' activity that henceforth will
be reported (Feldkamper, 1978: 86-87).

Lk 6:13 is closely related to the prayer notice of Lk
6:12. Jesus' prayer throughout the night is followed by his
activity during the day that occurs in two places: on the
mountain, and — after the descent in Lk 6:17 — at the
foot of the mountain (Schürmann, 1969: 320). Luke considers Jesus' activity in these two places as one. He expresses
this by reporting it in one sentence that stretches from Lk
6:13 to 18 (Feldkämper, 1978: 87-88; C.F. Evans, 1990: 318).

Regarding the expression "Simon, who was called the
zealot" (Lk 6:15), it has been observed that there is no
unambiguous evidence that zelotes/zelotai were terms in
current use as a designation for any specific group in the
time before A.D. 66. The conception of a zelotic "solidly
united party" is a construction without sufficient documen-
tary foundation. The view of a "zealot movement" (or "party"),
that early in the Jewish War (A.D. 66-70) was split up and
divided into "parties" (Hengel, 1989: 366) is untenable. Neither
in the pre-war years nor during the War itself, was there
such "solidly united party." There were, however, many coalitions at work. Some groups had started out as factions but
later developed into corporate groups of a family-clan type
like the group of Judas of Galilee, which persisted for several years. Lk 6:15 and Acts 1:13 do not suggest that these
"zealots" belonged to any zealotic "party"; they might rather
have been (former) individual zealots like Paul (cf. Gal 1:13;
Seland, 1995: 219).

In Lk 6:18a it is stated that the people came to hear
Jesus and to be healed. Subsequently it is reported how Jesus

responds to the desire of the people, first by his healing
activity (Lk 6:18b-19), and then by his proclamation in which
he refers explicitly to the multitude's desire to hear (Lk
6:278,47; 7:1). In Lk 7:1, then, begins a new sequence of
pericopes with another change of place (Capernaum) and
persons (centurion). As a result, Lk 6:13-49 should be interpreted in close relationship with the prayer notice in Lk
6:12 (Feldkämper, 1978: 88).

In Luke nothing is said about the purpose of the call,
namely, the close relationship with Jesus and the mission in
his service. What Mark connects here programmatically with
the call (Mk 3:14, "to be with him, and to be sent out to
proclaim the message"), Luke presents later in the course of
his account in Lk 8:1, "the twelve were with him," and Lk
9:2, "and he sent them out to proclaim the kingdom of God."
In Luke the call is thereby less concentrated on Jesus than
in Mark. The call expresses the relation between the praying Jesus and the disciples (Feldkämper, 1978: 91-92).

Jesus calls his disciples to him to select twelve from among
them. Shortly before Luke had referred already thrice to the
disciples (Lk 5:30,33; 6:1). Everytime it concerned their behavior criticized by the scribes and Pharisees but defended by
Jesus. Its justification lies ultimately in his person: because
he has come to call sinners (Lk 5:32), because he is the bridegroom (Lk 5:34f.), because as the Son of Man he is lord over
the Sabbath (Lk 6:5), they may do things that offend the
religious leaders. According to this Lukan presentation, the
disciples are a closer circle of followers of Jesus for whom
Jesus' word and praxis is decisive (Degenhardt, 1965: 31f.).
Jesus' circle of disciples is fundamentally a learning and living community. From the disciples he had called to him he
now selects twelve. In fact, in the Bible it is always God who
calls, and so Jesus does here something that otherwise only
God does. Jesus, who spent the whole night in prayer to God,
acts in God's power. The "choosing" of the Twelve is presented as a divinely guided election (Tiede, 1988: 134).

From these observations we may conclude that Luke has introduced the call of the apostles with a prayer vigil in order to stress that this act, which is saving-historically very important, is ultimately an act of God that Jesus has brought about. There is a "causal link" between prayer and call. God himself stands behind the call event; Jesus' action is grounded in his will (Dietrich, 1972: 86; Feldkämper, 1978: 92-93).

Luke alone makes explicit that the Twelve are chosen from a larger pool (Bock, 1994: 540). He is obviously less interested in the number "twelve" than Mark. He says merely that Jesus chose twelve disciples, whereas Mark stresses twice that "he apointed twelve" (Mk 3:14 and 16). Elsewhere too Luke mentions the Twelve less frequently than Mark (Mark: 11 times; Luke: 7 times). Nevertheless in Luke - in contrast with Mark — it is fairly often indicated that the number (*twelve*) of chosen ones gets its meaning from the relation to the twelve tribes of Israel. Whereas in Mark the people of Israel are not present in any significant way, and the Twelve are not mentioned together with Israel, this is the more clearly the case in Luke. In Acts 26:7, Luke makes mention of "our twelve tribes" (*dodekaphulon* — mentioned only here in the New Testament) in connection with the promises given to the fathers. According to Lk 22:30, the (twelve) apostles (Lk 22:14) will judge the twelve tribes of Israel as reward for their continuing with Jesus in his trials. Finally, in connection with the reconstitution of the Twelve (Acts 1:13 gives the list of the *eleven*) by the election of Matthias (Acts 1:26), mention is made of hundred and twenty brethren, a number that is ten times twelve. This makes it clear that the circle of the Twelve is the basic structure and the measure of the communinity of disciples that Jesus gathers around himself as germ cell of the future Church (Lohfink, 1975: 72; Feldkämper, 1978: 93-94).

According to Luke, Jesus calls the Twelve as a group "apostles." The verb *onomazō*, "to call," is rarely found in the New Testament and in the Septuagint. Only in Lk 6:13

("whom he also named apostles"; lacking in some manuscripts and in RSV; but see NRSV) and 6:14 ("whom he
named Peter") is it twice used for name-giving which is
usually expressed by other verbs. In Lk 6:13, one can speak
of name-giving only in a wider sense, because, in contrast
with Lk 6:14 (Peter), it is not a single person but a group
that receives a name.

Characteristic of the group is their being "apostles."
In the Synoptics, *apostolos* is found only at Mk 6:30 and
Mt 10:2 and six times in Luke. That Luke uses *apostolos*
more frequently is not surprising, since he narrates a se-
quel about the early Church and the key role of the apostles
(Lk 9:10; 17:5; 22:14; 24:10; Bock, 1994: 541). They are
authorized representatives of Jesus for well-determined tasks.
Luke emphasizes this by stating that, like Jesus (Lk 4:36;
5:17,24), the circle of the Twelve (Lk 9:1), apostles (Lk
9:10) — and only they — are equipped with power and
authority (Lk 9:1) for the task to continue Jesus' work in
word and deed (Lk 5:15,17; 6:18b,19,20-49; 9:12; 24:19;
Acts 1:1).

In the list of the apostles in Lk 6:14-16, Luke — like
Mark — lines up the names by a simple "and" [For a comparison of the four New Testament lists of the Twelve, Mk
3:16-19; Mt 10:2-4; Lk 6:14-16; Acts 1:13, see Bock, 1994:
543-547]. It is remarkable that Luke give more attention to
the first and the last name in the list. Only Simon and
Judas are further described by means of a relative clause:
"Simon, whom he named Peter" and "Judas Iscariot, who
became a traitor."

In Mark, the first place of Peter is somewhat relativized
in that he is grouped together with James and John into a
"triumvirate." They are distinguished from the others in that
all three receive a surname. But in Luke, as in Matthew,
the names of the three are separated from each other by
the name of Andrew. Thereby Peter is placed in parallel,
not with James and John, but with the twelve apostles:

"*twelve of them, whom he also named apostles
Simon, whom he named Peter.*"

In the previous pericopes we read that the leaders of
the people begin to reject Jesus and to discuss with one
another what they might do to him. Consequently — after
spending a night in prayer — Jesus chooses from among his
disciples twelve men who derive their significance from their
mission and function for the twelve-tribe people. Two among
them are given special attention: Peter who in the group of
twelve and among the "brethren" (Lk 22:31) will play a
special role, and Judas who will hand Jesus over to his enemies (Feldkämper, 1978: 95-98).

The social-science point of view distinguishes here between coalition and faction. A *coalition* is a type of impermanent group gathered for specific purposes over a limited
time period. In social-scientific terminology, it is a fluid,
impermanent, multidimensional network of relations focused
on limited goals. Coalitians characterized both elites (e.g.,
Herodians with Romans, Herodians with Pharisees) and non-
elites in the first-century Mediterranean world. In contrast
to coalitions stood "corpoprate groups" such as parties or
closed statuses among elites. Corporate groups were based
on enduring principles: for example, birth and marriage (the
Sadducee party and its priestly basis); birth and political
allegiance (Herodians); tested fictive kinship rooted in commitment to a common ideology (the purity fellowship of
the Pharisees, community members of Qumran's Essenes).
Corporate groups were rather formal, socially compulsory,
and tightly knit. Coalitions were informal, elective, and loosely
knit. Identifying with a coalition did not override membership or commitments to more fundamental groups such as
the family. But membership in a corporate group, such as
the Pharisaic movement groups, involved one's family as
well.

A *faction* is a type of coalition formed around a central

person who recruits followers and maintains the loyalty of a core group. Factions share the common goal of the person recruiting the faction. Membership is based on a relationship with that central personage. This relationship results in a core group of those with distinct and rather permanent, ongoing relationships. More loosely connected peripheral members often have distinct, fluid, and incidental relationships with the faction. Peripheral members sometimes divide their loyalty with other factions and their leaders and thus can threaten a faction's effectiveness. Rivalry with other groups is basic; hence hostile competition for honor, truth (an ideological justification), and resources is always present.

The recruitment of core disciples, beginning at Lk 5:1-11, clearly identifies the Jesus movement as such a faction and may also explain the rivalry with John the Baptist's faction, which Luke tries to put to rest in Lk 3:15ff. (see also Lk 5:33; 7:18ff.; 9:7ff.; 11:1; 16:16; 20:4ff.). Much of Luke portrayal of Jesus as the honored Son of God, especially his depiction of Jesus' success in the game of challenge-riposte, can be understood as justification of Jesus' leadership of the faction that followed him (Malina and Rohrbaugh, 1992: 321).

2. *The Assembling of the People* (Lk 6:17-19)

Verses 17-19: (17) He came down with them and stood on a
                         level place,
                    with a great crowd of his disciples
                    and a great multitude of people from all Judea,
                    Jerusalem, and the coast of Tyre and Sidon.
              (18) They had come to hear him and to be healed
                         of their diseases,
                    and those who were troubled with unclean
                         spirits were cured.
              (19) And all in the crowd were trying to touch him.
                    for power came out from him and healed all
                         of them.

According to a number of commentators Lk 6:17-19 is the fourth summary to appear in Luke's Gospel (Lk 4:14-15,31-32,40-41), but this has been denied on the ground that it does not summarize what occurs over an extended period of ministry, but rather pictures (with aorist verbs) a one-time gathering (Hamm, 1990: 37-38). It occupies a position in Luke's sequence very close to that of Mk 3:7-12 in that Gospel. The only difference is that Mark (3:13-19a) relates the choosing of the Twelve after giving his summary, while Luke (6:12-16) has the choosing of the Twelve first. Luke chose to let his summary introduce the sermon, while Mark has it in a slightly different position, possibly because he does not mention the sermon (Marshall, 1978: 237; Bock, 1994: 548). A comparison of Mk 3:7-12 and Lk 6:17-19 helps reveal Luke's theological emphases. The addition "went down" (Lk 6:17) and the setting on a mountain (Lk 6:12) tie the preceding account thematically as well as geographically and chronologically to the following sermon "on a level place" (Lk 6:17). Luke also emphasizes the presence of "power" (Lk 6:19) and Jesus' healing ministry (Lk 6:17-19). The addition of "had come to hear him" (Lk 6:18) also places greater emphasis on Jesus' message than we find in Mark's account (Stein, 1992: 195).

The dominant center of the scene is Jesus who has spent the night in prayer and has chosen his disciples. Since he does not descend from the mountain alone, but "with them," the single verbal forms "came" and "stood" (Lk 6:17: *katabas, este*) emphasize once more the social position of Jesus who is surrounded by a threefold audience: the twelve apostles, a great crowd of disciples, and a "great multitude of people" (Lk 6:17).

The circle of apostles is thereby clearly distinguished from the disciples and the people. Their relationship with Jesus is that of a living community. They are the companions of the one sent by God to proclaim good news to the poor (Lk 4:18). Their being-with-him becomes a mission community with him. Luke shows this step by step: In Lk 6:17 the Twelve stand with Jesus as distinct from the people from all Judaea and the seacoast; in Lk 8:1-3, they are with Jesus as he carries out his mission from place to place; finally in Lk 9:1-6, they are sent out to cities and villages, equipped with his authority and commission, and work "everywhere" (Lk 9:6).

The "great crowd of his disciples" is not mentioned in the Markan parallel. In Lk 19:37 too Luke speaks of the "whole multitude of the disciples" who praised God "for all the deeds of power they had seen." This looks back to the whole of Jesus' ministry which means that Luke envisages Jesus as surrounded by a great, constantly present circle of disciples. At the beginning of Acts this circle of disciples appears as "the believers" ("the brothers") — hundred and twenty in number (Acts 1:15). In this way Luke makes it clear that the faithful companions of Jesus were the prefiguration of the post-Easter Christian community. The "great crowd of his disciples" anticipates the expansion of the Church (see Acts 6:1; Danker, 1988: 136).

Luke then says where the "great multitude of people" came from. They came from "all over Judaea" (Fitzmyer, 1981: 622-624), by which he means the whole of Palestine, the territory of ancient Israel, in which Galilee, Idumaea and Transjordan are included. In "Tyre and Sidon" appears already the new Israel of Jews and Gentiles. Between the two stands "Jerusalem," the city where Jesus' way (of suffering; see Lk 6:11) comes to an end, but where also the apostolic message starts (Lk 6:13-16).

The people from these regions come to Jesus, not because they heard about his deeds (Mk 3:8), but, as in Lk 5:15, to listen to him and to be healed. As in Lk 5:17, here too Jesus responds to this twofold expectation, first by healing and then by preaching.

Compared to Mark several details of Jesus' healing activity are omitted, like the readiness of a boat (Mk 3:9;

compare Lk 5:2f.) and the imposition of silence in connection with the crying out of the possessed (Mk 3:11b,12;
compare Lk 4:41; C.F. Evans, 1990: 322). On the other
hand, Luke intensifies and generalizes Mark's account where
"many" (Mk 3:10) were healed by saying that "all in the
crowd were trying to touch him, ...and [he] healed all of
them" (Lk 6:19; Fitzmyer, 1981:624). Luke is fond of high-
lighting Jesus' pandemic outreach and frequently edits Mark
so as to bring out the theme. Greco-Roman readers, accustomed to the adulation of public benefactors, especially
physicians who embraced the general public with their generosity, would be impressed (Danker, 1988: 137).

Not just "many" (Mk 3:10), but "all" (Lk 6:19) were
cured. That happened through the power that came forth
from Jesus (see Mk 5:30 par Lk 8:46). What was said of
Jesus' power in Lk 5:17 is also valid here, without any need
to repeat it: it is the "power of the Lord." Jesus works in
the power of God. Without telling any specific healing story,
the evangelist has set a dramatic stage for the address that
is to follow (Tiede, 1988: 136).

The following discourse has been fittingly called the
"sermon at the mountain," or the "sermon at the foot of
the mountain," rather than the "sermon on the plain," thereby
expressing its connection with the events on the mountain
— prayer and election of the apostles (Feldkämper, 1978:
98-101).

3. The Sermon at the Mountain/on the Plain (Lk 6:20-49)

Introduction

The title "Sermon on the Plain," in obvious contrast to
the Matthean "Sermon on the Mount" (see Mt 5:1-2a), is
due to the clear indication in Lk 6:17 that after the choice
of the apostles Jesus descended with them from the mountain and came to a level place at the foot of the mountain

where the sermon was delivered. Some have contended that such a title is scarcely justifiable. They point out that there is no explicit mention of a "plain" (*to pedion*) in the context, or indeed anywhere in the New Testament, and that there is no evidence that the *topos pedinos* that is actually mentioned was at the foot of the mountain (Plummer, 1975: 176). Others prefer to call it the "Sermon at the Mountain." They insist that because of the unmistakable Sinai-typology present in the context, just as Moses could not have conveyed to the people on the mountain the message he received from God at the mountain top, but had to come down to the foot of the mountain, neither could Jesus. But at the same time, Moses' meeting with the people could not be pictured apart from the mountain. Neither could Jesus' for obvious reasons. Therefore, one should not speak of a "Sermon on the Plain" (Schürmann, 1969: 311; Malipurathu, 1994: 15 note 27), although for practical reasons we will continue to do so.

Luke now introduces into his Gospel a major sermon of Jesus. It is, in fact, Jesus' second sermon in Luke, unlike in Matthew where Mt 5:1-7:29 is the first. Luke's first sermon was recorded in Lk 4:16-30 and was addressed to the "crowds." Lk 6:20-49 is in the first place addresssed to Jesus' disciples (Lk 6:20; Stein, 1992: 197), but in the hearing of all the gathered people (Lk 6:17; 7:1): the boundary line between the two groups is permeable and Jesus speaks for the benefit of disciples and would-be disciples (Nolland, 1989: 288). The Sermon on the Plain is, therefore, not directed to isolated individuals or to an elite within the Church; neither is it in the first instance *immediately* addressed to the whole world. It is rather a guide for the Church, which is the true Israel. In this sense the sermon is also universal and directed to all of humankind (Lohfink, 1988: 38).

The title "Sermon on the Plain" or "Sermon at the Mountain" is commonly used to identify this sermon, and it does serve as a convenient label (but see above). It is important to remember, however, that what that label identifies is more like a collection of somewhat related teachings on a variety of themes, rather than a coherent argument or single "sermon" delivered at one time. Instead of speculating about why Luke did not include particular teachings found in Matthew's sermon or why he wove them into other parts of the Gospel narrative, it seems more helpful to work with the collection of teachings Luke does present, identifying points of emphasis and guiding themes of his sermon (Ringe, 1995: 90-91).

These sets of sayings are concrete in focus and purpose, and they are directed to the people generally. The beatitudes pronounce blessing upon a group defined by social and economic circumstances: poverty, hunger, sorrow and persecution (Kloppenborg, 1987: 188). Following that "programmatic statement" come a "body of instructions" addressed to the kind of concrete social-economic problems faced by just such people in their local communities (Lk 6:27-36,37-38,41-42; cf. Horsley, 1987: 265-273), and the complex concludes with general exhortation and sanction on the admonitions (Lk 6:43-45,46-49; Horsley, 1991: 184-185).

The sermon is a major policy statement of the kingdom. All who are "hearing" or "overhearing" this major policy address would be well advised to listen to both the warnings and the promises (Tiede, 1988: 137,142). Whereas Matthew's Sermon on the Mount is addressed to Jesus' "disciples" (Mt 5:1) and to "the crowds" (Mt 5:1; 7:28), Luke's sermon seems initially intended for the "disciples" only. But when Luke resumes the narrative after the sermon, he writes, "after Jesus had finished all his sayings in the hearing of the people, he entered Capernaum" (Lk 7:1). Consequently, it is the people, understood as representing all Israel, who constitute Jesus' audience. The woes would then be addressed to those in the gathering of the people who resist the invitation to discipleship (Hamm, 1990: 38,41).

The Lukan sermon is considerably shorter than the

Matthean sermon (Mt 5:3-7:27). Whereas the Lukan sermon consists of a mere thirty verses, Matthew's has at least a hundred and seven verses [some count a hundred and nine verses, but there are some text-critical problems that do not concern us here]. Despite many differences in the two sermons, there is a basic similarity in them that makes one argue to a nucleus sermon that was inherited by "Q" and that the two evangelists have reworked each in their own way (Fitzmyer, 1981: 627; Blank, 1982: 22), as a comparison of the contents of the two sermons clearly shows (Hendrickx, 1984: 3-4; Bock, 1994: 931-944). The central core of the underlying sermon (*Grundrede*) contains verbal agreement of approximately thirty percent (Bergemann, 1993: 73-229).

Commentators are far from unanimous about the structure of the sermon owing to the lack of clear breaks and to the variety of themes. Luke operates here, as elsewhere, with "bridging passages," so that a verse or paragraph may be reckoned as both closing one section and introducing another. This is probably the case with Lk 6:36 [for various divisions proposed, see Marshall, 1978: 243-244; C.F. Evans, 1990: 324-325; Malipurathu, 1994: 40-45].

The structure of the sermon is fraught with difficulties. However, the first part of it, viz., verses 20-26, stands out for its peculiar propositions. From a literary point of view, one half of these propositions are expressed through the genre of the *makarioi* formulations and the other half through that of the *ouai* ones. They are linked to one another through the device of antithetical parallelism. Problems abound mainly when we turn to the structuring of the rest of the discourse (Lk 6:27-49, divided into two subsections, Lk 6:27-38 and 39-49; Malipurathu, 1994: 38-39, 45-54). Commentators are generally agreed that the main body of the sermon is Lk 6:27-45. It is an exposition of Jesus' love commandment (Fitzmyer, 1981: 630; Kilgallen, 1988: 86-87).

The Sermon on the Plain is a sample of the preaching

of the Lukan Jesus. Its peculiar emphasis and theological import can only be judged from its place within the Lukan Gospel. Presented as an instruction to the "disciples" (Lk 6:20), it is intended to shape their conduct. But it has also to be related to the mission of Jesus as presented thus far in the Gospel: he has come to preach to the poor, the prisoners, the blind, and the downtrodden of his day (in the words of Isaiah, quoted in Lk 4:18). The teaching and the deeds of Jesus created a new world view for a group of people who most probably despaired because of their socio-economic and political situation. In their interpretation of the life and the works of Jesus, and of his message concerning the kingdom of God, followers of Jesus saw the basis for a new conception of happiness. Although it had a present aspect in that his coming gave reasons for happiness, his teaching about the kingdom of God most probably also included a future aspect — that real happiness would come in the end. After the death of Jesus, happiness was motivated christologically. His complete life was seen as the sole basis of happiness. Especially in the case of Luke, we notice how the life of Jesus from his birth to his resurrection is described from the perspective of joy and happiness. Jesus started his mission, according to Luke, with a sermon in the synagogue of Nazareth concerning good news of the liberation of the oppressed that he brings about (Lk 4:18-19,21). The Gospel ends on a happy note when the followers of Jesus are seized by the happiness of Easter (see *chara* in Lk 24:41,52; Vorster, 1990: 44-45).

In the last episode before the sermon, Luke stressed the flocking of people to him from all over, who wanted to "hear him" (Lk 6:18); now he presents Jesus responding and throwing out challenges even to them. The detail of Lk 6:18 is picked up in the sermon itself: "I say to you that listen" (Lk 6:27); "someone... who comes to me, hears my words, and acts on them" (Lk 6:47). We should realize that in collections of sayings, such as we have in Luke's sermon, it is extremely difficult, if not impossible, to identify original audiences. However, the use of "you" (plural) throughout the beatitudes and "woes" seems to imply the presence of both rich and poor in the group addressed. That is no clear certainty, and scholars continue to debate the matter (Schweizer, 1984: 120). Fortunately for us, while a reconstruction of the original audience for Lk 6:20-26 and the whole sermon is important from a historical and sociological point of view, the truth and the force of Jesus' words does ultimately not depend upon such a reconstruction (Craddock, 1990: 88).

It is a "spiritual" statement, but Luke's version of the "sermon" mightily resists the kind of "spiritualizing" of Jesus' address that would deny or diminish its claim on the here and now (Tiede, 1988: 138). Jesus' words in the sermon touch on the concerns of daily existence, poverty, hunger, grief, hatred, and ostracism; and the beatitudes and woes seek to raise those concerns to another dimension. That dimension is eschatological, perhaps less radically than the Matthean form, because Luke is less preoccupied with an imminent end, but the dimension is nonetheless there. His insertion of "now" (Lk 6:21a,c; 6:25a,c) reveals his concern for the Christian life here and now. Yet even these beatitudes and woes serve only as a starting-point for the heart of his message, the love that must dominate the life of the Christian disciple (Fitzmyer, 1981: 630).

A "Christianity of the Sermon on the Mount/Plain" is — from a historical point of view — no longer possible. But there will always be a "way of justice." It remains a task for all theological reflection, responding to the ethical challenge of the Christian faith, to develop this way also, but not exclusively, from the sermon and not allow it to be domesticated by a Christian theology (Berner, 1979: 108). It seems evident that the purpose of this inaugural discourse was to proclaim the kingdom or reign of God to the poor and to give instruction for social interaction within the renewed community(ies). The complex is not simply a collection of general sapiential exhortations or some sort of "radical ethic" (Horsley, 1991: 184).

a. *Exordium: Beatitudes and Woes* (Lk 6:20-26)

A number of recent literary studies dealing with New Testament Wisdom discuss the beatitudes and woes as examples of proverbs and aphorisms (e.g., Robbins, 1985: 35-61; Perdue, 1986: 30). In the intertestamental literature, beatitude formulas are used in two different ways. In continuity with Old Testament usage, macarisms appear in Wisdom literature, where they have a paraenetic function. They are also used in apocalyptic writings, where they are future oriented, and their function is to encourage. The difference between the two usages is important, since wisdom theology and apocalyptic theology are based on two different world views (Vorster, 1990: 46-47).

The five Qumran beatitudes cited below are found in a clearly sapiential text (Fitzmyer, 1992: 513). But the eschatological nature of the macarisms in the Gospels distinguishes them from wisdom beatitudes (Beardslee, 1970: 36). While Kloppenborg has made a convincing case that the material in Q 6:20-49 is predominantly sapiential in form, his analysis also suggests that continuation of the debate, sapiential versus prophetic, may not be all that decisive for understanding the material at the Q or pre-Q levels (Koester, 1990: 137-138). In both beatitudes and admonitions, materials that are typically sapiential in content stand in tension with sapiential forms. While not typically sapiential in content, the beatitudes could well be characterized as the "radical wisdom of the kingdom" (Kloppenborg, 1987: 188-189).

The beatitudes expand the message delivered at Nazareth (Lk 4:18-19). Isa 61 is considered by many the best commentary on these words (Danker, 1988: 138; Kramer, 1992: 59). A beatitude is a kind of congratulation, spoken by one human being to another (not God to human or human to God), the purpose being to affirm, encourage and hold up as an example those qualities for which the person is congratulated. Praise has the social function of promoting those values and behaviors which the community holds dear (or at least what the *speaker* holds dear; in the case of the biblical macarisms, because they are in the canon of Scripture, we know that they affirm the values held by the canonizing community). The point of biblical macarisms [from the Greek word *makarios*, "blessed"] may become clearer when we realize that most advertisements in today's media are, at bottom, secular beatitudes. The TV iconography of the retired home-run hitter enjoying a cool, sparkling mug of a certain beer is, at heart, a macarism. The message of the commercial might be paraphrased: "Happy those who drink 'Old....'! They not only quench their thirst. They also place themselves in the company of the likes of this all-time great" (Hamm, 1990: 12).

The beatitudes (Lk 6:20b-23) and the woes (Lk 6:24-26) form the exordium of the Lukan sermon; they are like two stanzas of a poem and correspond to Mt 5:3,6,4,11-12. The four beatitudes reflect the fourfold number of them in the nucleus sermon and in "Q." Of the four Lukan beatitudes the first three originally formed a unit, as their parallelism reveals, and the fourth was added only secondarily to it either in "Q" or in a pre-"Q" collection. So the fourth beatitude has not always been with the other three, but it is not necessary to attribute the formation of the beatitude to the later church period (Dupont, 1969: 359-365; Nolland, 1989: 280). These are not the only beatitudes in the Lukan Gospel (see further Lk 1:45; 7:23; 10:23; 11:27 28; 12:37,38,43; 14:14-15; 23:29). In fact, in the New Testament one counts at least forty-one beatitudes introduced by *makarios/ makarioi* (Fitzmyer, 1992: 509). In form, the beatitudes are related to macarisms found in Egyptian, Palestinian, Hellenistic, and Old Testament literature (Fitzmyer, 1981: 631).

A collection of beatitudes as a distinct literary form has turned up in Qumran literature and was fully reconstructed and published in 1991:

[Blessed is the one who speaks truth]
with a pure heart and slanders not with his tongue.
Blessed are those who cling to her statutes
and cling not to paths of iniquity.
Blessed are those who rejoice in her
and babble not about paths of iniquity.
Blessed are those who search for her with clean hands
and seek not after her with a deceitful heart.
Blessed is the man who has attained wisdom
and walks by the law of the Most High
and fixes his heart on her ways,
gives heed to her admonishments,
delights always in her chastisements,
and forsakes her not in the stress of [his] trou[bles];
(who) in time of distress abandons her not
and forgets her not [in days of] fear,
and in the affliction of his soul rejects [her] not.
For on her he meditates,
and in his anguish he ponders [on the law];
and in all his existence [he considers] her
[and puts her] before his eyes
so as to not to walk in the paths [   ]

Here we have a collection of five beatitudes. Such a collection of beatitudes in a pre-Christian Palestinian Jewish writing provides an interesting example of a literary form that until now was attested only in the Greek New Testament, or in literature dependent on it. It also provides a context for the collected beatitudes of Mt 5 and Lk 6, and thus allows us to understand better the gathering of Jesus' beatitudes into a collection in imitation of such a Palestinian Jewish convention. For Jesus' utterance of beatitudes was not simply an imitation of a well-known Palestinian

Jewish form, but the utterance of them in multiple form is now also seen as characteristic of that background (Fitzmyer, 1992: 512-513).

Before commenting on the Lukan form of the beatitudes (and woes) we present the Lukan and Matthean forms in parallel:

Mt 5:3-12	Lk 6:20b-26
3. Blessed are the poor in spirit, for theirs is the kingdom of heaven.	20b.BLessed are you who are poor, for yours is the kingdom of God.
4. Blessed are those who mourn, for they will be comforted.	
5. Blessed are the meek, for they will inherit the earth.	
6. Blessed are those who hunger and thirst for righteousness, for they will be filled.	21. Blessed are you who are hungry now, for you will be filled. Blessed are you who weep now, for you will laugh.
7. Blessed are the merciful, for they shall receive mercy.	
8. Blessed are the pure in heart, for they will see God.	
9. Blessed are the peacemakers, for they will be called children of God.	
10. Blessed are those who are persecuted for righteousness' sake, for theirs is the kingdom of heaven.	
11. Blessed are you when people revile you and persecute you	22. Blessed are you when people have you, and when they exclude you,

and utter all kinds of evil
against you
falsely on my account.
12. Rejoice and be glad,
for your reward is great in
heaven,
for in the same way they
persecuted
the prophets who were
before you.

revile you, and defame you
on account of the Son of
Man.
23. Rejoice in that day and
leap for joy,
for surely your reward is
great in heaven;
for that is what their
ancestors did to the
prophets.
24. Woe to you that are rich,
for you have received
your consolation.
25. Woe to you that are full now,
for you will be hungry.
Woe to you that are
laughing now,
for you will mourn and weep.
26. Woe to you when all
speak well of you,
for that is what their
ancestors did to the false
prophets.

We have dealt with Matthew's beatitudes elsewhere (Hendrickx, 1984: 16-36). Here we concentrate on the Lukan version.

Verse 20: (20a) Then he looked up at his disciples and said:
(20b) "Blessed are you who are poor,
for yours is the kingdom of God.

The Lukan beatitudes are addressed to the "disciples" as the real poor, hungry, grief-stricken, and outcasts of this world. Luke has not spiritualized the condition of the disciples as Matthew has done (in adding to Jesus' words distinctions that would suit the members of a mixed community. "poor in spirit," those hungering and thirsting "for righteousness"). Rather, poverty, hunger, weeping, hatred, and ostracism characterize the real condition of the Christian disciples whom the Lukan Jesus declares "blessed" (Fitzmyer, 1981: 631; Hamm, 1990: 47-50).

Luke is clearly addressing the poor and the despised of the earth in the literal sense of those words (Craddock, 1990: 89). But does Luke refer only to an economic condition, whereas Matthew leans toward a meaning parallel to "the meek" in Mt 5:5)? The distinction may be a modern one. Mt 5:3,5 appear to draw together references to the poor, the humble, and the meek that are found in such biblical texts as Isa 61:1; 66:2; Ps 37:11. In·fact, it can be said that the four Q-beatitudes recapitulate the themes of Isa 61:1-2 (Sampathkumar, 1996: 178). The words used in the Septuagint of such texts to identify the groups referred to are very similar in meaning and virually interchangeable. They refer to people who are economically destitute, who can claim no power in the prevailing economic system, and who reap no benefits from it. We might refer to them as "oppressed" or "marginalized." Luke uses here the word *ptochos* which means a person who has been reduced to the condition of a beggar. In the Septuagint it is used for the materially poor and needy in Israel, sometimes perhaps as a class, "the poor ones" (Ps 149:4). This poverty is often a scandal, especially when it is the result of oppression or dispossession by the wealthy, and it is to be removed by God (Ps 9:18; 72:2-4,12-13; 82:2-4, etc; C.F. Evans, 1990: 329). It is to such people that God's reign belongs. The blessing is part of the reversal of fortunes that characterizes God's project, as Luke has already made clear in the hymns and stories of the birth narratives and in the appropriation of the Jubilee text of Isa 61:1-2 in Lk 4:18-19. To see the beatitude as rewarding an attitude (as Mathew seems to imply) or an economic condition for its own sake (as Luke seems to imply) is to miss the principal point (Ringe, 1995: 92). It seems best, therefore, neither to spiritualize away the reference to actual poverty, nor to make the whole thing a matter of economic justice for the proletariat (Nolland, 1989: 288; see Dupont, 1969: 19-51).

There is no glorifying of poverty involved in the beatitudes. To be poor (hungry, and weeping) is not at all the situation that Luke envisages in the ideal state of Christian existence (Acts 2:43-47; 4:34). While renunciation is a very important theme of the Gospel of Luke, this is never thought of as making oneself poor. The beatitiude of the poor connects naturally in the Gospel not with the renunciation material but rather with the reversal motif and more particularly with the announcement of good news to the poor (Lk 4:18; 7:22; Nolland, 1989: 283).

"Blessed" is the usual translation of the Greek *makarios*. In the Greek world the adjective *makarios* denoted a person's inner happiness. In the Septuagint the beatitude-form was especially used in Wisdom literature, and took on a religious sense as the expression of God's favor toward persons. The beatitude thus ascribed often connoted a full life, a good wife (Sir 26:1), sons as heirs (Ps 127:3-5), prosperity and honor (Job 29:10-11). The beatitude admits that the happy condition results from God's blessing, but emphasizes the concrete manifestation of the blessing. In the New Testament the beatitudes rarely express practical wisdom, since they usually stress a reversal of values that people put on earthly things in view of the kingdom now being preached by Jesus. A paradox is often involved in them. The first part describes the condition of the disciples, but the second promises his/her eschatological lot, often formulated in the theological passive (i.e., with ther implied agency of God, "you shall be filled" [by God], Lk 6:21; Fitzmyer, 1981: 633).

It is a matter of debate whether the beatitudes were originally couched in the second or the third person. Some scholars think that they were originaly couched in the second person and changed by Matthew to the third (Grundmann, Schurmann, etc.). These commentators think that in using the third person Matthew has produced a "catalogue of virtues." This is far from certain, since the third person plural form has better Old Testament antecedents. More likely Luke has changed the third person to the sec-

ond, partly because of the added woes that are addressed to
"you" (Dupont, 1958: 274; Fitzmyer, 1981: 631-632). The
pervasive presence of the poor in the Lukan story probably
reflects the situation of an earlier stage of the tradition than
that of Luke himself. His knowledge of poverty is second-
hand, via the tradition, which he uses to crtiticize the rich
of his own community to which he writes.

The term "poor" should be understood in concrete though
not necessarily exclusively economic terms (Danker, 1988:
138; Bovon, 1991: 292); Luke does not spiritualize poverty
(C.A. Evans, 1990: 108). It is a social reality as well as an
economic one. Essential to understanding it is the notion of
"limited good." In modern economics, we make the assumption that goods are, in principle, in unlimited supply. If a
shortage exists, we can produce more. If one person gets
more of something, it does not automatically mean someone
else gets less, it may just mean the factory worked overtime
and more became available.

But in ancient Palestine, the perception was the opposite: all goods existed in finite, limited supply and all goods
were already distributed. This included not only material
goods, but honor, friendship, love, power, security, and status as well — literally everything in life. Because the pie
could not grow larger, a larger piece for anyone automatically meant a smaller piece for somebody else.

An honorable person would thus be interested only in what
was rightfully his/hers and would have no desire to gain anything more, that is, to take what was another's. Acquisition
was, by its very nature, understood as stealing. The ancient
Mediterranean attitude was that "every rich person is either
unjust or the heir of an unjust person" (Jerome, *In Hieremiam*
2.5.2; Corpus Christianorum Series Latina, LXXIV, 61). Profit-
making and the acquisition of wealth were automatically assumed to be the result of extortion or fraud, and the notion
of an honest rich man was a first-century incongruity.

To be labeled "rich" was, therefore, a social and moral

statement as much as an economic one. It meant having
the power or capacity to take from someone weaker what
was rightfully his. Being rich was, therefore, synonymous
with being greedy. By the same token, to be "poor" was to
be unable to defend what was yours. It meant falling below
the status at which one was born. It was to be defenseless,
without recourse.

In the New Testament poverty is often associated with
a condition of powerlessness or misfortune. In Lk 4:18-19
the poor are the imprisoned, the blind, the debtors. Lk
14:13,21 list the poor with the crippled, the blind, and the
lame. In Lk 16:19-31 the rich man is contrasted with poor
Lazarus, a beggar full of sores. In a society in which power
brought wealth [in our society it is the opposite: wealth
brings power], being powerless meant being vulnerable to
the greedy who preyed on the weak. The terms "rich" and
"poor," therefore, are not exclusively economic. Fundamentally they describe a social condition relative to one's neighbors: the poor are the weak, and the rich are the strong
(Malina and Rohrbaugh, 1992: 324-325).

Being "poor" (i.e., *ptochos*, "being a destitute beggar,"
not *penes*, or the general peasant audience of have-nots [see
Esler, 187: 180-181], having suffered a recent and severe
loss of means [Guelich, 1976: 426]) contains a social and
cultural component as well as a economic one. Clearly
"wealth" is a component of "honor"; and the loss of wealth
entails corresponding threat of loss of honor. When a person becomes *ptochos*, he loses the resources to maintain his
social status or honor rating. This loss of honor is more
serious to ancient peasants than the mere loss of wealth.
The scenario presented by the makarisnms in Q has to do
with both loss of honor (*makarios* = "honorable") as well as
a los of wealth But the question remains. why did a person
suffer loss of wealth according to the makarisms? The
makarisms contrast the way of Jesus with other "ways"
(Guelich, 1976: 416-419). Hence the general *Sitz im Leben*

envisioned is one of discipleship and loyalty shown to Jesus. But discipleship with a deviant like Jesus is costly. The four original makarisms should be seen as Jesus "honoring" of disciples who have paid the cost and been shamed by their kinship network (Neyrey, 1995: 153-154).

Luke, however, does no longer address the beatitudes and woes to Galilean peasants, but to urban poor (Hendrickx, 1992: 35), and on the level of the Third Gospel, these texts should be ʻread in that context. The Lukan Jesus addresses his message to the urban poor of Luke's time whose condition was reduced to that of beggars. For Luke, the "poor" are people who can find no security or hope in the structures of human institutions or plans of human rulers.

The division of human society into poor and rich reflects the conceptual world of the Hellenistic moralists, who tend to view the poor positively while castigating the rich. Taken together, the beatitudes amount to a social description of the type "poor," that is, of destitute individuals. Hunger, weeping, and discrimination are singled out as concrete situations. Such descriptions are known as well from other New Testament texts (see, e.g., Mk 12:41-44 par.; Lk 16:19-31; Jas 2:1-7) and from Greek literature elsewhere (Betz, 1995: 572).

In what sense can Luke (and Jesus) call the poor "blessed"? Not, as is often said, because their poverty would make them more naturally receptive to the kingdom of God, or would make them put their trust in God more easily than the rich (Hamm, 1990: 57-59). That would go against what the whole biblical message says about God and the poor and defenseless. Poverty is evil and has to be opposed and fought by all possible means. If the God of the Bible is said to be on the side of the poor, it is not because the poor would have virtues and religious attitudes that are by and large lacking among the rich, and that would make God owe it *to the poor* to be on their side. If God of the Bible is on the side of the poor and the defenseless it is because as the God of the covenant He owes it *to himself* to be on their side! Again, how can Jesus call the poor "blessed"? Because, if the message of the kingdom of God that Jesus has started to proclaim (Lk 4:43) is taken seriously and acted upon, changes are bound to take place of which the poor will be the first beneficiaries. So the poor are called "blessed," not because there would be anything good about their poverty, but because their condition will change! It is not a glorification of the nobility of poverty, hunger, grief, or dishonor. But it is a declaration of the priority of those in need in the policy of this reign (Tiede, 1988: 141).

It is only in the first beatitude that the "kingdom" is mentioned, and the initial mention of it relates the sermon to the kingdom-preaching of Jesus in Lk 4:43. But it scarcely gives to the sermon as a whole the emphasis that the theme has in the Matthean Sermon on the Mount (see Mt 5:3,10,19*bis*,20; 6:10,[13],33; 7:21; Fitzmyer, 1981: 630).

The first beatitude sets the tone. It is, first of all, a proclamation about the kingdom. The long-awaited messiah turns out to be at once the end-time prophet modeled in Isa 61 and the Son of God as well. He has been proclaiming to all Israel the good news of the kingdom of God and he has been promulgating it in his healing ministry. The beatitudes and woes are, first of all, statements about what God is doing, ushering in the opportunity for a new set of relationships (human and divine) mediated by Jesus (Hamm, 1990: 57).

Verse 21a: Blessed are you who are hungry now,
        for you will be filled.

The second beatitude, corresponding to the fourth in the Sermon on the Mount (Mt 5:6), promises relief to the hungry. The verb *peinan* can refer to any kind of want, but here the thought of physical hunger is uppermost (Marshall, 1978: 250; C.F. Evans, 1990: 330). The connection between poverty, the term used in the first beatitude, and hunger is traditional. Hunger and weeping are not to be considered as separate conditions from povery but as characteristic manifestations of poverty (Nolland, 1989: 283). The Old Testament tradition, continued in later sources, combines poverty and hunger, in both the real and the figurative sense (Schürmann, 1969: 331; Ernst, 1977: 218). As the wisdom texts point out, the immediate consequence of poverty is hunger (Job 22:7; 24:4-11; Prov 25:21, etc.). That such hunger dominates the present situation is emphasized by the adverb "now," conspicuously placed at the end of the statement (Dupont, 1973: 100-109). In contrast is the future tense of the following clause stating the rationale, "for you will be filled," that is, a "divine passive" meaning "by God."

The second and the third beatitudes continue Luke's theme of divine reversal; the present condition ("now") will be turned around in the future (Johnson, 1991: 106-107). In addition to echoing the motif of a reversal of fortune, the beatitude of the hungry affirms that the basic human need for food is both a specific example and a symbol of all the human needs that are met in the establishment of God's reign (Ringe, 1995: 93). The term for "being filled" (chortazō) will be used in the multiplication of the loaves (Lk 9:17) and the parable of the rich man and Lazarus (Lk 16:2; Johnson, 1991: 106). The future tense in "you will be filled" no doubt takes up the old prophetic promise (Isa 49:10,13; Ez 34:29; 39:17-20, etc.), but the question of whether the future is to be taken in the thisworldly or the eschatological, otherworldly sense is not automatically answered. The context (Lk 6:20c and 23) speaks in favor of the eschatological fulfillment of the promise by a heavenly meal, which was imagined to be a real meal (Schürmann, 1969: 331). But one should not be constrained by wrong alternatives. It is precisely the eschatological realism that does not exclude metaphorization of the language, so that the Sermon on the Mount with its metaphor (Mt 5:6) seizes on an interpretative possibility inherent in the language itself. Taken together, the divine passive and the future tenses in Lk 6:21-23 paint the verbal picture of an eschatological meal of joy comprising the consumption of good food, laughter, and dance (Stein, 1992: 201; Betz, 1995: 577).

A primary exhibition of royal beneficence in the Mediterranean world was assurance of a regular food supply. Emperors vied with one another in maintaining the grain supply for Rome's teeming citizenry.

According to some versions of Jewish apocalyptic scenario, the fortunes of the poor were to be redressed in a radical transformation initiated by God in an end-time cataclysm that was to spell the downfall of the mighty. In the popular mind this would inaugurate the long-awaited kingdom. Luke teaches that the kingdom is present reality, being here in the activity of Jesus' deed and word, which anticipates that those who wield the instruments of power will use them in the interests of the powerless.

Obviously the beatitudes in Lk 6:21-22 are not an endorsement for social or political inaction. The beatitudes rather stress that Jesus' presence is the realization of what the psalmists and prophets in Israel had proclaimed. Jesus was not of that breed of shallow idealists who with eyes fixed on tomorrow stumble over present reality. The liberation proclaimed by Jesus would indeed be hollow if it had no bearing on the depressing conditions of those who are victimaized by the powerful and exploited by vested interests. Jesus is unjustly attacked by the system for his association with publicans and sinners and for what traditionalists considered his unorthodox disinterest in their fasting regulations and sabbatical ordinances. Yet his companions, the "poor" in the land, are the very ones to whom the dream for ultimate victory expressed in popular apocalyptic applies (Danker, 1988: 139-140).

From another perspective the presence of the poor is an invitation to self-inventory by those who enjoy relatively greater benefits. The latter cannot take refuge in an interpretation that gives the poor assurance only a of a future recompense for present misery. Spiritualizing promises to the poor is a luxury that the rich can love too much. The promise to the poor is at the same time an invitation to the more prosperous to engage now in the proces of redistribution and help God do the "filling" (cf. Lk 16:19-31; Acts 2:44-45; 4:32-37; Danker, 1988: 140-141).

Verse 21b: Blessed are you who weep now,
             'for you shall laugh.

The third beatitude in the Sermon on the Plain corresponds to the second in the Sermon on the Mount (Mt 5:4), but they are independent formulations. The Old Testament background for weeping pictures a person in mourning for a variety of reasons, but primarily for the suffering of painful injustice in a world where God's people are persecuted, and exiled, just as the prophets were (Ps 126:5-6; 137:1; Fitzmyer, 1981: 634; Bock, 1994: 577). The weeping does not refer to one's lament about sinfulness (Lk 7:38, etc.), or to weeping as part of a burial ceremony (Lk 7:13; 8:52), or to other specific forms of grief, but to the weeping over the conditions of this world and the suffering resulting from them (Lk 19:41; 23:28). One can draw this conclusion from the juxtaposition of "laughing" with "mourning and weeping" in Lk 6:25. The verb "to laugh" (*gelaō*) is found only here in the New Testament. Weeping is part of poverty. "Surely one does not turn against the needy, when in disaster they cry for help. Did I not weep for those whose day was hard? Was not my soul grieved for the poor?" (Job 30:24-25). Although laughter is usually portrayed negatively as an expression of superiority or a sign of derision or joy over one's enemies, in Ps 126:1-2 it is a positive expression of joy for God having brought his people back to Zion (Stein, 1992: 202). Those who weep now will laugh with joy when the cause of sorrow has been removed.

The promise to the disciples follows in Lk 21d: "for you

shall laugh."Doubtless the reference is to the eschatological laughing of joy because of the fulfillment of the promise as it is opposed to the cynical laughter in verse 25d (Betz, 1995: 577).

There is no reason not to attribute the first three beatitudes to Jesus. They fit well with what we are able to determine concerning his proclamation of the kingdom of God. It is even possible that they are part of Jesus' inaugural sermon commencing his public ministry and of the original form of his proclamation of the kingdom. In them he refers to Isa 61:1-2. His reading of those words of Isaiah disclosed to Jesus that he himself was sent to "bring good news to the poor," and to "comfort all who mourn/weep." The beatitudes are misunderstood if we take them only as consolation to the poor, the hungry, and those who weep/mourn. They are rather *proclamation of God's new order before the forum of the entire world.* God is proclaimed as the God of the poor, and his kingdom as the kingdom of the poor. God's kingdom — and this is asserted unequivocally — is genuinely his kingdom only when in it the poor receive justice (Hoffmann, 1969: 117; Stenger, 1993: 154-155).

It is generally agreed that the first three beatitudes and the fourth did not form an original unity. This is evident from the various features of this beatitude (Kloppenborg, 1987: 172-173)

Verses 22-23: (22) Blessed are you when people hate you, and when they exclude you, revile you, and defame you on account of the Son of Man.

(23) Rejoice in that day and leap for joy, for surely your reward is great in heaven; for that is what their ancestors did to the prophets.

The first three beatitudes may have been put together in the tradition prior to the composition of the fourth, which introduces a concretization and an application to the disciples (Bultmann, 1972: 109-110; Grundmann, 1961: 143; Schürmann, 1969: 335; Marshall, 1978: 251-252; Fitzmyer, 1981: 631; Betz, 1995: 578). The content of the fourth beatitude suggests amplification of Jesus' words at a later stage in the tradition (Danker, 1988: 141). But, although some commentators doubt that Jesus said these words, it is not unreasonable that Jesus sought to encourage his closest followers, that is, not the crowd or the people to whom Luke addressed the first beatitudes, but those who followed him in such a manner near the end of his life (Krämer, 1992: 63). This theme certainly became important to the early post-Easter communities confronted with persecution (as 1 Pet 3:14; 4:13-14) makes clear. What is also certain is that the community that assembled the sayings of Jesus in the Q document kept the last beatitude with the other three and, by that means, made them explicitly Christian, that is, linked with the following of Christ. Even more certain is the fact that the evangelist Luke found the last beatitude characteristic of the Christian life as he knew it, for he made it thematic of his portrait of church life as sketched in his narrative (Hamm, 1990: 59). While in the first three beatitudes it may not be at once clear whether the disciples themselves belong to the poor, the hungry, and the weeping, this ambiguity is abandoned in the fourth beatitude. The persecution described in the conditional clauses ("when people hate you...," etc.) is not merely a possibility but describes the real experience of the early Church. The hatred will culminate in ostracism: "when they exclude you." This may refer to exclusion of Jewish Christians from synagogues (but this rejected by Hare, 1967: 48-56), and probably reflects the experience of early Christians in Luke's own day (Stein, 1992: 202). However, persecution of disciples because of Jesus may well be an idea that is to be traced back to Jesus himself, in which case it may have the more general sense of social ostracism (cf. Isa 66:5; Marshall, 1978: 252). "And revile you" refers to the slander and verbal attack that one might suffer for a commitment to Jesus (Bock, 1994: 579). "And defame you," literally, "reject your name as evil," does probably not refer to the personal names of the disciples, but to the name of "Christian," which Luke otherwise knows (Acts 11:26; 26:28; Dupont, 1973: 81-82; Fitzmyer, 1981: 635; C.F. Evans, 1990: 331; Stein, 1992: 203). But some scholars observe that the suggestion that the name is that of "Christian" makes the following "for the sake of the Son of Man" redundant (Nolland, 1989: 285).

Such incidents of persecution find explanation in their association with the first three beatitudes, which enable the disciples to identify with the poor, the hungry, and the weeping. Of them both the tradition and Jesus had spoken, and they are now applied to the disciples who suffer from suppression (Fitzmyer, 1981: 631; Betz, 1995: 578). The social ostracism in Lk 6:22 is always the fate of the poor in agrarian societies but will equally become the fate of the rich who join Christian communities that include the poor. Luke knows the terrible costs involved for rich Christians but is uncompromising in his demand that they be paid (Malina and Rohrbaugh, 1992: 323).

The phrase "on account of the Son of Man" is rather surprising in that it has no parallel in either the Sermon on the Plain or the Sermon on the Mount (Mt 5:11, "on account of me"). Is this phrase an original part of the text? Or is it the result of later redactional activity, either prior to Luke or Luke's own? If it is the latter, was it interpolated to identify the "name" used earlier in the sentence? There is no clear answer to these questions (Betz, 1995: 581). What would the phrase "on account of the Son of Man" mean in the context of the Sermon on the Plain? It could mean that the disciples mentioned at the beginning of the sermon would adhere to a Son of Man Christology, according to which they would regard Jesus of Nazareth, their master, as the Son of Man (Grundmann, 1961: 144). Does the term refer to the life of Jesus on earth (Fitzmyer,

1981: 635) or to his eschatological parousia as Son of Man? One can give no clear answer to this question, but because of the closeness to Q, the eschatological expectation of Jesus as the Son of Man seems more likely. At any rate, the Christology of the Son of Man marks one of the most important differences between Luke's sermon and the Sermon on the Mount, for the latter expects Jesus to be the eschatological advocate, but does not call him the Son of Man (Guelich, 1982: 95). Luke here connects the fate of the Christians to the narrative development of the figure of the Son of Man in Lk 5:24 and 6:5 (Johnson, 1991: 107).

An appeal to be joyful (Lk 6:23) stands between the beatitudes (Lk 6:20b-22) and the "woes" (Lk 6:24-26). The verb *skirtao*, "leap for joy," is peculiar, perhaps indicating a dance (cf. Lk 7:32; 15:25; Schurmann, 1969: 334 note 65). The kind of dance becomes clear when one realizes that the *skirtoi* are Satyrs, the jolly companions of Dionysos, whose grotesque dances were known in antiquity as "Sikinnis." Pictures of the Satyrs were a popular decorative motif on vases and walls. The allusion to such dances must have been obvious. For Gentile Christians, the positive reference to them must have induced chuckles; but for Jewish Christians, such a reference would have been repulsive, and that the Sermon on the Mount does not employ the term cannot be accidental. [Philo uses the term always in the negative sense in connection with imagery describing the unruly nature of passion]. Even amid persecution Christians can rejoice, and Luke gave illustrations of this in Acts 5:41; 165:25; 21:13f. (Stein, 1992: 203).

The verse has two parts: the appeal itself (Lk 6:23a) and the reason for it (Lk 6:23b). Is the appeal made in view of the present or of the future? In forming a judgment, one must keep in mind the whole composition of Lk 6:20b-26. The future tense of the verbs in verse 21b ("you will be filled") and verse 21d ("you will laugh") evokes an image of a feast in the heavenly kingdom (Lk 6:20c and

23b). It seems clear, then, that the phrase "in that day" refers to the well-known eschatological expression (Betz, 1995: 582).

By adding the temporal designation "in that day" to the imperative "rejoice," Luke introduces the idea of eschatological judgment and thereby sharpens the contrast between the present condition of being reviled and the future rejoicing over the heavenly reward. As in the beatitudes of the hungry and the weeping, where "now" is added in Luke, "in that day" thus introduces the Lukan schema of the eschatological reversal of fortunes. Luke also makes "people" the subject of the abuse suffered by the blessed. This is not just a closer identification of Matthew's indefinite "they." Rather, by adding this subject Luke distinguishes the generation of those who mistreat the blessed from the generation of their "fathers" (which also appears only in Luke, in the last clause of verses 23), those who treated the Hebrew prophets in the same manner. He thus underscores his view of salvation history in which the time of "the law and the prophets" is distinguished from the age of Jesus and the age of the Church (Stenger, 1993: 151).

Moreover, the promise of eschatological joy in the eternal kingdom of God does not exclude an anticipated joy here on earth. On the contrary, it is the motivation for such an earthly joy. The appeal to be joyful, therefore, is grounded in the eschatological conviction that there will be heavenly joy, a conviction that generates joy even in the present. The appeal to joy generally also belongs to the early Christian paraenetical theme of joy in persecution and suffering, a theme found as well, although in different form, in the Sermon on the Mount (Mt 5:11-12; Betz, 1995: 582-583).

One passage in Acts in particular works as a fulfillment of the last beatitude. After telling of the arrest, flogging, and warning of Peter and John, the narrator continues: "As they left the council, they rejoiced that they were considered worthy to suffer dishonor for the sake of the name. And every day in the temple and at home they did not cease to teach and proclaim Jesus as the Messiah" (Acts 5:41-42).

Besides the convergence with the last beatitude in the elements of rejoicing and being rejected because of the name of Jesus, the use of the word for preaching, *euangelizomai*, is an enhancement of the theme of the apostles extending the prophetic ministry of Jesus, for it is the word Luke took from Isa 61. It is used extensively in Acts to describe the mission of the Church. It describes the preaching of Philip (Acts 8:4,12,35), Peter and John (Acts 8:25), disciples in general (Acts 11:20), Paul alone (Acts 13:32; 16:10; 17:18), and Paul and Barnabas (Acts 14:7, 15,21; 15:35). Hence, for Luke (as for the Q community), the last beatitude climaxes the others and makes the following of Christ a matter of following Jesus the rejected Prophet (Hamm, 1990: 59-61).

Lk 6:23b states the reason not only for the promise of joy and the appeal in verse 23a, but for the entire position in Lk 6:20b-23. The initial "for surely" (*idou gar*) both indicates the character of the reason behind the statement and expresses a moment of surprise. Indeed, it must be a surprise for Gentile Christians (the element of surprise is missing in Mt 5:12) to learn that they can expect a reward in heaven, that is, in the sight of God: "for surely your reward is great in heaven." There is no idea of merit in this stastement, for even after perfect obedience and service to God (and fellow human beings), believers will only be able to say: "We are worthless slaves [better RSV: unworthy servants]; we have done only what we ought to have done" (Lk 17:10; Stein, 1992: 203). The phrase "your reward is great" (cf. Jer 31:16) does not intend to motivate their conduct through expectation of a reward. Rather, the words are consolatory. Their experience will be a sign that they are on the right track and that they have God's endorsement (see Acts 4:23-31). Reward as motivation is condemned in Lk 17:7-10 (Danker, 1988: 141). The promise, therefore, is the same as that made to Jewish Christians in Mt 5:12. How can such a promise be made and justified theologically?

The subsequent statement answers this question: "for that is what their ancestors did to the prophets." There are two ways of interpreting this statement. Believers should rejoice (1) because they will share God's kingdom with the prophets or (2) because their persecution assures them that they are indeed God's people; for God's people, the prophets, have suffered similarly. The latter interpretation is to be prefered due to the parallel in Lk 6:26 (Stein, 1992: 203-204).

This statement affirms the Jewish doctrine that the prophets of old suffered from oppression and persecution by their contemporary authorities. Such persecutions made of these prophets "righteous persons" who generated divine reward (Schürmann, 1969: 335). If the Christians, even Gentile Christians, experience the same persecutions, they are right in expecting reward because of the principle that equal merit leads to equal reward. Since the reward of the prophets was "great," as was generally agreed, so will the reward for Christians be "great." This theological argument is identical with that in Mt 5:12, except that in Luke it seems to apply to Gentile Christians. This conclusion follows from the expression "*their* ancestors," focusing on the Jewish forefathers of those prophets, and implying a non-Jewish perspective (Betz, 1995: 583-584).

For Luke, disciples are prophets (Fitzmyer, 1981: 636) who face the probable fate of persecution. Besides the places in Acts where certain disciples are called prophets because they have the special function of prophet within the community (e.g., Acts 13:1; 15:32; 21:10), there are other places where the followers of Jesus are associated with the prophetic tradition in a broader sense. For example, the very imagery which had earlier been assigned to Jesus in the Third Gospel, "a light for the nations," an image from Isa 49:6 describing Israel as prophetic Servant of Yahweh, is later applied in Acts to Paul and Barnabas in Acts 13:46-47. That prophetic image from Isaiah is tellingly employed once again in Acts 26:22-23, where Paul, in his defense before Agrippa, speaks of the events of Jesus fulfilling Old Testament prophecies "that the Messiah must suffer, and that, by being the first to rise from the dead, he would proclaim light both to our people and to the Gentiles." This is a clear identification of the ministry of the disciples as an extension of Jesus' own prophetic ministry. Indeed, their ministry is the very means by which Jesus as risen Prophet-like-Moses now continues his ministry.

That sense of prophetic mission is also expressed powerfully in a Q saying found among the woes in Lk 11:47-48. This passage places the Christian prophets and apostles in the line of God's messengers from the foundation of the world through the last book of the Hebrew canon. Later, in Lk 13:28, where Luke uses the Q saying about the eschatological banquet, Luke includes "all the prophets" as the first-mentioned guests of the patriarchs: There will be weeping and gnashing of teeth when you see Abraham and Isaac and Jacob *and all the prophets* in the kingdom of God and you yourselves thrust out." Three verses later, in response to the Pharisees' warning that Herod wants to kill him, Jesus says that he must continue on his way, "because it is impossible for a prophet to be killed outside of Jerusalem."

Verse 24:   But woe to you who are rich
            for you have received your consolation.

Only Luke has these four "woes," which match the beatitudes precisely in form and content (Johnson, 1991: 108). The "woes" are intimately linked with the blessings that precede, for those who have "woes" pronounced on them are the ones who must share a large portion of the blame for the negative conditions described in Lk 6:20b-23 (Danker, 1988: 142). It is not altogether excluded that Luke has taken the "woes" from another context. But in the present context they add sharpness to the beatitudes (like shading in a drawing) and intensify the sociological slant (Sampathkumar, 1996: 178).

The conjuction "but" (*plen,* "however") presages the turning point between promise of salvation and warning against disaster and marks the first of the four "woes." The "woes" in Lk 6:24-26 are the exact counterparts of the beatitudes. These "woes" address more directly the disciples for whom the Sermon on the Plain is composed and might seem almost like curses if they were not given on the condition that the addressees actually meet the descriptions of people rich, filled, laughing, and being liked by everyone. Since the disciples are warned against this condition, the "woes" may amount not to curses but to mere threats, although pronounced with solemnity and definiteness. Similar threats are found in Lk 17:1; 22:22. Series of beatitudes and "woes" are found in prophetic, apocalyptic, and wisdom literature (e.g., Isa 3:9,11; 5:8-11; Tob 13:12). The woes in Lk 6:24-26, however, serve a didactic and paraenetical; purpose, with eschatological but not highly apocalyptic overtones. In contrast the Sermon on the Mount has no "woes" at all but rather a long section of eschatological warnings (Mt 7:13-23; Betz, 1995: 585-586).

The "rich" play a thematic role in the Gospel as opposites of the poor. The term denotes economic well-being and security. It connotes belonging and power within the people, and, in the narrative, a sense of arrogance that does not require the visitation of God (see Lk 1:53; 12:16,21; 14:12; 16:1,19,21-22; 18:23,25; 19:2; 21:1; Johnson, 1991: 108).

The threat is a warning that the rich can expect no eschatological reward: "for you have already received your consolation." The verb "receive" (*apecho*) comes from the language of commerce and signifies the cashing in of a payment and the issuing of a receipt for a sum owed. The term also occurs in Mt 6:2,5,16. In what sense has the rich cashed in his consolation? Some scholars think that the rich are threatened because of their egotism (Grundmann, 1961: 144-145). One scholar says that "a certain shortsightedness, induced by that status, leads such persons to think that there is nothing more to have" (Fitzmyer, 1981: 636). In order to understand the argument, one must consider some social presuppositions held in antiquity, according to which the rich suffer from a whole catalog of aches and pains coming from luxurious living, including illnesses, worries, fear, anxieties, thefts, cheating and false friends. One must read Lucian's descriptions of the dreadful lot of the rich to understand the argument that they, more than others, need consolation. The plight of the rich is already the subject of the Old Testament wisdom literature (Eccl 5:10-6:9). Now Luke states that they have already cashed in on that consolation. The "consolation" of the rich is their wealth (Johnson, 1991: 108). The luxurious life itself is their consolation, that is, those things mentioned in Lk 6:25-26: the filled stomach, fun and laughter, and of course flattery, of which the rich can never get enough (cf. Lk 16:26, where Abraham says to the rich man: "Remember that during your lifetime you received your good things, and Lazarus in like manner evil things; but now he is comforted here, and you are in agony." This consolation is in itself a waste, illusion, and self-deception (cf. Lk 12:16-21, the story of the foolish rich man; Betz, 1995: 585). A New Testament passage remarkably similar to this is Jas 4:9, "Let your laughter be turned into mourning...."

Verse 25:   Woe to you who are full now,
             for you will be hungry.
             Woe to you who are laughing now,
             for you will mourn and weep.

This verse contains the second and the third "woes." In the second, the exclamatory "woe" is followed by the specification of the addressees, whose food consumption is described not without satirical sting as "filling up" either themselves or their stomachs. [Other New Testament passages use the term with a positive or neutral meaning: Lk 1:53; 15:16, etc.] In comedy and satire the flabby rich person who stuffs himself or herself with delicacies is a well-known character (e.g., in the works of Lucian). Moreover, critical descriptions of banquets of the wealthy and their parasites entertain readers with detailed episodes of gluttony, giving proper attention to the consequences of such gluttony. According to common belief, the situation can easily be reversed, either in this world or in afterlife (Eccl 120:16-17; Sir 18:32). The parable of the Rich Man and Lazarus (Lk 16:19-31) contains this teaching, according to which the rich man suffers in Hades from thirst (Lk 16:24; Betz, 1995: 586-587).

The third "woe" parallels the second: "Woe to you who are laughing now, for you will mourn and weep." Although not obvious from the context, the laughter seems cynical, expressing an eerie joy and even frenzy, the mark of the fool (Eccl 2:2, "I said of laughter, 'It is mad,'..."; Sir 21:20; 27:13; Fitzmyer, 1981: 637).The laughter is that of those who feel quite happy with their present lot in life. Theirs is a fool's paradise (Nolland, 1989: 288). Luke is describing people who are self-satisfied and indifferent to the needs of others (Marshall, 1978: 256). One should see this laughter of the rich in contrast to the grim lot of the poor (laughter equals contempt; see Prov 17:5, "Those who mock the poor insult their Maker"). The reason for this warning is again the eschatological reversal of roles, which has "mourning and weeping" ready for the laughers. The combination of the two is traditional. Apocalyptic literature and tales of the netherworld also substantiate that the laughing rich of this world have nothing to laugh about in the world to come (Isa 13:6; 65:13-14; Joel 1:8-10; Ex 22:24-31. etc.).

These things seem to have been the stock-in-trade of popular literature, proverbs, and folklore (Betz, 1995: 587-588).

Verse 26:   Woe to you when all speak well of you,
             for that is what their ancestors did to the false
             prophets.

The fourth "woe" is analogous to the fourth beatitude (Lk 6:22). Verse 26a describes yet another type of attitude typical of the wealthy, flattery: "Woe when all speak well of you." Obviously, the expression "speak well" (*kalos eipein*) refers to what we know from other texts as flattery. If *all* people speak well of someone, what they say must be flattery (Klostermann, 1929/1975: 80). One of the troubles of the rich is that they are continuously surrounded by flatterers; the upstarts and parasites in particular were known to fall prey easily to flattery. If defamation is already bad enough (Lk 6:22) flattery is even worse. Although such a situation is typical for the rich, the warning is directed to the disciples. It is a hypothetical situation as far as they are concerned, but other early Christian paraenesis confirms that such warning was not redundant (Gal 1:10; 1 Thess 2:4-5; Eph 6:6; Col 3:22).

The reason for the warning in verse 26 stands in juxtaposition to verse 23c: "for that is what their ancestors did to the false prophets." "False prophets" as described here are not people who teach wrong doctrine but are, rather, those who make hypocritical claims to being God's mouthpieces. They operate under the guise of established tradition and are highly respected in their religious communities for maintaining the status quo. They make no waves and rock no boats. Nevertheless, they are religious quacks, unable to offer a real remedy, while they exploit people for their own ends. Bogus prophets have always enjoyed popular acclaim, for they promise peace when there is no peace (cf. Jer 6:13-15; Danker, 1988: 143). This argumentation is a topos, known from the Old Testament (1Kgs 22:26-28;

Isa 28:7; Jer 5:31; 14:13-16; 23:16-17). Accordingly, the true prophets were always persecuted while the false prophets were always glorified. Prophets of old who enjoyed the esteem of their contemporaries turned out to be deceivers of Israel (Isa 30:10-11; Fitzmyer, 1981: 637). From this evidence anyone can see who the true and false prophets are. The true disciples of Jesus, therefore, must avoid attracting flattery toward themselves. Acting in such a way that *all* people praise them cannot be a Christian goal. Instead the people are to be moved by good deeds to praise God (cf. Mt 5:16; Betz, 1995: 588-589).

b. *Rules for Conduct of the Disciples* (Lk 6:27-45)

Many proposals have been presented concerning the structure of Lk 6:27-49, most of which are based on a threefold division whose contours are, however, different from scholar to scholar (Malipurathu, 1994: 40-46). Our division is close to that of Schmithals (1980: 82), but we take verses 27-38 and 39-45 as one section and do not agree with the author in interpreting verses 39-45 as addressed to false teachers.

Although the beatitudes and the woes are really intended as the exordium of the Sermon on the Plain and serve as the starting-point for the heart of Jesus' message subsequently laid out in the sermon (Fitzmyer, 1981: 630), there is an obvious break at Lk 6:26. This is not only because of the indication of the syntactic change provided by the expression, "But I say to you that listen," (*alla humin lego tois akouousin*) in Lk 6:27a, but more so because of the genre of the macarisms and the overtones of the prophetic language (Ernst, 1977: 215-216; Malipurathu, 1994: 21).

There is no direct link in thought between Lk 6:24-26 and 27ff. One can, however, see a possible catchword link with the beatitudes by means of "to hate" (*miseō*; Lk 6:22 and 27; Marshall, 1978: 259). Love of enemies is but one theme among many in Lk 6:27-45, but it is the dominant one: "Love your enemies" opens the series of instructions

(Lk 6:27), and the phrase is repeated in Lk 6:35 (Linskens, 1983: 19). In between is a compilation and not a single sermon. This judgment is supported by the shifts in the Greek text from plural "you" (verses 27-28), to singular (verses 29-30), and back to plural (verses 31-36), coupled with the fact that some of these sayings are found elsewhere in the other Gospels, and where paralleled in Matthew, they are found in a different order (Mt 5:39-42,44-48; 7:12; Craddock, 1990: 89). If the same source underlies both Matthew and Luke, one or both evangelists has/have considerably revised its order and contents. Luke's sequence in Lk 6:27-36 is less original than Matthew's (Linskens, 1983: 19). There are, however, places where each Gospel seems to have the more primitive wording (Lk 6:27; Mt 5:40), and hence there are grounds for suspecting that a simple solution in terms of one common source is inadequate (Wrege, 1968: 75-94).

As is sometimes noted, the phrasing of Luke's version stresses the element of violence in the situations that are depicted — being *struck* on the cheek, followed by when someone *takes away* your cloak, and when someone *takes away* your belongings. His descriptions seem to be of a mugging or robbery. How far has Luke, however, taken a step beyond Q? Has Luke's motive been to ensure that nonretalitation is not simply viewed as the response of those who were in any case defenseless and had no alternative but to tolerate oppression and try to make friends with the oppressors? The teaching on nonretaliation potentially represents a particularly challenging affront to ancient Mediterranean codes of honor and shame. Luke does not hesitate to confront those codes in other contexts, but the nonretaliation exhortations are distinctive in that they depict the *voluntary* vulnerability of the oppressed to *material and physical exploitation*. This seems to run counter Luke's concern for the poor. As such, these are potentially difficult sayings for Luke. Luke deals with them in two ways. First, he alters Q's context for the exhortations by placing them amid the positive teaching about loving one's enemies, in imitation of God who is kind and merciful. Effectively, he switches emphasis from the exploited being encouraged to accept further exploitation to the virtues of love and mercy (see Piper, 1989: 78-82). Second, he reduces the vulnerability demanded of those who are oppressed by his formulation of this teaching as related to isolated acts of violence. One's economic and physical vulnerability — the scale of exploitation — is more limited if the wrong that one suffers is a sporadic and unpredicted violent act (such as being mugged) rather than if it is part of an ongoing exploitative personal or contractual relationship. Acceptance of an ongoing material and physical vulnerability could hardly sit easily with Luke's concern for the poor. Regarding officials, see the experience of extortion against which John the Baptist warns soldiers in Lk 3:14 (Piper, 1995: 55-56,68).

The teaching on love in Lk 6:27-36 moves in one area, the love of one's enemies, but in Lk 6:37-45 it takes on a wider scope, i.e., demands regarding Christians among themselves: the prohibition of judging (or criticizing) is another application of the counsel of love. Judgment and condemnation must yield to forgiveness, bounteous generosity, upright conduct. Finally, in Lk 6:46-49 Jesus calls for realistic, effective action, based not only on such love, but on the word that he preaches (Fitzmyer, 1981: 630). In continuity with Lk 6:20-26, Luke here explores the theme of reciprocity, a basic factor in human relationships and integral to the politics of the new age. Greco-Roman readers would readily interpret Luke's recital via their benefactor-beneficiary model: goodness is to be reciprocated by recognition, and ingratitude is despicable. In many respects the injunctions of this part of the sermon are in harmony with the theme of the Jubilee expressed in Lk 4:18-19 (Danker, 1988: 143).

The actions commended ("expecting nothing in return") are those of generalized reciprocity typical of a household

interaction (Malina and Rohrbaugh, 1992: 323). Social interaction in agrarian societies fell across a spectrum run-
ning from reciprocity at one end to redistribution at the
other.

Reciprocal relations, typical of small-scale social groups
(for example, villages) involved back-and-forth exchanges
that generally followed one of three patterns: (1) Generalized reciprocity: open sharing based on generosity or need.
Return was often postponed or forgotten. Such reciprocity
characterizes family relations. (2) Balanced reciprocity: exchange based on symmetrical concern for the interests of
both parties. Here return was expected in equal measure.
Such reciprocity characterizes neighborly relations. (3) Negative reciprocity: based on the interests of only one party,
who expected to gain without having to compensate in return. This characterizes relations with strangers.

Redistributive relations are typical of the large-scale agrarian
societies of antiquity (Egypt, Palestine, Rome). They involved
pooling resources in a central storehouse (usually via taxation and tribute) under the control of a hierarchical elite
which could then redistribute them though the mechanisms
of politics and religion. Redistribution relations are always
assymmetrical and primarily benefit those in control. The
temple system of first-century Palestine functioned as a system of redistributive relations (Malina and Rohrbaugh, 1992:
324-325).

Verses 27-28: (27) But to you that listen,
                    Love your enemies,
                    do good to those who hate you,
               (28) bless those who curse you,
                    pray for those who abuse you.

In Lk 6:27-28 we find four commands in synonymous parallelism, in which the same thought is repeated in poetic
rhythm. The importance of these commands is evident in
that they are Jesus' first direct commands in the Gospel
(Nolland, 1989: 293; Stein, 1992: 206).

Enemies are usually treated with the same sort of hostility they have shown, and, one does good to one's benefactors. The principal point of Lk 6:27-35 is that, on the contrary, the behavior of the other person should not determine one's own involvement in a relationship. A dramatic statement of that change in the conduct of relationships is in the general principle, "Love your enemies." Statements of that general principle (Lk 6:27,35) frame a disparate collection of sayings about specific dimensions of the theme.

The intervening sayings fall into two general categories. The first develops the theme of one's response to mistreatment. The assumption underlying these sayings is that they are addressed to the "victims" and not to the victimizers. The point is that those on the receiving end of such actions are not to remain victims whose responses are dictated by the initial encounter. The second set of teachings (Lk 6:32-34) deals with the equally (if not actually more) difficult problem of relationships with benefactors. There the usual pattern of repaying one favor with another simply perpetuates relationships based on calculation and mutual advantage. Such relationships represent no more than business as usual, particularly in a society (like those in which both Jesus and Luke lived) defined by systems of "patronage." In a patronage system, a person's status in society is determined by those who have to depend on that person, and by those, in turn, on whom that person must rely. Since both one's status in the society and one's economic debts and credits are strictly calculated, the same dynamic that determines social status also undergirds the system of financial indebtedness that was so destructive to small landowners in rural Palestine of Jesus' day and to poor city dwellers elsewhere in the Empire in Luke's day as well. For Luke, an important aspect of the good news present in Jesus is that such calculation in both economics and social status is ended, and the patronage system in general is replaced by a social structure founded on generosity, respect, and equal treatment for everyone (Ringe, 1995: 94-95).

We assume that the moral maxims gathered together in Lk 6:27-35 were not initially proposed and subsequently appropriated by their first adherents simply to make life more miserable but, instead, to help these persons out by suggesting a better way of dealing with the various difficulties and displeasures facing them in life. In this regard, the language of the text has meaning only if and when it worked in practice. In other words, What made the imperative to "love your enemies" and the related recommendations in Lk 6:27-35 more than just "lousy" advice? (Vaage, 1994: 40). We will try to deal with this question in the following.

"But to you that listen" is Luke's introduction to a new part of the sermon (Lk 6:27-36). In a sense it is the introduction to the whole middle section of the sermon (Lk 6:27-45), the most important part, for which the exordium has been preparing. The initial particle *alla* (literally "but"; maybe here best translated by something like "and now") and the emphastic position of the "to you" mark the beginning of a new section. According to some scholars "but" at the begining of the verse contrasts with the preceding woes. It represents a shift back to the desired activity of disciples (Bock, 1994: 588). Others, however, see here a shift of audience from outsiders to insiders (Ernst, 1977: 224; Marshall, 1978: 258; but see Schmidt, 1987: 141).

The phrase that Luke uses here echoes that of Lk 6:18, "they had come to hear him"; it will be picked up again in Lk 6:47 (Fitzmyer, 1981: 637). All through this pericope, Luke seems to have emptied it of its Palestinian context and applied it to the situation of his community. Luke's situation in life has nothing to do with the situation of a defeated, humiliated Jewish people. His redaction is related to popular Hellenistic ethics. Luke maintains that Christian morality can compete with the world and is, indeed, far superior to it. Luke presents Gospel principles for those

who will be children of the Most High (Lk 6:35), and who
are told to be merciful as the Father is merciful (Lk 6:36).
They are about as practical as dying on the cross for others.
But they are decisively efficient in as far as in their aggres-
siveness they do not allow an enemy to be an enemy
(Linskens, 1983: 19-20).

It has been suggested that within the lives of charismatic wanderers, who adapted for themselves the words and
life-style of Jesus, these sayings must have had an existential relevance quite distinct from those transposed reinter-
pretations that they took on among the settled householders according to the Gospels of Matthew and Luke. The
Lukan community(ties) associated love of enemies with
conflicts between people who lent money and their debtors. Luke took the radical sayings of the wandering
charismatics and restructured them to provide divine guidance toward a greater social symmetry in the relationship
between rich and poor (Theissen, 1992, 141,144,146-148).

But recently it has been proposed that Matthew's identification of "enemies" as members of "one's own household" (Mt 10:36) holds a better promise for reconstructing
the social setting of Lk 6:27-36. Using this possibility to
good purpose, the opening rules of the two-ways manual of
the *Didache*, or Teaching of the Twelve Apostles, have been
held up as providing the clearest instance in which new
recruits had to be prepared for the backlash within their
extended families which their conversion might precipitate.
The *Didache* is considered to provide a clear instance wherein
young Gentile recruits were being equipped to defuse and to
counter the limited aggression of their elders that was sanctioned within the patriarchal family system. The Jesus movement was breaking up households. Parents, frustrated at being
unable verbally to persuade their children of the folly and
shame of their commitment, were driven to "strike them on
the cheek." Work relationships associated with family trade
or business also deteriorated. To prevent their children from

meeting with the despised Christians, parents "took their cloaks" — but to no avail — for they shamed them by surrendering to their parents their tunics as well. Finally, when parents discovered that their children had become absurdly generous and planned to share everything they had with outsiders, they resorted to seizing their children's goods so they would not squander family resources on outsiders who were regarded as inconsequential to the family welfare. Each of these steps, however, only served to further alienate their sons and daughters and to push them into the care and protection of those "brothers and sisters" ready to receive them (Milavec, 1995: 142).

There are strong grounds for suggesting that the wandering charismatics originally spoke of "loving one's enemies" and "turning the other cheek" as reflecting the opposition they often received from disgruntled hearers in the towns through which they passed (Theissen, 1992). When these sayings were later adapted and used by householders, however, the evidence of the *Didache* clearly signals that new recruits to the Jesus movement had to anticipate various forms of abuse as originating, not now from strangers in the marketplace but from members of their own household (Milavec, 1995: 142).

There is no evidence that Luke has in mind only persecutors from outside the Christian communities. With "enemies," "those who curse," and so forth, he may have in mind either community members or noncommunity members or both. Especially if the formulation of Lk 6:35 is Luke's and was not originally in Q, then his focus is clearly local intracommunity social-economic relations. He appears to envision situations less specific than local borrowing and lending in Lk 6:29b and 30b, perhaps situations of theft, but the context is still local social interaction. Certainly there is no indication of foreign enemies. This analysis of the sayings in Lk 6:27-36, whether in the Q form or in the Lukan adaptation, suggests that the context indicated by the content of the individual sayings is that of social-economic relations in a village or a city. It is easy to understand the "enemies, haters, cursers, abusers" in the context of local interaction but difficult if not impossible to understand them as referring to national or political enemies. This interpretation is confirmed simply by the kinds of relationships assumed in the following sayings: the insulting slap on the face, the local creditor's seizure of the token pledge given by the debtor, borrowing and begging among local community members, or doing good and lending to those who may be local adversaries. Finally, in the Lukan Sermon on the Plain, as well as in the sayings source Q, whether in this passage or in the sermon as a whole, Jesus' words touch on the concerns of daily existence, poverty, hunger, grief, hatred, and ostracism (Daube, 1956: 255-258; Horsley, 1992: 88-89).

At the same time, the sayings in Lk 6:27-36 seem to depict circumstances of severe economic hardship among those addressed. It assumes that some in the local community are asking for loans for which they have genuine need. Some to whom the sayings are addressed, already in debt, are unable to repay and fear that their creditors seize the security they have posted. Still others have been reduced to begging. It is not surprising that in such desperate economic circumstances, some people are at each other's throats, hating, cursing, and abusing. The picture given by the blessings and the woes (Lk 6:20-26), which must have immediately preceded the "Love your enemies" passage even in Q, is similar; those addressed are apparently poor, hungry, and in despair. What is more, they stand opposite others (their urban creditors?) who are wealthy, well fed, and satisfied with life.

In such circumstances one would expect a high degree of resentment of the wealthy. Indeed, the woes against the wealthy reflect just that. The sayings beginning with "Love your enemies," however, do not have the exploitative ruling class in mind. These sayings, rather, call people in the local communities to take economic responsibility for each other in their desperate circumstances. Those addressed may have little or nothing themselves. But they are called upon to share what they have willingly with others in the community, even with their enemies or those who hate them. They are not to seek damages from a formal insult. They are even to render up the pledge for a loan that the unmerciful creditor has no right to take. The message seems to be: take responsibility for helping each other willingly, even your enemies, in the local community.

Exploitation of the people by the Jewish priestly aristocracy and the Romans may well have been addressed in other sayings of Jesus. The focus of "Love your enemies" and the related sayings, however, is not on the Romans or even on domestic political enemies. Rather, they call for realization of the will of God and or imitation of the mercy of God in dealing with the squabbles of day-to-day life that were integrally related to the struggle for supreme values and that took place in circumstances where people had their backs against the wall. When the people have achieved such solidarity with regard to the supreme values of life focused on concrete social-economic relations, however, it has usually been highly threatening to the ruling groups. The movement gathered around Jesus appears to have been no exception (Horsley, 1992: 90-92).

Going beyond the scope of this immediate setting, it is tantalizing to imagine that the strategies and instincts perfected to counter intrafamilial aggression might have formed the tacit beginnings of an emergent policy designed for dealing with imperial aggression as well. In retrospect, therefore, while "turning the other cheek" and "loving one's enemies" might have initially had nothing to do with the naked aggression of a foreign army of occupation, it is not unthinkable that those very strategies that provided new recruits with a tested means for preventing intrafamilial aggression from interfering with their self-chosen "way of life" might have shaped the social character whereby Christians in a subsequent era were predisposed to respond to the much more menacing inperial aggression (Milavec, 1995: 142).

The first ethical rule cites the authoritative doctrine of Jesus (Lk 6:27b). The teaching of Jesus, however, is set forth not in one but in four parallel maxims (Lk 6:27-28). They are arranged by parallel lines. The first set of parallel lines is found in verse 27b-c. The first maxim states the famous command, "love your enemies." The wording is identical with Mt 5:44. The subsequent elaboration concerning the meaning shows that Jesus' love-command is regarded as more than simply his authoritative doctrine. Within themselves the four maxims contain an argument that stands in the place of the quite different argument made by Mt 5:43-48. The difference is that Luke makes no attempt to justify the love-command by reference to Torah tradition but assumes that it makes sense on its own terms. This assumption implies that as a maxim one is to regard it as self-evident. The Sermon on the Plain considers "love your enemies" as authoritative tradition and thus as well known to the Christian community. Hence the reason for citing it here is not to introduce it for the first time but to interpret it appropriately.

As already metioned above, many scholarly and semi-popular treatments of Jesus' teaching understand "enemies" in Lk 6:27 to refer to foreign or national enemies or to include national as well as personal enemies (Schottroff, 1978: 9; Klassen, 1984: 86; Theissen, 1992: 115-156). In fact, most studies of "Love your enemies" published in recent years have given little attention to the definition of "enemies" because they give little attention to the concrete social context. Some do not even raise the question of the enemies' identity (whether in Matthew, Luke, Q, or for Jesus). The command of loving enemies remains general, abstract, and susceptible of a variety of interpretations so long as the meaning of "enemies" remains imprecise. Specification of the enemies (whether in Matthew, Luke, Q, or for Jesus) requires investigation into the concretre social context as well as the literary context of the sayings and their transmission. Pursuit of such an inquiry, moreover, requires attention to the context indicated by the content of the sayings. In the few studies that note the context indicated in the sayings themselves, the interpreters still jump to the foreign/political interpretation (Seitz, 1969: 46-52; Horsley, 1992: 79-80).

In the Septuagint, which strongly influenced the Greek usage of the early churches, *echthros* can be used both for foreign, political enemies and for personal (and more local) enemies. More decisive for determining the meaning of this and other terms, however, is the usage in the individual Gospel writers. In two passages in Luke, the Song of Zechariah in Lk 1:71,74; and the lament over Jerusalem in Lk 19:43, the term refers to national enemies. In the other occurrences in Luke (and Matthew), none of the cases is a reference to foreign national or domestic political enemies. The "enemy" is, rather, a local adversary, for instance, one who sabotages a farmer's crop by sowing weeds among the grain (Mt 13:25,28). The crucial decision required in response to Jesus' preaching of the kingdom (bringing not peace but a sword/division) means that the members of one's own household may become "enemies" (Mt 10:34-36). Herod Antipas and Pilate had been personal enemies, although there may have been an element of political rivalry involved (Lk 23:12). In the immediate context of the saying in Lk 6:27-28 and in Q, there is nothing to suggest that foreign or political enemies were in view. Standing in isolation, "your enemies" is vague. Taken in connection with the parallel sayings in Luke, the phrase surely means those with whom one is in personal, local interaction. Although "those who hate" and "those who curse" could be anyone, whether local or distant, "those who abuse you" would have to be local. But with a few exceptions (Lk 1:71; Mt 24:9), "those who hate," although outside the community of Jesus' followers, are within the local sphere of social interaction. The "hatred" could

even be between family members, precisely as the result of
response to Jesus (Lk 14:26). Similarly, while one could bless
and pray for people at a distance, "doing good" presupposes
direct interaction (Horsley, 1992: 85-86).

The second line provides a parallel variation: "Do good
to those who hate you." The verb "to love" is now identified with "doing good," a general Greek moral term, while
the "enemies" are concretely explained as "those who hate
you." Thus loving and hating, doing good and being inimical, interpret each other. For the Greeks, the enemy is the
opposite of a friend. With the friend one is united in a
bond of love that consists of mutual acts of doing good.
Therefore, the variation of verse 27c means in effect that
the term "love" is interpreted here in the context of friendship. Since such an interpretation is somewhat unusual in
the New Testament, its purpose here can only be pedagogical. The disciples addressed by the Sermon on the Plain are
given to understand that Jesus' commandment to love the
enemy is not an alien and incomprehensible law but a part
of the familiar friendship doctrines. At the same time, Jesus'
love-commandment is shown to be a matter of reality. Lk
6:22 already has shown that the disciples were objects of
hatred. Those who hate them are now identified as the
enemies. They must be confronted by the disciples, who in
this confrontation need to learn what is the master's command (Betz, 1995: 592-593).

The second parallelism in verse 28a-b offers practical
ways faithful both to the teaching of Jesus and of the stan-
dards of ethics. The variation of Jesus' command in verse
28a identifies a form of hostility common in antiquity: cursing,
a magical application of enmity. The ordinary reaction would
be to respond in kind and to answer curse with curse. The
Sermon on the Plain, however, recommends the opposite
of the curse, namely, the blessing: "Bless those who curse
you." This command, that has no parallel in the Sermon
on the Mount, is known, however, from other early Chris-

tian sources. The earliest parallel to it occurs in Rom 12:14, "Bless those who persecute you; bless and do not curse them." What is the purpose of such an action? Ancient thought would indeed have judged it morally noble and an act worthy of imitation, not sentimental or stupid. One may assume, therefore, that an attitude such as the recommended one made moral sense to Greeks of the Hellenistic era. Furthermore, the passion narrative of Luke has made Jesus an example for his commandment when he prays on the cross, "Father, forgive them; for they do not know what they are doing" (Lk 23:34). One should note also that the verbs used in verses 27-28 circumscribe what is meant by an enemy: one who hates, curses, and abuses or mistreats. Thus, the Christian is asked to pray on behalf of the oppressor rather than to retaliate (Betz, 1995: 593-595).

Verses 27-28 express a principle of nonretaliation, not nonviolence. It must be kept in mind that these directions apply to communities that find themselves subject to social and religious persecution. Followers of Jesus ought to know before they take to the road of discipleship what the cost will be (Lk 14:25-35). Having opted for the consequences, they must be prepared to accept them. Retaliation would defeat their profession of faith. These verses say nothing about self-defense unrelated to religious persecution, nor do they speak to the question of the use of legal resources when they are available. A sample of Luke's own thinking on the latter topic is offered at Acts 16:35-40 where Paul cals on his Roman citizenship. The Christian, in other words, is not to be a simpleton but must judge circumstances in the light of the principle that vengeance belongs to the Lord (Rom 12:19), and that one is called not to curse but to bless (Danker, 1988: 144).

Verses 29-30: (29) If anyone strikes you on the cheek, offer the
                    other also;
                    and from anyone who takes away your coat
                    do not withhold even your shirt.

(30) Give to everyone who begs from you;
      and if anyone takes away your goods,
      do not ask for them again.

In verses 29-30 Luke gives four examples about how the
four commands of enemy love (verses 27-28) should be carried out. The four examples, however, do not correspond
exactly in content with the four commands in Lk 6:27-28
(Stein, 1992: 207). The four maxims of verses 27-28 are
followed by a set of four examples of abuse, exaggerated no
doubt for the sake of demonstration. Each example envisions both an act of violence and a recommendation for
reaction. The first two examples (verse 29a-b) are specific,
the last two (verse 30a-b) general in nature. The reactions
are stated in alternating fashion: positively (verse 29a),
negatively (verse 29b), positively (verse 30a), negatively (verse
30b). While the examples may originally have existed separately, they were combined already in the pre-Lukan source
(Schürmann, 1969: 347-349).

What do these four examples demonstrate? What is their
connection with the context? We are apparently entering
here into a more extended argument concerning the maxims (verses 27-28), of which they are a part. The examples
(verses 29-30) bring to the fore the paradoxical, even absurd, nature of these maxims, and in particular of Jesus' love-
command (verse 27b). Indeed, from the Greek perspective,
the absurdity of this command was too obvious to ignore or
easily explain away. While verse 28 presented the claim that
it is a reasonable ethical position to take, verses 29-30 seem
to serve primarily a pedagogical function by admitting what
would easily be the students' objections to the maxims. The
four imaginary and exaggerated cases (Tannehill, 1975: 67-
77) demonstrate the absurd consequences of Jesus' maxims
when put into practice. They leave one with the question:
Is this sort of thing really what Jesus demands and what
Christian ethics consists of? Indeed it is. Yet the following
section (verses 31-35) will point out that it is not as unrea-

sonable a position as would appear initially. Thus one should
not mistakenly understand these four examples as commands
in themselves. Although they are in fact commands grammatically; they are in reality merely illustrations in an ongoing argument exaggerated by design (Betz, 1995: 595).

Verse 29 contains the first example of beating or striking (*tupto*), a specific act of humiliation, and the proposed
reaction: "If anyone strikes you on the cheek, offer the other
also." The example must have been associated with the following one (verse 29b) even in the earlier tradition, because they appear together in a similar context in Mt 5:39-
40: "But I say to you, Do not resist an evildoer. But if anyone strikes you on the right cheek, turn the other also; and
if anyone wants to sue you and take your coat, give your
cloak as well." In this parallel, however, wording and argumentation are rather different. Some believe that Matthew
has preserved the more original form of the saying (Creed,
1957: 93), but Luke's fondness for the "right" hand/ear (Lk
6:6; 22:50) makes it difficult to think that he would have
suppressed the adjective here, if it were in his source (Fitzmyer,
1981: 638). Eight of the twelve occurrences of *tupto*, "to
strike" in the New Testament are found in Luke-Acts and
the use of this verb may reveal the hand of Luke at work
(Seland, 1995: 278; Mt 5:39 has *rapizo*, "to strike"). The
saying probably refers to an insulting blow, from one who
assails the Christian disciple for his/her allegiance to Christ
(Jeremias, 1963: 28). Far from being a symbol for violence
or evil (to which Jesus then counsels passive nonretaliation
or nonresistance), the slap on the cheek was a *formal insult*,
not a spontaneous act of violence (Perrin, 1967: 147). It
was a serious insult, but there is only insult and "no dam-
age to person" (Daube, 1956: 257). As has been noted, the
head or face is one of the most prominent places on the
"map" of the physical body as symbolic of honor. A physical affront is a challenge to honor, and all the more so if it
is directed to the head (Malina, 1981: 35). Luke is respon-

sible for applying this and the following offenses to acts of violence or compulsion (Piper, 1995: 58).

Luke has made a number of alterations in the Q version. He may have mistaken the striking as armed robbery [*tupto* is used in Homer mostly with weapons of war] and the response as submission: offer the other cheek to be pommeled. Consequently, he drops Matthew's "right" cheek, apparently not recognizing that "right" specifies the type of blow and that it is intended, not as an attack or injury, but as humiliation. Why the right cheek? A blow by the *right* fist in that right-handed world would land on the *left* cheek of the opponent. To hit the right cheek with a fist would require using the left hand, but in that society the left hand was used only for unclean tasks. Even to gesture with the left hand at Qumran carried the penalty of ten days' penance (1QS 7:15; Lapide, 1986: 121). The only way one could naturally strike the right cheek with the right hand would be with the back of the hand. We are dealing here with insult, not a fistfight. The intention is clearly not to injure but to humiliate, to put someone in his or her "place." On did not normally strike a peer thus, and if one did, the fine was exorbitant. A backhand slap was the usual way of admonishing inferiors. In all the examples given, Jesus' listeners were not those who strike, etc., but were their victims. There were among Jesus' listeners people who were subjected to these indignities, forced to stiffle their inner outrage at the dehumanizing treatment meted out to them by the hierarchical system of caste and class, race and gender, age and status. [But, in response, it has been pointed out that the backhanded insult is not necessarily confined to relations between superiors and inferiors. It could have been part of local quarrels and conflicts as well (Horsley, 1992a: 130)].

Why, then does Jesus counsel these already humiliated people to turn the other cheek? Because this action robs the oppressor of the power to humiliate. In a world of honor and shaming, he has been rendered impotent to instill shame in a subordinate (Malina, 1988: 3). He has been stripped of his power to dehumanize the other (Wink, 1992: 104-106).

If we also consider the principle of "focal instance," in which an extreme example is used to cover similar actions up to and including the literal case, then the insulting slap in the face (the formal insult) is the most extreme case envisaged in the saying. Thus, if the content of the saying concerns the insulting slap in the face and other lesser but similar actions, then the context is local village or town interaction (Horsley, 1992: 86-87).

If so insulted, the disciple does not go to court about it but bears the insult and is ready to take more in the spirit of love expected of a follower (Lk 6:27). This injunction and that in verse 30b thus cut through the old principle of retaliation (Ex 21:24; Lev 24:20; Deut 19:21), and this is all that Luke retains of what is found in the fifth Matthean antithesis (Mt 5:38-42; Fitzmyer, 1981: 638). The term *parechein*, "offer, give a gift," found only here in the Sermon on the Plain, is used with purpose. It indicates that the reaction consists of a gift offering, the other cheek. The one who *reacts* in such a way in fact *acts* by asking for a counteroffer of generosity, rather than more violence. To do this is by no means a sign of weakness but one of moral strength. The gesture exposes the act of the offender as what it is: morally repulsive and improper. In addition, it doubles the renunciation of violence by a person insulted; and finally, it challenges the striker to react with comparable generosity. A person who would ignore the gesture and strike again would reveal that person as an uncivilized brute. Thus the turning of the other cheek is a highly provocative challenge demonstrating the law of retaliation in reverse by taking the initiative in accordance with the Golden Rule (Betz, 1995: 290,596; different Strecker, 1988: 83-84).

The second example in verse 29b is constructed in the

same way as the first, except that the reaction is stated negatively: "and from anyone who takes away your coat do not withhold even your shirt." The example occurs also in Mt 5:40 but with a different interpretation. The Sermon on the Mount has a court action in mind (Mt 5:40 envisions a court case in which a creditor has filed suit for the shirt because the coat is exempt from debt service), while the Sermon on the Plain describes a robber who attempts to "take away" by force a person's coat. Instead of trying to prevent the robbery, the victim is told to hand over his shirt as well. According to the Torah (Ex 22:25-26; Deut 24:10-13; cf. Amos 2:8), "If you take your neighbor's cloak in pawn, you shall restore it before the sun goes down; for it may be your neighbor's only clothing to use as cover; in what else shall that person sleep?" Only the poorest of the poor would have nothing but a garment to give as a collateral for a loan. Jewish law strictly required its return every evening at sunset. The rights of the poor debtor were thus to some extent protected by Scripture. On the other hand, the creditor was permitted to harrass and shame the debtor by demanding the outer garment each morning. The *Mekilta de R. Ishmael* on Ex 22:25-27 shows creditors intensifying their demand by taking a night garment by day and a day garment by night (Wink, 1992: 119 note 16). The Torah thus covered the outer garment (cloak, *himation*), but not the undergarment (*chitōn*).

Why then does Jesus counsel the poor to give over their undergarment as well? This would mean stripping off all their clothing and marching out of court stark naked! Imagine the hilarity this statement must have evoked. There stands the creditor, covered with shame, the poor debtor's garment in the one hand, his undergarment in the other. The tables have suddenly been turned on the creditor. The debtor had no hope of winning the case; the law was entirely in the creditor's favor. But the poor man has transcended this attempt to humiliate him. He has risen above shame. At the same time, he has registered a stunning protest against a system that spawns such debt (Wink, 1992: 106-107).

For Luke who seems to think rather of robbery (Bock, 1994: 592-593) the whole episode resembles an absurd exchange of gifts, as in the previous example. The paradoxical reaction of the victim counters the violence by making a gift, no doubt a challenge to respond in kind. This response is the method of Christian ethics, not, as some may surmise, going naked! (Marshall, 1978: 261; Betz, 1995: 597). The point is that Jesus' ethical demand is strong, comprehensive, and serious (Bock, 1994: 594-595).

The third example (verse 30a) changes from specificity (verse 29a a-b) to generality: "Give to everyone who begs from you." "Every one" is more properly to be rendered as "any one." "Everyone" is not found in the parallel, Mt 5:42, and intensifies the command (Nolland, 1989: 296-297; Stein, 1992: 208). This verse anticipates the discussion on motivation for lending (Lk 6:34-35; Danker, 1988: 145). The same example is found in Mt 5:42a, and it is attested as well in other passages. The situation envisages a beggar who stretches out his hand. It has always been both common expectation and common habit not to pass by such a person, but to give him something. The recommendation, therefore, conforms to ancient morality, and especially to the whole complex of ideas and attitudes associated with giving and receiving (see, e.g., 2 Cor 9:7, "God loves a cheerful giver"), which is in turn related to the Golden Rule (verse 31). Absurdity enters the picture, however, when the demand is made that one give to *every* petitioner. The position of "every" (*panti*) at the beginning of the statement is underlining its importance. No amount is specified, but the assumption can only be (see verse 38 below) that it should be a generous gift. Whoever follows this advice will soon run out of things to give. Will such a giver not soon become the victim of cleverness, deception, and greediness on the part of petitioners? Will such a person not soon have

to go begging himself, as is the case with the main character of Lucian's *Timon the Misanthrope*? Or, to raise another
question, What can one give if one owns nothing that can
be given (compare Acts 3:6)? Is this obvious foolishness all
that Christian ethics demands? Indeed, it is, but as the ensuing discussion will reveal, the demand is not as unreasonable as it would appear (Betz, 1995: 597-598). [For practical considerations about how much to give see Mt 6:3; Lk
19:8; Acts 5:1-10; 2 Cor 8:11-12.] That these exhortations
do "not fit the topic of nonretaliation very well" (Furnish,
1972: 56) indicates that nonretaliation is not the subject of
the passage as a whole.

The fourth example (verse 30b), seemingly more violent than the third, is also general in nature: "and is anyone takes away your goods, do not ask for them again." But
the phrase "takes away" does not necessarily refer to force.
In view of the succeeding remarks (verses 32-35) that express the principle behind these statements in verses 27-30
and include words about lending, it is possible that Luke
had borrowing in mind. Lk 6:29, then, describes disciples
as debtors, and verse 30 views them as creditors. Mt 5:42b
contains a similar example but it is formulated very differently: "Do not refuse anyone who wants to borrow from you."
In the Sermon on the Plain, the fourth example is con-
joined with the second in verse 29b by catchword (e.g., "to
take away"), showing that all four examples are connected
by similar terms ("offer" [verse 29a], "not withhold" [verse
29b]. "not ask again" [verse 30b]). The Greek term behind
the phrase "Do not ask for them again" is a commercial
expression applied to one who makes demand for payment
and should be rendered: "Don't press continually for payment." That is, the disciple is not to dun the poor debtor
in the manner of the creditor described in Sir 20:15: "Today he lends and tomorrow he asks it back" (Danker, 1988:
146).

In Lk 6:30b, Luke may have a situation of theft in mind

(Fitzmyer, 1981: 639; Stein, 1992: 207). In the more original wording (Mt 5:42), the sayings are straightforward exhortations to give one who begs and to loan to one who seeks to borrow. The exhortation to lend is repeated in Lk 6:34 and 35a. It thus has a certain prominence in the passage as a whole, at least in Luke, and perhaps in Q as well (depending on one's reconstruction). The context and the content of the sayings clearly presuppose local social-economic relationships (Horsley, 1992: 87).

Compared to verse 30a, verse 30b presents the opposite case: if verse 30a has as the focal person a servile beggar, verse 30b shows a brutal expropriator. The recommended reaction assumes the victim is somehow in a position to recover the stolen goods [the verb *apaiteō* means "demand something back"]. Yet he is advised to forego this chance for recovery, thereby turning the theft into a generous gift. Is this cheerful indifference to one's property the demand of Christian ethics? Apparently so, but the Sermon on the Plain does not advocate lack of responsibility. The intended meaning is that by giving up the chance of retrieval, the victim takes the initiative and offers a generous gift to the offender, no doubt expecting the perpetrator to respond in kind (Betz, 1995: 598-599).

Jesus' command to love the enemy cannot be reduced to an inner disposition that requires no concrete deeds. This love cannot be a private affair. Its effects must reach to the society structure of the state, to international relations. There can be no talk of a compromise that would interfere with the radicalness of Jesus' command. Every deficiency in this area is ethically reprehensible, unchristian, sinful. What Jesus requires is unconditional love for fellow humans. As soon, however, as my nonviolence itself becomes the cause of injustice to someone other than the enemy, as soon as a hostile deed against myself or society threatens a third person, it is then not excluded that the intent of Jesus might best be reached (paradoxically) by the use of resistance and, if needed, counterviolence. But we should warn against the ease with which people with good intentions can be swept up in delusions and slide into violence (Lambrecht, 1987: 301-302).

Verse 31:   Do to others as you would have them do to you.

Matthew has this statement later in the Sermon (Mt 7:12) and ties it specifically to the Law and the Prophets (Bock, 1994: 595). Since the eighteenth (Fitzmyer, 1981: 639; Guelich, 1982: 360) and maybe even the sixteenth century (Bovon, 1991: 314-315 note 64), the sentence in Mt 7:12 and Lk 6:31 has been called "The Golden Rule," golden in the sense of most precious and important. Indeed, the Golden Rule was regarded as one of the ground rules of human civilization, its truth being beyond questioning. This wide acceptance was not limited to Christian tradition. In the West, the Golden Rule is first attested by Herodotus; and in the East, Confucius knew it (see Bock, 1994: 596-597).

The sentence is transmitted in various forms. It can be stated positively, "Do to others what you would have them do to you!" or negatively, "Do not do to others what you would not want them to do to you!" Is there a difference between the positive and the negative formulation of the Rule? If there is, what is the difference?

It is commonly assumed that the two forms differ significantly in that the positive form prescribes an initiative and substantial contribution, while the negative form implies mere abstention without initiative and contribution. Others have argued, however, that the difference is simply a matter of formulation, not substance; one can state a wish or desire positively or negatively without changing the basic meaning. Thus, the difference between positive and negative would amount to no more than rhetoric or preference (Singer, 1963, 293-294). But more than rhetoric or personal preference seems to be involved.

The question may be raised whether the Golden Rule

is, strictly speaking, a *principle* that stands on its own terms,
or a *maxim* that is in turn based on other principles. According to many ancient and modern philosophers, one cannot regard the Golden Rule as a self-evident principle of
ethics (Betz, 1995: 509-510). [Augustine called it a "common proverb," and Kant dismissed it as "trivial"!]. The negative
form permitted the priest and the Levite to pass by the
wounded person (Lk 10:29-37). On the other hand, even
the positive form does not encompass the possibilities of
creative moral action. For I may do to another what I would
wish for myself, but my need may not be the other's need,
nor my interest the other's interest. Most people do in fact
live by the Golden Rule: "I want to be left alone, so I leave
others alone." Therefore, unless one has the motivation of
the "poor" (Lk 6:20), even the Golden Rule can become
an instrument of self-congratulation and selfish morality. What
Jesus himself understands by the rule is shockingly radical,
and verses 32-35 cancel out most of those who crowd in to
espouse it on a shallow prudential level (Danker, 1988: 146-
147).

  After the important studies of Albrecht Dihle (1962)
and Hans Reiner (1974), Paul Ricoeur (1990: 392-397) has
presented a new interpretation of the Golden Rule. His
interpretation is part of a comprehensive theory of ethics,
which defines philosophical ethics as responsible action in
a field of tension constituted by the metaphorical poetics
of love, on the one side, and the formality of the law, on
the other side. Ricoeur argues against Dihle when he sees
the Golden Rule as open to two interpretations, one ego-
tistical/utilitarian and another altruistic/nonutilitarian. For
this concept of ethics he prefers the latter, nonutilitarian,
interpretation. In his view it is based on the love-command
of Jesus. As such the love-command is not without its presuppositions but is based, in Ricoeur's terms, on an "economy
of abundance." This "economy of abundance" is a "supra-
ethical," cosmic, and quasi-theological process, by which

human beings experience life in its totality as an abundant gift requiring a concurrent response of generosity. This "economy of abundance," while itself not a principle, can be summed up in the form of a principle. Against Dihle, Ricoeur further argues that one must not understand Jesus' love-command as an abrogation of the Golden Rule. Rather, the love-command is a corrective, to which the Golden Rule is made to conform. Thus, one must interpret the Golden Rule in accordance with the "economy of abundance." As a result, ethical action originates in real-life situations that occur in the midst of the "logic of abundance" and the "logic of the exchange of gifts." Such ethical action can, therefore, justify the requirements of justice and at the same time engage in the "poetics of love." Love must not be confused with ethics, according to Ricoeur, but the "poetics of love" is indispensable for any formation of ethical action.

Ricoeur regards the Golden Rule as expressing the logic of equivalence and human reciprocity, and thus in creative tension with the logic of superabundance expressed in the command to love one's enemies (Lk 6:35; Mt 5:44) that arose from an economy of gift and from a reverence to God. But there is a logic of excess where love is at work in ethical solicitude that allows one to place oneself in the place of the other. The solidarity implied by the Golden Rule creates a dynamism that can go beyond the demands of justice. The Golden Rule is the place where God hides and at the same time appears in ethical spontaneity of the human conscience (Theobald, 1995: 43-59).

There seems to be no reason to rule out the hypothesis that Jesus appropriated the Golden Rule in its positive version from the tradition. Furthermore, one can have no real doubt that the Rule was a constitutive part of his teaching; a number of independent witnesses affirm it (Betz, 1995: 515-516). Even when one grants this point, however, one must still examine the interpretation of the Golden Rule in the Sermon on the Plain.

After the serious questioning of Jesus' commands (verses 27-28) in verses 29-30, a positive argument begins to demonstrate their reasonableness. This positive argument first explains the ethical principles underlying Jesus' way of thinking, beginning with the statement of the Golden Rule. The argument assumes, therefore, that this principle underlies Jesus' commands (verses 27-28) as well as their subsequent discussion. This assumption is far from evident, however, especially since the Golden Rule can be, and often is, misunderstood. Therefore, to facilitate a proper understanding, a commentary on the Golden Rule is supplied in Lk 6:32-35.

Like Mt 7:12, the Sermon on the Plain also cites the Golden Rule in its positive form. But there are important differences. Textual examination indicates that: (1) Lk 6:31 has no parallel to Mt 7:12c: "For this is the law and the prophets." The omission implies that the Sermon on the Plain as a whole shows no interest in matters of Jewish law. (2) While the Sermon on the Mount is primarily concerned with the justification of the ethics of Jesus by obedience to the Torah, the Sermon on the Plain focuses on personal attitudes (Schürmann, 1969: 350 note 55). (3) The use of "all" (*panta*), typically emphasized in the Sermon on the Mount, is given somewhat less emphasis in the Sermon on the Plain. *Pas* occurs four times in Lk 6:20-49 as compared to sixteen times in the Sermon on the Mount.

These differences indicate that for the Sermon on the Plain, the Golden Rule serves as an ethical principle, the truth of which is self-evident and not in need of support by authorities such as "the law and the prophets." It functions in the Sermon on the Plain as it usually functions in Greek ethical discussions. The parallels and the differences between the Sermon on the Mount and the Sermon on the Plain demonstrate how the ethics of Jesus could be negotiated simultaneously within the cultural and religious contexts of both Jewish and Gentile Christianity. Verse 31a insinuates that the Christians wish to be treated in a friendly manner by the outsiders, called here "people" (*hoi anthropoi*; Schürmann, 1969: 351; Merklein, 1978: 244-245), while verse 31b recommends taking the initiative and treating "people" in just that friendly way (Betz, 1995: 599). Jesus' commands are reasonable because one can understand them properly in the light of the Golden Rule, a principle widely accepted in antiquity (Schürmann, 1969: 350-352; Betz, 1995: 600).

Verse 32-34: (32) If you love those who love you,
what credit is that to you?
For even sinners love those who love them.
(33) If you do good to those who do good to you,
what credit is that to you?
for even sinners do the same.
(34) If you lend to those from whom you hope to receive,
what credit is that to you?
Even sinners lend to sinners, to receive as much again.

In the three following illustrations of Lk 6:32-34, Jesus uses negative examples to show that the disciples' love is to be different from the "sinner's" love (Bock, 1994: 598). More specifically, in these verses Luke explores the heart of the Greco-Roman reciprocity system. Jesus challenges his hearers to transcend reciprocal love, "doing good," and so forth. Mt 5:46 may well reproduce the more original wording from Q; "sinners" occurs often in Luke, and Matthew has the term only where clearly following Q or Mark. But the "gentiles" in Mt 5:47 is clearly a distinctive Matthean term, occurring elsewhere only in another Sermon on the Mount text (Mt 6:7) and in the church-discipline discourse (Mt 18:17). Thus it is only Matthew who uses non-Jews (outsiders) as a contrast for the transreciprocal relations Jesus is calling for. In Luke and Q the sayings draw their comparison and contrast within the broader Jewish community (with "sinners" and/or "toll collectors"). And, in the case of either "sinners" or "toll collectors," the contrast is drawn from people with whom the hearers would have been familiar in their local communities (Horsley, 1992: 87-88).

The commentary on the Golden Rule begins with a refutation of its misinterpretation (Lk 6:32-34). This refutation consists of three rhetorical questions, each followed by an implicit answer. The three arguments are remarkably Greek in nature. Their logic is that of Hellenistic moral discussions on benevolence (*charis*; van Unnik, 1966: 284-300).

The first question considers the notion of love (*agapan*, Lk 6:27b) as it is conventionally understood — and misunderstood: "If you love those who love you, what credit is that to you?" What is stated here as a hypothetical assumption is in fact a misunderstanding of the Christian concept of *agape* as an exchange of favors. Greek ethics did understand love and friendship in terms of an exchange of favors; but the Greeks construed the granting of such favors merely as responses to favors received to be false love and friendship, as for instance, stated by Plato in his *Symposion*. True love and friendship do not wait for another to act and do not cease, even when rejected (Rom 5:8,10; 1Cor 13:4-7; 2Cor 12:15b; Gal 4:12-20). The question of verse 32b, "What credit is that to you?" (repeated in verses 33 and 34) must, therefore, be answered: "None." That the credit is established with people, not with God, disqualifies the exchange of favors from being an adequate definition of love (*agape*; Schurmann, 1969: 353; Betz, 1995:600-601). The proof of the argument is derived from life experience: "For even sinners love those who love them" (Lk 6:32c). Indeed, sinners — even criminals [a possible meaning of *amartolos*] — exchange favors; in their own way, they love who love them. The practice described in verse 32c is not only common but also non-Christian. It is thereby disqualified from having any value for Christian ethics, or, indeed, for ethics in general (Betz, 1995: 601).

The second rhetorical question is constructed parallel to the first (verse 32) but with significant differences. Conspicuous is the change of the verbs in verse 33a: "If you do good to those who do good to you, what credit is that to you?" The change of the verb from "love" to "do good" (*agathopoiein*) parallels the similar change of the same verb in Jesus' commandment in Lk 6:27b to "do good" (*agathopoiein*), which is a common term in Hellenistic ethical texts. The Sermon on the Plain uses it only here and in verse 35; the Sermon on the Mount does not use it at all, while elsewhere in the New Testament it is prominent in passages showing heavy Hellenistic influence (Lk 6:9; Acts 14:17, etc.). "To do good" referred in ancient society primarily to conferral of some private or public benefit. The remarkable feature in Luke's account is Jesus' acute exposure of the broad application of the system in its crasser forms, especially in the private sector. Verses 32-34 cut through the bargaining system that characterizes much of substandard ethics: Do good to those who can return the favor. "He never did anything for me" is a complaint often heard (Danker, 1988: 147-148). The argument reported is parallel to that in verse 32, but the change of verb leads to a change as well in the statement in verse 33c: "For even sinners (criminals) do the same." If sinners and criminals do good toward each other, the very meaning of the term "good" is lost. In this sense verse 33 goes beyond verse 32 in that now the self-contradiction is evident.

While the first two questions verses 32a, 33a) are of a general nature, the last one (verse 34a) considers a specific case, the lending of money: "If you lend [money] to those from whom you hope to receive [it back], what credit is that to you?" The basic argument is the same as that of the previous two questions, but there are some fine points of difference. Formally, the identity of the verbs in the description of mutuality is given up. Regarding content, there is a sudden turn to a specific issue. Doubtless this turn is planned, probably for pedagogical reasons, because it keeps the reader alert (Black, 1967: 137-138).

Nevertheless, the question remains: Why is the issue of

moneylending brought in at this point? Moneylending was certainly a widely discussed issue at the time, both in Judaism and in Hellenistic ethics. The change of topic to the issue of moneylending may be suggested by the previous questions, especially that of verse 33. If the exchange of favors exists even among "sinners," such exchanges are business operations. All commerce amounts to an exchange of goods. There is no better demonstration of commerce than the process of lending money. The main reason for introducing the issue of moneylending here is that it has traditionally been connected with the topic of commerce, both in Judaism (Ex 22:25; Lev 25:35-38; Deut 15:2-6; 23:19-20; 24:10, etc.) and in Greek ethics. Luke has joined here the saying concerning lending not only to supplement a forgotten topic but because it is somewhat akin in the Greek context. Lending for the purpose of getting a return is good business practice; lending without requiring a return is benevolence. One should note that verse 34 does not criticize the lending of money in itself as ethically objectionable; it simply describes the process.

The evidence stated in verse 34b makes yet another point: "Even sinners lend to sinners, to receive as much again." The point does not appear to be the taking of interest as a moral issue, but the equivalency of the exchange, so that "as much" or "the equal amount" must refer to the sum of money the lender hopes to regain [For the most important interpretations of this statement, see Bock, 1994: 601]. The implication is that in the lending of money, one does nothing to another person that one can ethically call "love" or "doing good." Nothing is given to or bestowed on the other person, and there is no exchange of favors as is constitutive of love or friendship. The lending of money is simply a business transaction, enacted out of self-interest; it is not an exchange of anything. Thus it is a grave misunderstanding to confuse such business transactions with compliance to the Golden Rule (Betz, 1995: 602-604).

Verse 35:   But love your enemies,
              do good, and lend, expecting nothing in return.
              Your reward will be great,
              and you will be children of the Most High;
              for he is kind to the ungrateful and the wicked.

This verse summarizes the preceding discussion (Bock, 1994: 602). After refuting the incorrect understanding of the Golden Rule (Lk 6:31) and its misapplication to the commandment of Jesus (Lk 6:27), the commentary moves to the presentation of the correct understanding. This highly condensed argument is made in two parts. First, a set of three imperatives restates Jesus' commandment, now including the important interpretation (verse 35b-c), for which a theological rationale is provided (verse 35d). Verse 36 then presents the conclusion to the entire argument of Lk 6:27-35.

In verse 35a, the turning point is marked by "but (*plen*): "But love your enemies, do good, and lend expecting nothing in return." The three imperatives employ the same verbs as do verses 32-34; they are formulated positively, the first and the second being general, the third, specific. The restatement of Jesus' commands takes into account the Golden Rule, properly understood, and affirms them as conforming to that Rule (Marshall, 1978: 263-264).

The critical difference from verse 34 is expressed by the additional phrase "expecting nothing in return" [a phrase which presents text-critical and lexicographical problems; Betz, 1995: 604-605]. But is reference being made here to general benevolence or to a specific prohibition of taking interest on loans, or the practice of usury? To answer this question, one should first of all consider the general context of ethics and also be aware of the issues of law and business as they were practiced in antiquity and later times (see Betz, 1995: 605-609). The renunciation of return in Lk 6:35 is not an expression of "pure altruism." Rarther, it is part of a doctrine of reward that is Jewish in origin. Forgoing a reward in this world is justified in that it preserves the reward for the world to come. The argument is thus similar to that in the Sermon on the Mount, especially Mt 6:1-6,16-18, which states that since one can claim reward and suffer punishment for a deed only once, forgoing such claims in this life establishes the "right" to them in the world to come. Therefore verse 35b-c constitutes not two superfluous promises but an integral part of the argument. The only remarkable thing is that this doctrine, Jewish in nature, is being applied to Gentile Christians.

The first of the promises reads "Your reward will be great" (Lk 6:35b). The text does not spell out the details of the reward, and the silence is powerfully suggestive. Luke's auditors bring to the text their understanding that the Supreme Benefactor's award will certainly outweigh anything that an earthly benefactor might be able to offer (Danker, 1988: 151).

The second promise does not appear to be a separate promise in content: "and you will be children of the Most High" (Lk 6:35c; Guelich, 1982: 96; Schweizer, 1984: 124; differently, Bock, 1994: 602). This promise is known from Mt 5:9b,45a, and seems to come from older Jewish tradition. Again, the surprising thing here is that the promise is made to Gentiles. If such a promise is made here, then, it reflects an older doctrine of the Church rather than later Lukan redaction (Schurmann, 1969: 355; Marshall, 1978: 264-265). Verse 35d offers the soteriological reason for granting the reward to the Gentiles: "for he is kind to the ungrateful and the wicked." Divine benevolence stands in stark contrast to human failure to respond in kind. Disciples who love their enemies visibly demonstrate their pedigree to the Father. In Judaism, a relationship with God was seen as a privilege of members of the divine era (Schurmann, 1969: 355 note 94; Danker 1988: 149). For the early Church, love was seen as a mark of that relationship (1 Jn 3:1; 4:7-12; Fitzmyer, 1981: 640; Bock, 1994; 603).

What does all this mean for the Sermon on the Plain?

In sum, the difference between common behavior and Christian ethos is that the former merely reacts to favors received while the latter takes an initiative, acting first. The Christian can be generous because God deals with humankind, especially with the ungrateful and the wicked, with the same generosity. Moreover, since such spontaneous conduct imitates the divine philanthropy, the Christian is promised a great reward in heaven.

The result of the whole argument thus far is that Jesus' love-command (Lk 6:27b), if properly interpreted by the Golden Rule (Lk 6:31), corresponds to God's philanthropy. God also loves his enemies and does not expect anything in return. The proper ethical conduct for the Christian can therefore only be to imitate God in his philanthropy. This point basically concludes the argument in Lk 6:27-35. Jesus' command to love the enemy has been shown to be by no means stupid or absurd but in conformity with the basic idea of Hellenistic religion and morality (Betz, 1995: 610-612).

Verse 36:   Be merciful, just as your Father is merciful.

Luke's "merciful" is surely closer to Q than Matthew's "perfect" (compare Mt 19:21). But opinions remain divided on the relationship between the two (Schürmann, 1969: 360 note 119; Bock, 1994: 605). Luke's concluding summary follows the form found in Lev 19:2. As the concluding exhortations, both terms "be merciful" and "be perfect," in imitation of God, however, indicate that the context of the whole group of sayings is the covenant people who are called to practice justice in imitation of God's justice (Horsley, 1992: 88; Stein, 1992: 209).

Some link verse 36 with what follows and others with what precedes. The latter is to be preferred (Nolland, 1989: 300). Verse 36 is a hinge verse (Fitzmyer, 1981: 640-641; Danker, 1988:151) but the emphasis goes backward (Bock, 1994: 587). The statement concluding the section Lk 6:32-

36 is a maxim. The imperative of verse 36a, "be merciful" (*ginesthai oiktirmones*) is formulated as a periphrastic construction of *ginomai* with the present participle, denoting "the beginning of a state or condition." The motivation or the command follows in the second clause, where "just as" resumes the idea of verse 35d and now states expressly the concept of the imitation of God (Schürmann, 1969: 358-359; Zeller, 1977: 110-113). The Golden Rule of "do as you would want done" is not the ultimate norm here, but rather, "do as God would do" (Johnson, 1991: 112). Where in verse 35 to be a child of God is the goal of one's actions, in verse 36 having God as Father is the starting point from which imitation proceeds (Nolland, 1989: 300).

The imperative is based on the premise that the Father is merciful. This theological doctrine is presupposed as well known and acceptable. It must have been prominent in the circles where the Sermon on the Plain originated, but one should also note the close parallels in Jas 5:11, "...how the Lord is compassionate and merciful," in the letters of Paul (Rom 9:15; 2Cor 1:3, etc.), and in Eph 4:32-5:1, which has developed it in a new form of Deutero-Pauline theology. It is likely that the historical Jesus also held this *theologoumenon*, and this not only because it was generally Jewish (see, e.g., Mt 18:23-35). It is prominent in the Sermon on the Plain because the mercifulness of the deity was also a generally recognized element of Hellenistic religiosity. We have here another instance in the Sermon on the Plain explaining the teaching of Jesus in Hellenistic terms, whereas the Sermon on the Mount couches the same teaching in Jewish terms (Schürmann, 1969: 356 note 99). Verse 35, though not repudiated, is superseded by the motivation in verse 36: not heavenly reward but imitation of God is the higher and more important doctrine motivating Christian ethics (Betz, 1995: 612-614).

Those existential interpretations of the love command and the call to nonviolence that center on what goes on internally in the heart of the one who loves do not do justice to the text. Indeed, we should be wary of a form of pacifism that is more concerned with the purity of the pacifist than winning justice for the oppressed. We are not disposed to take Jesus' teachings as a law that says a follower "cannot" engage in violence, though we cannot really get away from Jesus' nonviolence as in some sense normative either. We believe that we cannot be delivered from having to discern the will of God for our own unique modern situations and that Jesus' teaching cannot be simply transferred to our problems today in an unmediated way (Wink, 1992a: 133).

What does do justice to the text is the view that the Christian is really looking to the effect that nonviolence will have in the heart of the enemy. This sees love of the enemy as a concrete social event (Schürmann, 1969: 344,349; Schottroff, 1978: 12). One should note, however, that this is not a universally applicable ethical rule, but the attitude expected of Christians when they encounter resistance. It can be practiced only by the weak toward the strong. Only those involved in resistance of the weak toward the strong can preach or demand it. When it is recommended or imposed from outside, it is perverted into a demand to give up resistance (Schottroff, 1978: 13; Helgeland, 1985: 14).).

This understanding of love of enemy can be verified as a valid interpretation of Lk 6:27–36. But if love of enemy is not passive, but rather an active seeking to convert the enemy, to turn evil into good, how can we explain it in relation to the clear prohibition of resistance in Lk 6:29? Why is resistance forbidden and active love of enemy enjoined? To see this merely or primarily as an attack on the zealot position does not make much sense chronologically. But there are clear political implications in this. To see what they might be requires one to see the call both to renounce resistance to evil *and* actively to love the enemy in the context of the ways in which antiquity conceived "loving one's enemy."

In non-Christian antiquity, one can find at least three somewhat parallel situations and themes. There is the renunciation of revenge by the powerful. Whether motivated by magnanimity or political expediency, this reflects a situation fundamentally different from that of the early Christians. Then there is the philosopher's (e.g., Socrates) nonviolent protest or acceptance of abuse in order to proclaim the rottenness of society. This is obviously not what is going on in the Gospels. Finally there are the attitudes and reactions of the powerless underdog. This does fit the situation of the early Christians. Yet no early Christian source discusses and explicitly treats the situation of dependence that gave Christians no other option but to submit to injustice peaceably. Thus the question, on this level, remains open: Is this a universal ethic for everyone, or only for Christians in a similar situation of powerlessness? This is obviously a key question for Christians attempting to form their attitudes and consciences on issues regarding nonviolence and the use of force, pacifism, and military service. But it is also a question that might never be raised if one were not alert to the concrete social situation of the original human authors and audience of these texts.

Analyzing the matter further, one discovers that at all levels of the New Testament tradition loving "your enemies" and doing good to "those who persecute you" are understood in an active, even aggressive, sense of a missionary attitude toward enemy and persecutor. It is an appeal to bring enemy and persecutor into the Christian fold (cf. Rom 12:21; Schottroff, 1978: 23). Whether the identification of enemies with persecutors goes back to the historical Jesus cannot be determined. But in any case, the clear meaning of Jesus' teaching, as found in all levels of the New Testament tradition, is that we should love our enemies, that is, strive to make them our brothers and sisters in the Lord. This gives the love commandment a public and implicitly political dimension because it explicitly refers to the identity of social groups (Schottroff, 1978: 25; Helgeland, 1985: 15).

But at this point biblical exegesis leaves us at an impasse, unable to explain how an aggressively active love can be consistent with a passive, nonviolent acceptance of injustice. It seems that we must, as Schottroff suggests, go beyond exegesis to find an answer to this question. We are not going against exegetical evidence, but simply going beyond what exegesis can clearly prove, one way or another, when we see nonresistance in these texts as applying specifically and concretely in an area of politics, especially insurrectional or revolutionary politics. Christians are not revolutionaries, but they do resist evil. The prohibition is not a fundamental rejection of every type of resistance. In fact, as Tertullian put it, Christians are, precisely because they are Christians, factors of resistance in society (*Apology*, 37; cf, Schottroff, 1978: 27). They resist injustice, driven by an aggressively missionary love that impels them to try to bring all, including the persecuting enemy, into the fold of Christ.

If this is so, it relativizes somewhat the New Testament call to nonviolence and its modern political counterpart, pacifism. It locates the absolute, nonnegotiable center of the Christian message in the positive call to love and not in its negative counterpart and normal mode of realization, nonviolence. This does not imply, for example, that the just-war theory is equally well grounded in the New Testament as is nonviolence. But it does suggest that one cannot assume that any attempt to observe the love command which does not live up to the ideals of nonviolence is a betrayal of the Gospel (Helgeland, 1985: 15-16).

We believe that the demands of nonviolence and nonresistance in Lk 6:27-36 do not prevent us at the end of the second millennium from asking the question whether the principle of Christian love cannot lead to the decision of a justified rebellion of the exploited against structures that are created to perpetuate oppression and exploitation, provided that they are not inspired by hatred or revenge (Linskens, 1983: 24). A good example of such enterprise are the events in recent years in South Africa.

Verses 37-38: (37) Do not judge, and you will not be judged;
                    do not condemn, and you will not be
                    condemned.
                    Forgive, and you will be forgiven;
            (38)   give, and it will be given to you.
                    A good measure, pressed down, shaken
                    together, running over.
                    will be put into your lap;
                    for the measure you give, will be the measure
                    you get back.

In verses 37-38 we move beyond what is strictly the theme of love of enemies. These verses have, however, been introduced at this point because the starting point for their exhortations is a recognition of the merciful ways of God. There is thus an easy transition from verses 35-36 (Nolland, 1989: 300). Verses 37-38 present a set of sentences (*sententiae*): four parallel maxims which in a real sense need to be taken together (verses 37-38a ; Bock 1994: 605), a gnomic saying on measure (verse 38b), and a concluding maxim (verse 38c). Verses 37-38 introduce traditional paraenesis for which the preceding sections have prepared us. The four parallel maxims, verses 37-38a, explicate concretely what it means to love the enemy and to be merciful in situations of judging, condemning, setting free, and giving. All four are formulated as paradoxes, but the reader who has understood the argument presented in Lk 6:27-36 will now be able to clarify them. One will recognize all four maxims as applications of the Golden Rule (verse 31), correctly understood (verses 32-35); one will see in their implementation the imitation of God's treatment of humankind (verse 36). The passage, Lk 6:37-38, is thus another part of the interprtetation of Jesus' love-command (Schürmann, 1969: 359; Stein, 1992: 211; Betz, 1995: 614).

In the carefully composed verses 37-38a, the four sentences are arranged as two sets of parallel lines. The first of the couplets (verse 37a and b) begins each maxim with a negative prohibitive imperative, which is then followed by an emphatic denial. The second couplet (verses 37c and 38a) gives positive commands, in asyndetic form, followed by predictions in the future tense connected only by "and."

Verse 37a presents the first maxim: "Do not judge, and you will not be judged." The imperative "judge not" proposes the appropriate action: it recommends the opposite of common practice. One should understand the term *krinō* ("judge") here in its general sense as "passing judgment" on another. The theme is traditional in moral exhortation, based on the observation that people constantly pass judgment on one another and that this practice destroys human relationships (Betz, 1995: 615). The kind of judgment one passes on others comes back to the person who started it. The prudent person, so goes the advice, will break the vicious cycle by withholding such judgment because the same mechanism will work in the reverse direction as well. Restraint will motivate others to exercise equal restraint. In fact, the use of the present imperative in this and the next prohibition can better be translated "stop judging" and suggests that the readers stop what they are presently doing, rather than that they should guard themselves against ever doing this sometime in the future (Stein, 1992: 211).

This reciprocity implies that the verb *krinein*, "pass judgment," is taken as negative and destructive conduct. The context clearly implies that *krinein* refers to the perpetual human obsession to criticize and correct the behavior of other people, in particular those with whom one is closely associated. What is wrong with passing judgment in this manner? It is true that human conduct inevitably involves taking the measure of each other; in this way human society establishes place, rank, affiliation, and rewards. This all-penetrating activity is the way human beings identify themselves and their place in family, group, and society. This activity is acknowledged by the saying, but it is not condemned; it is observed as part of life.

What is criticized, then, is the degeneration of this process. This happens when a person denigrates another by harsh and unfair criticism, with a lack of sympathy and understanding. In doing so, people put themselves into the role of judges, working themselves up into a position of "holier than thou" (cf. Lk 15:25-32; 18:9-14). Once one gets into this mold, pedantry and self-righteousness become the norm. Self-righteoussness, lack of mercy and compassion, and antisocial destructiveness are attitudes that are incompatible with the ethics of the Sermon (Betz, 1995: 490-491). Faultfinding is a mark of the mean-spirited person and ill befits a person who aspires to the extraordinary excellence portrayed in the Sermon on the Plain (Danker, 1988: 151; Stein, 1992: 211).

The second maxim follows strictly parallel to the first, but its force is climactic: "Do not condemn, and you will not be condemned" (Lk 6:37b). It suggests that censoriousness necessarily leads to condemnation. The parallel in Jas 5:6 continues the logic: "You have condemned and murdered the righteous one."

The second parallelism is postively formulated. The first line (verse 37c) commands an act that appears to be the opposite of condemning, namely, setting free: "Forgive, and you will be forgiven." The meaning of *apoluo* is not immediately clear. Does it refer to the freeing of prisoners or to the forgiving of debts? If it refers to the latter — the more likely meaning — then the parable of the Unforgiving Servant (Mt 18:23-35) offers the strongest illustration, especially verse 27: "And out of pity for him, the lord of that slave released him and forgave him the debt." Was this parable designed to explicate this interpretation of Lk 6:37c in narrative form? (Betz, 1995: 616). The two commands, "forgive...give," are also present imperatives and thus emphasize that forgiving and giving are seen as actions that are to be done continually (Stein, 1992: 211). In living this way one is not to pretend that another person is innocent when he or she is guilty; but rather one is not to hold an action permanently against that other person (Schürmann, 1969: 361 note 127; Bock, 1994: 607).

The last of the four maxims (Lk 6:38a) is climactic, turning from "letting go" to the more active "giving": "Give, and it will be given to you." We mentioned the topic of giving in verse 30; we note now that the ethical context of the entire text consistently is giving and receiving (Mott, 1975: 60-72). The fourth maxim, however, presents the act of giving as the culmination of Jesus' teaching as explained through the Golden Rule (Lk 6:31). In that context, all of Christian ethics is a form of giving. The imagery relates to the oriental grain market. Grain is measured out to overflowing in order to ensure the purchaser a full measure (Danker, 1988: 152).

The saying in verse 38b is extraordinary for several reasons. Its literal translation reads: "Good measure, pressed down, shaken together, overflowing — they will give (it) into your lap." The first part of the sentence presents a word picture of the good measure, followed in the second part by a rather puzzling predication. The vivid image, almost a still life of the measure of grain, is conveyed by three perfect participles, none attested elsewhere in the New Testament. The image represents generosity and abundance beyond measure (Klostermann, 1975: 83). Although the concluding part of the sentence undeniably breathes action into the still life, the subject of the verb *dosousin* ("they give") is unclear. Who are "they"? Are "they" generally "people," or is the word a reference to God, as many commentators assume? (Grundmann, 1966: 150-151; Schürmann, 1969: 362-363; Fitzmyer, 1981: 626, 641; Stein, 1992: 212). We would suggest that the people who give have first received the full measure from God before offering it to another (Betz, 1995: 618).

The concluding maxim states the principle underlying the whole set of sentences (*sententiae*, verses 37-38): "For the measure you give will be the measure you get back." Even a cursory examinatioin indicatres the close relationship of this principle to the Golden Rule: the Golden Rule states a general ethical principle while verse 38c considers the narrower focus of the exchange of gifts. Verse 31 establishes the acts appropriate to the daily conduct of human life; verse 38c describes actual situations surrounding the issue of giving and receiving.

In conclusion, one can see that in its entirety, the argument (verses 27-38) has demonstrated that Jesus' commandment to love enemies conforms to the Golden Rule (verse 31), to the doctrine of the imitation of the benevolence of God (verse 36), and to the social customs connected with the exchange of gifts (verse 38c). All three issues concern fundamental laws of religion, ethics, and social relations in the Greco-Roman era (Betz, 1995: 619).

Verses 39-42: (39) He also told them a parable:
                    "Can a blind person guide a blind person?
                    Will not both fall into a pit?
            (40)   A disciple is not above the teacher,
                    but everyone who is fully qualified will be
                        like the teacher.
            (41)   Why do you see the speck in your neighbor's
                        eye,
                    but do not notice the log in your own eye?
            (42)   Or how can you say to your neighbor,
                    'Friend, let me take out the speck in your eye,'
                    when you yourself do not see the log in your
                        own eye?
                    You hypocrite, first take the log out of your
                        own eye,
                    and then you will see clearly
                    to take the speck out of your neighbor's eye.

It must be conceded that the literary indication contained in verse 39a, "He also told them a parable," imparts a special character to the last part of the sermon, as a sort of a parabolic illustration (Jeremias, 1980: 146). Although there are authors who insist that the themes treated here are of a very different kind from those recounted until now (Goulder, 1989: 348), too drastic a break with what has gone before cannot be maintained in the face of the general meaning conveyed by the metaphors contained in it. There is definitely a thematic link between Lk 6:39-45 and what precedes (Malpurathu, 1994: 52-54).

The Sermon on the Plain concludes with three parables — the first of which is Lk 6:39-42 — that warn the disciples to take Jesus' words seriously and use them as a basis of self-examination (Bock, 1994: 609). Luke explores further the theme of self-centered moral exclusiveness that was suggested in verses 31-35 and maintains connection with the central thought of Lk 6:20-26 (beatitudes and woes), which stressed the ultimate vindication of the poor through God's intervention. Verses 39-40 introduce the illustration of speck and beam found in verses 41-42 and anticipate the expanded exposition of the student-teacher relationship in verses 46-49. The imagery of the good and the bad tree of verses 43-45 balances the imagery of the speck and the beam of verses 39-42, which in turn formulate an answer to the verdict pronounced by the enemies in Lk 6:22 (Danker, 1988: 153).

Verse 39a clearly marks the beginning of a new section (Schürmann, 1969: 367; Fitzmyer, 1981: 641; Betz, 1995: 619) that includes verses 39-42 and consists of rules for the community of the disciples, specifically rules delineating the purpose of the text of the Sermon on the Plain as a whole. Verse 39 introduces these rules by stating both the need for and the goal of the learning process. Stated as a narrative reference, the phrase, "He also told them a parable," this early testimony (of pre-Lukan origin?) to Jesus' teaching methods is important to the continuing debate whether the original addressees of the parables in the Gospels were the disciples of Jesus or the people of Israel in general (Sider,

1981: 453-470; Cuvillier, 1991: 25-44). For the Sermon on the Plain, the answer is clear: the parables are meant as an instrument of their education. The notion of parable (*parabole*) is used here in the broader sense. The "parable" is, properly speaking, a proverb (compare Lk 4:23; 5:36; Johnson, 1991: 114; Stein, 1992: 212).

Verse 39b-c comprises another word picture, this time formulated as a set of rhetorical questions. The first question is both proverbial and comic: "Can a blind person guide a blind person?" Of course not, and if he tries, disaster will follow. The second question describes just such a disaster: "Will not both fall into a pit?" They certainly will. For the debate as to the referent of the blind leader, see Bock, 1994: 610-611].

What is the purpose behind this comic image? The form of the two rhetorical questions presupposes prior knowledge of the material. The proverb of "the blind leading the blind" is known since classical antiquity. The expression "blind leader" is an example of oxymoron, a literary device commonly employed in antiquity to express incompetence, in teachers particularly. The meaning of the passage in the present context should be clear. The questions are to be answered by students being trained as leaders, either generally as exemplars of the faith or more specifically as leaders in the Christian community. What kind of leaders will they be? Will they join the ranks of those who, because of their blindness, their ignorance, and their stupidity, will lead others astray? Some scholars (cf. Schürmann, 1969: 365-379) take the whole section Lk 6:39-45 to be a warning against false prophets, but this is in fact interpreting the Sermon on the Mount (Mt 7:15-20) into the Sermon on the Plain (Betz, 1995: 620-621 note 274). The "blind guide" is unquestionably entirely unsuitable for Christian discipleship or leadership (cf. Mt 15:14,16-17; 23:16,17,19,24,26); but one might look askance at a special plea justifying education as incorporated into an educational text written for Gentile Christians. Yet one can see from similar, if much more comprehensive and explicit, defenses of education (such as Plutarch's *De liberis educandis* and Seneca's *Epistulae* 88 and 90) that education was under attack at the time, and such plea was therefore in order. The implication of verse 39 is that without education the disciples will remain blind, as they were blind before their conversion. Thus education ensures the development of "vision" (see verses 41-42 for the attention being paid to the eye). It is noteworthy that this movement from blindness to vision, interpreted in the metaphorical sense, also occurs in some miracle stories in the synoptic tradition (e.g., Mk 10:46-52). Perhaps Lk 6:39 points to the social context of these interpretations (Betz, 1995: 621).

The three rules presented in the following verses expose cases of blindness to enlightenment.

The first rule concerns the relationship between student and teacher and consists of two statements prescribing the status of the student at two stages of education. The first statement, formulated negatively, regards the student prior to graduation: "A disciple is not above the teacher" (Lk 6:40a). Does this rule state a general educational principle, or does it define in Christological terms the student's relationship to Christ? One should not simply read back into the earlier tradition its later Christological interpretation (Fitzmyer, 1981: 642). Since verse 40 refers to the general school setting and precedes the second, similar rule, most scholars rightly prefer to interpret it as a general educational principle. That the context does not allude to higher Christology strengthens this interpretation. Although the focus is on "the disciple" in the singular, the statement includes all converted church members for whom the Sermon on the Plain serves as teaching material.

Verse 40b further specifies: "But everyone who is fully qualified will be like the teacher." The disciple can become "fully trained" and thus able to teach as the teacher does

(Johnson, 1991: 114). But the meaning of this verse seems to have remained somewhat obscure for translators, resulting in great variety among major translations (Plummer, 1977: 190; Marshall, 1978: 269-270; Betz, 1991: 623). As varied as these translations are the interpretations of meaning (Dupont, 1957: 53-58; Dodd, 1968: 30-40; Betz, 1995: 624-625). Verse 40 envisages three levels of education: the level of the disciple-in-training (*mathētēs*); the graduate (*katerismenos*), whose training is completed; and the teacher (*didaskalos*), who is entrusted with the training of the disciples. That the Sermon on the Plain is directed toward the present disciples-in-training is underscored by the focus of verse 40 on the future: the Sermon on the Plain is the teaching material of the supervising teachers. This material is not the end of education, however, so that the postgraduate would presumably turn to the other means of instruction beyond the text of the Sermon on the Plain. One must not overlook the final phrase, "like the teacher." The adjectival *hos* ("as, like") has a comparative force, expressing equality or difference. Here it expresses equality with a difference: not every student who graduates becomes a teacher (cf. Jas 3:1 "Not many of you should become teachers"), but the graduates are told that they can count on being treated as a person of social status equal to that of a teacher, and of all teachers. The rule does also regulate the relationship between former students and teachers in the community, where both have equal status but different vocations (cf. 1Cor 12:28-29; Rom 12:6-8; Betz, 1995: 625-626).

Whereas the rule concerning the relationship between teacher and student in verse 40 has implied the need for self-criticism, the next textual unit, verses 41-42, takes self-criticism as its primary theme. The passage concerns the relationship between student and fellow student. Its composition is in the diatribe style, addressing the readers in the second person singular, thus underscoring the educational function of the Sermon on the Plain as a whole. Verses

41 and 42a contain two parallel rhetorical questions followed by the epithet "hypocrite" and a gnomic sentence in two parts employing the form "do this..., and then." The close parallel with Mt 7:3-5 vitually assures a common source (Bultmann, 1972: 47,79-80,86-87; differently, Wrege, 1968: 129-131). The parallels reveal that the cluster of sayings was employed in various contexts for different purposes related to education. In Lk 6:41-42, the cluster is part of the rule regulating the relationships between students (Betz, 1995: 626; differently, Schürmann, 1969: 372).

Jesus' proverbial speech was stocked with humorous contrasts. The picture is purposely overdrawn in order to make the point that any effort at moral improvement of others without taking stock of oneself is utterly ridiculous (Danker, 1988: 153). Jesus made repeatedly use of hyperbolic language (Stein, 1990: 133-220).

The meaning of the first rhetorical question, "Why do you see the speck in your brother's eye, but do not notice the log in your own eye?" is clear: it criticizes the common but absurd habit of readily observing the faults of others while overlooking one's own. The first part of the question (verse 41a) describes the human readiness to assess the faults of others as writ large, while the second part (verse 41b) discloses the absence of self-criticism. The question is not answered. The reason for this omission is not that the answer is self-evident. Rather, the epithet, "hypocrite" in verse 42b discloses what verse 41b implies.

The second question, "Or how can you say to your neighbor [Greek: "brother"], 'Friend [Greek: "brother"] let me take out the speck in your eye, when you yourself do not see the log in your own eye?" (verse 42a), is closely parallel to Mt 7:4. The designation "brother" (*adelphos*), that is, a fellow member of the community, introduces a dramatic element and intensifies the disclosure of hypocrisy. The question in verse 42a thus moves from the issue of self-criticism to the issue of self-correction, and once again observes the bad habit of eagerly correcting others while overlooking the need to correct oneself.

The two questions (verses 41 and 42a) are answered in the direct address "hypocrite." The word is frequently associated with play-acting and here connotes one who plays a role that does not bear up under scrutiny in real life. In its anglicized usage the term bears a stronger negative tone than the Greek term probably conveyed. Posturing or dissembling is here indicated (Danker, 1988: 154). The contradictions observed earlier are now identified by the correct term, and the conduct is judged to be unethical and unreasonable. Remarkably, the epithet "hypocrite" is usually reserved for outsiders, but is here used in criticism of the disciple's behavior (Betz, 1995: 627). So its use here takes the listeners/readers by surprise and tells them rather bluntly that being a disciple of Jesus does not make one any different from other people. Also the disciple of Jesus is obsessed with criticizing and correcting others while failing in one's own self-criticism and correction (Betz, 1995: 493). The term "hypocrite" also introduces the rule proper in verse 42c: "First take the log out of your own eye, and then you will see clearly to take the speck out of your neighbor's [Greek: brother's] eye." The rule takes the form of sayings employing the pattern "do first..., and then..." It recommends self-correction first, as it is the more difficult to accomplish. Once one has accomplished self-correction, one is assumed to have gained a sufficiently clear perspective (*diablepein*) to evaluate the faults of others in order to correct them. Jesus' teaching has many cultural parallels (Marshall, 1978: 270; Fitzmyer, 1981: 642-643; Bock, 1994: 615).

Lk 6:42 puts the verb *ekballein* ("remove, take out") at the end, a position expressing the view that the actual correction of others is an act separate and distinct from the acquisition of a right perspective for evaluation, and that this correction of others can occur only at the end of this process (Betz, 1995: 627). Some scholars argue that the disciple is being discouraged entirely from correcting others (Schürmann, 1969: 371-372).

It has been suggested that answers to the questions raised by Lk 6:37-42, and especially Lk 6:41-42, must be sought by combining information from several quarters. First, a popular saying known in more than one culture expressing that critics forget their own faults while criticizing others', and which the Jews could quaintly phrase in terms of specific obstructions of the eye of the crticic as well as his victim. Second, the behavior of the eye. All Jesus' sayings about the eye have one substratum that most commentators have ignored, namely, that the eye appears to give light; it is the great communicator, exchanging impressiions (Psalms of Solomon 4:5), and is even capable of asking questions. In fact, Hebrew and Aramaic use "eye" for every emotion. Third, the Jewish views on reproof as expressed in Lev 19 which Jesus had almost certainly in mind. It is a universally accepted theory that one should correct one's own faults first, but that does not mean that a rebuke is not merited because of the quarter from whence it comes. An offender will seldom doubt the justice of the rebuke in theory, even if he repels, perhaps violently, the voice that utters it. It is to this that Jesus has applied his mind. He is not saying that rebuke is wholly impossible (Derrett, 1988: 271-274). It is further suggested that *karphos* means "chaff" rather than splinter. Chaff is refuse (Isa 41:15). If not burnt, it will be blown away by the wind, as the enemies of God are (Job 21:18; Isa 17:13l 29:5; 41:16). It can get into one's eye and hinder one's sight. But the one who volunteers has a pole, that is, a construction- beam or a roofing material in the eye. As Jesus puts it, someone with a pole in his eye (disposition) has presumed to admonish one who has mere chaff in his. But both of them are subject to God's wrath. No wonder that Jesus is amazed ('how?") that any disciple could be like them. Jesus agrees that a brother should rebuke a brother. Only he should remember before whom he himself stands (Derrett, 1988: 274-276).

The implications should be clear. Behind these arresting images lies a theory, according to which any attempt at self-correction leads to self-knowledge, to the knowledge of one's own limitations and faults. Such knowledge in turn increases one's sensitivity regarding the difficulties in correcting oneself and others, limits the temptation to self-righteousness, and facilitates compassion (Betz, 1995: 627-628).

Verses 43-45: (43) No good tree bears bad fruit,
                    nor again does a bad tree bear good fruit;
              (44) for each tree is known by its own fruit.
                    Figs are not gathered from thorns,
                    nor are grapes picked from a bramble bush.
              (45) The good person out of the good treasure of
                        the heart produces good,
                    and the evil person out of evil treasure
                        produces evil;
                    for it is out of the abundance of the heart
                    that the mouth speaks.

Verses 43-45 amplify the thought expressed in the illustrations in verses 41-42 (Danker, 1988: 154). The final rule concerns the disciple's relationship to him/herself (Betz, 1995: 628; differently in Schürmann, 1969: 373-379). The rule consists formally of descriptive rather than imperatival statements; verses 43-45 form a well-structured composition of two sets of three statements each: (1) a set of three sentences (*sententiae*) comparing plants with human beings (verses 43-44), and (2) a set of three anthropological statements (verse 45). All are united by the underlying assumption that what holds true for plants also holds true for people, an assumption fundamental to much of ancient moral and ethical thought.

Verse 43a introduces the first sentence of the first set. Formulated as parallel lines, it employs both a double negative and an instance of *homoioteleuton* (lines ending with similar words). The couplet is proverbial, presented as a kind of agricultural rule. It is not the purpose of the saying to teach agricultural wisdom, however, but to reveal a particular state of human affairs. Thus it presages verse 45 and the moral application of the rule. Verse 43a is simply an instance of a culture's proverbial wisdom deriving clues from peasant lore. Verse 43b by repeating the message of verse 43a simply reverses it chiastically, a result from gnomic [= characterized by or expressive of aphorism or sententious wisdom especially concerning human condition or conduct] poetry rather than from a somewhat pedantic logic.

The second statement (verse 44a) is a presupposition based on the first: "For each tree is known by its own fruit." The sentence would appear to be another proverb derived from agricultural wisdom and loosely connected to the preceding proverb (verse 43) by "for" in a positive formulation. The difference between verses 43 and 44 lies in the focus of verse 44 on the "knowing" (*ginoskō*, its only occurrence in the Sermon on the Plain), thereby introducing a further concept necessary to the understanding of verse 45.

Verse 44b appears to add what may have been originally a separate proverb. It supports the proverbs in verses 43 and 44a but makes its own point as well: ""Figs are not gathered from thorns, nor are grapes picked from a bramble bush." This proverb also offers agricultural wisdom, focusing on experience rather than on knowing (verse 44a), Stated negatively, the proverb sums up impossibilities, revealing the category of proverbs called *impossibilia*, to which it belongs (Crenshaw, 1979: 96-111). The agricultural reference once again serves to illustrate a moral point. The language of verse 44b employs technical terms that emphasize knowledge of harvesting (Betz, 1995: 629).

Verse 45 is the climax of the composition Lk 6:43-45: the lesson learned from the plants is applied to human existence. The sentence has three parts, formulated positively (cf. the three parts of verses 43-44). The first two parts comprise antithetical parallel lines, contrasting the good person (verse 45a) and the bad person (verse 45b); the third part presents a concluding maxim (verse 45c). The style of

definition indicates that the text has now changed from proverbial illustrations to the major concept toward which the
Sermon on the Plain has been consistently moving. The
emphasis is not on "doing" (unlike the parallel in Mt 7:15-
20) but on "being." The ideal of the "good person" was
famous in ancient Greek moral and philosophical thought,
and this concept has no doubt intentionally been chosen as
an appeal to disciples from a Greek cultural background (Betz,
1995: 629-630).

Once adopted from the Hellenistic environmernt, the
concept of the "good person" is reinterpreted according to
the theology of the Sermon on the Plain. Thus, verse 45
constitutes an attempt to formulate a Christian answer to
the question, Who is a good person?

Of primary concern is the use of the term *anthrōpos* ("a
human being"), replacing the usual term *aner* ("a man").
Indeed, Socrates had pointed out that the answer to the
question of the good person cannot be *manliness* but only
humanity. The Sermon on the Plain does not generally define who is or who is not a good human being; rather it
poses the question, How can the disciple of Jesus become a
good person? Tradition helps to answer the question. The
factor determining how one can become a good human person
is the condition of the heart. The word "heart" (*kardia*) is
commonly used by Luke to refer to the inner being of an
individual out of which attitudes (Lk 2:35; 16:15) and values come (Lk 12:34; Stein, 1992: 215). According to the
Sermon on the Plain, two kinds of people exist, those of
good and those of evil heart, and the character of the heart
determines the character of the person throughout his or
her life. The good person is thus good because his or her
heart is a treasure of goodness, which "produces" (*propherei*)
the goodness characteristic of the person. Goodness can
neither be achieved nor imposed on one; plainly and simply, goodness is the external manifestation of the internal
quality of the heart. How the heart obtains, or fails to ob-

tain, such a quality is not considered (Betz, 1995: 633-634; differently in Marshall, 1978: 273).

Verse 45b goes on to contrast the good person with the bad, and it is noteworthy that the bad person is not even designated as a "human being" (*anthrōpos*). An evil human being was apparently felt to constitute a contradiction in terms. Why? The answer is logical. The evil person does not hold a treasure in the heart.

Verse 45c concludes the argument with a maxim: "For it is out of the abundance of the heart that the mouth speaks." What does this final sentence contribute? Apart from confirming the preceding material with what originally may have been a proverb, it observes that the most important evidence for a person's constitution — one's "goodness" or "badness" — rests in one's words: not deeds but words reveal one's true nature. The maxim, then, presents a theory concerning human language and its relation to the individual. Every individual has a distinctive language, the character and quality of which are determined by the heart, the center of human identity. That language reveals "the good" and "the bad" of which verse 45a-b speaks.

Which conclusions, then, can one draw from the entire composition of verses 43-45? To be a "good human being" is affirmed as the goal of the disciple, and through this affirmation the Church adopts and confirms the ethical ideals of Greek culture, albeit modified under the impact of the Jesus-tradition.

c. *The Parable of the Two Builders* (Lk 6:46-49)

The final section of the Sermon on the Plain begins in verse 46 and includes two subsections: (1) a rhetorical question that functions as a warning against misconceptions concerning discipleship (verse 46), and (2) a double parable, also a warning, describing in powerful images both success and failure (verses 47-49). While the previous section (verses 43-45) argued the need for self-recognition, the peroration (verses 46-49) establishes the need for action. This sequence of self-knowledge and action again indicates the Hellenistic outlook of the Sermon on the Plain (Betz, 1995: 636).

Verses 46-49: (46) Why do you call me "Lord, Lord."
and do not do what I tell you?
(47) I will show you what someone is like who comes to me,
hears my words and acts on them.
(48) That one is like a man building a house,
who dug deeply and laid the foundation on rock;
when a flood arose, the river burst against that house
but could not shake it because it had been well built.
(49) But the one who hears and does not act
is like a man who built a house on the ground without a foundation.
When the river burst against it,
immediately it fell, and great was the ruin of that house.

Verses 46-49 evidently function as the conclusion of the whole sermon. Once again verse 46 raises the question of the bridge verse. Though in its Lukan formulation verse 46 has thematic links to what precedes (Schürmann, 1969: 323-324) in view of the thought content, the verse seems to go bether with the following parable of the two housebuilders. The literary link evident in verse 46, "and do not what I tell you," on the one hand, and in verse 47, "and acts on them [does them]," and verse 49, "and does not act [not do]," on the other, further contributes to the unity of the cluster of verses. As a matter of fact, in verse 46 we have a climax of all that precedes, and at the same time those words serve as a transition to the concluding paragraph (Danker, 1988: 90; Malipurathu, 1994: 54).

A number of terms determine the close relation between Lk 6:46-49 and the rest of the Sermon. There are mainly four key terms that serve as conductor-threads in all the teaching of Jesus and reveal the function of the present pericope in its context: "come" (*erchomai*; see Lk 6:18: *elthon*), "say" (*legein*), "listen" (*akouein*), and "do" (*poiein*). The four terms are found in Lk 6:46-49, and are plastically interrelated by means of the example of the construction of a house. Moreover, it should be noted that the term "word," which appears in the sermon only in Lk 6:47, alludes to the relative pronoun "which" (*ha*), direct object of "doing" and "saying." The relative pronoun *ha* is the key word which relates this pericope to the teaching of Jesus in general, and with the totality of the Sermon on the Plain, in particular. Jesus refers clearly to his previous words by means of the expression "what I tell you" (Lk 6:46: *ha lego*). In the light of the above it seems reasonable to think that the function of Lk 6:46-49 is to confront the audience of Jesus with the fundamental content of his message: the acknowledgement of Jesus as the Lord is not accomplished by following him and listening attentively to his words, but by the radical practice of his teaching. Whoever proceeds thus builds his house on a solid foundation (Garcia, 1993: 8-10).

Verse 46 in a sense climaxes the preceding exhortation and serves as a transition to the concluding paragraph (verses 47-49; Danker, 1988: 155). It addresses itself pointedly to all who profess discipleship but settle for a less demanding way than that proposed by Jesus in his call to love of enemy and nonjudgment (Nolland, 1989: 309). Marked off from the preceding material by *de* ("but"; not translated by NRSV), verse 46 asks a rhetorical question. In fact, there is no answer to this question; the reader must draw his or her own conclusions. All one can say is that the query discloses an absurd habit of the disciples, a habit for which the text gives neither reason nor excuse. The first part of the sentence presents a caricature of a formal devotional habit of the disciples toward their teacher, a habit actually no more peculiar to Jesus. The disciples address Jesus as "lord" (*kurios*; Schürmann, 1969: 380-381) continuously, to the extent of absurdity. The confession of Jesus as "lord," no matter how exuberant, when unaccompanied by obedience to God's will, will not hold one's life when the storm hits. It is in the storms — and the faithful seem to face more of them than anyone else — that the difference between interested listeners and obedient disciples will be evident (Craddock, 1990: 93)

The verse discloses two essential facts: (1) the description is typical of the behavior of immature students; (2) such behavior is actually, although regrettably, found among the disciples of Jesus so addressed. The question reveals that the disciples envisioned in the Sermon on the Plain are still in a state of general, not to mention specifically Christian, immaturity, and that the road toward "graduation" is lengthy (Fitzmyer, 1981: 643-644; Betz, 1995: 637).

The double parable of the two builders concludes the peroration, and thus the entire Sermon on the Plain. It closely parallels Mt 7:24-27, the conclusion of the Sermon on the Mount. Some scholars have pointed correctly to the Greek character of the Lukan passage (Klostermann, 1975: 85). The double parable depicts a contrast that would be easily recognized by people from areas where long droughts are interrupted by torrential rains that turn dry river beds into flood waters. The point is not to teach sound building strategies, but rather to make clear how life-encompassing Jesus' message is. What is needed to ground a person in Jesus' teachings is to move from learning as an intellectual or emotional achievement to learning embodied in action (Ringe, 1995: 97).

The introductory sentence states explicitly the purpose of the first parable (verse 47). The parable that follows describes the successful student whose resolute efforts parallel the safety and sturdiness of a house built on rock (verse 48). The contrasting second parable describes the failing student using the same metaphors and images, the builder constructing not on rock but on sand (verse 49). Each parable presents the characteristics of the successful and the failing student, in that order (verses 47a,49a), so as to demonstrate success and failure through contrasting imaginative images and metaphors (verses 48b,49b).

The introductory sentence (verse 47) contains two parts: first the definition of the qualities of the good disciple (verse 47a), and then the literary definition of the subsequent double parable: "I will show you what someone is like who comes to me, hears my words, and acts on them." Three characteristics identify the good disciple.

First, like all disciples, the good disciple "comes to" Jesus (Marshall, 1978: 275; Bock, 1994: 620-621), an expression denoting the initiative leading to discipleship. The present tense of the participles in verse 47 indicates an ongoing process; the contrasting aorist tense of the participles in verse 49 indicates an action or an event situated in the past. Scholars have often commented that one's approaching Jesus in order to become a disciple is contrary to Jesus' understanding of discipleship. Rather, it is Jesus who takes the initiative and calls his disciples into his service (Bornkamm, 1960: 144-152). The call narratives of the Gospels make this point. Students who themselves take the initiative in approaching Jesus are often rebuffed as failures (Mk 10:17-22 par.; Lk 9:57-62 par.). Thus, the narratives of the Gospels assume that Jesus himself called the historical disciples, later named apostles. [The concept of apostle does not appear in the Sermon on the Plain]. But the great numbers of new Christians came without doubt on their own initiative. It seems likely that verse 47a regards these new Christian converts, for whom the text of the Sermon on the Plain was composed, as those who "come to" Jesus (Betz, 1995: 637-638).

The second and third characteristics of the good disciple concern hearing and acting on the sayings of Jesus. Verse 47b provides literary information, instructing that one should read the subsequent "parable," as it is usually called, as a demonstration of the point made in verse 47a, that is by implication, the point of the Sermon on the Plain as a whole. The verb *hupodeiknumi* is used here with the meaning "to demonstrate by a story of the *hupodeigma* type," indicating that one is not to read verses 48-49 in the usual manner of Jesus' parables.

The first parable (verse 48) consists of two sections: first, a narrative picture of the good builder constructing a house (verse 48a); and second, a further narrative picture describing an attack on the house by the forces of nature (verse 48b). The introductory words "that one is like" use the form common to the parables of Jesus (Jeremias, 1963: 100-103). The builder of the house is simply called "a man" (*anthropos*, "human being") with no further distinctive attributes (verses 48a, 49a). The Sermon on the Plain seems to focus on the building process, while the Sermon on the Mount focuses on the types of builders. The Sermon on the Plain is characterized, then, because of the careful description of the building process, by the laying of foundations in particular. The verbs describing this construction are simultaneously metaphors of intellectual activity (Betz, 1995: 638-639). "Building a house" points to the disciple's own life as follower of Jesus. Every person is presumably building his or her house of life. This house consists of thoughts, speech, and practice; it begins with one's education as a disciple and ends only with death. These things determine whether one is "at home" in life (Betz, 1995: 563).

Verse 48b assumes that the attack by the forces of nature occurs upon completion of the building: "When a flood arose, the river burst against that house, but could not shake it, because it had been well built." The course of events differs characteristically from those of the Sermon on the Mount (Craddock, 1990: 93; Betz, 1995: 639). The account in Matthew envisions the torrential autumn and winter rains in Palestine, accompanied by a storm, that produce rising streams, i.e., wadis swollen with rainwater descending from the hills. In contrast Luke envisions a storm that causes a river to rise and the torrent or flood to hit the house. Luke also may have been describing a house with a basement ("dug deeply") that fits well Hellenistic houses that typically had basements (Jeremias, 1963a: 194 note 4; Nolland, 1989: 310; Stein, 1992: 215; Bock, 1994: 621-622). Thinking only of the present, the foolish builder imagines that the hard alluvial sand of the summer will remain in that state throughout the winter months, whereas the wise builder digs a deep foundation (Franz, 1995: 6-11).

The second parable in verse 49 presents the counterpicture of verse 48, describing the failing student through the image of the careless builder. The first part of the sentence describes the man and his activities: "But the one who hears and does not act is like a man who built a house on the ground without a foundation." The initial clause identifies the failing student by noting that he only "hears" but he fails to "do." That no objects are mentioned can only mean that such a student, although he listens to the sayings of the master, does not really hear them. The sayings go in one ear and out the other. He misses the appeal to act in what he hears, and thus he misses the point. His major identifying trait is nonaction.

The parable itself stands in analogy to its predecessor in verse 48. The man's building activities are judged careless because he sets the house directly on the surface of the earth. [The metaphorical meaning suggests superficiality]. The additional remark "without a foundation" reveals the thrust of the story, the question being whether a foundation exists. Such a focus concerns the intellectual, doctrinal, and ethical foundations presented throughout the Sermon on the Plain.

Verse 49b describes with quick strokes the effects of the flood on the house: "When the river burst against it, immediately it fell, and great was the ruin of that house" The description assumes events identical to those in verse 48, but now the flood hits the house built on the foundationless surface. Predictably, the house quickly collapses, its supporting structure completely eroded by the raging river. One cannot ignore the metaphorical applications of the term "fall, collapse." Thus the last line brings the drama to a fatal conclusion and leaves the hearer with a final warning that one cannot disregard (Betz, 1995: 640).

In verses 47-49 Jesus couples "doing" with "hearing" of his words (cf. Lk 8:21; 10:37). His words are not theoretical statement. They are not presented as discussion themes, as theses for ecclesiastical committee work designed to make the Church think that it is doing God's will because it spends so much time talking about it (Danker, 1988: 155).

In spite of the paradoxical (or at least challenging!) character of the Sermon's virtues, duties, ethical principles, and paraenesis, most scholars simply lay out an exegesis of the various verses without coming to grips with the sermon's ethics as a whole, except for a few occasional comments, like, e.g., that there is a connection between the beatitudes and the love of enemy. But one must treat the Sermon on the Plain in the context of all Jesus' teachings, especially in connection with his words on the imminent inbreaking of the kingdom of God and the *metanoia* it requires (Kahlefeld, 1962; Topel, 1981: 50).

The various sections of the Sermon on the Plain do not fit together into a single argument or theme. They do, however, form an interesting introduction to the training program that Jesus' disciples are receiving. The blessings and woes recall what is emerging as the dominant theme of Luke's Gospel, namely, the sort of reversal of fortunes that constitutes "good news to the poor" — those who have been left on (or pushed to) the margins of the part of society that has benefited from the status quo. That theme sets the stage for specific teachings about aspects of personal conduct and relationships that affect the quality of a person's or community's life in general, and especially the quality of the ministry of those chosen as apostles. Their preparation for their work begins with hard lessons about personal interactions and accountability in their daily life, not with academic theories or training for leadership in public events. The very purpose of the gospel as "good news" depends on the coherence and integrity of the lives of those who bear its word of justice and liberation (Ringe, 1995: 97).

BIBLIOGRAPHY

(The books and articles presented in the bibliography of Volume I are not repeated here).

Abraham, M.V. "Good News to the Poor in Luke's Gospel," *Bible Bashyam* 14 (1988), 65-77.

Albertz, Rainer. "Die Antrittpredigt Jesu im Lukasevangelium auf alttestamentlichem Hintergrund," *Zeitschrift für die neutestamentliche Wissenschaft* 74 (1983), 182-206.

Allison, Dale C. "The Baptism of Jesus and a New Dead Sea Scroll," *Biblical Archaeology Review* 18 (1992), 58-60.

Ascough, Richard S. "Narrative Technique and Generic Designation: Crowd Scenes in Luke-Acts and in Chariton," *Catholic Biblical Quarterly* 58 (1996), 69-81.

Bachmann, Michael. *Jerusalem under der Tempel: Die geographisch-theologischen Elemente in der lukanischen Sicht des jüdischen Kultzentrums.* Stuttgart: Verlag W. Kohlhammer, 1980.

Bailey, James L. and Lyle D. VanderBroek. *Literary Forms in the New Testament: A Handbook.* Louisville: Westminster/John Knox Press, 1992.

Bajard, J. "La structure de la péricope de Nazareth en Lc., IV, 16-30. Propositions pour une lecture plus cohérente," *Ephemerides Theologicae Lovanienses* 45 (1969), 165-171.

Balch, David L. "Rich and Poor, Proud and Humble in Luke-Acts," in White, L. Michael and O. Larry Yarbrough. eds. *The Social World of the First Christians. Essays for Wayne A. Meeks.* Minneapolis: Augsburg/Fortress Press, 1995. 214-233.

Banks, Robert, *Jesus and the Law in the Synoptic Tradition.* Cambridge: Cambridge University Press, 1975.

Barrett, Charles K. *The Holy Spirit and the Gospel Tradition.* London: SPCK, 1954.

Bauckham, Richard. "The Messianic Interpretation of Isa 10:34 in the Dead Sea Scrolls, 2 Baruch and he Preaching of John the Baptist," *Dead Sea Discoveries* 2 (1995), 202-21

Beardslee, William A. *Literary Criticism of the New Testament.* Philadelphia: Fortress Press, 1970.

Bergemann, Thomas. *Q auf dem Prüfstand. Die Zuordnung des Mt/ Lk-Stoffes zu Q am Beispiel der Bergpredigt.* Göttingen: Vandenhoeck & Ruprecht, 1993.

Berner, Ursula. *Die Bergpredigt. Rezeption und Auslegung im 20. Jahrhundert.* Göttingen: Vandenhoeck & Ruprecht, 1979.

Betz, Hans Dieter. *The Sermon on the Mount.* Hermeneia - A Critical and Historical Commentary on the Bible. Minneapolis: Fortress Press, 1995.

Betz, Otto. "The Kerygma of Luke," *Interpretation* 22 (1968), 131-146.

Black, Matthew. *An Aramaic Approach to the Gospels and Acts.* Third Edition. Oxford: Clarendon, 1967.

Blank, Josef. "Die Seligpreisungen," in Hochgrebe, Volker. ed. *Provokation Bergpredigt.* Stuttgart: Kreuz Verlag, 1982.

Blomberg, Craig. "The Law in Luke-Acts," *Journal for the Study of the New Testament* 22 (1984), 53-80.

Bocher, O. "Lukas und Johannes der Taufer," *Studien zum Neuen Testament und seiner Umwelt* A4 (1979), 7-44.

Bock, Darrell L. "The Son of Man in Luke 5:24," *Bulletin for Biblical Research* 1 (1991), 109-121.

_____. "Framing the Account: Alleviating Confusion on the Lukan Portrait of Jesus," in Lovering, Eugene H. ed. *SBL 1994 Seminar Papers.* Atlanta: Scholars Press, 1994a. 612-616.

Borg, Marcus J. *Conflict, Holiness and Politics in the Teachings of Jesus.* New York: The Edwin Mellen Press, 1984.

Bornkamm, Günther. *Jesus of Nazareth.* New York: Harper & Row, 1960.

Bouwman, Gijs. "De wonderbare visvangst (Lc 5, 1-11). Een proeve van integrale exegese," in Weren, Wim and N. Poulssen. eds. *Bij de put van Jacob. Exegetische opstellen.* Tilburg: University Press, 1986. 109-129.

Bovon, François. "The Role of the Scriptures in the Composition of the Gospel Accounts: The Temptations of Jesus (Lk 4:1-13 par.) and the Multiplication of the Loaves (Lk 9:10-17 par.)," in O'Collins, Gerald and Gilbert Marconi. eds. *Luke and Acts*. New York: Paulist Press, 1993. 26-31.

Brawley, Robert L. *Luke-Acts and the Jews. Conflict, Apology, and Conciliation*. Atlanta, GA: Scholars Press, 1987.

_____. "Canon and Community: Intertextuality, Canon, Interpretation, Christology, Theology, and Persuasive Rhetoric in Lk 4:1-13," in Lovering, Eugene H. ed. *Society of Biblical Literature 1992 Seminar Papers*. Atlanta, GA: Scholars Press, 1992. 419-434.

Bretscher, Paul C. "Exodus 4:22-23 and the Voice from Heaven," *Journal of Biblical Literature* 87 (1968), 301-311.

Brown, Raymond E. *New Testament Essays*. Milwaukee: The Bruce Publishing Company, 1965.

_____. "The Beatitudes According to St. Luke," *New Testament Essays*. Milwaukee: Bruce, 1965. 265-271.

_____ et al. eds. *Peter in the New Testament*. New York: Paulist Press, 1973.

Brown, Schuyler. *Apostasy and Perseverance in the Theology of Luke*. Analecta Biblica 36. Rome: Pontifical Biblical Institute, 1969.

Bruners, Wilhelm. *Die Reinigung der zehn Aussätzigen und die Heilung des Samariters, Lk 17,11-19*. Forschung zur Bibel 23. Stuttgart: Verlag Katholisches Bibelwerk, 1977.

Buchanan, George Wesley. "The Age of Jesus," *New Testament Studies* 41 (1995), 297.

Burkett, D. "The Nontitular Son of Man: A History and Critique," *New Testament Studies* 40 (1994), 504.

Busse, Ulrich. *Die Wunder des Propheten Jesus: Die Rezeption, Komposition und Interpretation der Wundertradition im Evangelium des Lukas*. Forschung zur Bibel 24. Stuttgart: Katholisches Bibelwerk, 1977.

_____. *Das Nazareth-Manifest Jesu. Eine Einführung in das lukanische Jesusbild nach Lk 4,16-30*. Stuttgarter Bibelstudien 91. Stuttgart: Verlag Katholisches Bibelwerk, 1978.

Carroll, John T. "Luke's Portrayal of the Pharisees," *Catholic Biblical Quarterly* 50 (1988), 604-612.

Carson, D.A. "Jesus and the Sabbath in the Four Gospels," in Carson, D.A. ed. *From Sabbath to Lord's Day: Biblical, Historical and Theological Investigation*. Grand Rapids: Zondervan, 1982. 57-97.

Casey, P. Maurice. "Culture and Historicity: The Plucking of Grain (Mark 2:23-28)," *New Testament Studies* 34 (1988), 1-23.

Catchpole, David R. "The Anointred One in Nazareth," in De Boer, Martinus C. ed. *From Jesus to John: Essays on Jesus and New Testament Christology in Honor of Martinus de Jonge.* Sheffield: JSOT Press, 1993. 231-251.

Chiappini, A. "Jésus de Nazareth, Prophète et Libérateur, Luc 4,16-30," in *Peuple parmi les Peuples: Dossier pour l'animation biblique.* Geneva: Labor et Fides, 1990:229-237.

Claudel, Gerard. *La confession de Pierre: Trajectoire d'une péricope évangelique.* Etudes Bibliques. Paris: J. Gabalda, 1988.

Conroy, Charles. "Methodological Reflections on Recent Studies of the Naaman Pericope (2 Kings 5): Some Background to Luke 4:27," in O'Collins, Gerald and Gilberto Marconi. eds. *Luke and Acts.* New York/Mahwah, N.J.: Paulist Press, 1991:32-47.

Conzelmann, Hans. *The Theology of St. Luke.* New York: Harper & Row, 1960.

Crenshaw, James L. "Questions, dictions et épreuves impossibles," in Gilbert, M. ed. *La Sagesse de l'Ancient Testament.* BETL 51. Louvain: Leuven University Press, 1979. 96-111.

Crockett, Larrimore. "Luke 4:25-27 and Jewish-Gentile Relations in Luke-Acts," *Journal of Biblical Literature* 88 (1969), 177-183.

Cross, Frank M. *Ancient Library of Qumran and Modern Biblical Studies.* New York: Doubleday, 1958.

Cuvillier, Elian. "*Parabole* dans la tradition synoptique," *Etudes Théologiques et Religieuses* 66 (1991), 25-44.

Dalman, Gustav. *Von der Ernte zum Mehl. Arbeit und Sitte in Palästina III.* Hildesheim: Georg Olms, 1964.

Daniel-Rops, Henri. *Daily Life in the Time of Jesus.* New York: Hawthorne Books, 1962.

Daube, David. *The New Testament and Rabbinic Judaism.* London: Athlone Press, 1956.

_____. "Responsibilities of Master and Disciples in the Gospels," *New Testament Studies* 19 (1972-1973), 1-15

Davies, William D. *The Gospel and the Land: Early Christianity and Jewish Territorial Doctrine.* Berkeley: University of California Press, 1974.

Degenhardt, Hans-Joachim. *Lukas Evangelist der Armen. Besitz und Besitzversicht in den lukanischen Schriften.* Stuttgart: Verlag Katholisches Bibelwerk, 1965.

de la Potterie, Ignace. "L'onction du Christ," *Nouvelle Revue Théologique* 80 (1958), 225-252.

Delobel, Joel. "La rédaction de Lc., IV,14-16a et le "Bericht vom Anfang," in Neirynck, Frans. ed. *L"Evangile de Luc—The Gospel of Luke.* Revised and Enlarged Edition. Louvain: Leuven University Press, 1989), 113-133, 306-312.

Delorme, Jean. "Luc V.1-11: Analyse structurale et histoire de la rédaction," *New Testament Studies* 18 (1971-1972), 331-350.

Denaux, Adelbert. "Criteria for Identifying Q-Passages. A Critical Review of a Recent Work by T. Bergemann," *Novum Testamentum* 37 (1995), 105-129.

Derrett, J. Duncan M. "Christ and Reproof (Matthew 7:1-5/Luke 6:37-42," *New Testament Studies* 34 (1988), 271-281.

_____. "Getting on Top of a Demon (Luke 4:39)," *Evangelical Quarterly* 65 (1993), 99-109.

_____. "The Baptist"s Sermon: Luke 3,10-14," *Bibbia e Oriente* 37 (1995), 155-165.

Dewey, Joanna. "Jesus' Healings of Women: Conformity and Non-Conformity to Dominant Cultural Values as Clues for Historical Reconstruction," in Lovering, Eugene H. ed. *Society of Biblical Literature 1993 Seminar Papers.* Atlanta: Scholars Press, 1993. 178-193.

Diefenbach, Manfred. *Die Komposition des Lukas-Evangeliums unter Berücksichtigung antiker Rhetorikelemente.* Frankfurt am Main: Verlag Josef Knecht, 1993.

Dietrich, Wolfgang. *Das Petrusbild der lukanischen Schriften.* Stuttgart: Verlag W. Kohlhammer, 1972.

Dihle, Albrecht. *Die Goldene Regel: Eine Einfuhrung in die Geschichte der antiken und fruhchristlichen Vulgärethik.* Göttingen: Vandenhoeck & Ruprecht, 1962.

Dillon, Richard J. "Easter Revelation and Mission Program in Lk 24:44-46," in Durken, D. ed. *Sin, Salvation and the Spirit.* Collegeville: The Liturgical Press, 1979.

Doble, Peter. *The Paradox of Salvation. Luke's Theology of the Cross.* SNTSMS 87. Cambridge: Cambridge University Press, 1996.

Dodd, Charles H. *According to the Scriptures: The Substructure of New Testament Theology*. London: Collins Fontana Books. 1965.
_____. *More New Testament Studies*. Grand Rapids: Eerdmans, 1968.

Dunn, James D.G. "Spirit-and-Fire Baptism," *Novum Testamentum* 14 (1972), 81-92.

Dupont, Jacques. "L'arrière-fond biblique du récit des tentations de Jésus," *New Testament Studies* 3 (1957), 287-304.
_____. *Les Béatitudes. Le problème littéraire – Les deux versions du Sermon sur la montagne et des Béatitudes*. Louvain: E. Nauwelaerts, 1958.
_____. *Les Béatitudes*. Tome II: *La bonne nouvelle*. Paris: J. Gabalda, 1969.
_____. *Les Béatitudes*. Tome III: *Les Evangélistes*. Paris: Gabalda, 1973.
_____. "The Temptations of Jesus in Luke," *Theology Digest* 14 (1966), 213-217.
_____. *Les tentations de Jésus au désert*. Studia Neotestamentica 4. Bruges: Desclée de Brouwer, 1968.

Erickson, Richard J. "The Jailing of John and the Baptism of Jesus: Luke 3:19-21," *Journal of the Evangelical Theological Society* 36 (1993), 455-466.

Ernst, Joseph. *Johannes der Täufer – Interpretation – Geschichte – Wirkungsgeschichte*. Berlin/New York: de Gruyter, 1989.

Esler, Philip F. *Community and Gospel in Luke-Acts: The Social and Political Motivations of Lucan Theology*. Cambridge: Cambridge University Press, 1987.
_____. ed. *Modelling Early Christianity: Social-Scientific Studies of the New Testament in Its Context*. New York: Routledge, 1995.

Farmer, William R. in Buttrick, G.A., Th. S. Kepler, et al. eds. *Interpreter's Dictionary of the Bible*. Four Volumes. Nashville, TN: Abingdon Press, 1962.

Feldkämper, Ludger. *Der betende Jesus als Heilsmittler nach Lukas*. St. Augustin: Steyler Verlag, 1978.

Feuillet, André. "Le récit lucanien de la tentation," *Biblica* 40 (1959), 613-631.

Finkel, Asher. "Jesus' Preaching in the Synagogue on the Sabbath (Luke 4:16-28)," *Sidic* [Rome] 17 (3, 1984), 4-10.

Fitzmyer, Joseph A. "The Lucan Picture of John the Baptist as Precursor of the Lord," in *Luke the Theologian*. Mahwah, NJ: Paulist Press, 1989. 86-116.

_____. "A Palestinian Collection of Beatitudes," in Van Segbroeck, Frans et al. eds. *The Four Gospels 1992 – Festschrift Frans Neirynck*. Louvain: Leuven University Press. 1992. 509-515.

Flusser, David. "Do You Prefer New Wine?" *Immanuel* 9 (1979), 26-28.

_____. "Die Versuchung Jesu und ihr jüdischer Hintergrund,"*Judaica* 45 (1989), 110-118.

Franz, G. "The Parable of the Two Builders," *Archaeology in the Biblical World* 3 (1, 1995), 6-11.

Freyne, Sean. *Galilee from Alexander the Great to Hadrian (323 B.C.E. to 135 C.E.)*. Notre Dame: University of Notre Dame Press, 1980.

Fuchs, Albert. "Exegese im elfenbeinernen Turm. Das quellenkritische Problem von Mk 1,2-8 par. Mt 3,1-12 par. Lk 3,1-17 in der Sicht der Zweiquellentheorie und von Deuteromarkus," *Studien zum Neuen Testament und seiner Umwelt* 20 (1995), 23-129.

Fuliga, Jose B. "The Temptations of Jesus: A Class Struggle," *Asia Journal of Theology* 8 (1994), 172-185.

Garrett, Susan R. *The Demise of the Devil: Magic and the Demonic in Luke's Writings*. Minneapolis: Fortress Press, 1989.

Garcia, Miguel A. "Committed Discipleship and Jesus' Lordship. Exegesis of Luke 6:46-49 in the Context of Jesus' Discourse in the Plain," *African Christian Studies* 9 (2, 1993), 3-10.

Geldenhuys, N. *Commentary on the Gospel of Luke: The English Text with Introduction, Exposition and Notes*. Grand Rapids: Eerdmans, 1951; reprint 1988.

Geninasca, Jacques. "To Fish/To Preach: Narrative and Metaphor (Luke 5:1-11)," in The Entrevernes Group. *Signs and Parables: Semiotics and Gospel Texts*. Pittsburgh: The Pickwick Press, 1978. 185-222.

Gerhardsson, Birger.*The Testing of God's Son*. Lund: Gleerup, 1966.

Gibson, Jeffrey B.*The Temptations of Jesus in Early Christianity*. Sheffield: Academic Press, 1995.

Gordon, Cyrus H. "Paternity at Two Levels," *Journal of Biblical Literature* 96 (1977), 101.

Goulder, Michael D. *The Evangelists' Calendar: A Lectionary Explanation of the Development of Scripture.* London: SPCK, 1978.

Gowler, David B. "Characterization in Luke: A Socio-Narratological Approach," *Biblical Theology Bulletin* 19 (1989), 54-62.

_____. *Host, Guest, Enemy, and Friend. Portraits of the Pharisees in Luke and Acts.* New York: Peter Lang, 1991.

Grant, Robert M. *Historical Introduction to the New Testament.* New York: Harper, 1963.

Grelot, Pierre. "Les tentations de Jésus," *Nouvelle Revue Théologique* 117 (1995), 501-516.

Grollenberg, Lucas. "Mensen 'vangen' (Lk 5,10): hen redden van de dood," *Tijdschrift voor Theologie* 5 (1965), 330-336.

Grundmann, Walter. "Die Bergpredigt nach der Lukasfassung," in Aland, Kurt and Frank Cross. eds. *Studia Evangelica I.* Texte und Untersuchungen 74. Berlin: Akademie-Verlag. 1959. 180-189.

_____. *Das Evangelium nach Lukas.* Theologischer Handkommentar zum Neuen Testament 3. Berlin: Evangelische Verlagsanstalt, 1966.

Guelich, Robert. *The Sermon on the Mount: A Foundation for Understanding.* Waco, Texas: Word Books, 1982.

_____. "The Matthean Beatitudes: Entrance Requirements or Eschatological Blessings," *Journal of Biblical Literature* 95 (1976), 415-434.

Hamm, Dennis. "Sight to the Blind: Vision as Metaphor in Luke," *Biblica* 67 (1986), 457-477.

_____. *The Beatitudes in Context: What Luke and Matthew Meant.* Zacchaeus Studies: New Testament. Wilmington, DE: Michael Glazier, 1990.

Hanson, K.C. "The Herodians and Mediterranean Kinship. Part I: Genealogy and Descent," *Biblical Theology Bulletin* 19 (1989), 75-84.

Hanson, Paul D. *The Dawn of Apocalyptic.* Philadelphia: Fortress Press, 1975.

Hare, Douglas R.A. *The Theme of Jewish Persecution of Christians in the Gospel according to St. Matthew.* Cambridge: Cambridge University Press, 1967.

Helgeland, John, Robert J. Daly and J. Patout Burns. *Christians and the Military: The Early Experience*. Philadephia: Fortress Press, 1985.

Hengel, Martin. *The Zealots: Investigations into the Jewish Freedom Movement in the Period from Herod I until 70 A.D.* Edinburgh: T. & T. Clark, 1989.

Hendrickx, Herman. *The Sermon on the Mount.* Studies in the Synoptic Gospels. Revised Edition. London: Geoffrey Chapman, 1984.

_____. *The Miracle Stories of the Synoptic Gospels.* London: Geoffrey Chapman, 1987.

_____. *A Key to the Gospel of Luke.* Quezon City, Philippines: Claretian Publications, 1992.

Hill, David. "The Rejection of Jesus at Nazareth (Luke IV 16-30)," *Novum Testamentum* 13 (1971), 161-180.

Hoffmann, Paul. "'Selig sind die Armen...' Auslegung der Bergpredigt II (Mt 5:13-16)," *Bibel und Leben* 10 (1969), 111-122.

Hollenbach, Paul W. "The Meaning of Desert Symbolism for Civilization in Ancient Israel," *Iowa State Journal of Research* 49 (1974), 169-179.

_____. "Social Aspects of John the Baptizer's Preaching Mission in the Context of Palestinian Judaism," in Haase, W. ed. *Aufstieg und Niedergang der römischen Welt* II: *Principat* 19.1. Berlin: Walter de Gruyter, 1979. 850-875.

_____. "John the Baptist," in Freedman, David Noel. ed. *The Anchor Bible Dictionary* Vol. 3. New York: Doubleday, 1992. 887-899.

Holtz, Traugott. *Untersuchungen über die alttestamentlichen Zitate bei Lukas.* Berlin: Akademie Verlag, 1968.

Horsley, Richard A. "Popular Messianic Movements around the Time of Jesus," *Catholic Biblical Quarterly* 46 (1984), 471-495.

_____. "'Like One of the Prophets of Old': Two Types of Popular Prophets at the Time of Jesus," *Catholic Biblical Quarterly* 47 (1985), 435-463.

_____. "Q and Jesus: Assumptions, Approaches, and Analyses," *Semeia* 55 (1991), 175-212.

_____. "Ethics and Exegesis: "Love Your Enemies" and the Doctrine of Nonviolence," in Swartley, Willard M. ed.

The Love of Enemy and Nonretaliation in the New Testament... Louisville, KY: Westminster/John Knox Press, 1992. 72-101.

_____. "Response to Walter Wink, "Neither Passivity nor Violence: Jesus' Third Way," in Swartley, Willard M. ed. *The Love of Enemy and Nonretaliation in the New Testament.* Louisvile, KY: Westminster/John Knox Press, 1992a. 126-132.

_____. *Galilee: History, Politics, People.* Valley Forge, PA: Trinity Press International, 1995.

_____. *Archaeology, History, and Society in Galilee: The Social Context of Jesus and the Rabbis.* Valley Forge, PA: Trinity Press International, 1996.

Horsley, Richard A. and John S. Hanson. *Bandits, Prophets, and Messiahs: Popular Movements in the Time of Jesus.* Minneapolis: Winston Press, 1985.

Huber, A. "*Hōs peristera.* Zu einem Motiv in den Tauferzählungen der Evangelien," *Protokolle zur Bibel* 4 (1995), 87-101.

Hull, John M. *Hellenistic Magic and the Synoptic Tradition.* Studies in Biblical Theology. Second Series, 28. London: SCM Press, 1974.

Humphrey, Hugh M. "Temptation and Authority: Sapiential Narratives in Q," *Biblical Theology Bulletin* 21 (1991), 43-50.

Isenberg, Sheldon R. "Power Through Temple and Torah in Greco-Roman Palestine," Neussner, Jacob. ed. *Christianity, Judaism and Other Greco-Roman Cults: Studies for Morton Smith at Sixty.* Part 2: *Early Christianity.* Leiden: Brill, 1975. 24-52.

Jeremias, Joachim. "Das Gebetsleben Jesu," *Zeitschrift für die neutrestamentliche Wissenschaft* 25 (1926), 123-14

_____. *Jesus' Promise to the Nations.* Studies in Biblical Theology 24. London: SCM Press, 1958.

_____. *The Sermon on the Mount.* Facet Books, Biblical Series 2.Philadelphia: Fortress Press, 1963.

_____. *The Parables of Jesus.* London: SCM Press, 1963a.

_____. *Jerusalem in the Time of Jesus: An Investigation into Economic and Social Conditions During the New Testament Period.* Philadelphia: Fortress Press, 1969.

_____. *New Testament Theology: The Proclamation of Jesus* London: SCM Press, 1971

Johnson, Marshall D. *The Purpose of the Biblical Genealogies.* Second Edition. With Special Reference to the Setting of the

Genealogies of Jesus. Cambridge: Cambridge University Pres, 1988.

Kahlefeld, Heinrich. Der Jünger. Eine Auslegung der Rede Lk 6:20- 49. Frankfurt: Knecht, 1962.

Karris, Robert J. "Poor and Rich: The Lukan Sitz im Leben," in Talbert, Charles H. ed. Perspectives on Luke-Acts. Danville, VA: Association of Baptist Professors of Religion, 1978. 112- 125.

Kavunkal, Jacob. "Jubilee the Framework of Evangelization," Vidyajyoti 52 (1980), 181-190.

Kazmierski, Carl R. "The Stones of Abraham: John the Bapttist and the End of Torah (Mt 3:7-10 par. Lk 3:7-9)," Biblica 68 (1987), 22-39.

_____. John the Baptist: Prophet and Evangelist. Collegeville: The Liturgical Press, 1996.

Kilgallen, John J. A Brief Commentary on the Gospel of Luke. Mahwah: Paulist Press, 1988.

Kinman, B. "Luke's Exoneration of John the Baptist," Journal of Theologivcal Studies 44 (1993), 595-598.

Kirchschläger, Walter. Jesu exorzistisches Wirken aus der Sicht des Lukas: Ein Beitrag zur lukanischen Redaktion . Klosterneuberg: Österreichisches Katholisches Bibelwerk, 1981.

Kissinger, Warren S. The Sermon on the Mount: A History of In- terpretation and Bibliography. Metuchen, NJ: The Scarecrow Press, 1975.

Klassen. William. Love of Enemies: The Way to Peace. Philadel- phia: Fortress Press, 1984.

Klinghardt, Matthias. Gesetz und Volk Gottes. Das lukanische Verständnis des Gesetzes nach Herkunft, Funktion und seinem Ort in der Geschichte des Urchristentums. Tübingen: Vanden- hoeck & Ruprecht, 1988.

Kloppenborg, John S. The Formation of Q: Trajectories in Ancient Wisdom Collections. Philadephia: Forterss Press, 1987.

Koester, Helmut. Ancient Christian Gospels: Their History and Development. Philadelphia: Trinity Press International, 1990.

Koet, Bart J. Five Studies on Interpretation of Scripture in Luke- Acts. Louvain: Leuven University Press, 1989.

Krämer, Michael. Die Überlieferungsgeschichte der Bergpredigt. Eine synoptische Studie zu Mt 4,23-7,29 und Lk 6,17-49. 3. erweiterte

Auflage. Deutsche Hochschulschriften 433. Egelsbach: Hänsel-Hohenhausen, 1994.

Kuhn, H.W. *Altere Sammlungen im Markusevangelium.* Göttingen: Vandenhoeck & Ruprecht, 1971.

Kurz, William S. "Luke 3:23-38 and the Greco-Roman and Biblical Genealogies." in Talbert, Charles H. ed. *Luke-Acts: New Perspectives from the SBL Seminar.* New York: Crossroad, 1984. 169-187.

Kyo-Seon Shin, Gabriel. *Die Ausrufung des endgültiges Jübeljahres durch Jesus in Nazaret. Eine historisch-kritische Studie zu Lk 4,16-30.* Bern/New York: Peter Lang, 1989.

Lambrecht, Jan. *The Sermon on the Mount: Proclamation and Exhortation.* Wilmington, DE: Michael Glazier, 1985. 11-13

—————. "The Sayings of Jesus on Nonviolence," *Louvain Studies* 12 (1987), 291-305.

—————. "Is Active Nonviolent Resistance Jesus' Third Way? An Answer to Walter Wink," *Louvain Studies* 19 (1994), 350-351.

Lapide, Pinchas. *The Sermon on the Mount: Utopia or Program for Action?* Maryknoll, N.Y.: Orbis Books, 1986.

Leaney, A.R.C. *The Gospel According to St. Luke.* Black's New Testament Commentaries. London: Adam & Charles Black, 1958.

Lentzen-Deis, Fritzleo. *Die Taufe Jesu nach den Synoptikern. Literarkritische und gattungsgeschichtliche Untersuchungen.* Frankfurt am Main: 1970.

Liebenberg, J. "The Function of the *Standenpredigt* in Luke 3:10-14: A Response to E.H. Scheffler's, The Social Ethics of the Lukan Baptist (Lk 3:10-14)," *Neotestamentica* 27 (1993), 55-67.

Linskens, John. "A Pacifist Interpretation of Peace in the Sermon on the Mount?" in Elizondo, Virgil, et al. eds. *Church and Peace − Concilium* 164. New York: Seabury Press, 1983. 16-25.

Lohfink, Gerhard. *Die Sammlung Israels: Eine Untersuchung zur lukanischen Ekklesiologie.* Munich: Kösel-Verlag, 1975.

—————. *Wen gilt die Bergpredigt? Beiträge zu einer christlichen Ethik.* Freiburg/Basel/Vienna: Herder, 1988.

McKnight, Edgar V. *Meaning in Texts: The Historical Shaping of a Narratrve Hermeneutics.* Philadelphia: Fortress Press, 1978.

McVan, Mark. "Rituals of Status Transformation in Luke-Acts: The Case of Jesus the Prophet," in Neyrey, Jerome, ed. *The Social World of Luke-Acts: Models for Interpretation.* Peabody, MA: Hendrickson, 1991. 333-360.

Mahnke, Hermann. *Die Versuchungsgeschichte im Rahmen der synoptische Evangelien.* Frankfurt am Main: Peter Lang, 1978.

Maisch. Ingrid. *Die Heilung des Gelähmten.* Stuttgarter Bibelstudien 52. Stuttgart: KBW Verlag, 1971.

Malina, Bruce J. "The Individual and the Community—Personality in the Social World of Early Christianity," *Biblical Theology Bulletin* 9 (1979), 126-138.

——————. "Patron and Client: The Analogy Behind Synoptic Theology," *Forum* 4 (1988), 2-32.

——————. "Mary—Mediterranean Woman: Mother and Son," *Biblical Theology Bulletin* 20 (1990), 54-64.

Malipurathu, Thomas. *The Beatitudes According to Luke: An Exegetico-Theological Study of Luke 6:20-26 in the Perspective of the Sermon on the Plain and the Designation of Luke as the "Evangelist of the Poor."* Rome: Pontifical Gregorian University, 1994

März, Claus-Peter. *Das Wort Gottes bei Lukas.* Erfurter Theologische Schriften. Leipzig: St. Benno-Verlag, 1974.

Matson , David L. *Household Conversion Narratives in Acts: Pattern and Interpretation.* Sheffield: Academic Press, 1996.

Mauser, Ulrich W. *Christ in the Wilderness: The Wilderness Theme in the Second Gospel and Its Basis in the Biblical Tradition.* Naperville, IL: Allenson, 1963.

Meier, John P. "John the Baptist in Matthew's Gospel," *Journal of Biblical Literature* 99 (1980), 383-405.

——————. "John the Baptist in Josephus: Philology and Exegesis," *Journal of Biblical Literature* 111 (1992), 225-237.

Merklein, Helmut. *Die Gottesherrschaft als Handlungsprinzip: Untersuchungen zur Ethik Jesu.* Forschung zur Bibel 34. Würzburg: Echter Verlag, 1978.

——————."Die Umkehrpredigt bei Johannes dem Täufer und Jesus von Nazaret," *Biblische Zeitschrift* 25 (1981), 29-46.

Meynet, Roland. *Initiation à la rhétorique biblique.* Paris: Editions du Cerf, 1982.

Milavec, Aaron. "The Social Setting of 'Turning the Other Cheek' and 'Loving One's Enemies' in Light of the Didache," *Biblical Theology Bulletin* 25 (1995), 131-143.

Miller, Robert J. "Elijah, John and Jesus in the Gospel of Luke," *New Testament Studies* 34 (1988), 611-622.

Miyoshi, Michi. *Der Anfang des Reiseberichts Lk 9:51-10:42. Eine redaktionsgeschichtliche Untersuchung.* Rome: Biblical Institute Press, 1974.

Moessner, David P. "'Eyewitness,' 'Informed Contemporaries,' and 'Unknowing Inquiries': Josephus' Criteria for Authentic Historiography and the Meaning of *parakoloutheo,*" *Novum Testamentum* 38 (1996), 105-122.

Monshouwer, D. "The Reading of the Prophet in the Synagogue of Nazareth," *Biblica* 72 (1991), 90-99.

Moon, Sheila. *Joseph's Son.* Francestown, N.H.: Golden Quill Pres, 1972.

Morgen, Michèle. "Jésus descendit à Capharnaum: Il étonne par la puissance de sa parole (Lc 4,31-32 et ses sources)," *Revue des Sciences Religieuses* 66 (1992), 233-248.

Mott, Stephen Charles, "The Power of Giving and Receiving: Reciprocity in Hellenistic Benevolence," in Hawthorne, Gerald F. ed. *Current Issues in Biblical and Patristic Interpretation: Studies in Honor of Merrill C. Tenney.* Grand Rapids: Eerdmans, 1975, 60-72.

Müller, Paul-Gerhard. *Lukas-Evangelium.* Suttgarter kleiner Kommentar. Neues Testament 3. Stuttgart: Verlag Katholisches Bibelwerk, 1984.

Murphy-O'Connor, Jerome. "Why Jesus Went Back to Galilee?" *Bible Review* 12 (1996), 20-29,40.

Neale, David A. *None But Sinners. Religious Categories in the Gospel of Luke.* Sheffield: JSOT Press, 1991.

Nebe, Gottfried. *Prophetische Züge im Bilde Jesu bei Lukas.* Stuttgart: Verlag W. Kohlhammer, 1989.

Neirynck, Frans. "Jesus and the Sabbath: Some Observations on Mark II,27," in Dupont, Jacques, ed. *Jesus aux origines de la Christologie.* BETL 40. Louvain: Leuven University Press, 1975. 227-270.

_____. "The First Synoptic Pericope: The Appearance of John the Baptist in Q?," *Ephemerides Theologicae Lovanienses* 72 (1996), 41-74.

New, David S. *Old Testament Quotations in the Synoptic Gospels, and the Two-Document Hypothesis.* Septuagint and Cognate Studies 37. Atlanta: Scholars Press, 1993.

Neyrey, Jerome H. *The Passion According to Luke: A Redaction Study of Luke's Soteriology.* Wilmington, DE: Michael Glazier, 1985.

_____. "Unclean, Common, Polluted, and Taboo," *Forum* 4 (1988), 72-82.

_____. "Loss of Wealth, Loss of Family and Loss of Honor. The Cultural Context of the Original Makarisms in Q," in Esler, Philip F. ed. *Modelling Early Christianity: Social-Scientific Studies of the New Testament in Its Context.* New York: Routledge, 1995. 139-158

Nolland, John. "Impressed Unbelievers as Witnesses to Christ (Luke 4.22a)," *Journal of Biblical Literature* 98 (1979), 219-229.

Noorda, Sijbolt Jan. "'Cure Yourself Doctor' (Luke 4,23). Classical Parallels to an Alleged Saying of Jesus," in Delobel, Joel. ed. *Logia. Les Paroles de Jésus. The Sayings of Jesus.* Louvain: Leuven University Press, 1982. 459-467.

_____. *Historia Vitae Magistra. Een beoordeling van de geschiedenis van de uitleg van Lucas 4,16-30 als bijdrage aan de hermeneutische discussie.* Amsterdam: VU Uitgeverij, 1989.

O'Fearghail, Fearghus. "Rejection in Nazareth: Lk 4:22," *Zeitschrift für die neutestamentliche Wissenschaft* 75 (1984), 60-72.

Okorie, A.M. "The Gospel of Luke as a Polemic Against Wealth," *Deltion Biblikon Meliton* 23 (1994), 75-89.

_____. "The Characterization of the Tax Collectors in the Gospel of Luke," *Currents in Theology and Mission* 22 (1995), 27-32.

Olson, D.T. "Temptations and Trials in Deuteronomy 6-11, Luke 4, and Luke 22-24: The Significance of a Recurring Threefold Pattern," in Hultgren, Arland J., Donald H. Juel, Jack D. Kingsbury, eds. *All Things New: Essays in Honor of R.A. Harrisville.* St. Paul, MN: Word and World, 1992. 21-28.

Osiek, Carolyn. "The Family in Early Christianity: 'Family Values' Revisited," *Catholic Biblical Quarterly* 58 (1996), 1-24.

_____. "Jesus and Galilee," *The Bible Today* 34 (May 1996), 153-159.

Overman, J. Andrew. "Who Were the First Urban Christians? Urbanization in Galilee in the First Century," in Lull, David J. ed. *Society of Biblical Literature 1988 Seminar Papers*. Atlanta, GA: Scholars Press, 1988. 160-167.

_____. "Recent Advances in the Archaeology of the Galilee in the Roman Period," *Currents in Research: Biblical Studies* 1 (1993), 35-58.

O'Toole, Robert F. "Does Luke Also Portray Jesus as the Christ in Luke 4,16-30?," *Biblica* 76 (1995), 498-522.

Paffenroth, K. "The Testing of the Sage: 1Kings 10:1-13 and Q 4:1-13 (Lk 4:1-13)," *Expository Times* 107 (5, 1996), 142-143.

Page, Sydney, H.T. *Powers of Evil: A Biblical Study of Satan and Demons*. Grand Rapids: Baker Books, 1995.

Pagels, Elaine. *The Origin of Satan*. New York: Random House, 1995.

Perdue, Leo G. "Wisdom Sayings of Jesus," *Forum* 2 (1986), 3-35.

Perkins, Pheme. *Peter: Apostle for the Whole Church*. Columbia, SC: University of South Carolina Press, 1994.

Perrin, Norman. *Rediscovering the Teaching of Jesus*. London: SCM Pres, 1967.

Perrot, C. "Luc 4,16-30 et la lecture biblique de l'ancienne Synagogue," *Recherches de Science Religieuse* 47 (1973), 324-340.

Pesch, Rudolf. *Der reiche Fischfang: Lk 5:1-11/Jo 21:1-14. Wündergeschichte – Berufungserzählung – Erscheinungsbericht*. Düsseldorf: Patmos – Verlag, 1969.

_____. *Jesu ureigene Taten?* Quaestiones Disputatae. Freiburg – Basel – Vienna: Herder, 1970.

_____. "Luke's Formulation of the Saying on the Fishers of Men (Lk 5:10a), *Bible Bhashyam* 2 (1976), 44-59.

_____. "La rédaction lucanienne du logion des pécheurs d'hommes (Lc V,10c)," in Neirynck, Frans. ed. *L'Evangile de Luc – The Gospel of Luke*. Revised and Enlarged Edition Louvain: Leuven University Press, 1989. 135-154.

Pilch, John J. "Biblical Leprosy and Body Symbolism," *Biblical Theology Bulletin* 11 (1981), 108-113.

_____. "Sickness and Healing in Luke-Acts," in Neyrey, Jerome H. ed. The Social World of Luke-Acts: Models for Interpretation. Peabody: Hendrickson, 1991. 181-209.

Pilgrim, Walter E. Good News to the Poor: Wealth and Poverty in Luke-Acts. Minneapolis: Augsburg Publishing House, 1981.

Piper, Ronald A. Wisdom in the Q-Tradition. The Aphoristic Teaching of Jesus. SNTSMS 61. Cambridge; Cambridge University Press, 1989.

_____. "The Language of Violence and the Aphoristic Sayings in Q: A Study of Q 6:27-36," in Kloppenborg, John S. ed. Conflict and Invention: Literary, Rhetorical and Social Studies on the Sayings Gospel Q. Valley Forge, PA: Trinity Press International, 1995. 53-72.

Pittner, Bertram. Studien zum lukanischen Sondergut. Sprachliche, theologische and formkritische Untersuchungen zu Sonderguttexten in Lk 5-19. Erfurter Theologische Studien. Leipzig: St. Benno-Verlag, 1992.

Prior, Michael. Jesus the Liberator: Nazareth Liberation Theology (Luke 4:16-30). Sheffield: Sheffield Academic Press, 1995.

_____. "Jesus and the Evangelization of the Poor," Scripture Bulletin 26 (1996), 34-41.

Radl, W. Das Lukas-Evangelium. Erträge der Forschung. Darmstadt: Wissenschaftliche Buchgesellschaft, 1988.

Reiner, Hans. "Die 'Goldene Regel': Die Bedeutung einer sittlichen Grundformel der Menschheit," in Grundlagen der Sittlichkeit. Third Edition. Meisemheim am Glan: Hain, 1974. 348-379.

Rese, Martin. Alttestamentliche Motive in der Christologie des Lukas. Gütersloh: Gütersloher Verlaghaus Gerd Mohn, 1969.

Rhoads, David M. Israel in Revolution, 6-74 C.E.: A Political History Based on the Writings of Josephus. Philadelphia: Fortress Press, 1976.

Rice, George E. "Luke 4:31-44: Release for the Captives," Andrews University Seminary Studies 20 (1982), 23-28.

Ricoeur, Paul. "The Golden Rule. Exegetical and Theological Perplexities," New Testament Studies 36 (1990), 392-397.

Rijkhoff, Martin. "De duivel en het Rijk van God (Lucas 4)," JOTA 9 (1991), 30-40.

Ringe, Sharon H. Jesus, Liberation, and the Biblical Jubilee: Images for Ethics and Christology. Philadelphia: Fortress Press, 1985.

_____. *Luke*. Westminster Bible Companion. Louisville. KY: Westminster/John Knox Press, 1995.

Robbins, Vernon K. *Jesus the Teacher: A Socio-Rhetorical Interpretation of Mark*. Philadelphia: Fortress Press, 1984.

_____. "Pragmatic Relations as a Criterion for Authentic Sayings," *Forum* 1 (3, 1985), 35-61.

_____. "Plucking Grain on the Sabbath," in Mack, Burton L. and Vernon K. Robbins. *Patterns of Persuasion in the Gospels*. Sonoma, CA: Polebridge Press, 1989. 107-141.

Robinson, John A.T. "The Temptations," in *Twelve New Testament Studies*. London: SCM Press, 1962. 53-60.

Robinson, William C. *Der Weg des Herrn. Studien zur Geschichte und Eschatologie im Lukas-Evangelium*. Hamburg-Bergstedt: Herbert Reich Evangelischer Verlag, 1964.

Rohr, Richard. *The Good News According to Luke: Spiritual Reflections*. New York: Crossroad, 1997.

Rohrbaugh, Richard L. "Legitimating Sonship—A Test of Honour. A Social-Scientific Study of Luke 4:1-30," in Esler, Philip F. ed. *Modelling Early Christianity: Social-Scientific Studies of the New Testament in Its Context*. New York: Routledge, 1995.

Rousseau, John J. "Jesus, an Exorcist of a Kind," in Lovering, Eugene H. ed. *Society of Biblical Literature 1993 Seminar Papers*. Atlanta:Scholars Press, 1993. 129-153.

Safrai, S. "Sabbath Breakers?," *Jerusalem Perspective* 3 (1990) 3-5.

Safrai, S. et al. *The Jewish People in the First Century: Historical Geography, Political History, Social, Cultural and Religious Life and Institutions*. Two Volumes. Philadelphia: Fortress Press, 1974-1976.

Sahlin, Harald. *Studien zum dritten Kapitel des Lukasevangeliums*. Uppsala: A.B. Lundequistska Bokhandeln, 1949.

Sampathkumar, P.A. "The Rich and the Poor in Luke-Acts," *Bible Bhashyam* 22 (1996), 175-189.

Sanders, Ed Parish. "Jesus and the Sinners," *Journal for the Study of the New Testament* 19 (1983), 5-36.

Sanders, Jack T. *The Jews in Luke-Acts*. Philadelphia: Fortress Press, 1987.

Sanders, James A. "Isaiah in Luke," in Mays, James Luther and Paul J. Achtemeier. eds. *Interpreting the Prophets*. Philadelphia: Fortress Press, 1987. 75-85.

_____. "Sins, Debts, and Jubilee Release," in Evans, Craig A. and James A. Sanders. *Luke and Scripture. The Function of Sacred Tradition in Luke-Acts.* Minneapolis: Fortress Press, 1993. 84-92.

Seitz, Oscar J.F. "Love Your Enemies: The Historical Setting of Matthew V.43f.; Luke VI.27f.," *New Testament Studies* 16 (1969), 39-54.

Scheffler, Eben H. "The Social Ethics of the Lukan Baptist (Lk 3:10-14)," *Neotestamentica* 24 (1990), 21-36.

_____. "Reading Luke from the Perspective of Liberation Theology," in Hartin, P.J. and J.H. Petzer. eds. *Text and Interpretation. New Approaches to the Criticism of the New Testament.* Tools and Studies 15. Leiden: Brill, 1991. 281-298.

Schlatter, Adolf. *Das Evangelium des Lukas.* Stuttgart: Calwer Verlag, 1960.

Schmidt, Thomas E. *The Hostility to Wealth in the Synoptic Gospels.* JSNT Supplement 15. Sheffield: JSOT Press, 1987.

Schmithals, Walter. *Das Evangelium nach Lukas.* Zürcher Bibelkommentare. Zürich: Theologischer Verlag, 1980.

Schottroff, Luise. "Non-Violence and the Love of One's Enemies," in *Essays on the Love Commandment.* Philadelphia: Fortress Press, 1978. 9-39.

Schramm, Tim. *Der Markus-Stoff bei Lukas. Eine literarkritische und redaktions-geschichtliche Untersuchung.* Cambridge: Cambridge University Press, 1971.

Scobie, Charles H. H. *John the Baptist.* Philadelphia: Fortress Press, 1964.

Seland, Torrey. *Establishment Violence in Philo and Luke: A Study of Non-Conformity to the Torah and Jewish Vigilante Reactions.* Leiden: E.J. Brill, 1995.

Senior, Donald. *The Passion of Jesus According in the Gospel of Luke.* Wilmington, DE: Michael Glazier, 1989.

Shelton, James B. *Mighty in Word and Deed: The Role of the Holy Spirit in Luke-Acts.* Peabody, MA: Hendrickson, 1991.

Sider, John W. "The Meaning of *Parabole* in the Usage of the Synoptic Evangelists," *Biblica* 62 (1981), 453-470.

Siker, Jeffrey S. "'First to the Gentiles': Literary Analysis of Luke 4:16-30," *Journal of Biblical Literature* 111 (1992), 73-90.

Singer, Marcus G. "The Golden Rule," *Philosophy* 38 (1963), 293-314.

Smith, Dennis E. "The Historical Jesus at Table," in *Society of Biblical Literature 1989 Seminar Papers*. Atlanta: Scholars Press, 1989. 467-486.

Staley, Jeffrey L. "'With the Power of the Spirit': Plotting the Program and Parallels of Luke 4:14-37 on Luke-Acts," in Lovering, Eugene H. ed. *Society of Biblical Literature 1993 Seminar Papers*. Atlanta: Scholars Press, 1993. 281-302.

_____. "Narrative Structure (Self-Structure) in Lk 4:14-9:62: The United States of Luke's Story," *Semeia* 72 (1995), 173-213.

Stegner, William Richard. "The Temptation Narrative: A Study in the Use of Scripture by Early Jewish Christians," *Biblical Research* 35 (1990), 5-17.

Stein, Robert H. *Difficult Passages in the New Testament*. Grand Rapids: Baker, 1990.

Stendahl, Krister. *The School of St. Matthew*. Philadelphia: Fortress Press, 1968.

Stenger, Werner. *Introduction to New Testament Exegesis*. Grand Rapids: Eerdmans, 1993.

Strecker, Georg. *The Sermon on the Mount: An Exegetical Commentary*. Nashville: Abingdon Press, 1988).

Strobel, August. "Pladöyer für Lukas: Zur Stimmigkeit des chronistischen Rahmens von Lk 3:1," *New Testament Studies* 41 (1995), 466-469.

Swartley, Willard M. ed. *The Love of Enemy and Nonretaliation in the New Testament*. Louisville, KY: Westminster/John Knox Press, 1992.

Sweetland, Dennis M. *Our Journey with Jesus: Discipleship According to Luke-Acts*. Collegeville: The Liturgical Press, 1990.

Talbert, Charles H. *Reading Luke. A Literary and Theological Commentary on the Third Gospel*. New York: Crossroad, 1982.

Tannehill, Robert C. "The Mission of Jesus according to Luke 4:16-30," in Eltester, Walther. ed. *Jesus in Nazareth*. Berlin; Walter de Gruyter, 1972. 51-75.

_____. *The Sword of His Mouth*. Philadelphia: Fortress Press, 1975

Theissen, Gerd. *The Miracle Stories of the Early Christian Tradition.* Philadelphia: Fortress Press, 1983.

_____. "Nonviolence and Love of Our Enemies," in *Social Reality and Early Christians.* Minneapolis: Fortress Press, 1992. 115-156.

Theobald, C. "La regle d'or Chez Paul Ricoeur: Une interrogation théologique," *Recherches de Science Religieuse* 83 (1995), 43-59.

Tiede, David L. *Prophecy and History in Luke-Acts.* Philadelphia: Fortress Press, 1980.

_____. "Luke 6:17-26," *Interpretation* 40 (1986), 63-68.

Topel, L. John. "The Lukan Version of the Lord's Sermon," *Biblical Theology Bulletin* 11 (1981), 48-53.

Tuckett, Christopher M. "Luke 4,16-30, Isaiah and Q," in Delobel, Joel. ed. *Logia: Les Paroles de Jesus—The Sayings of Jesus.* Louvain: Leuven University Press, 1982. 343-354.

_____. "The Temptation in the Q Narrative," in Van Segbroeck, Frans et. al. eds. *The Four Gospels 1992—Festschrift Frans Neirynck.* Louvain: Leuven University Press, 1992. 479-507.

_____. *Luke.* New Testament Guides. Sheffield: Sheffield Academic Press, 1996.

_____. *Q and the History of Early Christianity.* Studies on Q. Edinburgh: T. & T. Clark, 1996a.

Twelftree, Graham H. *Jesus the Exorcist: A Contribution to the Study of the Historical Jesus.* Peabody, MA: Hendrickson, 1993.

Tyson, Joseph B. "The Opposition to Jesus in the Gospel of Luke," *Perspectives in Religious Studies* 5 (1978), 144-150.

_____. *The Death of Jesus in Luke-Acts.* Columbia: University of South Carolina Press, 1986.

Vaage, Leif E. *Galilean Upstarts: Jesus First Followers According to Q.* Valley Forge, PA: Trinity Press International, 1994.

Van der Loos, H. *The Miracles of Jesus.* Novum Testamentum Supplement 9. Leiden: Brill, 1985.

van Unnik, Willem C. "Die Motivierung des Feindesliebe in Lukas vi.32-35," *Novum Testamentum* 8 (1966), 284-300.

Via, E. Jane. "Women, the Discipleship of Service, and the Early Christian Ritual Meal in the Gospel of Luke," *Saint Luke Journal of Theology* 29 (1985), 37-45.

Vorster, Willem S. "Stoics and Early Christians on Blessedness," in Balch, David L; Everett Fergusan; Wayne A Meeks. eds. *Greeks, Romans, and Christians*. Essays in Honor of Abraham J. Malherbe. Minneapolis: Fortress Press, 1990. 38-51.

Voss, Gerhard. *Die Christologie der lukanischen Schriften in Grundzugen*. Studia Neotestamentica. Bruges: Desclée de Brouwer, 1965.

Weatherly, Jon A. *Jewish Responsibility for the Death of Jesus in Luke-Acts*. Sheffield: Sheffield Academic Press, 1994.

Webb, Robert L. "The Activity of the Baptist's Expected Figure at the Treshing Floor (Matthew 3:12 = Luke 3:17)," *Journal for the Study of the New Testament* 43 (1991), 103-111 (a).

_____. *John the Baptizer and Prophet: A Socio-Historical Study*. JSNT Supplements 62. Sheffield: JSOT Press, 1991 (b).

_____. "Juan el Bautista: Un profeta de su tiempo," *Kairos* [Guatemala City] 16 (1995), 23-38.

Wilckens, Ulrich. *Die Missionsreden der Apostelgeschichte. Form- and traditions-geschichtliche Untersuchungen*. Neukirchen-Vluyn: Neukirchener Verlag, 1961.

Wilson, S.G. *Luke and the Law*. Cambridge: Cambridge University Press, 1983.

Wink, Walter. *John the Baptist in the Gospel Tradition*. Cambridge: Cambridge University Press, 1968.

_____. *Unmasking the Powers: The Invisible Forces That Determine Human Existence*. Philadephia: Fortress Press, 1986.

_____. "Neither Passivity nor Violence: Jesus' Third Way (Mt 5:38-42 par.)," in Swartley, Willard M. ed. *The Love of Enemy and Nonretaliation in the New Testament*. Louisville, KY: Westminster/John Knox Press, 1992. 102-125.

_____. "Counteresponse to Richard Horsley," in Swartley, Willard M. Ed. *The Love of Enemy and Nonretaliation in the New Testament*. Louisville, KY: Westminster/John Knox Press, 1992a. 133-136.

_____. "Jesus and the Nonviolent Struggle of Our Time," *Louvain Studies* 18 (1993). 3-20.

Witherington III, Ben. *Women and the Genesis of Christianity*. Cambridge: Cambridge University Press, 1990.

_____. *The Christology of Jesus*. Minneapolis: Fortress Press, 1990a.

Wolter, Michael. "'Reich Gottes" bei Lukas," New Testament Studies 41 (1995), 541-563.

Wrege, Hans-Theo. Die Überlieferungsgeschichte der Bergpredigt. WUNT 9. Tübingen: J.C.B. Mohr (Paul Siebeck), 1968.

Young, Brad H. Jesus and His Jewish Parables. Mahwah: Paulist Press, 1989.

_____. Jesus the Jewish Theologian. Peabody, MA: Hendrickson, 1995.

Zeller, Dieter. Die weisheitliche Mahnsprüche bei den Synoptikern. Forschung zur Bibel 17. Würzburg: Echter Verlag, 1977

Ziesler, J.A., "Luke and the Pharisees," New Testament Studies 25 (1979), 146-157.